# Practical Microsimulation Modelling

**Practical Econometrics**

**Series editors**
Jurgen Doornik and Bronwyn Hall

Practical econometrics is a series of books designed to provide accessible and practical introductions to various topics in econometrics. From econometric techniques to econometric modelling approaches, these short introductions are ideal for applied economists, graduate students, and researchers looking for a non-technical discussion on specific topics in econometrics.

**Books published in this series**

*An Introduction to State Space Time Series Analysis*
Jacques J. F. Commandeur and Siem Jan Koopman

*Non-Parametric Econometrics*
Ibrahim Ahamada and Emmanuel Flachaire

*Econometric Methods for Labour Economics*
Stephen Bazen

*A Practical Guide to Price Index and Hedonic Techniques*
Ana M. Aizcorbe

*Practical Microsimulation Modelling*
Cathal O'Donoghue

# Practical Microsimulation Modelling

Cathal O'Donoghue

OXFORD
UNIVERSITY PRESS

Great Clarendon Street, Oxford, OX2 6DP,
United Kingdom

Oxford University Press is a department of the University of Oxford.
It furthers the University's objective of excellence in research, scholarship,
and education by publishing worldwide. Oxford is a registered trade mark of
Oxford University Press in the UK and in certain other countries



First Edition published in 2021

Impression: 1



Published in the United States of America by Oxford University Press
198 Madison Avenue, New York, NY 10016, United States of America

British Library Cataloguing in Publication Data
Data available

Library of Congress Control Number: 2021935786

ISBN 978–0–19–885287–2

DOI: 10.1093/oso/9780198852872.001.0001

Printed and bound by
CPI Group (UK) Ltd, Croydon, CR0 4YY

*Dedicated to my peers and students in the microsimulation community*

# Preface

This book describes the lessons that I have learnt over the course of developing my skills as a microsimulation modeller and co-generating knowledge and experience with Ph.D. and master's students and with industry clients.

While I have built many models over the course of my career, the research in this book draws on lessons from four models:

- SWITCH–the tax-benefit microsimulation model of the Economic and Social Research Institute, in Dublin, Ireland (Callan et al. 1996)
- EUROMOD–the European tax-benefit model (Immervoll et al. 1999; Immervoll and O'Donoghue 2009; Sutherland and Figari 2013)
- LIAM–Lifecycle Income Analysis Model (dynamic microsimulation framework) (O'Donoghue et al. 2009; de Menten et al. 2014)
- SMILE–Simulation Model of the Irish Local Economy (spatial microsimulation model) (O'Donoghue et al. 2012)

Figure 0.1 describes my knowledge-tree equivalent to a genealogical tree of these models and their link to earlier models in the literature.

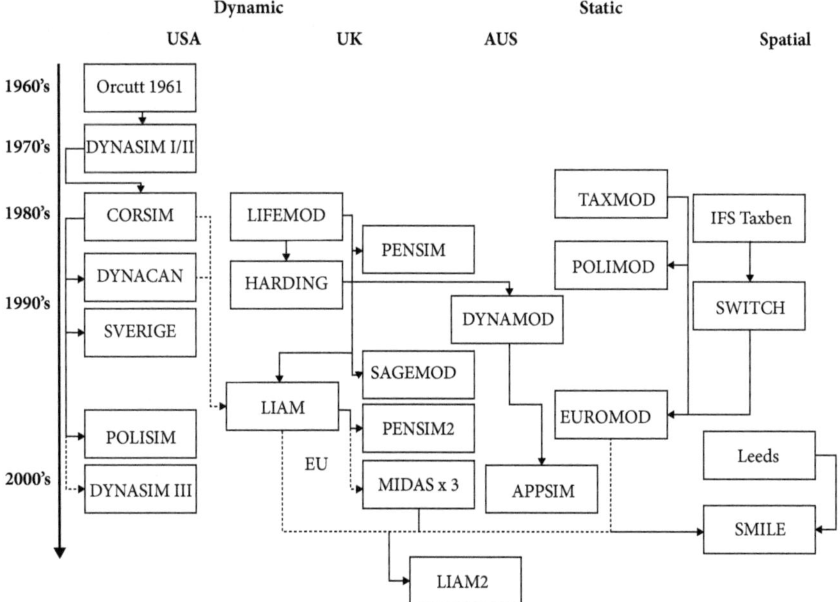


Figure 0.1 Model Knowledge Tree

These models span many of the main methodological areas of microsimulation modelling, covering static, dynamic, cross-country, and spatial models. Starting with static modelling, which ignores behaviour, time, and place, the first model I worked on was the SWITCH static microsimulation model at the Economic and Social Research Institute, in Dublin, Ireland, working with Tim Callan and his team to develop and use the Irish SWITCH static tax-benefit model (Callan et al. 1996). This work was heavily influenced by the Institute for Fiscal Studies' Taxben model (Blundell et al. 2000).

Extending the dimensionality of the modelling to incorporate the time dimension in a dynamic microsimulation model, I developed a dynamic-cohort model LIAM (O'Donoghue 2002) during a Ph.D. at the London School of Economics (LSE), under the supervision of Celia Phillips and Jane Falkingham. LIAM built upon the family of dynamic-cohort models developed at the LSE for the UK (LIFEMOD, Falkingham and Hills 1995) and Australia (HARDING, Harding 1993). This model was also influenced by the work of Steve Caldwell at Cornell University (where I had the pleasure of spending some time during the course of my Ph.D.), who developed the CORSIM model (Caldwell 1996). Caldwell's model is a direct link to the first microsimulation models in the field, when he partnered with Guy Orcutt (Orcutt et al. 1958; Orcutt 1960) on the DYNASIM model at the Urban Institute, Washington DC, in the early 1970s.

Caldwell had a particular way of building very sophisticated models with relatively limited resources, working with Ph.D. students and with partners in other countries. One of these partnerships was with the Canadian government to build the DYNACAN model, along with Rick Morrison and his team (Caldwell and Morrison 2000). The joint meetings between CORSIM–DYNACAN teams were one of the leading fora for the exchange of knowledge in dynamic microsimulation modelling at the time.

I also worked with Holly Sutherland's team at the Microsimulation Unit, in the Department of Applied Economics, University of Cambridge, together with partners such as Tony Atkinson and Francois Bourguignon, to create a cross-country microsimulation model, EUROMOD (Atkinson et al. 2002). Other partners, such as Gert Wagner at the Deutsches Institut für Wirtschaftsforschung (DIW),[1] provided a link back to the cutting-edge Sfb3 models in Germany in the 1980s (Galler and Wagner 1986). In addition, the early version of the EUROMOD framework was developed together with Herwig Immervoll, who now heads up microsimulation analysis at the OECD (Immervoll and O'Donoghue 2009), although later versions are more flexible

[1] German Institute for Economic Research.

and powerful (Sutherland and Figari 2013). Extensions of EUROMOD involved collaborations with Andre Decoster to incorporate modelling consumption and indirect tax (Decoster et al. 2010), and also collaborations with Ugo Colombino to incorporate labour supply (Colombino et al. 2010).

Extending microsimulation modelling to incorporate the spatial dimension, I developed, on returning to Ireland, SMILE, working in partnership with Graham Clarke and Dimitris Ballas of the University of Leeds (Ballas et al. 2005). SMILE has a focus on rural- and agricultural-policy analysis (O'Donoghue et al. 2013). In parallel, my Ph.D. framework, LIAM (O'Donoghue et al. 2009), was generalized to be applied to other countries (Dekkers et al. 2010), which eventually led to the development of a new and faster, more-powerful framework, LIAM2 (de Menten et al. 2014), with the methodologies influencing the development of the UK's dynamic-microsimulation model Pensim2, at the Department of Work and Pensions (Edwards 2010; O'Donoghue et al. 2010).

Progress in research is based on building upon the achievements and learnings of others. Much of the learning in microsimulation has been by word of mouth, via interpersonal interactions, or via documentation in conference proceedings or books, many of which are now out of print, such as the excellent Orcutt et al. (1986).

Without personal interactions with leading figures in this fast-growing and relatively novel field, it would have been more challenging for me to develop these models. In essence, I had to rely largely on an oral exchange of knowledge and experience. Across the microsimulation field, much of the knowledge has been transmitted verbally between people on teams, at conferences, and through networks. In developing further, the microsimulation field faces a challenge to find more-effective ways of transferring knowledge.

In transferring knowledge, there are two main types of knowledge transfer:

- codified knowledge, where specific knowledge is written down
- tacit knowledge, where more-abstract information may be more difficult to transmit

For much of the period since the foundation of the field, knowledge has been codified mainly through the following forms:

- documentation that aims to facilitate other team members utilizing the models
- published material, mainly books and conference presentations, which may have been non-peer reviewed, had limited coverage, and often went out of print

- documents that may have only been available to those who attended an event and were rarely included in the usual citation indices and searchable databases
- papers published in peer-reviewed formats, which were typically in journals where the focus was on the application rather than the methodology

A significant proportion of the methods used in the field are not formally codified, meaning that new models have had to reinvent the wheel and redevelop existing methods over and over again. Where methods were formally codified, they were often codified in non-peer-reviewed technical notes or discussion papers and thus lack the quality assurance that peer review can help to achieve. Another issue is that publication in a research-centre technical paper or note carries risks associated with the ending of funding, retirement of staff, or the end of the life of a model. Thus, there is a sustainability risk for the field in respect to its core methodological foundations.

A classic example of this is the methodology in relation to alignment, used in dynamic microsimulation models. It is a calibration mechanism used to align simulated totals to external control totals, and has been used since the 1970s. It is, thus, a core methodology within the field. However, there is relatively little documentation or guidance as to how to undertake alignment. Where it exists, it is published in non-peer-reviewed technical papers (Bækgaard 2002) as team-specific internal documentation (Johnson 2001; Morrison 2006), conference papers (Kelly and Percival 2009; Chénard 2000a), or in relatively hard-to-find volumes based on conferences (Neufeld 2000; Chénard 2000b). It should be noted that all these references date from 2000 onward, despite the methodology being used since the 1970s. Most are not peer reviewed and most are hard to find, and, given the dissolution of some of the teams, are impossible to access. One of the first peer-reviewed journal articles that aims to assess the performance of a part of the methodology was only published in 2014 (Li and O'Donoghue 2014). This chapter covers the alignment of only a single variable type. Is it any wonder that the methodology has received serious criticism (Winder 2000)?

It is arguable that the development of a method cannot be trusted until it has been road-tested through publication and rigorous peer review. There is, thus, a need for a literature to be developed to document, test, and provide rigorous quality assurance for the alignment of the many other variables that are found in the literature. The example above cites an issue in relation to one specific aspect of the methodology. This criticism could be extended to many other methods used within the field of microsimulation.

This book is an attempt to codify and describe many of the main techniques utilized in microsimulation modelling, and to present examples of how they are used.

I am grateful both to my many peers in the field of microsimulation and to students that I have learned from and taught over the past twenty-five years. I am also grateful to helpful comments by anonymous referees and to my colleague Mary Ryan for extensive comments on the draft document. I hope this book provides a helpful guide for those wishing to develop models within the field. I would like to acknowledge the understanding and support of Rosaleen and Jude as I prepared this book.

# Table of Contents

## PART III. BEHAVIOURAL MODELS



## PART IV. DYNAMIC AND SPATIAL MODELS

# List of Figures

# List of Tables

# PART I
# INTRODUCTION

# 1
# Introduction

## 1.1 Introduction

Public policy design increasingly expects and relies upon a body of evidence to make decisions. Better evidence can produce better and more focused policies. It can allow for better targeting of resources, improving the cost of achieving a particular policy objective, or improving the effectiveness of a policy for a given resource. Targeted policy interventions require better information on who is affected, how they are affected, and where those who are affected are located. For example, a transfer programme targeted at a group that are generally poor, such as the elderly, may cost more than an instrument that is targeted on the basis of income, and so is targeted specifically at the poor. However, this targeting or means testing may introduce negative incentives. Thus, designing effective policy requires a *micro-based* unit of analysis, containing information on how a policy will affect individuals differentially.

While there is a large range of methodologies utilized in undertaking evidence-based policy analysis, they can be classified broadly into the following categories:

- Ex-post analysis (Heckman et al. 1999; Todd 2007; Vedung 2017; Benhassine et al. 2015), focusing on evaluating the impact of a policy after it has been implemented.
- Ex-ante analysis, assessing the potential impact before roll out (Hertin et al. 2009; Figari et al. 2015; De Agostini et al. 2018).

Increasing use is being made of pilot initiatives using randomized experiments and then evaluated using ex-post methods, for example in the case of the main worldwide pilot projects for child-related conditional cash-transfer programmes (see Gertler 2004; Fernald et al. 2008; Pearce and Raman 2014; Haskins and Margolis 2014). However, political constraints and/or time or resource constraints frequently do not allow this to take place. Thus ex-ante simulation-based methods are often used for public policy design as they are cheaper, being undertaken on a computer without incurring large piloting

*Practical Microsimulation Modelling*. Cathal O'Donoghue. Oxford University Press. © Cathal O'Donoghue 2021.
DOI: 10.1093/oso/9780198852872.003.0001

costs. They are less accurate than ex-post methods as the structure of behaviour may change in response to policy instrument or they may be based upon historical data. However, the methodology may be the only one possible in many circumstances.

Microsimulation modelling is a potential simulation-based tool with a micro-unit of analysis that can be used for ex-ante analysis (O'Donoghue 2014). It is a micro-based methodology, typically utilizing micro-data units of analysis, for example taking surveys or datasets containing micro-units such as households, individuals, firms, and farms, etc. It is a simulation-based methodology that utilizes computer programs to simulate public policy and economic or social changes on the micro-population of interest. While microsimulation models have taken firms (Eliasson 1991; Buslei et al. 2014) or farms (O'Donoghue 2017) as the micro-unit of analysis, most have carried out analysis at the level of individuals or households (see Mot 1992; Sutherland and Figari 2013)

As a research field, microsimulation has its roots in the work of Guy Orcutt (1957, 1961). However, it was only the advent of the personal computer in the 1980s and the availability of micro-data that have allowed the field to develop. Whether formally defined as microsimulation modelling or not, micro-based, ex-ante simulation-based analysis is now used extensively around the world for policy analysis and design.

There have been a number of survey articles written such as Merz (1991, 1994), Mot (1992), Martini and Trivellato (1997), Bourguignon and Spadaro (2006), Dekkers and van Leeuwen (2010), and Anderson and Hicks (2011). Generally, Sutherland (1995) covered static models; Klevmarken (1997) behavioural models; O'Donoghue (2001), Zaidi and Rake (2001), Spielauer (2007), and Li and O'Donoghue (2013) dynamic models; Rahman and Harding (2016), Rahman et al. (2010), Hermes and Poulsen (2012), Tanton and Edwards (2013), Tanton (2014), and O'Donoghue et al. (2014) spatial models; Creedy and Duncan (2002), Creedy and Kalb (2005), and Bargain and Peichl (2013) labour supply models; Figari and Tasseva (2013) a special issue on the cross-country EUROMOD model; Brown (2011) health models; and Ahmed and O'Donoghue (2007), Cockburn et al. (2010), and Bourguignon et al. (2010) covered macro-micro models. The O'Donoghue (2014) handbook brings together developments across a variety of different areas. Given the growth in microsimulation over the past twenty years, there is a need for a text book to assimilate this literature and describe the development and implementation of current practice in the microsimulation field.

Public policy is broad, with many objectives and associated targets. Microsimulation modelling can in principle be applied to assess the micro impact of many policy areas, subject to data availability and to the capacity to quantify the impact of the policy. This book will focus primarily on policies associated with the distribution of income such as poverty, income inequality, and labour supply incentives. These are the areas in which the methodology has seen most use over time. However, there are also many other areas in which the methodology has been widely used, particularly in the areas of transport (Miller 2014), health (Schofield et al. 2014), urban planning (Waddell et al. 2003), and farm-level modelling (O'Donoghue 2017; Shrestha et al. 2016).

Microsimulation models can be produced in different programming environments. Relatively simple models can be programmed in Microsoft EXCEL, while more sophisticated models use statistical software such as SAS or Stata, or programming languages such as C++, VB, and Java (Hancock 1997). There are no specific software packages for undertaking microsimulation, but a number of frameworks have been used to build models for different purposes, for example the EUROMOD (Immervoll and O'Donoghue 2009), MODGEN (Spielauer 2011), and LIAM2 (De Menten et al. 2014) frameworks.

Other modelling methods, such as computable general equilibrium models (CGE) (De Melo 1988; Van Ruijven et al. 2015), overlapping generations models (OGM) (Lambrecht et al. 2005; Bommier and Lee 2003), or agent-based models (Tesfatsion and Judd 2006; Gatti et al. 2018), incorporate behaviour in a more detailed or consistent way than microsimulation models, but typically do not have the same heterogeneity of population or detail in relation to policy. Linking these models with microsimulation models can generate some of the advantages of both methods, illustrated by attempts to link more detailed behavioural models such as CGE (Cockburn et al. 2014) with microsimulation models.

### 1.1.1 Complexity and Microsimulation Models

As a modelling framework, microsimulation modelling is a mechanism of abstracting from reality to help us understand complexity better. Figure 1.1 outlines potential sources of complexity in a static, single-time-period microsimulation model.

In the context of policy design and evaluation, complexity can take the form of:

- population structure
- behavioural response to the policy
- policy structure

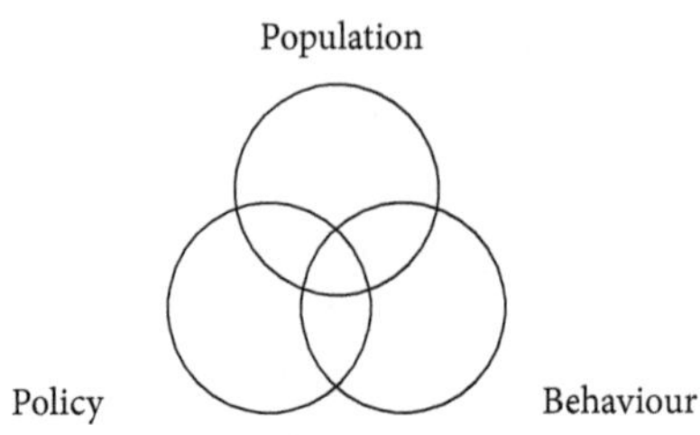


**Figure 1.1** Sources of Complexity in Policy Design and Evaluation

These levels of complexity themselves interact with each other, resulting in a degree of complexity that is difficult to disentangle without recourse to a model.

Consider first the dimension of complexity, for example policy complexity or the range of different policy or socio-economic impacts. Many microsimulation models try to replicate the fine detail of legislation in their simulations, as opposed to a more generic form of simulation. These include the areas of tax and benefit policy, indirect taxation, health policy, pension policy, rural policy, transport policy, or macroeconomic change. Different geopolitical contexts may influence the nature of the policy complexity. For example, the set of policies simulated in an OECD country may be different to those simulated in a developing country, with the former typically having a greater reliance on income-related systems such as income taxation and means-tested benefits, and the latter being more reliant on consumption-based taxes and in-kind instruments.

The next dimension of complexity in relation to population is whether an analysis takes place on a population with limited or extensive heterogeneity. Many analyses focus merely on the impact of policy on typical families, abstracting almost entirely from population complexity, such as the OECD tax-benefit model based upon workers at the average production wage (Immervoll and Pearson 2009). Another dimension of population complexity considered is the unit of analysis. Some microsimulation models have taken businesses such as firms (Buslei et al. 2014) or farms (O'Donoghue 2017) as the micro-unit of analysis, however most have carried out analysis at the level of individuals or households (Bourguignon and Spadaro 2006).

The third dimension of complexity is behaviour. Many policies are explicitly aimed at influencing behaviour, as in the case of work incentives, in-work benefits, or environmental incentives. Models that abstract from behavioural response are known as static microsimulation models, while models that incorporate behaviour include labour participation and supply, consumption decisions, benefit take-up, tax evasion, transport decisions, or farm- and firm-level investment decisions.

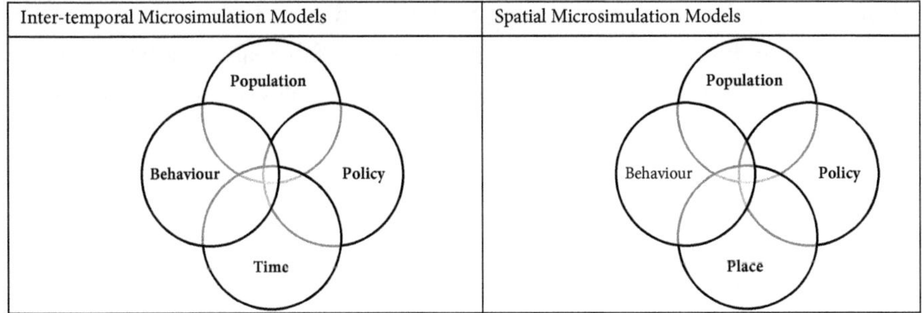


**Figure 1.2** Enhanced Complexity in Inter-Temporal and Spatial Microsimulation Models

In the case of models that incorporate either spatial dimensions (O'Donoghue et al. 2014) or inter-temporal dimensions (Li and O'Donoghue 2013), the level of complexity is further increased (Figure 1.2). Land use and spatially targeted policy or spatially targeted socio-economic effects require spatial models. Analysis of policies which depend upon long-term contribution histories, such as pensions and long-term care policy, or require long-term repayments (as in the case of education financing), utilize inter-temporal or dynamic models.

Finally, across all dimensions there may be an interest in understanding the performance of policies in different country contexts. Multi-country models and comparative analyses have been developed to analyse such questions of differential complexity.

### 1.1.2 Population Complexity

Policy analysis frequently tries to understand how a policy will impact the 'average' family. The OECD's average production worker examination of comparative tax and social policy is an example of such analysis (Pearson & Scarpetta 2000; Burlacu et al. 2014). However, familiarity with micro-data makes one realize that there is in fact no average family, such as a single-earner couple with children and living on the average wage. For example, looking at the structure of the Irish population in 2005 using the Survey of Income and Living Conditions, there are 33.5 per cent of the population living in households defined as a couple with children. Of these, 13.1 per cent are single-earner couples and of these less than 2 per cent have earnings at or close to the average wage. Thus, the so called 'average' contains only a tiny fraction of the population, reflecting the high degree of heterogeneity-derived complexity within the population. Decomposing into other dimensions, such as time or income source, further add to this complexity. For this reason, policy analysts require micro-datasets containing representative samples of the population.

### 1.1.3 Policy Complexity

Public policy often starts with simple objectives, perhaps in response to a crisis or a specific social-policy objective. However, unexpected effects or 'mission creep' can often lead to a policy becoming more complicated. Take for example an anti-poverty strategy. A desire to reform poor laws in Britain and Ireland saw the introduction of contribution-based unemployment insurance to combat poverty in 1911. However, the cost of extending the instrument to fill coverage gaps saw the introduction of means-tested unemployment assistance in 1933 (Figure 1.3). This added further complexity, requiring information about the income of an individual, instead of evidence of having paid sufficient social insurance contributions.

As the value of the instrument rose to improve the poverty effectiveness of the instrument over time, the impact was to increase the proportion of the population covered by the means-tested instrument, thus increasing what is known as the 'unemployment trap', whereby individuals are not better off in work. To counter this, an in-work benefit, the Family Income Supplement (FIS)—similar to instruments such as the EITC and Family Credit/WTC in the US and the UK respectively—was introduced in 1984 (Figure 1.4). This

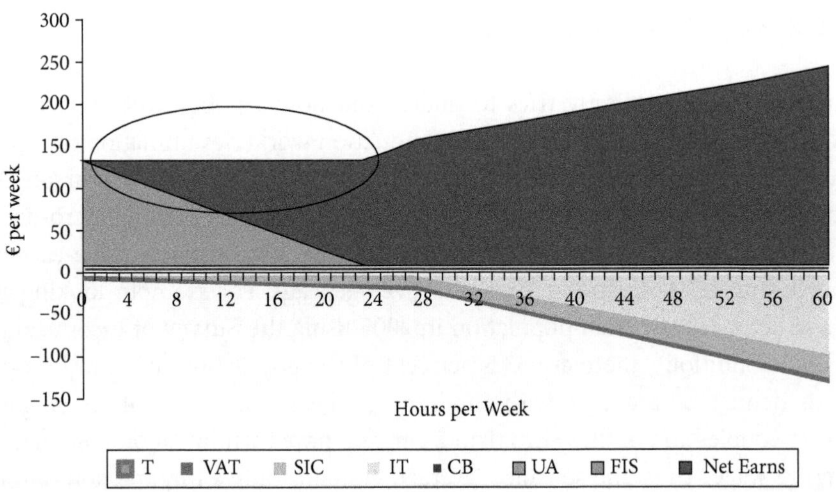


**Figure 1.3** Unemployment Trap from Means Testing

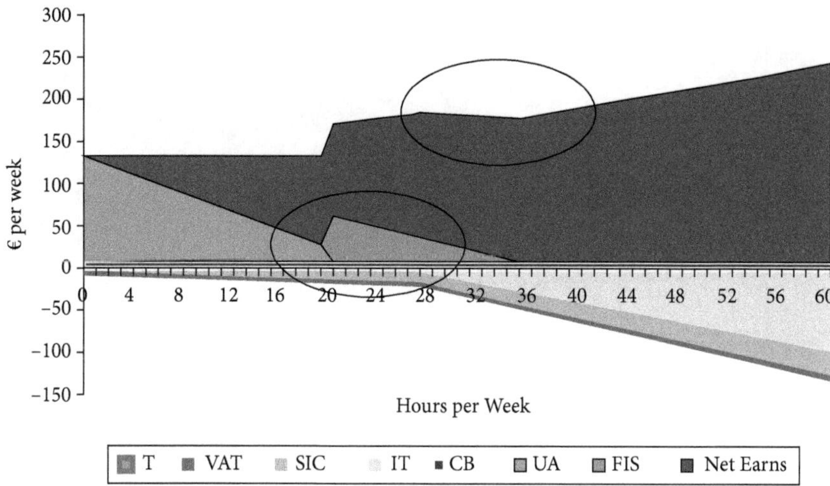


**Figure 1.4** Poverty Trap

instrument was targeted at families working more than twenty hours per week, with the objective of reducing the unemployment trap. It too was means tested at the rate of 60 per ent, however it also extended means testing higher up the income distribution. At the same time, reforms were made to take low-income individuals out of the tax net, but with a relatively high, marginal tax rate of 40 per cent.

This system of policies, all with relatively straightforward and reasonable objectives, evolved over time. However combined, this system produced significant complexity and unintended interactions. Here, quite a significant proportion of low-income families with children faced a withdrawal rate of 60 per cent of the FIS, combined with a marginal income-tax rate of 40 per cent and a social-insurance contribution rate of about 8 per cent, combining to produce a marginal effective tax rate of 108 per cent (Callan et al. 1995) (Figure 1.5). This resulted in a 'poverty trap' where individuals have no incentive to increase their working hours even if they wished to, as earning an extra pound would result in their net income falling by eight pence. Capturing the detail of actual legal rules, microsimulation models allow for complex interactions between different policy instruments to be identified.

### 1.1.4 Behavioural Complexity

Since the 1980s, a significant amount of tax-benefit policy reform across the OECD has targeted improved work incentives to counter some of the problems identified above. However, microeconomic theory identifies

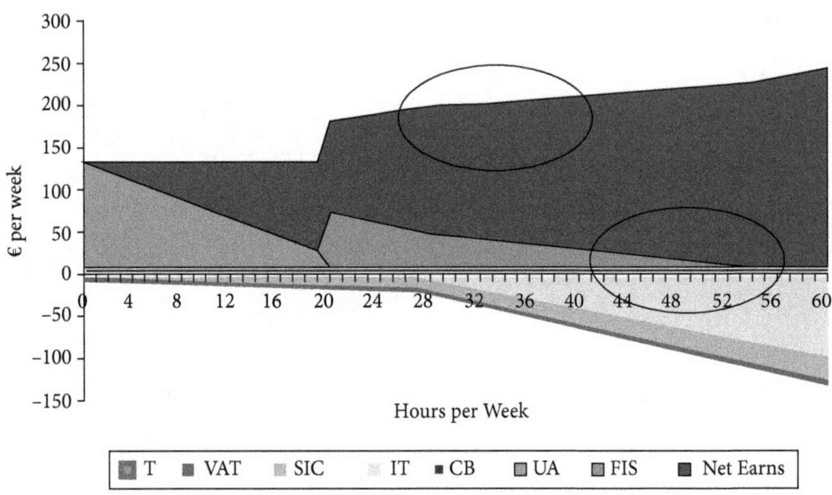


**Figure 1.5** Reducing the Poverty Trap

complex competing forces resulting in what is known as a backward-bending labour supply curve, as a result of the impact of a substitution effect, whereby a reduction in the marginal return from labour will increase the attractiveness of leisure, and an income effect incentivizing an individual to work more. The net impact of these forces in terms of labour supply depends upon the relative preferences of the individual, which may be both idiosyncratic or a function of personal characteristics, such as the presence of children, their gross wage rate, or age. In addition, labour-demand constraints may result in labour-force outcomes that are different to desired labour supply.

Combined, these sources of complexity can result in a 'spaghetti' of different issues. While it may be feasible to use pen-and-paper analytical methods to analyse average or simplistic situations or sets of policies, it is often very difficult or impossible to disentangle the impacts of more complex policies, population groups, or behaviours. In such cases, it is often the unintended consequences that cause the policy maker the greatest headaches, as the recipients of these consequences are often those who will be most likely to complain, resulting in negative media coverage and thus undermining the political support for what may be generally worthy policy objectives. A microsimulation model facilitates the ironing out of some of these difficulties in policy prior to implementation. Microsimulation allows for the examination of drivers of behaviour using a static model, as in the case of replacement rates (O'Donoghue 2011) or marginal effective tax rates (Mertens and Montiel Olea 2018).

### 1.1.5 Analytical Objectives

In the field of income maintenance policy, and the associated financing of these policies, what are the dimensions of analysis in which policy makers are interested?

Cost is often top of the priority list in designing a policy reform, albeit as a constraint or indirect policy objective due to a limited budgetary envelope. Targets associated with this objective include public finance indicators of balance and sustainability. A model with this objective will in general have the requirement of both (a) utilizing a dataset which is representative of the population of concern to the policy and (b) modelling the policy in sufficient detail to be able to undertake accurate costings.

As microsimulation models incorporate a micro-population, the distributional impacts of a policy are another primary focus. Models may look at the distributional impacts of a policy or policy change across different income categories, either in the case of a vertical redistributive analysis or across different family types in the case of horizontal redistribution. Estimations of the impact of changes on low incomes, as in the case of a poverty analysis, are commonplace. The capacity to estimate the numbers of potential winners and losers as a result of a policy change is also very important, particularly to politicians.

Policies often have a behavioural dimension. Strategies to reduce labour-supply incentives associated with interactions of the tax-benefit system in OECD countries are highlighted above (Aaberge and Colombino 2014). There is a priority objective within policy reform in many developing countries to add conditionality to other anti-poverty policy. For example, in the Bolsa Familia programme in Brazil school attendance of children is a requirement for eligibility for an anti-poverty instrument (Bourguignon et al. 2003; Cury et al. 2016). It thus has multiple objectives, namely increasing education participation and reducing both child labour and poverty. In order to model these analyses, an econometric behavioural model will be required, or at a minimum, a capacity for scenario analysis.

Sometimes, the induced behaviour that is targeted relates to consumption. This may include the achievement of minimum consumption baskets (Capéau et al. 2014) or the reduction of consumption of goods with negative consumption such as excessive fatty foods (Cappacci et al. 2012) or polluting fuels (Labandeira and Labeaga 1999; Berry 2019). This type of model will require a base dataset that contains consumption expenditures and an econometric model of consumer behaviour.

Poverty and social exclusion can be concentrated in particular places in addition to being associated with particular socio-economic characteristics, such as age, disability, or unemployment. Policy targets in this dimension include the UK's target of 'tackling disadvantage by reviving the most deprived neighbourhoods, reducing social exclusion, and supporting society's most vulnerable groups' (Tanton and Clarke 2014). In this case, the microsimulation model will require spatial coordinates.

A related spatial dimension that is useful in policy development is policy learning from developments in other countries. It is the basis of comparative research which has become increasingly important, particularly as part of the objectives of international organizations. The OECD Making Work Pay programme focuses on cross-country comparisons of tax-benefit policy (Pearson and Scarpetta 2000). Comparative research places challenging demands on microsimulation models as datasets, and models in different countries are not necessarily compatible and can require significant work to be made comparable (Sutherland 2014).

Another dimension of relevance to policy development is time. Some policies, such as pensions, are affected through the accumulated influence of labour-market status and policy change over time. Given increasing life expectancy, changes in fertility and mortality rates can have long-lasting impacts. Thus, the impact of policy changes may be very slow to be visible, while demographic changes that occur now can have influences a long time into the future. Interacting with these forces are policy targets to improve the sustainability of public pension systems and to reduce old-age poverty (Li et al 2014).

## 1.2 Types of Microsimulation Models

In this section, the types of model considered throughout this book are introduced.

### 1.2.1 Hypothetical Family Models

When governments publish their budgetary policy changes, it is often evident the impact that these policy changes have on hypothetical families. These are the simplest type of 'microsimulation model', as they abstract from the complexity of the population or their behaviour to try to simulate the impact of policy on hypothetical families. These models, described in

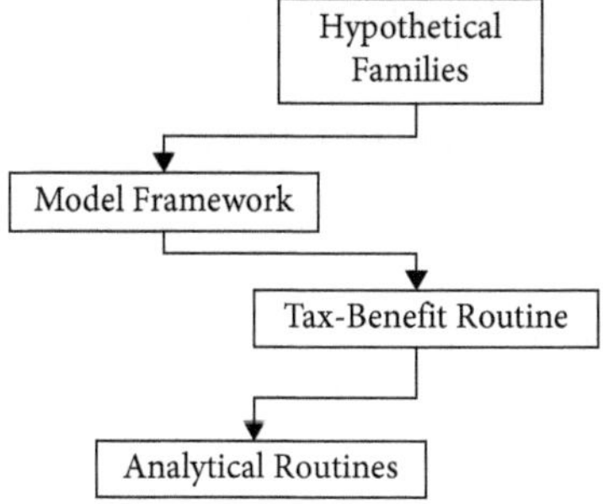


**Figure 1.6** Hypothetical Model

Figure 1.6, typically therefore contain a simple database containing one or more hypothetical families and generally use a stripped-down version of the tax-benefit system.

As noted, the simplest type of microsimulation model is one that abstracts from population complexity entirely, analysing the static impact of policy and policy change on hypothetical families. Burlacu et al. (2014) describe the main focus of these models which include:

- illustrative purposes
- validation
- cross-national comparisons
- replacement of insufficient or lack of micro-data
- communication with the public

Hypothetical family models have been applied to many fields, but the dominant policy area is that of social security and taxation. Given their relative simplicity, their geographic spread has been widespread, with the UK, the US, Australia, and Ireland having the highest share of such models. Methodologically, the chapter on hypothetical models focuses on a variety of choices, including the unit and period of analysis, updating, and analytical output measures, which are common to other types of model, as well as modelling choices specific to hypothetical models, such as the unit of variation by which heterogeneity is introduced to hypothetical models.

Due to their simplicity, they are very useful communication devices, as is evident from their use in media reports. As a developer of models, they are also specifically useful as validation models for testing components. The more complex a model, the more difficult it is to validate, so running a simulation on a small set of families can help to identify any bugs. When data are not available for a particular analysis, as in the case of some life-cycle analyses, hypothetical family models can be utilized for analysis (Rake et al. 1999).

Lastly, because of their relative simplicity, hypothetical family models are extensively used in international comparative analysis. Tax-benefit calculations for stylized households have been widely used in international comparisons of many different aspects of tax-benefit systems. Comparing the situations of similar household types, they provide valuable information about differences in national systems and illustrate some of the effects of actual or hypothetical policy changes (Pearson and Scarpetta 2000).

There are, however, problems with this approach because it attempts to reduce complex tax-benefit systems to single (or a few) point estimates.[1] By using 'average household' characteristics, the analysis is likely to miss many of the important features of the tax-benefit system which, although not applicable to the 'average household', may affect a significant part of the population. The 'stylized' approach does, by definition, not take into account the details of the structure of the population and is thus problematic if used as a basis for summarizing the actual situation in a given country.

### 1.2.2 Static Tax-Benefit Microsimulation Models

A second dimension of complexity that is considered relates primarily to population complexity (Di Nicola et al. 2015). These models are typically defined as static models, focusing on the impact of policy change before there is an opportunity for a behavioural reaction; i.e., the 'day-after effect'.

Static tax-benefit microsimulation models are similar to the hypothetical family models described above. The primary difference is that they incorporate greater heterogeneity in the population database, typically via representative samples of the population (Figure 1.7). Static microsimulation models involve the interaction of population and policy complexity, but abstract from behavioural response or other endogenous change in the model, and as such they model the day-after effect of a policy change. Li et al. (2014) consider the uses and methodological choices of static models.

Like other types of microsimulation model, static tax-benefit models examine in detail the policy system with the aim of understanding how policy impacts at the individual and household level, thus modelling the interaction of population and policy complexity. Given the complexity of tax and

1. See Immervoll and O'Donoghue (2009).

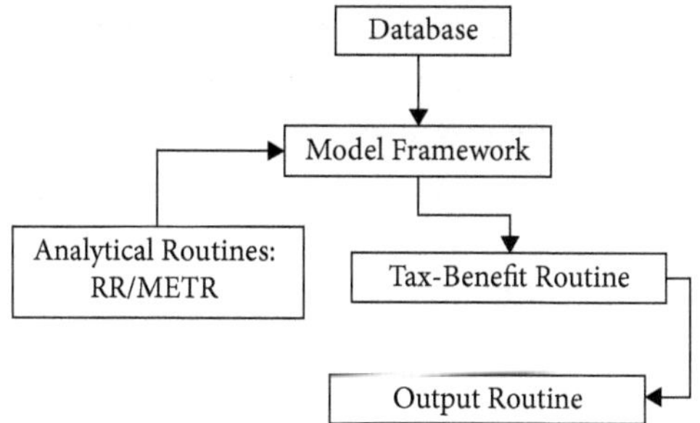


**Figure 1.7** Static Tax-Benefit Model
*Note*: RR (replacement rates); METR (marginal effective tax rates).

benefit policy legislation, these models, even ignoring behavioural responses, can be highly complicated. Being representative of the population, they require a full representation of the tax-benefit system. They are sometimes known as arithmetical models (Redmond et al. 1998).

In terms of their policy focus, while historically tax and social-security policy has been the main focus, there is an increasing importance of other policy areas, particularly in relation to health and social care. The geographical spread of these models has increased as the availability of micro-data has increased. Given their relative policy complexity and availability of data, static microsimulation models have proliferated in OECD countries, however with improved data availability the field has expanded outside of OECD countries in recent years (Joust and Rattenhuber 2018). In terms of analytical scope, static models focus on distribution and redistribution incidence, as well as on the drivers of behaviour, even if behaviour is not modelled endogenously.

Simulating the fine detail of tax-benefit policy legislation, these static models are thus in a position to evaluate existing tax-benefit policies and aid in the design of new individual schemes or entire systems. They calculate applicable amounts of each element of the tax-benefit system in the legal order, so that interactions between different elements of the system are fully taken into account. The resulting taxes, benefits, and income measures for each individual, family, or household are weighted to provide results at the population level. Such microsimulation models have been developed, and are in use, in many OECD countries (Li et al. 2014).

By incorporating the interactions of different elements of the tax-benefit system, and by taking full account of the diversity of characteristics in the population, this approach allows a very detailed analysis of the revenue, the distributional and incentive effects of individual policy instruments, and the system as a whole. In particular, they provide a powerful means of performing 'what if' analyses by allowing the analyst to manipulate all relevant parameters of the system such as tax rates, thresholds, amounts, and income concepts (see Redmond et al. 1998).

Static models do not, however, incorporate behaviour, treating simulations as the first-round, 'next-day' effects, before any behavioural response. Bourguignon and Spadaro (2006) argue that these first-round effects are 'a good approximation of final welfare effect if changes are small enough and individuals may be thought to operate in perfect markets'. However, when a large behavioural response might be expected, results will be biased in relation to the impact of a policy reform. Yet, even though such a 'static' simulation cannot measure the direct impact on behaviour of reforms, it can be used to determine the pressures on behaviour ('incentive effects'), such as marginal tax rates and replacement rates (see Figure 1.7).

Bourguignon and Spadaro (2006) also highlight other sources of potential inaccuracy in this approach, including the ignoring of the production side of the economy, which may react to changes in tax-benefit policy. Furthermore, static tax-benefit models generally assume that there is no tax evasion and assume full benefit take-up.

### 1.2.3 Behavioural Models: Labour Supply

Many public policies have the objective of changing behaviour in addition to financing or distributional objectives. Behavioural objectives include the reduction of work disincentives and the reduction of pollution. It is unsurprising, therefore, that part of the field of microsimulation has focused on behavioural response.

Labour market behaviour in relation to labour supply is one of the most important areas for behavioural analysis in the microsimulation field. Aaberge and Colombino (2014) describe the development of the field of labour-supply-focused microsimulation models and methodological choices.

There are three methodologies for modelling labour supply:

- the reduced form approach
- the structural 'marginalist' approach
- the random utility maximization approach

Figure 1.8 describes the structure of a labour-supply microsimulation model. In many senses, there is an overlap with the static microsimulation model outlined in Figure 1.7. A behavioural labour-supply model utilizes a static

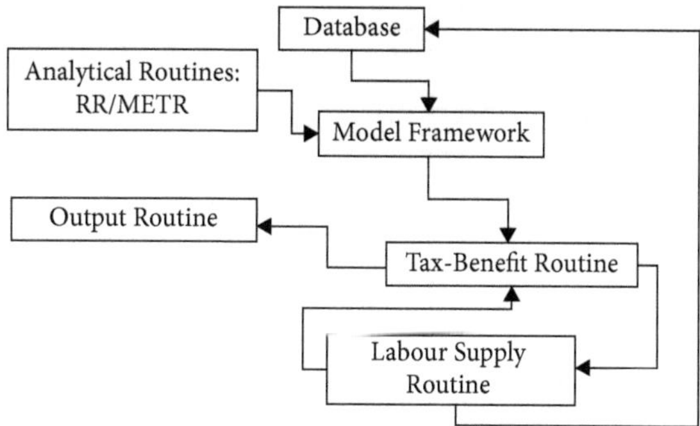


**Figure 1.8** Labour-Supply Behavioural Models

microsimulation model to simulate the budget constraint associated with alternative choices. This is required for the econometric estimation of a labour-supply utility function, which is then in turn used to model the behavioural responses of policy changes that are simulated in the static part of the model.

Labour supply is central not only to modelling behavioural responses, but also to modelling optimal tax-benefit systems, with a focus on a computational approach, given some of the challenges of the theoretical approach. Combining labour-supply results with welfare functions enables the social evaluation of policy simulations (Kleven et al. 2009).

## 1.2.4 Behavioural Models: Consumption Behaviour

While the modelling of policy measures that depend on current income (such as direct taxation and social transfers) has been the focus of most of the models described thus far, indirect taxation or taxation that is a function of expenditure is also quite important. Capéau et al. (2014) review models that depend on consumption and indirect tax. Indirect tax is one of the more important sources of tax revenue in OECD countries and frequently the most important in non-OECD countries, while there have been substantial reforms in the past fifteen years.

Figure 1.9 defines the structure of consumption-based microsimulation models. They are similar in structure to a labour-supply model, however the base dataset and the policy model are different. The base data requires information about expenditures, while the policy algorithm incorporates indirect taxation such as valued-added tax and excise duties. The behavioural module incorporates an econometric model, based on a demand system, that allows for the consumption response to price changes to be determined.

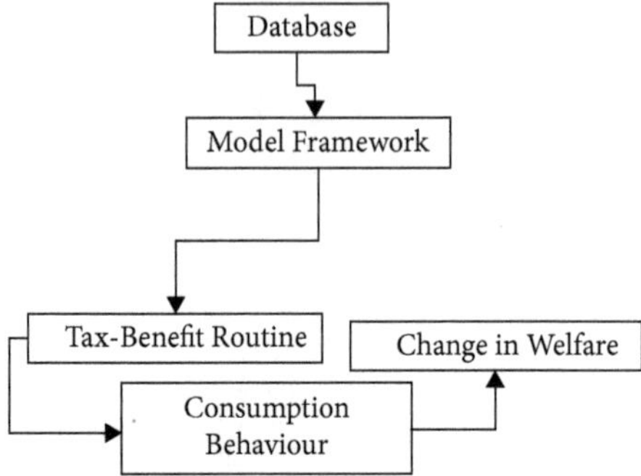


**Figure 1.9** Consumption-Behaviour-Based Models

Given the choice between changing consumption or savings rates when prices or taxes of goods change, behavioural assumptions or models (whether behaviour is explicitly modelled or not) are intrinsic to all indirect-tax models. Methodologically, most current indirect-tax models take the household as the unit of analysis, with some extensions into firm-level units. There are a variety of welfare analyses that are utilized in indirect-taxation modelling, including the modelling of potential winners and losers, the progressivity of a reform, and distributional analyses involving both direct- and indirect-tax reform.

## 1.2.5 Environmental Models

The environment as a policy issue has increased dramatically over the past four decades. Research in this area extends from global challenges, such as climate change, access to water and soils, ozone emissions, and biodiversity loss, to issues with a smaller geographical scope, such as water quality and traffic congestion to the impact of the environment on health. Hynes and O'Donoghue (2014) describe the use and development of environmental microsimulation models.

The use of microsimulation modelling in the realm of the environment overlaps with many traditional areas of such modelling, such as the distributional incidence of public policies or the impact on behaviour in relation to the incidence of these policies. Within the environmental and natural-resource economics literature, the interaction between human activity and the environment has also been shown to be strongly influenced by spatial location. In this regard, the use of spatial microsimulation models has proven

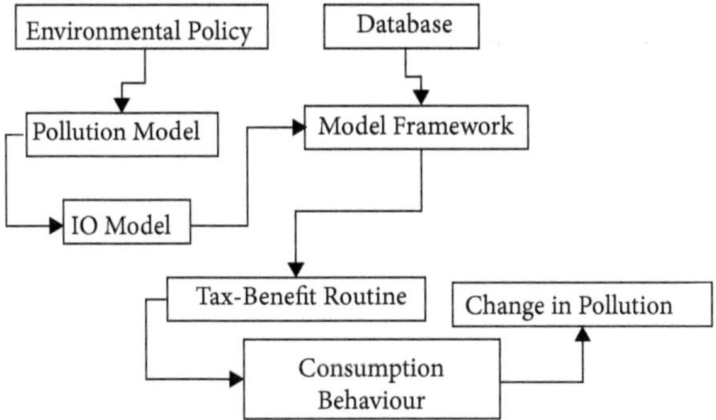


**Figure 1.10** Environmental Models

a useful tool for modelling socio-economic environmental interactions and policies.

Figure 1.10 describes the structure of a microsimulation model that is used to simulate environmental fiscal policy such as carbon taxation. It is similar in many respects to a consumption-based model. However, the price changes that are modelled as part of the policy are different. In dealing with a carbon tax, the initial price change depends upon the polluting equivalent of the good consumed. So, for example, coal is more polluting than gas and so would incur a higher carbon tax. The impact of a carbon tax can be both direct and indirect. Households purchase fuels which produce carbon emissions, but also purchase other goods and services which themselves have carbon inputs and so on. Incorporating both direct and indirect effects requires an input-output model, which is in effect a map of flows between different sectors in an economy and can be used to produce these direct and indirect impacts of the price change resulting from a carbon tax. Once the price change for household consumption at the detailed level is produced, a simulation can be undertaken in the same way as a consumption-tax model. However, in addition to revenue or budget impact, the impact of the policy change on pollution outputs can also be modelled.

### 1.2.6 Decomposing Inequality

Given the capacity to model the incidence of policy on a population, microsimulation models have been used to understand in greater detail the way in which policy impacts upon the income distribution. Bargain (2014) considers the methodology used to decompose the drivers of the income distribution. Traditionally, models have modelled inequality with and without particular policies, or modelled the impact of an actual policy change.

Bargain highlights challenges in relation to the decomposability of inequality and poverty indices and the decomposition of changes contemporaneously into factor and income components. It considers a methodology developed in recent years using microsimulation to construct counterfactual situations and to disentangle the pure effect of a policy change from changes in the environment in which the policy operates. The methodology decomposes inequality change into policy, income growth, and other effects, although linearity in tax-benefit systems sees the income-growth component eliminated.

The methodology has been applied to study the effect of policy changes in France and Ireland, policies implemented in the UK under the Labour government of 1997–2001, and the effect of tax-benefit policies on non-welfarist aggregated measures that value leisure in addition to disposable income. In addition, the role of policy developments occurring during 2008–10, the first 'dip' in the Great Recession, in four European countries and over the long term in the UK and the US, have also been examined using the methodology.

Increasing availability of data in developing countries has allowed for the field to be extended beyond OECD countries over the past two decades. Essama-Nssah (2014) consider microsimulation techniques commonly used to assess variations in individual and social outcomes associated with the process of development to try to explain distributional change by decomposing it into its various determining factors.

Figure 1.11 describes the structure of a model used for decomposing inequality. It essentially compares two datasets, relating either to two separate countries or two separate time periods. Income-generation models (IGM) are estimated for both countries to describe the labour and capital markets and to describe the distribution of market-income components of both periods or countries. Tax-benefit models describe the generation of disposable income. IGMs are swapped to simulate the impact of alternative market incomes and swap the tax-benefit systems, in order to simulate the impact of alternative systems to get eight different combinations. Alternatively, the IGM could be separated into market participation and market income to give sixteen combinations. Inequality can be calculated for each combination to describe the impact of individual components on the distribution of disposable income.

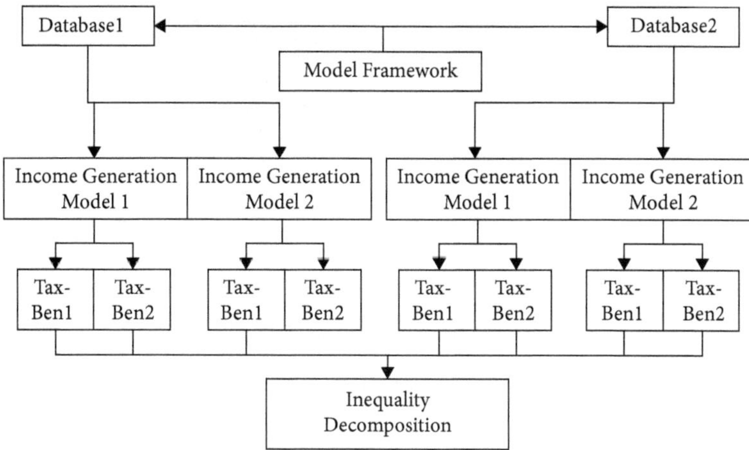


**Figure 1.11** Decomposing-Inequality Model

## 1.2.7 Inter-Temporal Dimension: Dynamic Microsimulation Models

Thus far, the focus has been on models that utilize datasets for a specific point in time and a specific place. However, policies often have a temporal dimension, as in the case of the accumulation of pension entitlement over time, the impact of long-term demographic change, or location-specific policy and behaviour, as in the case of urban renewal, rural development, or migration behaviour.

Dynamic microsimulation models simulate inter-temporal transitions in the population for use in policies that require this information, such as for pensions and student loans, or to provide an inter-temporal analytical dimension, such as life-cycle redistribution.

Li et al. (2014) describe the methodological choices faced by builders of these models, and Figure 1.12 describes this structure. At the core of the model lies a system of equations or behavioural routines that age the characteristics of a population (e.g., mortality, fertility, labour market, incomes, tax-benefits, and family formation, etc.). In that way, the population is projected forward though time at a micro-level. Some behavioural routines may, in a similar way to labour-supply routines, react to policy changes in, for example, retirement-choice decisions.

The main applications of dynamic microsimulation modelling are unsurprisingly, given the life-cycle nature of pensions, life-course redistribution, and inter-generational redistribution. However, the methodology is broadening to include health and spatial- and education-focused models.

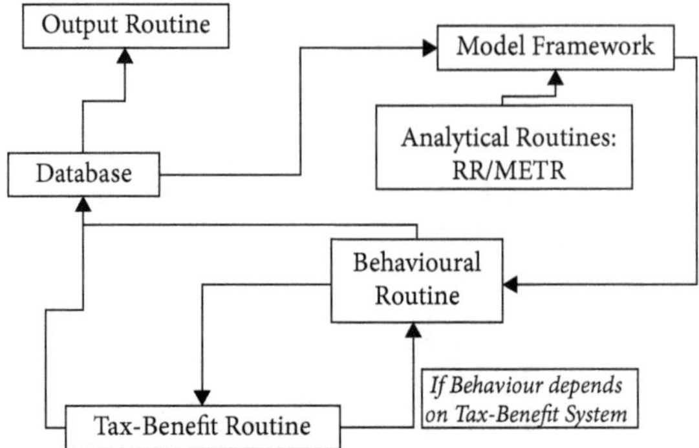


**Figure 1.12** Dynamic Microsimulation Models

Most models are aligned, closed cross-section models focused using discrete time. In relation to the last choice, about one-third of the models incorporate endogenous behaviour, incorporating this dimension of complexity discussed in the previous sub-section.

## 1.2.8 Spatial Microsimulation Models

Location also adds a dimension of complexity over which the population varies, such as with different labour markets, on which policy can vary as in the case of localized development policy, where distance may have an effect in terms of commuting behaviour, or where behaviour may vary, with spatial clustering of preferences (Tanton and Clarke 2014).

One of the main methodologies used in the field relates to spatial micro-data generation. Typically, there are data gaps in relation to data that are both representative at the unit of analysis, such as the individual or household, and also representative at the spatial scale. Data that are rich in terms of individual contextual information may have poor locational information, or due to sample size may not be representative at a fine spatial resolution. On the other hand, data that have a fine spatial resolution may have limited contextual information. Occasionally, as in the case of administrative data in the Nordic countries, both may coincide.

Figure 1.13 describes the structure of a spatial microsimulation model. The model takes nationally representative micro-data from, say, a household budget survey, and reweights or re-samples the data to be consistent with small-area census data. Geographic information systems can be utilized to link other spatial data, such as physical information, e.g., roads or rivers. Many studies then merely undertake descriptive analyses of the combined

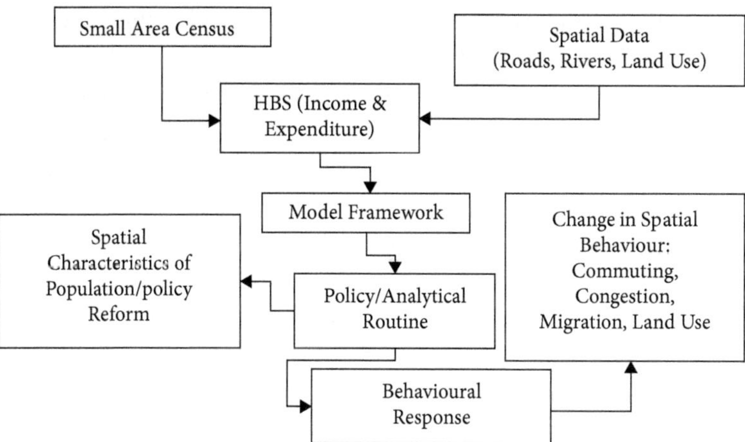


**Figure 1.13** Spatial Microsimulation Models

data, while it is also possible to incorporate behavioural responses, such as changes in commuting, congestion, land use, or migration behaviour as a result of policy changes, e.g., road construction.

Model applications are divided up into the simulation of the spatial incidence of socio-economic phenomena, such as income and poverty, crime, housing stress, obesity, water demand, smoking rates, well-being, trust, and disability on the one hand, and policy reform on the other. Spatial models are sometimes linked to other models, such as static tax-benefit microsimulation models, CGE models, location-allocation models, and to spatial interaction models. Spatial microsimulation models can also be used for projections.

## 1.3 Overview

This section presents an overview of the topics that will be covered in the book. The focus of the book relates to the practical development of microsimulation models, highlighting in turn policy context, issues associated with the preparation of data used in the model, issues associated with validation, and how to measure outcomes generated in the model, with each chapter containing a specific policy simulation.

The primary policy focus of the book is on using microsimulation modelling for policy-related inequality analysis. Drawing upon the complexity analogy, the book concentrates initially on social-protection policy for hypothetical families, abstracting from most aspects of complexity, thus focusing solely on policy complexity. Population complexity is then added when reflecting on tax policy and redistribution.

Behavioural complexity is next introduced, when considering labour-supply responses to tax-benefit policy change. Behavioural impacts of policy are also considered when analysing the impact of indirect taxation and environmental taxation.

In the final chapters, an IGM is introduced to describe the distributional structure of market income, when decomposing the inequality impact of an economic crisis, introducing temporal complexity into the dynamic microsimulation analysis of pension policy. Spatial complexity is also introduced when using a spatial microsimulation framework to analyse spatial inequality.

The early chapters of the book utilize a relatively simple Microsoft EXCEL-based model, XLSIM, which is a modelling framework developed for use as a teaching tool to help students quickly build their own models. In later chapters, bespoke models developed in Stata are utilized to undertake microsimulation.

Researchers interested in developing expertise in the field may wish to participate in the International Microsimulation Association and read articles from the *International Journal of Microsimulation*. The Association holds bi-annual world congresses, with regional meetings in different parts of the globe in intervening years.

# 2

# XLSIM: Developing a Software Tool to Assist Training and Learning in Microsimulation Modelling

## 2.1 Introduction

With increasing numbers of researchers and analysts using microsimulation models, there is merit in developing a tool to train modellers.[1] Microsimulation tax-benefit models are computer programs that simulate policy on representative household datasets, so as to give a representative picture of the impact of these policies on populations (O'Donoghue 2014). This chapter describes the development of a training model built upon on the Microsoft Excel© platform and utilized extensively in education and training.

The most common type of model is a static tax-benefit model (Li et al. 2014), i.e., models that focus on the policy and population complexity, ignoring behaviour by focusing on the day-after effect of a policy change. Until the advent of the EUROMOD system (Sutherland and Figari 2013), most modellers had to create a program in a specific computer language in order to develop a static tax-benefit microsimulation model from scratch (Hancock 1997).

The EUROMOD system is an effective program for developing microsimulation models, containing a particularly useful interface. However, in developing microsimulation modelling skills it is useful to be able to write basic code to understand the structure of policy instruments, although

[1] Acknowledgements: The author gratefully acknowledges financial assistance from the National University of Ireland, Galway Millennium Fund. This chapter was partially written while an ICER Visiting Fellow at the University of Turin. The author acknowledges the hospitality shown. I am grateful to my EUROMOD colleagues Francois Bourguignon, Jose Sastre Descals, Amedeo Spadaro, and Francesca Utili for comments and interactions in earlier work developing a prototype Excel-based model, and to Tony Atkinson, Herwig Immervoll, Holly Sutherland, and other members of the EUROMOD team in more-recent tax-benefit model developments. I am also grateful to comments from students who have taken my courses on social policy modelling using various versions of the model. The author is responsible for all remaining errors.

*Practical Microsimulation Modelling*. Cathal O'Donoghue. Oxford University Press. © Cathal O'Donoghue 2021.
DOI: 10.1093/oso/9780198852872.003.0002

more-complicated frameworks may inhibit learning if there are too many steps to undertake to learn how to model.

While more challenging for large-scale model development, spreadsheet-based models can be a useful tool to learn microsimulation modelling. This chapter describes the structure of XLSIM, a simple Excel-based model that can be used for training and learning how to develop a microsimulation model. It has been used by the author in providing training in a number of universities (Galway, Maastricht, Turin), where it has been possible in relatively short courses to train students how to undertake microsimulation-based analyses. It has also been used by a number of Ph.D. students to develop models for a variety of countries, including Ireland (O'Donoghue 1998), Lithuania (Stirling and Lazutka 2006), Estonia (Lüpsik et al. 2006), Nigeria (Osunde 2015), Brazil (Immervoll et al. 2006), and Pakistan (Ahmed and O'Donoghue 2009).

In the next section, the theoretical requirements of developing a microsimulation model are described, while in Section 2.3 the choice of software used for training purposes is evaluated and the structure of the model described. Section 2.4 describes in more detail the components of microsimulation models—and some of the advantages and constraints of these models—along with the databases used and the structure of the individual worksheets of the model, while Section 2.5 concludes the chapter.

## 2.2 Theoretical Objectives

The objective of the model discussed in this chapter is to develop a modelling framework for teaching and learning purposes.

We can categorize learners into a number of different types:

- Undergraduate and master's students who are learning about policy and the basics of trying to simulate them. Their learning is likely to be a short course over a semester with limited contact hours. Learning is likely to occur in group situations.
- Ph.D. Students who will develop a project over three or four years and gain a depth of knowledge in a particular policy area and a specific methodology, and will probably prioritize one software package. Learning will be through a combination of group, individual tuition, and self-learning.
- Policy professionals with high-level policy knowledge who want to learn how to do microsimulation analysis, and who will rerun models

regularly, implementing policy changes, but may not change functionality substantially. Learning will be through a combination of group, individual tuition, and self-learning.

- Microsimulation professionals with high-level policy and analytical knowledge, who will want to utilize a specific tool for a specific purpose, and who will rerun models regularly and may change functionality for particular purposes. Learning will be probably mainly through self-learning and learning from colleagues and peers.

In order to define how the framework should meet these objectives, let us first define a microsimulation model in simple terms. The key elements of a tax-benefit microsimulation framework are defined in Immervoll and O'Donoghue (2009):

- The set of variables to be used in the framework as well as their characteristics, such as whether they are to be simulated (e.g., taxes), or read from the data (e.g., employment income), or whether they are monetary variables.
- The definition of the fiscal units relevant for an instrument (e.g., who belongs to a 'family' receiving the instrument, who belongs to a 'couple' whose income is taxed jointly, who counts as a 'child' for the purpose of computing child benefits).
- The definition of sharing rules within the unit (i.e., which unit member receives what part of a benefit, and how tax burdens are shared between members of the tax unit).
- Policies and 'policy spine',[2] the structuring mechanism within the framework. The parameters relate to the types of module/policy (i.e., which modules make up a policy, and which policies make up the tax-benefit system) as well as their order.
- Modules, the primary building blocks of the model. Components to be parameterized include the definition of parameters directly related to the tax-benefit algorithm relevant for each module (e.g., rates, band thresholds, type of income concepts, fiscal units).
- The definition of aggregate income concepts that combine income variables used either by an instrument (e.g., 'taxable income' such as market incomes plus benefits minus deductions and allowances) or as an output of the model (e.g., 'disposable income').

[2] Policy spine: the list of policies and the order in which they are simulated (see Immervoll and O'Donoghue 2009).

- Updating. Here it is possible to specify 'uprating' factors for each monetary variable. In other words, if the data were collected in 1996 and the policy we wish to examine is for 1998, then we need to alter the data to bring all monetary variables forward to 1998 (accounting for say, inflation, earnings growth, etc.).
- Output functions, including the variables to be written to the output file, as well as the types of summary statistics required as output.

As a micromodel, we start with an input dataset or matrix $X$, containing a series of variables. Although not exclusively so, this is typically a rectangular matrix, where the columns are input variables and the rows are micro-units. In a model with a household unit of analysis, we will wish to scale up any results for welfare analysis at the household scale. In this case:

- The rows may contain separate rows for each individual in the household, grouped by a household identifier where the instruments to be simulated are instruments that depend upon individual characteristics such as income taxes, social insurance contributions, social protection instruments, etc. Thus, they combine household and individual units of analysis.
- There may be a single row, where the instruments to be simulated depend upon household-level characteristics such as housing benefits or indirect taxes.
- There may be a single row, where groups of columns denote sets of variables for each adult in the household.

While the fiscal unit and the way in which incomes or policies are shared within a unit can be parameterized in a general format in a generalized microsimulation framework, it is not necessary in a model developed for a specific purpose or in a training module.

In a hypothetical microsimulation model, the matrix $X$ may contain a single family or household, where a single parameter such as wage rate or hours worked varies. In a model that utilizes a representative sample of the population, the matrix $X$ will contain many different households representing the distribution of households in the country. Microsimulation models such as static non-behavioural models or behavioural tax-benefit models will be of this type, combining household and individual units of analysis. A model that focuses on household instruments such as indirect taxes or environmental taxes will have a household unit of analysis. Models that interact with the direct-tax or benefit system for more-comprehensive reforms will be similar to the static model. These datasets may be created by statistically matching an expenditure survey with a household unit of analysis $X_h$ with an income survey with a combined individual and household unit of analysis $X_{h,p}$.

An inter-temporal or dynamic model, where the period of analysis is multi-period, will either start with multiple matrices $X_t$ for separate times $t$, or simulate separate matrices over time $t$. A model with a spatial focus again will either start with multiple matrices $X_s$ for different spatial locations $s$, or generate separate matrices across places $s$, perhaps combining a cross-sectional dataset $X$ with spatial-aggregate characteristics $S$.

As a simulation model, it will contain a series of functions $g_i(\ )$ that simulate $n$ operations that combine to a policy instrument $G_j$:

$$G_j = \{g_1(\ ), g_2(\ ), \ldots, g_n(\ )\}$$

In a static or non-behavioural model, the operations are deterministic. In other words, they take the form of:

- basic operations +, -,/, *
- Boolean operations >, <, ≥, ≤, ≠
- power operations $(\ )^2, (\ )^3, (\ )^{\frac{1}{2}}, \ldots$
- comparative operations $Max(\ ), Min(\ )$
- logical operations $if(\ ), then(\ ), else(\ )$

Each operation $g_i(\ )$ is relatively straightforward, depending upon the nature of the legislative rules for the policy instrument $G_j$.

Utilizing the terminology of Immervoll and O'Donoghue (2009), where a series of $m$ policies $G_j$ combine through a policy spine to form a tax-benefit system $G$:

$$G = \{G_1, G_2, \ldots, G_m\}$$

For ease of organization, Immervoll and O'Donoghue group operations into modules, e.g., breaking up a social protection instrument up into:

- eligibility
- means calculation
- equivalence scale
- gross benefit
- means test

In this case, the policy instrument may be grouped as follows, with module 1 comprising operations $g_{1,j}(\;)$:

$$G_j = \{g_{1,1}(\;), g_{1,2}(\;), \ldots, g_{1,n_1}(\;), g_{2,1}(\;), g_{2,2}(\;), \ldots, g_{2,n_2}(\;), \ldots\}$$

Some operations combine a series of variables, such as incomes, into an aggregate income $Y_d$ concept, such as disposable, gross, or taxable income, or individual benefit means, by applying a vector of 1s, 0s, -1s, $\beta$ to the matrix:

$$Y_d = \beta' X$$

Immervoll and O'Donoghue refer to operations such as this as aggregate income concepts or income lists.

Behavioural or probabilistic models used in behavioural microsimulation or dynamic microsimulation models incorporate stochastisc components using random numbers $\varepsilon$ and statistical operations $f(\;)$.

In other words, a stochastic simulation takes the form:

$$Y = f(\beta' X + \varepsilon)$$

Each of these calculations applies to each unit of analysis and combine to produce the final analytical or welfare variable of interest $Y_i$, such as disposable income, expenditure less indirect taxes, labour supply, or environmental pollution, for each unit, $i$. However, each microsimulation model has a model environment $M$ that handles the data operations, to produce a vector of analytical variables $Y$:

$$\begin{aligned} &M: \textit{for each i population } N\{ \\ &\quad Y_i = G_i X_i = \{G_{1,i} X_i, G_{2,i} X_i, \ldots, G_{m,i} X_i\} \\ &\quad \} \end{aligned}$$

The model architecture essentially takes the input dataset $X$, applies the rules of the model $G$, and outputs the analytical variables $Y$. To this may be added some tabulations $T$ to summarize the output.

This is a generalized structure for many types of microsimulation model. However, there are many routines that are specific to individual models, which we ignore for now. These include:

- a demand system for indirect-tax and consumption microsimulation models
- an input-output and pollution model for an environmental tax model
- an alignment routine and marriage market for a dynamic model
- a spatial sampling or reweighting routine for a spatial microsimulation model
- a policy-swapping routine for microsimulation based inequality decomposition

For our purposes here in evaluating the requirements of a teaching- and learning-focused microsimulation model, it is sufficient to take a stylized version. This is particularly the case as more-sophisticated modelling requires more-sophisticated software and thus limits the potential choice of software to be used.

## 2.3 Software Evaluation for a Microsimulation Development

In this section, we take the stylized microsimulation model described above and assess the potential of different software types relative to the objectives described. As Hancock (1997) described, there are many options for building microsimulation models. Many different software options can achieve the objectives set, and Hancock (1997) reviews the computing and software options in developing microsimulation models. Microsimulation models can be developed in many different computing environments from program languages, such as C (e.g., EUROMOD in the EU and SWITCH in Ireland) and Visual Basic (ESPASIM in Spain) to statistical packages such as R (Lovelace and Dumont 2016), SAS (PSM in the UK and STINMOD in Australia), and Gauss (MITTS in Australia), and spreadsheet software such as Eur6, the EUROMOD prototype framework and used in this model.

We evaluate a number of different options:

- a spreadsheet software such as Microsoft Excel©
- a statistical package such as Stata or R
- a computer programming package such as C++ or Java
- a bespoke microsimulation software platform such as EUROMOD or LIAM2

In Table 2.1, we assess the attributes of the different software tools. In summary, there is a trade-off between flexibility of potential functionality, together with speed of computer programs and ease of use, versus actual functionality and slower speed of software packages.

Each needs to be able to undertake all of the components required above. In addition, Immervoll and O'Donoghue (2009) describe some desirable criteria that can be used to benchmark different software options, such as:

- flexibility
- ease of use
- robustness
- transparency
- maintainability
- cost effectiveness

Flexibility refers to the capacity to simulate a range of non-linear, legislation-based policy rules. Hancock (1997) argues that flexibility is probably the most important cornerstone of the computing strategy. Taking into account diverse skillsets, which may be limited for novice developers and students, ease of use is a key requirement to ensure that all relevant features of the model are accessible to a wide range of users, rather than just programmers. Flexibility and generalization can come with a cost in terms of ease of use. Robustness requires the program to balance flexibility and ease of use. The more complex a model gets, the greater the complexity of the model. As a result, it can become a 'black box'. In model development, it is necessary to maximize transparency, both in the way the code is defined and in terms of parameterizing the model. Maintainability refers to the capacity of the model to be updated as new policy rules are developed and for ease of use in terms of validation against external sources.

Another characteristic that should be added to these desirable features of microsimulation frameworks is that of speed.

Table 2.2 characterizes each software tool for these different characteristics:

- Excel is relatively easy to use, cost-effective, and reasonably flexible with most analysts having a good level of familiarity. While easy to use, with equations in cells, it has relatively low transparency, particularly as a model gets complicated. It is also the slowest of the four options.
- Statistical software presumes statistical knowledge, and for those with experience of using a particular software package, it may present a relatively easy-to-use route into microsimulation. With explicit code, it is

**Table 2.1** Microsimulation Functionality of Different Software Tools

| Model Type | Deterministic Calculations | Stochastic/Statistical Calculations | Model Environment | Microsimulation-Specific Routines |
|---|---|---|---|---|
| Excel | Very strong functionality that is relatively easy to use | Some functionality | Possible to develop model environment in the associated VBA. Very slow | All need to be modelled explicitly |
| Statistical Software | Strong functionality, but programming required | Strong functionality with lots of pre-programmed algorithms | Good availability of loops etc. and file handling. Slower than Programme Code | All need to be modelled explicitly |
| Computer Programming | Unlimited functionality, but relatively big overheads in setting up data structures etc. | Unlimited functionality, but relatively big overheads in writing algorithms from scratch | Unlimited functionality, but relatively big overheads in writing database and data-handling routines | All need to be modelled explicitly |
| Microsimulation Software | Available but clunky. Very strong library of existing routines in EUROMOD. Knowledge required of policy structures and parameters | Limited functionality in EUROMOD, stronger in dynamic microsimulation software | Good functionality and faster than Excel or statistical programs | Good, specific to the type of purpose: static, dynamic etc. |

**Table 2.2** Characteristics of Different Software

| | **Flexibility** | **Ease of Use** | **Robustness** | **Transparency** | **Maintainability** | **Cost-Effective** | **Speed** |
|---|---|---|---|---|---|---|---|
| Excel | Medium | High | Low-medium | Low | Medium | High | Low |
| Statistical Software | High | Medium | Medium | High | Medium | Medium-high | Medium |
| Computer Programming | High | Low | Medium | High | Medium | Medium | High |
| Microsimulation Software | High for specific purpose, but low-medium for other purposes | Medium | Medium | Medium | High | Medium | High |

quite transparent, although it may be less robust, as the complexity of the code can grow quite rapidly as the scale of the model expands. Depending upon the cost of licenses, it varies from medium cost-effectiveness for those which require a fee to high cost-effectiveness for open-source programs such as R.

- Programming languages such as C++ are highly flexible with the ability to more or less do anything an analyst wishes, providing they have the necessary skills. However, they come with the high overhead that the user must be proficient in programming, which is beyond most analysts, and for many that learn, their skill levels are lower than professional programmers. Depending upon the level of programming skills, code can become complicated and difficult to manage. Validation can, as a result, be very time consuming. Again, with appropriate skills, computer programs can be very fast.
- Microsimulation software can be very flexible for the purpose for which the model was built, with significant parameterization. With a library of components to learn, the software can save an analyst time in putting a model together, but may take effort to understand the library of measures and associated functionality. Optimized for microsimulation, they are typically faster than spreadsheets or statistical software for running microsimulation, and so are particularly suited for those who have to rerun models or run multiple times.

### 2.3.1 Software Options for Students and Professionals with Different Needs

Given the different attributes and requirements, there may be a differential optimal solution for analysts of different experiences for different purposes:

- For undergraduate and master's students, without statistical, policy, or programming experience, and with limited requirements to rerun models many times, and also with a focus on learning the basics of microsimulation, it is likely that Excel-based platforms are easier to engage with. They are also typically available in university computer suites. Coding calculations in the model itself can help the student to understand how policies actually work. They are probably the easiest to engage with in a short period with limited experience.
- For Ph.D. students, it may depend upon the purpose of the course of study. A Ph.D. student of microsimulation with a focus on policy

analysis would be well served by using EUROMOD and undertaking a training course. They will presumably develop a detailed knowledge of policy design and so have the capacity to engage with the library of policy routines in EUROMOD. For those with an interest in dynamic microsimulation modelling, they will have the time to learn about the individual simulation methodologies to be able to engage with tools such as LIAM2. Many Ph.D. students build extensions on existing modelling analyses, e.g., through labour-supply econometric models or inequality-decomposition or consumption modelling. It is likely, therefore, that they will also use a statistical package. It is also likely that, depending upon their skillset and interests, they will either link the statistical package to the microsimulation software tool or instead utilize the statistical software tool for both stochastic statistical processes and deterministic-policy modelling processes. With much of the learning undertaken informally with their supervisor and fellow students, or formally at workshops and summer schools, they have the time to engage with more-complex programs than Excel.

- Policy professionals, who work in the policy sphere, undertaking simulations to aid policy development, will have the skillset to use a microsimulation software tool, and, given the number of runs in developing a policy, will be concerned about speed. They are also generally interested in learning from policy experimentation undertaken in other countries, accessible through the library of policy routines in the software. They are unlikely to have the time to program additional functionality into software tools, contracting out these developments to others. Much training will be on the job, learning from peers or undertaking specific modelling workshops. The software they use needs to be complementary to their skillsets. Excel, however, is probably not transparent enough for their purposes if their main role is policy modelling, but may be sufficient for ad hoc analytical tasks.
- Microsimulation professionals are likely to have the skillset to engage with most of these software options, albeit as social scientists, their programming skills being generally weaker than software professionals. They are likely to have a greater interest in methodological development than a policy professional. As a result, they may wish to combine the range of libraries and routines in microsimulation software, with the power and functionality of being able to change the source code. Where microsimulation software is not open source, there may be incentives for experienced professionals to develop their own tools. In order to avoid the proliferation of modelling tools that has been seen in the field,

consideration should be given to encouraging model developers to provide access to source code for professionals with these more-advanced needs.

### 2.3.2 Software Tools for Different Modelling Objectives

In addition to user type, the choice of software may vary depending upon the modelling objective. The choice of modelling tool is considered for different objectives below:

- Hypothetical microsimulation. As the least-complex type of model, these have the possibility of utilizing a range of different solutions. Covering only a subset of population heterogeneity, their policy environment may also be less complex than a full population model. Therefore, a hypothetical model constructed for a specific purpose can use most options. Often, hypothetical microsimulation models are add-ons to existing tools, e.g., to do validation runs or single-family scenarios in EUROMOD. It is probably 'overkill' to use a computer language to develop a hypothetical model. Excel is often perfectly sufficient, and sometimes where replicability is required, as in the case of the OECD models, statistical software is used.
- Static models. Utilizing a population dataset requires static models to have some degree of sophistication in relation to data handling. Excel can be used for prototyping and teaching. However, longer-term projects require more-substantial software. Run speed is probably sufficient for a single-country model in a statistical software package. Nevertheless, building upon the community that has developed both EUROMOD and spin-offs such as SOUTHMOD, the EUROMOD framework is faster for static tax-benefit-model development.
- Behavioural labour-supply models. Requiring econometric estimation, it is inevitable that a statistical software package will be used. In a single-country setting, it may be preferable to add a static tax-benefit routine within a statistical software package to avoid having to learn multiple tools. However, in using labour supply in a cross-country setting, it makes sense to link statistical routines to a cross-country policy model such as EUROMOD. Computer-program tools can be useful for large datasets, where there is replication, or where very time-consuming estimation routines are used, given the speed advantages over statistical software tools.

- For consumption models and environmental models, with relatively simple policy environments, but with statistically estimated or derived demand systems, it makes sense to utilize a statistical software tool rather than use a microsimulation modelling tool, particularly taking advantage of their matrix-manipulation tools. Utilizing Excel, while possible, can become quite cumbersome given the multiplicity of different matrices. Computer programming software may be over-specified for this purpose.
- The increasing use of microsimulation for inequality decomposition has different requirements. Decomposing between policy and market income, particularly across countries, requires a microsimulation software tool, combined with a statistical software tool. On the other hand, where the balance shifts more towards decomposition of components of market income, such as demography, labour markets, and market incomes, and in particular the case where intra-country, inter-temporal decompositions are considered, then there may be merit in solely using a statistical software tool. Although not impossible, the use of Excel is impractical, while the use of a computer-program tool imposes too much model-environment development overheads on the model developer, particularly as speed is not of great concern. This, however, may change if additional layers of complexity are included, such as the interaction with structural labour-supply equations or finer degrees of disaggregation that require more iterations. In that case, the capacity of computer programs for speed and data optimization may become the dominant requirement.
- Dynamic microsimulation modelling, running over multiple years, is, by definition, more time intensive than many other areas, particularly if it also incorporates structural behavioural equations such as retirement choice. As a result, speed is an issue. In effect, Excel is ruled out for these reasons. It is possible to develop a small-sample-size, dynamic microsimulation model with a statistical package, but larger-scale models will put the package under pressure in terms of both speed and, potentially, size. Until the advent of specialized, dynamic microsimulation tools, such as LIAM2 or Modgen, it was inevitable that computer-program tools would be used for dynamic microsimulation models.
- The most time-intensive components of spatial microsimulation models are the reweighting or sampling algorithms used in generating the spatial data. For city-scale models, and for the simplest methods, such as iterative, proportional fitting, Excel is feasible. However, for more-complicated methods or for larger sample sizes, quicker packages, such

as those based upon computer programs or statistical software, are used. Lovelace and Dumont (2016) have recently developed a bespoke program in R for spatial microsimulation. While much of the literature thus far has focused on spatial-incidence analysis, with a focus on generating the spatial data and using geographic-information-system (GIS) tools for mapping and spatial analysis, there is merit in linking with other microsimulation tools for greater policy or behavioural analysis.

The choice of software tool, as a result, depends also on the nature of the microsimulation modelling.

### 2.3.3 Choice of Software for Students

The purpose of this chapter is to devise a software tool and approach to facilitate learning by students at the entry level. The conclusion of the analysis so far is that it is likely that students and practitioners with different skills and analytical needs will have different requirements. Similarly, different modelling objectives will require different tools.

Aiming to support students with limited analytical backgrounds, the model has quite specific objectives:

- It should enable students to learn how to do basic tax-benefit calculations.
- It must be able to take an external dataset, apply these calculations, and enable the student to run a simulation.
- It must enable the student to run post-simulation tabulations and calculations to evaluate a simulation.
- It shouldn't presume significant experience in computer programming or statistics.
- It must allow for group teaching, with perhaps mixed ability, as is typically the case in a computer suite, and typically with relatively short time available for interaction.

Given these requirements, it is likely that entry-level students from a practical perspective may only be able to engage with hypothetical and static microsimulation modelling in an initial course. Students with interests in other aspects of microsimulation are likely to progress on to other aspects in more-advanced courses, perhaps subsequent to having undertaken a statistical or econometrics course.

Weighing up the different issues above, and given potentially limited statistical skills and limited policy knowledge, an Excel-based framework makes most sense as a starting tool. It has the advantage of being relatively quick to engage with, while also having the benefit of familiarity to some degree for almost all students. Although Excel doesn't have a library of routines to draw from, if the objective is to first learn how policy instruments are structured, then starting with basic coding of instruments is a good learning objective. Similarly, for teaching purposes initially, as much of the pre-processing of data will be done before the class, the data-handling and manipulation advantages of statistical software are not a major issue.

As it is unlikely, although not impossible, that publication-grade analyses, with associated sample sizes, will be undertaken with the software, the speed of the framework is not so much of an issue. However, speed has two dimensions: the speed of simulation and the speed of development. While slower for simulation purposes, and more cumbersome and slightly less transparent than programming languages and statistical packages, spreadsheet software packages such as Microsoft Excel© have the advantage that most policy analysts are familiar with them. As a result, the speed of initial development of a basic model may be quicker than using other software, making it a suitable tool for development in a computer-practical environment as part of an introductory course. Spreadsheets also include an important set of features such as graphs, tabulations, and other in-built analytical tools.

The biggest issues that may impede learning are:

- transparency of the code
- data handling
- ease of use of the model environment

The later part of this chapter will focus on these issues. Next describes the development of a microsimulation model, with a focus on static or non-behavioural analyses using an Excel platform.

## 2.4 Methodology: The Computing Framework of XLSIM

### 2.4.1 Static Tax-Benefit Microsimulation Models

Static microsimulation models allow for policy and population complexity to be considered in a simulation-based analysis on micro-units, in this case, households and individuals. Due to the great diversity observed among the population, and the complexity of the tax-benefit systems, the redistributive analysis of the impact of social and fiscal policies requires that a high level of disaggregation should be used, in order to capture in fine detail their effects on the various types of individuals, families, and households.

Ultimately, it is the social and economic diversity typically found in the national populations that determines how economic agents will be affected by the tax and benefit rules. On the other hand, as different social programmes interact with each other and with the tax system, it is crucial to explicitly take into account the interdependencies within the whole tax-benefit system. The lack of analytical tools properly focused on the poor, and the neglect of the issue of how the programmes are to be financed, are major reasons why social and economic policies may fail to significantly reduce poverty.

The model described in this framework can be used to simulate policy on both hypothetical households and the population distribution. Typically, hypothetical families have been used to examine the operation of taxes and benefits and the impact of reforms (Burlacu et al. 2014). For example, the OECD uses this method to calculation the tax position of average workers. Although a useful method for illustration purposes, and for comparison across countries, the approach is not very satisfactory for looking at tax-benefit policy within a country, as families that are considered to be 'typical' may in fact form only a very small proportion of the population. It is desirable, therefore, to look at the population as a whole, using representative micro-datasets.

As static tax-benefit microsimulation models are computer programs that calculate tax liabilities and benefit entitlements for individuals, families, or households, in a nationally representative micro-data sample of the population, they require mechanisms to simulate policy rules and to store and work with data. A static tax-benefit microsimulation model calculates each element of the tax-benefit system in the legal order so that interactions between different elements of the system are fully taken into account. Calculations for each individual, family, or household are weighted to provide results at the population level.

By incorporating the interactions of different elements of the tax-benefit system, and by taking full account of the diversity of characteristics in the population, this approach allows a very detailed analysis of the revenue, the distributional and incentive effects of the individual policy instruments, and of the system as a whole. In particular, they give a great deal of flexibility to analysts. First, they simulate policy instruments that may not already exist in the micro-datasets on which they are based. They also have the capability of looking at the incidence of existing policy on actual populations to examine the efficiency of anti-poverty measures in actually reducing poverty. Additionally, as a simulation mechanism, they are well placed to look at the incentive impacts of existing policy, even in a static framework, where it is possible to measure the pressures on behaviour, such as marginal tax rates and replacement rates.

The primary advantage of microsimulation models, however, is that they can simulate policy reform. They can thus be used to compute the first-round revenue effects, and containing both social protection programmes and taxation instruments, models of this kind can look not only at changes to social policy programs but also examine different methods of financing:

- The first-round distribution of resulting winners and losers, particularly with reference to specific target populations, can also be found.
- Capturing the heterogeneity of government law, they can examine the interaction of different instruments.

Incorporating micro-data, they can also be used to look at the distributional impact of policy reform. Thus, it is possible to see how reforms affect households of different incomes, and to examine horizontal redistribution by focusing on families with children, the elderly, or the sick. Exploiting the hierarchical nature of households, they can also focus on gender dimensions by looking at within-household sharing and the impact of government policy.

The use of static microsimulation models can, therefore, greatly contribute to improved design and efficacy of policies (see for example Atkinson et al. 2002). The models provide a powerful aid to policy design and assessment, allowing users to consider how expenditure aimed at certain targeted groups is to be financed, how social spending is distributed among the population, and how fiscal and social policies impact on the different groups of the population. Thus, working with a microsimulation model, policy designers and analysts can simulate changes in the existing tax-benefit system, performing 'what if' experiments and examining their distributional and revenue implications (Redmond et al. 1998).

## 2.4.2 Computer Language

The origin of the modelling framework developed in this chapter resulted partly from a prototyping mechanism designed as part of the development of EUROMOD (Bourguignon et al. 2000) and partly from the author's need to develop a framework to train students and model developers. Its development grew from the technical challenges experienced by students and collaborators in utilizing microsimulation models that were developed in programming languages and statistical packages.

In developing the microsimulation tool to create a prototype model for six countries of the EU (Bourguignon et al. 1997), spreadsheets were used because of the speed with which a model could be developed. Within eighteen months, models were constructed for six countries and utilized for a range of policy analyses (e.g., Bourguignon et al 2000; Atkinson et al. 2002; Spadaro 2001). Excel was not used for the creation of the full EUROMOD model because it posed problems when dealing with some of the more-complicated requirements of a larger model. However, one has to weigh up the cost of development, which took at least four person-years for the development of the C-based model engine alone (see Immervoll and O'Donoghue 2009).

### 2.4.3 Model Structure

A static microsimulation model contains three elements: a policy calculator, a database, and a computing framework to undertake the simulation. This section describes the computing framework of the model XLSIM.

As described already, a microsimulation model is a model that takes micro-input data, applies tax-benefit rules and other calculations, such as behavioural equations, and simulates public policy, such as taxes and benefits, to produce output variables, such as disposable income.

Figure 2.1 describes the structure of an XLSIM microsimulation model. The model consists of three sets of Microsoft Excel© workbooks comprising:

- input data, containing the input data worksheets
- the model, containing the tax-benefit rules calculators, the data dictionaries, the parameter sheets, and the Visual Basic for Applications (VBA) simulation engine
- output data, containing the output-data worksheets

The core architecture of the model has many similarities with the Eur6 framework (see Bourguignon et al. 1998). The common feature of this framework, as with Eur6, is the use of VBA as the model environment, moving data between different input sources, modelling, and output for further analysis. While the code is visible to users, it is not necessary to understand

VBA to run the model, as these features are run via a button and associated parameters.

### 2.4.4 Generalization and Parameterization

While core architecture has many similarities with the Eur6 framework, there are many extra features that have been added to make the framework easier for analysts to develop new models from scratch, removing some of the complexities involved in model development. Also, the model allows for multiple units of analysis, so that results can be analysed both at family and household levels.

The main objective of the additional features were to deal with the challenges identified above and to adopt, where possible (and within the constraints of the framework), the features recommended by Immervoll and O'Donoghue (2009). Namely, they argue that a microsimulation model should incorporate flexibility, ease of use, robustness, transparency and consistency of structure and concepts, maintainability, and cost-effectiveness.

Extensive use is made of parameterization, ensuring that the model is flexible and easy to maintain and use. While the accessibility of Excel enhances the flexibility of the model, the fact that the tax-benefit rules are written in cells reduces the transparency, as one has to click on the cell to see the code.

Three particular aspects are utilized within Excel to improve transparency, robustness, and ease of use.

First, in relation to transparency, row names and variable names are used extensively to avoid using cell references, particularly as a model becomes more complicated. Depending upon their use, variables can be categorized as input, simulation, and output variables. In addition, variables can be combined into aggregate concepts, such as disposable income or tax bases etc. Variable characteristics, and the full variable list, also need to be stored.

Second, because of these requirements, introducing an additional variable can require changes in up to ten parts of the model. In order to facilitate the student or practitioner in adding or deleting variables of different types, and to give them variable names in Excel (without creating errors and without imposing greater Excel skill requirements), most of the model engine, written in VBA, focuses on assisting the user in these development objectives. Therefore, in addition to data-handling routines, most of the work of the VBA programs aims to assist the user to create the model. This speeds up development and learning in class.

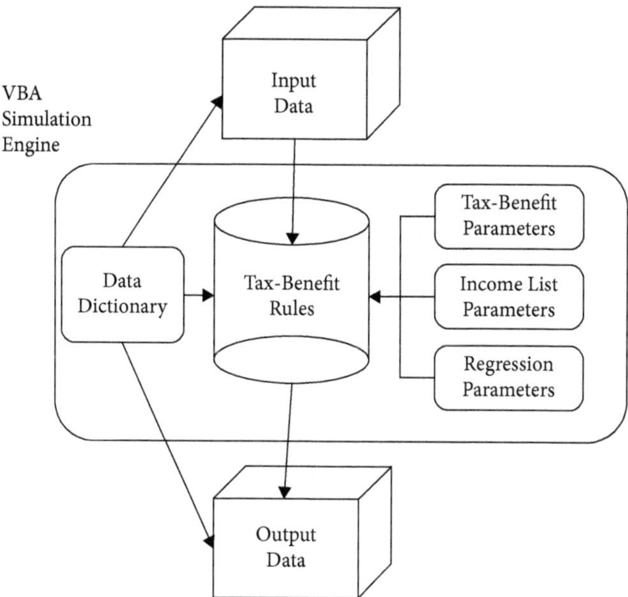


**Figure 2.1** Model Structure

Third, the VBA macros contain some error checking to prevent duplicates being inserted and a number of other errors being introduced.

## 2.5 Summary

In this chapter, we have described the structure of a new generic microsimulation model. The model is designed generically so as to be able to be applied to different countries, having been used at the time of publication to construct models for Estonia, Nigeria, Brazil, Ireland, and Pakistan. In order to facilitate ease of use, flexibility, and accessibility to students, policy analysts, civil servants, and academics, the model has been created in Microsoft Excel© utilizing the inbuilt VBA programming language. However, previous knowledge of this language is not required by the user as the principal functions have been automated utilizing easy-to-use buttons.

Utilizing macros in this way is an intermediate stage between doing all simulations manually using the Excel interface and designing a fully fledged graphical user interface (GUI). While creating a GUI is relatively straightforward, and was developed as part of an earlier version of the model, the author found it inconvenient, slowing down the creation of simulations. Nevertheless, this intermediate step has been created to allow for the advantages of an interface in terms of macros, but without cumbersome dialogue boxes.

## 2.6 Appendix

### 2.6.1 The Model Workbook

The model is constructed in Microsoft Excel© and consists of a set of VBA macros and a number of worksheets.

Command—this worksheet contains the buttons and initial parameters to run the model, such as what tax-benefit system to run, which dataset to use etc. There are also utilities for adding new variables, tax-benefit systems, parameters, and income lists.

TaxBenRules—this worksheet contains rules of the tax-benefit system and is where the calculations take place.

Parameters—this worksheet contains the features such as income-tax allowances, rates and bands, child-benefit amounts, social-insurance contribution rates, and indirect tax rates, required for particular instances of the tax-benefit system.

InclistBase—this worksheet contains the vectors detailing the components of aggregate income concepts (income lists), such as disposable income, taxable income, etc.

RegressParameters—this worksheet contains features for regression equations used in the models such as those of expenditure, labour supply, and benefit take-up.

There are three types of variables used in the model:

- input variables that are imported from the external database
- simulated variables that are simulated in the TaxBenRules worksheet
- outputted variables such as disposable income, total taxation, and benefits are outputted after a simulation

Some simple tabulations are calculated on these data, or alternatively they can be exported to specialized statistical or tabulation software for more-detailed analyses of the results.

#### 2.6.1.1 VBA Macros

The VBA routines are responsible for running the model and for assisting the user in creating the model as follows:

Run Model—this macro does the data handling, which runs the model. It copies each family in turn from the output-data workbook and pastes it into the <TaxBenRules> worksheet of the model workbook. The tax-benefit calculations are then carried out. The macro allows for both family- and household-level output variables to be calculated, with the output variables then transferred to the output (family and household) workbooks. The method used is based upon a technique suggested by Sastre-Descals in Bourguignon et al. (1997).

Insert Simulation Variable—when a user wants to create a new simulation variable or calculation, this macro can be used to carry out all the steps necessary to include the variable in the model, including adding to the <TaxBenRules> tax-benefit calculations worksheet, the creation of variable names, the addition to the <IncListBase> income list worksheet, the addition to the <SimVardesc> simulation variable-data-dictionary worksheet, and the addition to the <RegressParameters> simulation variable-data-dictionary worksheet.

Insert Input Variable—when a user wants to add a new input variable, this macro can be used to carry out all the steps necessary to include the variable in the model, including adding to the <TaxBenRules> tax-benefit calculations worksheet and the creation of variable names, the addition to the <IncListBase> income-list worksheet, the addition to the <InpVardesc> simulation variable-data-dictionary worksheet, and the addition to the <RegressParameters> simulation variable-data-dictionary worksheet.

Insert Output Variable—when a user wants to add a new output variable, this macro can be used to carry out all the steps necessary to include the variable in the model, including adding to the <TaxBenRules> tax-benefit calculations worksheet and the creation of variable names, the addition to the <IncListBase> income-list worksheet, the addition to the <OutVardesc> simulation variable-data-dictionary worksheet, and the addition to the <RegressParameters> simulation variable-data-dictionary worksheet.

Insert Income List—this macro adds a new column in the income-list <InclistBase> worksheet and creates a name for the income list and for both spouse-sets of variables as described below. This allows for aggregate income concepts to be created in the <TaxBenRules> tax-benefit worksheet.

Insert System—this macro allows the parameters for a new system to be added in the <Parameters> parameters worksheet. The initial parameters are based upon a copy of the existing parameters specified by the user.

Insert Parameter—this macro inserts new policy parameters in a row specified by the user in the <Parameters> parameters worksheet and creates a variable name for the new parameter.

Insert Regression—this macro takes regression coefficients specified by the user, checks to make sure that the variables exist in the model, adds the coefficients to the <RegressParameters> regression-parameters worksheet, creates a prediction variable, and then carries out the simulation of the regression, including a Monte Carlo-generated error term if necessary.

Delete Macros—for each of the 'insert macros' there is a corresponding delete macro that removes the component from the model.

### 2.6.2 The Datasets

We now describe the structure of the data sheets.

#### 2.6.2.1 Input Data

The input data is stored in a separate Microsoft Excel© workbook with file name defined in DataFile and worksheet name defined in DataSheet in the <COMMAND> worksheet. Each row in the dataset represents a different 'family'. By family, we mean the nuclear family, the head of the family plus (where they exist) a spouse and dependant children. Households can have multiple families, where non-dependant children, other relatives, and other household members have separate rows in the dataset, together with their spouses and children.

The definition of a dependant child varies with the objectives and use of the model. For example, one that looks only at the tax-benefit system may include children up to the age determined by the policy system, say sixteen. However, in considering the impact of the policy system on child labour, it may be necessary to identify children separately from the age of ten.

There are three sets of variables for each family: household-level variables, variables of the first spouse, and, where they exist, variables for the second spouse. The set of variables for both spouses are the same, with suffixes '1' and '2' for each spouse respectively. The set of compulsory variables that the model requires for it to run are defined below. The user can of course add extra variables where required.[3]

Note when creating the input dataset to sort the families so as to have the head of household (HOH) in the last family. This is because the household calculations occur during the last family of the household.

[3] Contact the author for a copy of the Stata code to generate this dataset.

For validation and illustration purposes, it is often useful to calculate the tax-benefit system for synthetic data. We enclose with the model a dataset with the following synthetic families, each with twenty income points:

- working-age single person
- working-age single parent
- working-age couple
- pension-age single person
- pension-age couple
- working-age couple with children

The incomes are points representing a proportion of the average wage. Therefore, to use the synthetic data, multiply by the average wage.

Note also that the model is calculated in terms of monthly income. Therefore, incomes will need to be converted to average monthly amounts.

When the model is run, it will check to make sure that the input variables in the dataset are the same as the expected input variables in the <TaxBenRules> worksheet.

#### 2.6.2.2 Output Data

Output variables are stored in two separate workbooks for households and families, with the default workbook names <Country Name> + <Reform Policy Name> and <Country Name> + <Reform Policy Name> + <TU>.

The household output data are copied form row 13 and the family output data are copied from row 7 in the <TaxBenRules> worksheet. In each workbook, there are separate worksheets for the baseline and reform-policy runs. If there is more than one input-data worksheet, then there will be the same number of output-data worksheets.

### 2.6.3 The Model Worksheets

#### 2.6.3.1 TaxBenRules

Table 2.3 shows part of the <TaxBenRules> worksheet. The row numbers on the left-hand side of the worksheet are shown for illustrative purposes and are not coded in the actual sheet.

The <Run Model> macro takes data from the input dataset and pastes each family line-by-line into row 3. In order to identify when the next household starts, we also paste the next family into row 4.

This data is then transformed from one line per family to data about the first spouse in column 3 and the second spouse, if they exist, in column 4, with family aggregates in column 2. Calculations for each spouse take place directly in the relevant column.

Row 14, column 1 is a model-generated cell which is used to indicate whether the baseline or reform-policy system is being simulated. As we shall see later, because of the interest in examining the impact of policy reforms, the model runs two policy systems at a time. This cell stores the value 1 when a baseline analysis is being run and a value 2 if a reform analysis is being run.

The data are organized so that the name of the 'simulation variable' is stored in column 1. In the model, variable names are used for calculations to aid transparency. In Microsoft Excel©, the row-name feature is utilized so that the name in column 1 refers to the variable name used to access the information in the relevant row, remembering that calculations take place for each spouse in the same column. Note that by default, the naming convention used for simulation variables is <Sim_> + <Variable Name>, in order to differentiate it from tax-benefit parameters.

Although not visible in Table 2.3, the calculations and simulation variables are grouped into different blocks, again to aid transparency. It is recommended that these are grouped into the following blocks (although users may use their own discretion here):

- data-input variables, containing incomes, labour market, demographic, and household characteristics
- policy simulations, containing sub-blocks in turn of the simulated policies
- regression simulations, containing the simulations of the desired regressions

Output Variables contains all the output variables. When adding new output variables, the model does not give the user a choice about where these variables are added as they are required to be stored in the Aggregate Output block at the end of the model. This is so that when the reform analysis is being run, the output from the baseline analysis can be copied and stored, in order that comparisons necessary for winner/loser and welfare losses can be calculated.

Once the tax-benefit policies and regressions have been simulated, the outputs are then passed into row 7 of the <TaxBenRules> worksheet. These are family-level outputs. In order to produce household-level outputs, the outputs of all families within the household need to be summed. To do this,

**Table 2.3** General Structure of TaxBenRules Worksheet

| 1. INPUT VARIABLES | | | | |
|---|---|---|---|---|
| 2. Input-Variable Names | | | | |
| 3. Input-Variable Values of Family (i) | | | | ... |
| 4. Input-Variable Values of Family (i+1) | | | | ... |
| 5. OUTPUT VARIABLES | Family Unit-Level Variables | | | |
| 6. Output (Family Level)-Variable Names | | | | |
| 7. Output-Variable Values of Family (i) | | | | ... |
| 8. | Household Unit-Level Variables | | | |
| 9. | Output (Household Level)-Variable Names | | | |
| 10. Current Family Unit | Output-Variable Values of Family (i) | | | |
| 11. Previous Family Units in Household | Cumulative Sum of Output-Variable Values of Previous Families in Household | | | |
| 12. | Output (Household Level)-Variable Names | | | |
| 13. Total Household | Cumulative Sum of Output-Variable Values of Previous and Current Families in Household | | | |
| 14. 1.00 | Baseline/Reform Scenario | | | |
| 15. | | | | |
| 16. | Family | Spouse 1 | Spouse 2 | Description |
| 17. Employment Income | | | | |
| 18. Sim_empy | 0 | 5,000 | 0 | ABC |
| 19. Sim_slfemy | 0 | 0 | 0 | ABC |
| 22. | | | | |
| 23. Other income | | | | ABC |
| 24. Sim_prvpen | 0 | 0 | 0 | ABC |
| 25. Sim_invy | 3 | 3 | 0 | ABC |
| 26. Sim_propy | 4 | 2 | 2 | ABC |
| 27. Sim_mainty | 0 | 0 | 0 | ABC |
| 28. Sim_prvtrn | 0 | 0 | 0 | ABC |
| 29. Sim_regy | 0 | 0 | 0 | ABC |
| 30. Sim_othery | 0 | 0 | 0 | ABC |
| 31. Sim_lumpy | 3 | 1 | 2 | ABC |
| ⋮ | ⋮ | ⋮ | ⋮ | ⋮ |

current family output is passed into row 10 and then added to the cumulative sum of previous family outputs to produce total household output. For this reason, it is advised to have the HOH in the final family. Both the family output and the household output are then copied into the relevant output files at the end of the baseline and reform runs.

What follows includes some example code for a hypothetical country.

## Tax base

```
Sim_taxbase = max(0, SUMPRODUCT(iltaxbableY,sp1taxbableY) - SUMPRODUCT(iltaxallowance,sp1taxallowance))
```

In the above case, we subtract the income list of tax allowances from the income list of taxable incomes, ensuring that the tax base does not go negative.

Tax calculation (with two tax bands)

Sim_tax = Par_tax1*min(Par_taxband1, Sim_taxbase) + Par_tax2*max (0,Sim_taxbase—Par_taxband1)

In this case, the lower tax (Par_tax1) is levied on the income in the first tax band up to the maximum of the value of the band (Par_taxband1), with remaining income taxes at the higher rate, (Par_tax2).

Child benefit (CB)

Sim_CB = Par_cb_rate*Sim_numchildren

Here, CBs are equal to the CB rate times the number of children in the family.

#### 2.6.3.2 Parameters

Associated with each tax-benefit calculation is the associated parameters, containing information regarding the actual rates and bands of income taxation etc. In Figure 2.2, we outline an example parameter sheet.

Alternative policy systems are archived between column <first_system> and <last_system>. At present, there are two systems, but one could store as many as an Excel worksheet allows, approximately two-hundred-and-fifty columns. The names of each policy parameter are located in column A. The default naming convention is <Country Name> + <"_"> + <Parameter Name>. To access one of these parameters, simply refer to them as an Excel variable (e.g., =Par_ub_rr*Sim_empy). Column B refers to the column that is accessed by the <TaxBenRules> worksheet and is transformed using information in column C from column D. The code in column C relates to the period of the parameter stored in the archive (e.g., 1 for year, 2 for month, 3 for week, 4 for rate). The values in column D are transformed into monthly figures in column C, as it is assumed that calculations in the model are done with a monthly accounting period.

When the model is run, the baseline and reform systems specified in the <COMMAND> worksheet are copied into the BaselineColumn column E and ReformColumn column F respectively. Then, each in turn is copied into column D as the baseline and reform analyses are run.

#### 2.6.3.3 Income Lists and Regressions

These two worksheets, <InclistBase> and <RegressParameters>, are handled together because their operation is similar. Each sheet contains three parts:

| Policy Paramter | Parameter val. (weeklified) | Period | RunColumn | Baseline Column | ReformColumn | | | |
|---|---|---|---|---|---|---|---|---|
| Number of Systems (nSYS) | Base params pw | 1:y, 2:m 3:w, 4:r | 2003 | 2010 | 2010 | first_system | 2010 | last_system |
| 1 | | | | | | | | |
| Year | | | 2003 | 2010 | 2010 | | 2010 | |
| **Child Benefits** | | | | | | | | |
| **Other Beneifts** | | | | | | | | |
| Par_pov_ben_rate | 0 | 2 | 0 | 0 | 0 | | 0 | |
| Par_means_rate | 0 | 2 | 0 | 0 | 0 | | 0 | |
| **Calculations** | | | | | | | | |
| Par_poverty_rate | 0.00 | 2 | 0 | 0 | 0 | | 0 | |
| **Net-to-Gross Calculation (Switch)** | | | | | | | | |
| Par_do_ntg | 1.00 | 2 | 1 | 1 | 1 | | 1 | |
| **EquvilanceScales** | | | | | | | | |
| Par_es_child | 0.00 | 2 | 0 | 0 | 0 | | 0 | |
| Par_es_adult | 0.00 | 2 | 0 | 0 | 0 | | 0 | |
| **Poverty Line Calculations** | | | | | | | | |
| Par_povline_perc_median | 0.00 | 2 | 0 | 0 | 0 | | 0 | |
| **Uprating** | | | | | | | | |
| Par_update_default | 1.00 | 2 | 1 | 1 | 1 | | 1 | |
| Par_update_default1 | 1.00 | 2 | 1 | 1 | 1 | | 1 | |

**Figure 2.2** Parameter Worksheet

- the income-list or regression-coefficient vector $(\beta)$
- the vector of spouse1 characteristics $(X_1)$
- the vector of spouse2 characteristics $(X_2)$

In both cases, the resulting simulated variable (Y) is of the form:

$$Y_i = \beta' X_i, i = 1,2$$

The income-list vector $(\beta)$ contains normally (although not necessarily) a set of (1,0,-1) and is used to generate a set of aggregate income concepts. For example, the disposable-income list would contain 1s for market incomes and benefits, -1s for taxes, and 0s for other variables. Occasionally, other values are used. In the UK tax-benefit system, half of private pension contributions are deductible, in which case the income-list coefficient would be -0.5. It is important to remember that non-income variables should not be added, and so should in general should have a 0 coefficient.

The regression-coefficient vector $(\beta)$, meanwhile, has the usual meaning in regression models. However, because the vector includes all variables in the model, the variables not in the regression equation have a zero vector value. Nevertheless, for convenience, as outlined below, regression coefficients are inputted only for the variables used in the regression model, and the model by default stores a value of zero for each variable not in the model. There is a separate column for each of the $(\beta)$ vectors, each with its own table name in the form il or regress + <name>, e.g., ilmarkety or Regresstotexp. These are created automatically by the model when new income lists or regressions are added in the <COMMAND> worksheet.

Meanwhile, in both cases, the model stores the values of the spouse characteristics from columns C and D in $X_1$ and $X_2$ respectively. These vectors exist for each income list or regression vector, although they are the same for each vector, as each represents the current value of the relevant variable. The vectors spouse1 and spouse2 also have vector names in the form sp1 or sp2 + <name>, e.g., sp1markety or sp2totexp.

In order to use income lists in the worksheet <TaxBenRules>, it is necessary to use the Excel SUMPRODUCT command. For example, for market income:

```
=SUMPRODUCT(ilmarkety,sp1markety) for spouse 1 in column C
=SUMPRODUCT(ilmarkety,sp2markety) for spouse 2 in column D
```

For regressions, the operation is more complicated, and so the VBA program in the model does more of the work for the user. Here, when the user specifies a regression model, the VBA program creates three simulation variables in the <TaxBenRules> worksheet.

First, the BX variable, which merely multiplies the sp1 or sp2 X vectors with the coefficient vector $(\beta)$. The variable has the naming convention <Sim_BX_> + <Regression Name>.

Next, the error-term variable. In Monte Carlo simulation, the user may want to sample from the distribution of the error term $\varepsilon$ of the $Y = f(X\beta + \varepsilon)$ regression model. The type of error term will depend upon the regression type defined in the <COMMAND> worksheet: Regression, Regression with logged dependent variable, Logit model, or Probit model. It depends upon the value of the standard error of the error term also defined by the user. The variable has the naming convention <Sim_error_> + <Regression Name>. If the error term is not to be used, so that each individual is given the average value for the simulated variable of those with the same characteristics, then the error term is assigned a zero value.

Lastly, the model determines the simulated value of the dependent variable. In the case of regressions, it sums the error term and the BX term. In the case of regressions with log-dependent variables, it takes the exponent of the sum of the error term and the BX term. In the case of Logit or Probit models, it transforms the BX term into predicted probabilities (p) using the appropriate F() transformation and sets the simulated value equal to 1, if the simulated uniformly distributed variable in the error term is less than p and 0 otherwise. The variable has the naming convention <Sim_> + <Regression Name>.

Note that the user should remember to avoid circularities when using income lists, i.e., do not include variables as inputs to income lists or regressions, which in turn depend upon the income list or regression.

#### 2.6.3.4 *Data Dictionaries*

There are three data-dictionary worksheets, <SimVardesc>, <InpVardesc>, and <OutVardesc>, for the three types of variables, respectively simulated variables, input variables, and output variables. These worksheets initially simply record the variable name and description, but allow for increased information about variables as the model is extended.

#### 2.6.3.5 *Command*

The <COMMAND> worksheet is the worksheet where the user specifies how the model is run and what is included in the model. Figure 2.3 shows part of this worksheet.

#### 2.6.3.6 *Running the Model*

In order to run the model, the user needs to specify the following information:

- baseline policy run—the column name from the <Parameters> worksheet to be run as the baseline policy
- reform policy run—the column name from the <Parameters> worksheet to be run as the reform policy
- number of families—specify the number of families to be run
- data file—specify the name of the Excel workbook containing the input data

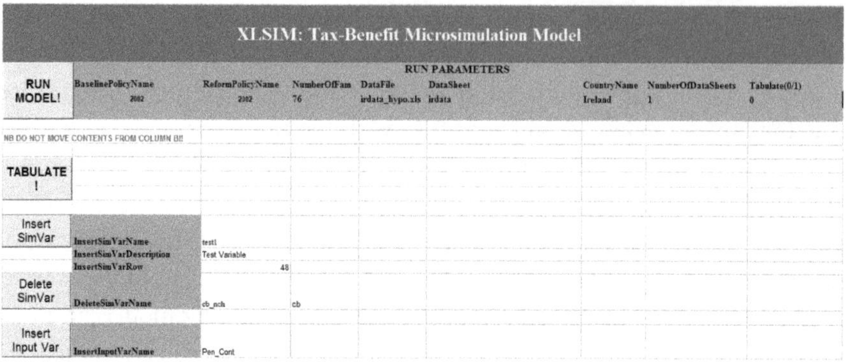

**Figure 2.3** The Command Sheet

- data sheet—specify the name of the worksheet containing the input data within the data file
- country name—specify the two-character name of the country being simulated, e.g., IR, US, UK, JP, and BR
- number of data sheets—normally this is only one
- tabulate (0/1)—this is switch which tells the model to calculate some simple output statistics (note, this feature only works if there is one input-data sheet!)

Once the parameters have been specified, click RUN MODEL! This button invokes the Run Model VBA macro. The model runs the baseline and reform systems in turn that are specified for each household and stores them in an output workbook with the name of the reform-policy system.

#### 2.6.3.7 Inserting and Deleting Variables

There are a number of buttons for inserting the different types of variables. Except for Regressions, the model allows more than one parameter, variable system, etc. to be inserted or deleted at a time. In each case, add the parameters between the parameter name in column B and the cell containing the text 'end'.

Simulation Variable—pressing the Insert SimVar button invokes the macro Insert Simulation Variable. It places the variable, with the name convention <Sim_> + <Variable Name> InsertSimVarName, in the worksheet <TaxBenRules> in row InsertSimVarRow and utilizes the description InsertSimVarDescription. To delete a variable, place the variable's name in InsertSimVarName and click the button Delete SimVar.

Input Variable—pressing the Insert Input Var button invokes the macro Insert Input Variable. It places the variable, with the name convention <Sim_> + <Variable Name> InsertInputVarName, in the worksheet

<TaxBenRules> in row InsertInputVarRow and utilizes the description InsertInputVarDescription. If the variable is a categorical variable, write the values of the categories in InsertInputVarCategorizations (for non-income variables, write 'n/a'). In addition, in order to uprate an income variable, store the parameter value (e.g., par_default_update) in InsertInputVarUprate Parameter. It also adds a column for the variable to the input-data rows 3 and 4 in the worksheet <TaxBenRules>. Note that an input variable also needs to be added to the input-data file for the model to run. To delete a variable place, place the variable's name in InsertInputVarName and click the button Delete InputVar.

Output Variable—pressing the Insert Output Var button invokes the macro Insert Output Variable. It places the variable, with the name convention <Sim_> + <Variable Name> InsertOutputVarName, in the worksheet <TaxBenRules> in the final row in the aggregate-output section of the model and utilizes the description InsertOutputVarDescription. It also adds a column for the variable to the output-data rows (6–13) in the worksheet <TaxBenRules>. To delete a variable place, the variable's name in InsertOutputVarName and click the button Delete OutputVar.

The model will not allow a variable to be added with the same name as an existing variable. It will create variable names in the <TaxBenRules> worksheet. One can then refer to this cell up or down the column relating to the first or second spouse by referring to the created variable name (e.g., =Sim_ABC+2).

#### 2.6.3.8 Inserting Income Lists

In order to add an income list, add the name of the new income list in the InsertILName. The model will not allow the user to add a new income list with the same name as an existing income list or regression parameter. The initial coefficients of the income list are 0. The coefficients will have to be inputted manually by the user. Similarly, to delete an income list, include the name in DeleteILName.

#### 2.6.3.9 Inserting Systems

When inserting a new system for a new policy year or a reform policy, decide on a unique name and include it in InsertSystemName and click the button Insert System. In many cases, for example in a reform-policy run, the user will only wish to change a small number of parameters; therefore, in order to save time, this can be achieved by including the name of an existing system in TemplateForNewSystem, and the new system is thus a copy of this existing system. If you wish to start with a blank system, then simply write 'n/a' in this cell. The changed parameters will then have to be entered manually. To delete a system, write the name of the system to be deleted in DeleteSystemName and click the button Delete System.

#### 2.6.3.10 Inserting Parameters

When inserting a new parameter, include it in InsertParameterName, decide on the row in the <Parameters> worksheet for it to be included in InsertParameterRow, and click the button Insert Parameter. To delete a parameter, write the name of the parameter to be deleted in DeleteParameterName and click the button Delete Parameter.

#### 2.6.3.11 Inserting Regressions

There are a number parameters that need to be included to insert a regression model in XLSIM.

First, the name of the dependent variable InsertRegressionName. This name (in the usual format) is added to the row InsertRegressionRow in the <TaxBenRules> worksheet. As highlighted above, three variables are in fact inserted, relating to the BX and error components of the regressions, in addition to the dependent variable.

Next, the regression type RegressType is selected from the set of Regression (Regress), Regression with a Log-Dependent Variable (LnRegress), Logit Model (Logit), and Probit Model (Probit).

Third, in relation to whether an error term is to be used in the model (ErrorTerm_0/1), write a '1' or '0' in the cell to indicate whether or not it is to be included.

Fourth, the value of the standard error of the error of regression equation is defined as SE.

Last, the variables and associated coefficients of the model need to be stored between first_varname and end_varname. The model will check to ensure that each variable name specified is a simulated variable. Although the example sheet contains standard errors, t-values, and p-values, as well as confidence intervals (as per Stata output), the program will work if at least the variable name and coefficients are included.

### 2.6.4 Uprating

We have already mentioned the issue of uprating in passing. As the year of simulation may not necessarily be the same as the year of simulation (the year from which policy rules are taken), it will be necessary to uprate the dataset to account for differences in the intervening period. For this purpose, external information will be needed.

The model allows for income variables to have variable-specific uprating indices, stored as parameters in the worksheet <Parameters>. When adding new income variables, ensure that the uprating parameter exists first, as otherwise the model will not allow you to add the variable.

## 2.6.5 Tabulations

On the basis of the output sheets, the model calculates a number of basic tabulations if the Tabulate(0/1) parameter is set to 1 in the <COMMAND> worksheet. For the tabulations to run, the model requires the following variables to be outputted:

- family unit ID (FUID)
- household unit ID (HUID)
- weight (Weight)
- disposable income (DisposableY)
- number of persons in the unit (nPers)
- number of families in the unit (nCh)

The user specifies the equivalence scale in the OECD format with parameters (par_es_adult, par_es_child) in the <Parameters> worksheet.

Calculations are produced both at the family and household units of analysis, while the difference in disposable income between the runs is regarded as the net effect of the reform. The calculations produced are:

- mean disposable income before and after the reform
- cost of a reform (comparing weighted total disposable income in both runs)
- poverty headcount for both runs
- poverty gap for both runs
- the target efficiency of the reform
- the Gini coefficient for both runs
- redistributive and progressivity impacts of the reform
- the distributive impact of the reform by equalized, disposable-income decile

The distribution of replacement rates is calculated so that the user can define the potential in-work wage for unemployed people to be either a flat amount or a predicted amount, using a wage regression. The replacement rate reported is that of the head of the family.

The distribution of marginal effective tax rates is calculated where the marginal increase in incomes is applied to the empty variable of the head of family of one currency unit.

These statistics are reported in the <Tabulation> worksheet of the output-data workbooks.

# PART II
# STATIC MODELS

# 3
# Anti-Poverty Policy

## 3.1 Introduction

Reducing poverty is one of the main objectives of the welfare state. Microsimulation models, which simulate the legislative detail of poverty-reduction instruments at the level of the individual or family, can be used to make social-protection instruments more effective in this objective by helping to improve the targeting of these instruments.

Microsimulation models are used extensively to design policy to meet these targets and to evaluate progress towards achieving these targets. For example, in the UK, the Institute for Fiscal Studies has established itself as an independent and influential analytical institute which extensively uses microsimulation models (Crawford and Johnson 2015). Similarly, Holly Sutherland, at the University of Essex, with colleagues in the EUROMOD network, developed tools to look at the poverty impact of policy at the European level (Sutherland and Figari 2013). Prior to 2010, much of the social-protection research using microsimulation models was undertaken in OECD countries (de Lathouwer 1996; Martini and Trivellato 1997; Frick et al. 2000; Sutherland 2002; Atkinson et al. 2002). In recent years, however, much of the use of microsimulation models for social-protection analysis has moved from OECD countries to developing countries (Mideros et al. 2016; Bastagli 2015; Decoster 2019; Osei et al. 2017).

A range of government policy mechanisms are being used to try to achieve poverty targets, including benefits targeting low-income families with children, and efforts to reduce work disincentives faced by families with children, such as child-care support and active labour-market polices, which try to make it easier for people to return to the labour market. While many policy interventions (from social-protection instruments, through labour-market policy, to public health, education, and child-care interventions) can impact upon poverty objectives, in this chapter the design and development of social transfers with the aim of reducing poverty is the main focus. These policy examples are used as a case study to take the first step in developing a simple microsimulation model.

*Practical Microsimulation Modelling.* Cathal O'Donoghue. Oxford University Press. © Cathal O'Donoghue 2021.
DOI: 10.1093/oso/9780198852872.003.0003

Here, some of the initial steps required in the development of a hypothetical non-behavioural or static microsimulation model for anti-poverty analysis are discussed, starting first with the structure of the dataset required for microsimulation modelling. Later, an understanding of the structure of social transfers is developed, and the concept of a hypothetical microsimulation model (Burlacu et al. 2014) is utilized to illustrate this. Although it abstracts from the population complexity, as described in Chapter 1, it allows us in a simpler way to understand the targeting and structure of anti-poverty policies. These models are used both for analysis in their own right and as a means of validating more-complex models.

Data quality and structure is a key input into a microsimulation model. In Section 3.3 of this chapter, some of the issues that arise in creating a base dataset for a microsimulation model are discussed. Given the dimensions of complexity in microsimulation models identified in the introduction to this book, validation, debugging, and error checking are paramount. In Section 3.4, the development of a hypothetical family model to use for validation purposes is introduced, while in Section 3.5 some concepts used to calculate the poverty efficiency of a social-protection instrument are discussed. Finally, Section 3.6 details the development of a simple, static-benefit microsimulation model and an analysis of the data.

## 3.2 Policy Design: The Design of Social Transfer

In order to contextualize the development of microsimulation models to simulate the impact of policy transfers on poverty, we firstly define what we mean by social transfers and present an overview of how they are classified.

Social transfers can have many objectives, including, among others, income maintenance, income smoothing, poverty alleviation, and vertical redistribution and horizontal transfers. The complex set of objectives, together with national, design, historical, and administrative constraints, can result in a wide range of potential policy designs. There are many studies, such as Esping-Anderson (2013), that categorize these types of social transfers, usually into contribution-based social insurance, means-tested social assistance, and universal benefits. Welfare regimes are then categorized depending upon the importance of different types of instruments within a system.

A slightly different approach, however, is taken in microsimulation modelling. Rather than a high-level focus on general objectives, or focusing on

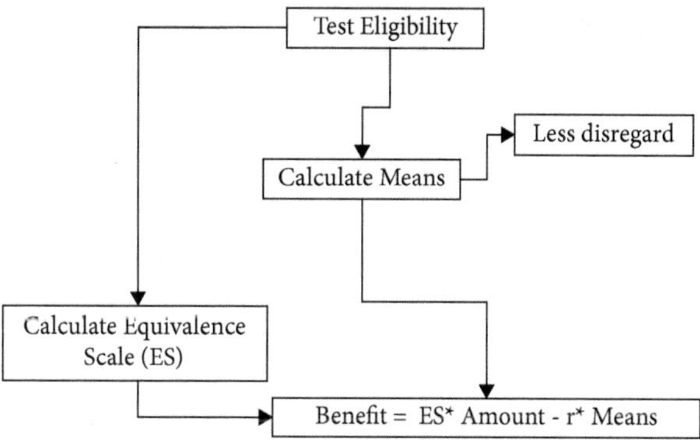


**Figure 3.1** Social-Benefit Modules
See Eardley et al. (1996), Matsaganis et al. (2006), and Gough et al. (1997).

the system, the focus is on the legislative detail of individual policy instruments, and, as such, focuses more on the mathematical structure to aid programming.

In modelling social benefits within a microsimulation model, components are classified into a number of discrete steps. Figure 3.1 shows the main common elements of social benefits, and they can be further described:

- The first component is eligibility. This component determines whether the relevant unit is eligible for the benefit.
- If the benefit depends upon the 'means' of an individual (i.e., the income that is set against a benefit), the means are calculated.
- Next, the 'equivalence scale', for determining the benefit amount as a function of characteristics of the fiscal unit (such as age, number of children, etc.), is specified.
- In general terms, the amount of payment as the base amount times the equivalence scale minus the means times a withdrawal rate (r) is defined.

Almost all social benefits can be coded using these components. It is also a useful categorization device for comparing the operation of different benefits over time and across countries.

A basic-income policy is an extreme version of this, with potentially limited eligibility criteria and no means test. In addition to being an important policy objective, given reduced work disincentives, it is also a useful comparator for the functioning of tax-benefit systems (Browne and Immervoll 2017).

### 3.2.1 Unit of Analysis

Within microsimulation modelling, an important concept is the unit of analysis. It relates to the level of aggregation to which the instrument applies. For example, the eligibility or means of the relevant unit may be taken into consideration in calculating the amount of benefit, if any, to which a unit is entitled. There are a number of potential levels of aggregation or unit of analysis:

- The individual is the lowest unit of aggregation, where only the eligibility of an individual is used for the calculation. Similarly, their means are incorporated into a potential means test. This is typically the case in social-insurance benefits where eligibility depends upon personal social-insurance contributions.
- The benefit unit or tax unit is perhaps the most common unit of analysis used in tax-benefit systems. It typically refers to a nuclear-family unit, including spouses, sometimes cohabiting partners, and dependant children. The definition of a child can vary substantially across characteristics such as age, income, education, or disability status. This is the case in the UK and French systems.
- In some situations, the unit of analysis is the household, where perhaps the means of all individuals within a household are considered. The German social-assistance system has a household unit of analysis.
- Occasionally, the unit of analysis can go beyond the limits of a household, where one is expected to rely on the wider family before recourse to benefits.

Some instruments have mixed units of analysis. For example, a social-insurance benefit may depend upon individual contributions, but the payment may depend upon the characteristics of the family of the recipient when, for example, adult dependant payments are made. Similarly, a social-assistance benefit may be paid to a nuclear family but be dependent upon the incomes of the wider household, as in the case of Italy or Ireland.

### 3.2.2 Eligibility

Regardless of the nature of the instrument, the first component in the simulation of a social benefit is the determination of eligibility. The principal characteristics that influence eligibility for a benefit include:

- contingency related to income loss—eligibility for many benefits, rather than depending solely on low income, requires a low income-related contingency to have occurred (such as unemployment, disability, widowhood, retirement)
- demographic characteristics, such as gender, age, marital status, number of children, pregnancy, citizenship, residency, household structure, contribution history
- income in a certain income range
- work test (seeking work) or particular hours of work
- exclusions (self-employment status, education participation, public sector)
- duration in receipt of the benefit
- conditionality, such as attendance of children in education

The eligibility condition can interact with the unit of analysis. For example, eligibility may depend upon at least one member of the unit being eligible, with the wider family being eligible if one member is eligible. Conversely, the family may not be eligible if one member is ineligible.

Combining these eligibility components will determine the coverage of the benefit. A basic-income-type benefit will have 100 per cent coverage due to universal eligibility, but many instruments will have quite limited coverage for various reasons, such as low coverage or particular income limits. An instrument with limited eligibility may have a low coverage if many groups are excluded from entitlement (such as students, self-employed, civil servants). As a result, Ferrera (1996) argues that transfers in Mediterranean countries should not be categorized with those in Central Europe in benefit typologies, even if ostensibly they are earnings-related, social-insurance benefits. Benefits in Southern Europe often have significantly shorter durations or limited eligibility or lower income thresholds, and as a result have significantly lower coverage than equivalent instruments in Central Europe.

### 3.2.3 Maximum Amount

For benefit units that are eligible for the benefit, the maximum amount possible, the gross benefit ($Benefit_{Gross}$), is first calculated. The maximum benefit amount relates to the amount of benefit that can be received on condition of eligibility, but before any means test is applied.

Factors that may influence the size of the benefit include:

- structure of family
- replacement rate
- duration in receipt of benefit
- contributions paid

The structure of the family may influence the size of the benefit through what is known as an equivalence scale (Cowell and Mercader-Prats 1999; Van de Ven et al. 2017). While at one extreme, the benefit may provide a flat amount to the beneficiary unit, regardless of size (per unit), and at the other extreme, the benefit may provide an amount to each member of the unit (per capita), it is common for benefits to be paid taking economies of scale into account.

The equivalence scale used in practice depends upon the level of need implicit within the tax-benefit system. For example, the system may regard a second adult as having 50 per cent of the need of the first adult, so that a couple would get 150 per cent of the resources of a single-benefit recipient. If children were deemed to have 30 per cent of the need of the first adult, then a couple with two children would receive 210 per cent of the benefit of a single person. However, the equivalence scale may depend upon other characteristics that influence need, including disability, living alone, age, the existence of specific living costs such as rent etc.

Where the value of a benefit depends upon previous income, then a replacement rate is required. The replacement rate is the ratio of benefit to the previous income. However, this amount may be subject to a floor, to avoid the receipt of a very-low benefit amount, or a ceiling, to place a cap on benefit receipt and expenditure.

In Figure 3.2, a range of alternative replacement rates are outlined. These include:

- ER45, where one receives 45 per cent of previous income
- flat, where one receives €450 in benefit, regardless of previous income
- ER60, where one receives 60 per cent of previous income, subject to a floor of €200 and a ceiling of €1,000
- ER40, where one receives 40 per cent of previous income, subject to a floor of €200 and a ceiling of €1,000
- ER50, where one receives 50 per cent of previous income, subject to a floor of €200 and a ceiling of €600

Thus, the operation of the benefit changes a great deal depending upon the floor, ceiling, and replacement rate, although, except for the flat-rate payment, all are earnings-replacement benefits. Nevertheless, the outcomes are

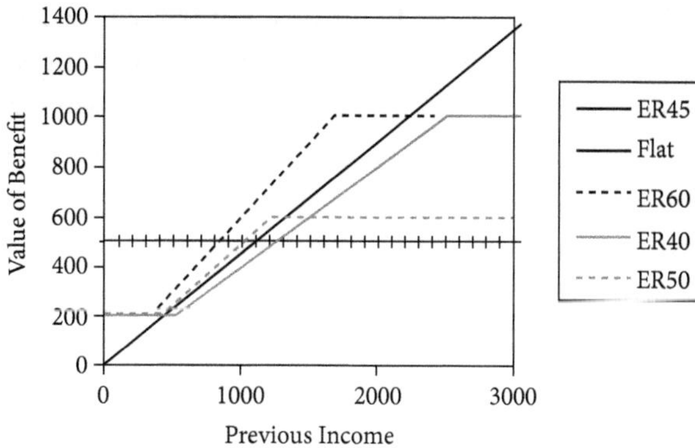


**Figure 3.2** Replacement Rates
*Note*: ER (earnings-related) percentage in replacement rate.

quite different depending upon the parameters of the benefit amount. So while ER50 is an earnings-related benefit, the net impact for much of the previous earnings distribution is not significantly different from a flat-rate benefit, due to the low ceiling.

In addition to eligibility, the value of a benefit may also depend upon duration of receipt, and may be time limited. It may also change over time, perhaps decreasing with increasing length of receipt, as in the case of unemployment-related, social-insurance benefits in France, or rising, particularly where need is deemed to increase, as in the case of unemployment social-assistance benefits in Ireland. Finally, in the case of a social-insurance benefit, the amount of contributions paid may influence the size of the benefit.

### 3.2.4 Targeting

The value of a benefit may depend upon the presence of other incomes. This enables a benefit to be targeted in relation to income. The means test is the way in which means are offset against the maximum benefit payable.

There are a number of factors that influence the size of the means. These include:

- income base or definition of the means test
- unit of analysis or group over which the benefit applies
- disregards—deductions or exemptions from the income base
- days or hours worked—some benefits limit entitlement to a certain number of days, as in the case of Jobs Seekers Allowance in the UK

The income base relates to the types of incomes that count towards the means. In a comprehensive means test, the value of most incomes counts as means. At the other extreme, in the case of a part-time worker in receipt of unemployment benefits, means may be as narrow as personal, earned income. Means can also be determined by net or gross income, where the former depends upon incomes after income taxes or social-insurance contributions have been deducted. Sometimes, a benefit applicant can deduct particular expenses, such as those related to work or travel, from the means. To avoid unemployment traps, some benefits allow income disregards, where the first part of any income earned is not counted as means.

The means are also subject to a unit of analysis, where the means depends upon the incomes of the relevant unit for assessment. This may be the individual in a social-insurance benefit, or the benefit unit in the case of a social-assistance benefit.

The way in which the level of means influences the value of the benefit depends upon the type of means test. These are detailed in Figure 3.3. The most common type of means test in OECD countries can be defined as follows:

$$Benefit_{Net} = Max(Benefit_{Gross} - r.Means, 0) \tag{1}$$

where $r$ is the withdrawal rate. This is frequently 100 per cent, meaning that benefits are reduced by one euro for every euro of means. The dotted line in Figure 3.3 utilizes a means test with a 100-per-cent withdrawal rate. However, sometimes this amount is lower, to avoid problems associated with the unemployment trap, where an individual does not gain financially from returning to work. This may arise as a result of generous welfare levels relative to typical earnings levels (de Lathouwer 2017).

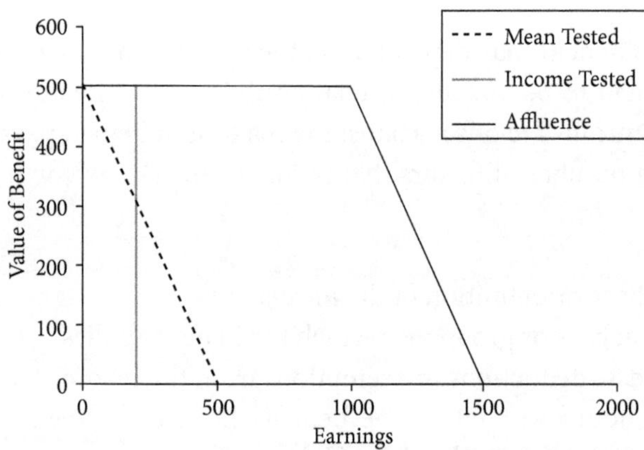


**Figure 3.3** Means Tests

In an alternative way to define a means test, the benefit depends upon a percentage of the difference between a limit and the means as follows:

$$Benefit_{Net} = r.Max(Benefit_{Gross} - Means, 0) \quad (2)$$

Occasionally, the value is subject to a minimum payment as long as the net benefit is non-zero.

However, calculating a means test in these ways depends upon administrative sophistication. Frequently, it is not possible to assess incomes reliably. In this case, a less-sophisticated income test is used (as per the grey line in Figure 3.3), and the benefit is paid if incomes are below a threshold, with a zero payment otherwise:

$$Benefit_{Net} = Benefit_{Gross} \text{ if Means} < \text{Limit; 0 otherwise} \quad (3)$$

This method is thus simpler to administer. However, it has relatively negative incentive effects, as moving from just under the threshold to a euro over the threshold can result in a reduction in income of hundreds of euros. It thus has a very high marginal effective tax rate.

The third type of means test highlighted in Figure 3.3 is an affluence test. The calculation is very similar to the means test in Equation 1, but here there is quite a high disregard:

$$Benefit_{Net} = Max(Benefit_{Gross} - r.Max(Means - Disregard, 0), 0) \quad (4)$$

The existence of this disregard allows the benefit to be targeted at a significant part of the population, but excludes those on the highest incomes.

## 3.3 Data Issues: Creating the Base Dataset

The generation of the base dataset to be used in a microsimulation model is one of the most critical tasks required in the model-development process. It is the source of the representativity of the microsimulation model, and will drive both the quality of results and the scope of the model. For new model builders, it is often one of the most underestimated tasks. Because it is difficult to publish in journals, the detail of this part of the model-building process is often ignored. For many, therefore, it can be a process of learning by doing.

A number of papers discuss some of the practicalities of generating a base dataset. Li and O'Donoghue (2012) and Zaidi and Scott (2001) describe the construction of the base dataset for dynamic microsimulation models. Martini and Trivellato (1997) and Wright et al. (2011) describe the production of base datasets for static microsimulation modelling. Sutherland et al. (2002) describe how to link different datasets together to produce a base dataset for their static microsimulation model. Peichl and Schaefer (2006) describe the base dataset for linked macro-micro models and Abello et al. (2008) describe the base dataset for a health microsimulation. In addition, the appendix in Redmond et al. (1998) gives a comprehensive description of the base data requirements of the UK tax-benefit model POLIMOD.

The base dataset for a static microsimulation model typically comes from a household survey, although in some cases administrative datasets are utilized, or sometimes a combination of both, e.g., where the survey contains the social-insurance number. The choice of dataset type, however, will depend upon the objectives of the model. For example, if the dominant instruments to be considered are family and social-assistance benefits and/or income taxes and social contributions, as is the case in many OECD countries, then a dataset that has strong current income, family labour market, and demographic characteristics will be important. Alternatively, where the instruments to be simulated are expenditure based, such as subsidies or indirect taxes, then an expenditure survey will be required.

As datasets are different, both in quality and in structure, and models are different in terms of purpose and data structures used, there are no hard-and-fast rules to developing a base dataset. In the following, the necessary steps to create a base dataset are discussed:

- Restructure the raw dataset. Frequently, there are many input files for an income survey. They may have different units of analysis (e.g., household, individual). Some files may only contain adult observations. Some files may not be in rectangular format, where each variable is one column, having the row as the relevant unit. This is often the case with expenditure data, where there may be one row per expenditure item rather than one column. In general, but not always, it will be necessary to restructure data into a rectangular format with the data in a single file. This may involve merging on identification numbers or converting non-rectangular formats to rectangular. In doing this, one needs to note the unit of analysis used in the microsimulation model.
- The next step is to have a healthy scepticism about the data quality in a survey. Do not presume that the data are clean just because they come from a reputable supplier. Always thoroughly check the data for errors. It is almost impossible to eliminate all sources of error in producing

micro-data, but preliminary data analysis will help. Do the individual incomes sum to total income? Are variables within expected ranges? Identify missing value codes! It may be possible to clean the data oneself. Occasionally, it may be necessary to return the data to the supplier to have it corrected.

- There may be issues with the data that do not result from error. For example, there may be differences of period of analysis between variables, such as when labour market status may depend upon current characteristics, while incomes are based on the previous year. This can result in inconsistency between variables such as hours and earnings. Typically in microsimulation models, the income variables are more important than the status variables, as the focus is on assessing the distributional impact of policy. Therefore, one may want to clean the labour-market data to be consistent with the income data. Another income-related issue that is relatively common is top-coding of income variables, so as to preserve anonymity.
- Occasionally, and particularly when collecting benefit data, individuals report private incomes that relate to a benefit contingency as a benefit rather than a source of private-sector income. For example, unemployment redundancy payments may be classified with unemployment benefits, or occupational pensions may be classified as pension income. Some benefits may also be miscoded as another benefit. The main way to deal with income miscoding such as this is to have a detailed understanding of the benefit system, in order to identify their presence. One may in fact use the tax-benefit microsimulation model itself to undertake this imputation.
- A common problem that arises with micro-data is that of missing values. This may be due to either a variable not being relevant, such as employment earnings for a retired person, a refusal by a survey respondent to reply to this question, or where a member of a household is missing. There should not be any missing values among the variables used in the microsimulation model. There is a choice, therefore, to drop the individual or the entire household if there is a missing value. However, this could significantly reduce the sample size and affect the distribution of outcomes, and may require reweighting. Alternatively, the missing value could be either imputed or modelled. There is a large literature describing methods for doing this that is beyond the scope of this book. See Rubin (1987) for a description of alternative methods.
- Most survey datasets report household and individual units of analysis. However, the tax-benefit system may utilize different units of analysis,

such as a tax unit. This will require that it be defined within the base dataset. Typically, income-survey data contain a variable indicating the relationship to the head of household (HOH). Unfortunately, this may not provide full information as to the composition of tax units within a household with multiple tax units. For example, in a three-generation household where the HOH is the oldest generation and there are multiple children, it will not be possible to allocate someone whose relationship to the HOH is that of grandchild, as there are multiple potential parents. Although not affecting many households, it can take a disproportionate amount of time to impute the tax unit, utilizing other variables, or in the end arbitrarily assigning a child to a parent.

- The next step is to create the necessary derived variables required for a tax-benefit microsimulation. These depend on the instruments to be simulated.
- The simulation of taxes and social contributions typically require gross incomes (e.g., incomes before the deduction of taxes). However, in many cases data are recorded net of taxes or contributions. In Chapter 4, an algorithm to convert net incomes to gross values is described.
- Due to non-response bias in surveys, weights are required. Typically, these are generated by the data provider. However, sometimes an analyst may wish to adjust these weights to account for changes in the structure of the population. The production of weights is beyond the scope of this book; however, interested readers are directed towards Creedy (2004) and Cai et al. (2006) for further information.
- There is frequently a time lag in the production of micro-data for use in microsimulation models. There may thus be a difference between the year that data have been collected and the year of the policy to be simulated. Incomes and other variables may require adjustment or updating to account for income or price inflation.
- The final stage of the data-creation process is to transform the data into the relevant data structure required for the model, whether it be as a rectangular file for most models or a hierarchical structure in some cases.

## 3.4 Validation: Hypothetical Families

Before simulating tax-benefit policy on real households, with all the complexity entailed therein, we first abstract from the complexity of the data in order to validate the coding of the system. This is done by using hypothetical households, which are designed in such a way as to test each component of the system of interest.

Varying a single parameter, such as hours worked, employment wage, age, number of children etc., the sensitivity of simulated policy to these changes can be tested. Also, performing relatively simple changes will enhance our ability to find errors in the code. Spikes in results may be due to badly written code. The challenge is to identify the dimensions of variability in the hypothetical data that can help us track down these bugs in the code.

Once the tax-benefit system has been coded, the hypothetical data are passed through the model. At this stage, one discovers whether all the variables required by the model algorithms have in fact been included in the dataset, and whether they are in the correct format. Once this works, one must determine whether all the interactions between the simulated components operate correctly.

The validation process is, therefore, one of the largest components in building a microsimulation model. Frequently, the validation takes multiples times that taken to build the first (pre-debugged) version of the model. The greater the complexity of the model, the greater the length of time to validate, in a non-linear, possibly exponential way.

In Figure 3.4, the hours worked by a family with two children in the UK tax-benefit system are varied. It is then possible to observe how, as income increases, the range of different means-tested benefits—jobseekers allowance (JSA), income support (IS), working tax credit (WTC), child tax credit

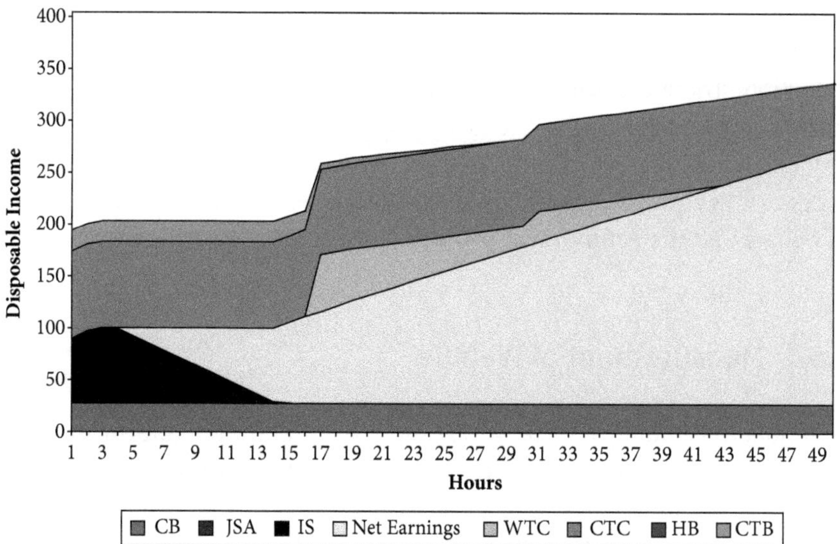


**Figure 3.4** UK Tax-Benefit System

(CTC), housing benefits (HB), and council tax benefit—taper away. Child benefits (CB), which are not means tested, do not vary with income.

Hypothetical microsimulation models, as discussed in Chapter 1, are both a mechanism for validation and an analytical tool in their own right (Burlacu et al. 2014). They can be used as communication mechanisms in the popular media at the time of national-government, budgetary-planning processes. They are also frequently used for cross-national comparisons; the OECD (1996) uses hypothetical family calculations based on workers earning a percentage of the average production wage (APW) to evaluate the performance of similar policies in different countries (Pearson and Scarpetta 2000). They are thus useful ways to describe the functioning of a tax-benefit system and are applied in a wide variety of contexts (Leonard et al. 2017; Ryan et al. 2017).

## 3.5 Measurement Issues: Poverty Efficiency

In this section, indicators frequently used to assess the performance of social transfers are considered. Standard measures used in understanding the impact of a static microsimulation analysis of a reform in social transfers include:

- the cost of the reform
- the incidence of the reform across the income distribution
- the numbers and types of winners and losers from the reform

One of the primary aims of reforms to social-transfer policies is poverty reduction. There is a substantial literature on poverty measurement, which shall be touched on briefly. The focus here is on measures related to the poverty efficiency of an instrument. However, in order to assess this, it is first necessary to address a number of relevant concepts related to the definition of welfare and the definition of poverty.

### 3.5.1 Measurement of Welfare

In simulating a policy reform, we are interested in how the reform affects the welfare of the unit of analysis (e.g., individual, family, household). Money income is the most common proxy used for measuring welfare, and 'in a given period' income is defined by Atkinson (1983) as being 'the amount a person could have spent while maintaining his wealth intact'. Two individuals with the same money income may have different welfares, due to drawing on savings for consumption. Money income also does not take into account non-money sources of income, such as non-cash state benefits (education and health services), non-cash benefits in kind, imputed rent from owner occupation, the value of household production and consumption of services, and non-pecuniary benefits from work. It is, however, very difficult to measure accurately the value of non-monetary income, and so, for this reason, money income, or a similar measure, is usually used for calculating an individual's welfare, standard of living, or well-being.

There are many practical decisions to be made when comparing the welfare of different units. These include:

- the measure to be used
- the unit of analysis
- the size of the household
- the type of income
- the period of analysis

Both income and consumption (or the related measure of expenditure) can be used as measures of standard of living. Consumption is a direct measure of living standard, in that it measures the value of goods consumed on which material well-being depends. Expenditure relates to purchased consumption. Income is an indirect measure, in that it measures the resources available to spend on material well-being. Current income may understate current living standards because individuals can draw on borrowings or savings. Expenditure is therefore often seen as a better measure. However, the simulation of cash-based policy instruments will simulate the impact on cash outcomes, and without a demand system, as described in Chapter 6, it may be difficult to infer the impact on expenditure.

Market income is not suitable for use as a measure of living standards, as it ignores taxes paid or transfers received, which significantly alter the resources available for consumption. Atkinson et al. (1995) outline different stages in calculating disposable income or the income available for consumption:

- market income—wage and salary income, self-employment income, investment-property income, occupational-pension and other cash income, such as regular private transfers, alimony, CBs
- gross income—market income plus social insurance, social assistance, and universal cash transfers

- disposable income—gross income less direct taxes and social-security contributions
- final income—disposable income less indirect taxes

Expenditure can be defined as disposable income minus net savings-based consumption items. Typically, disposable income is the welfare measure used in microsimulation models.

The welfare of an individual will depend upon the capacity to share resources within the household unit in which they live. However, as noted above, different policies frequently apply to different units of analysis, such as the family, tax, or benefit unit. While there are studies that try to understand the sharing of resources within a household (Woolley and Marshall 1994), most policy-incidence studies and microsimulation analyses make the assumption of sharing of resources within a household. Household incomes are typically adjusted by an equivalence scale to produce an equivalized income:

$$Y_{Eq} = \frac{\sum_{Individual,i} Y_i}{EquivalenceScale}$$

There is a substantial literature on measuring or defining equivalence scales, e.g., Cowell and Mercader-Prats (1999). Typically, in microsimulation analysis, variants of the following are used:

- OECD – (head (1) + adults (0.7) + aged 14 or younger (0.5))
- modified OECD – (head (1) + adults (0.5) + aged 14 or younger (0.3))
- single parameter scale—(number of persons in household)$^a$, a varies from 0 ~ total economies of scale (e.g., household income), to 1 ~ no economies of scale (e.g., individual income)
- equivalence scales used in national policy

The accounting period, which is the period over which income is measured, can also substantially alter the measure of standard of living. Typical accounting periods used in microsimulation models include the current week or month and annual or lifetime income.

Shorter-period incomes will overestimate the impact of temporary income changes. For example, when using current income, survey data will not differentiate between a long-term unemployed person and someone temporarily between jobs with access to savings.

A longer-term income measure captures the permanent income or long-term standard of living of an individual. However, simulating longer-term incomes can be more difficult in a microsimulation model as it requires the incorporation of income volatility.

Market-income volatility typically has an impact on the amount of taxation paid or benefits received. Given the complexity of modelling this, a static microsimulation model will typically focus on current income, while dynamic microsimulation models can capture inter-temporal income changes.

However, even current income can pose difficulties for microsimulation models due to intra-period variability. Many income surveys have an accounting period of a year in representing current income, while an employment status and consequential benefit entitlement and tax liabilities may vary across the year. Models such as EUROMOD take the status for a particular time period to represent current income, rather than varying status within a period such as a year.

### 3.5.2 Definition of Poverty

The tools described here are primarily used for policy design with anti-poverty objectives. In this section, the definition of poverty is considered, looking at in turn the concepts related to the definition of poverty. Different assumptions about this definition can radically alter the conclusions we draw. Atkinson et al. 2002 provides the following meanings:

- Poverty is a relative concept in that poverty is defined relative to the standard of living in the country.
- Poverty is multidimensional in that it does not relate solely to insufficiency of resources but also reflects 'cumulative deprivation in relation to income, housing, education, and health care'.

A standard definition of poverty is that a household is considered poor if the equivalized household disposable income is below the poverty line. The question is: how is the poverty line defined? Atkinson (1998) highlights the sensitivity of poverty measurement to assumptions made. These include:

- relative versus absolute poverty
- the level of the poverty line
- the income definition

An absolute poverty line is the level of resources required for an individual to remain alive and healthy. The only reasons for this to change over time are inflation and the substitution of new goods if older goods no longer exist. Relative poverty lines, on the other hand, are usually expressed as a proportion of average disposable earnings, and they increase over time as average earnings increase. In Figure 3.5(a), the impact on the level of poverty in the UK is reported if one takes poverty as 50 per cent of average income in 1979 and is either (a) held at this line in constant purchasing power—the absolute poverty approach—or (b) calculated on the basis of relative poverty. While under the absolute measure, poverty rates remain constant, but poverty rates increase substantially under the relative measure.

Relative poverty lines have become the norm in measuring poverty in OECD countries, as the measure reflects the definition outlined above more closely. If an absolute poverty line was used, then as the standard of living of society increases, the potential participation of the poor in society would fall relative to the rest of the population. Also, as the standard of living of society increases, shops cease selling cheaper types of goods. Therefore, even with the same purchasing power, poor people would be less able to purchase the same range of goods as before.

An analyst has a choice when using a relative poverty measure as to the poverty line to be used:

- The first decision is whether to use the mean or median as the reference income. The median is typically more robust to changes at the top of the distribution.
- Second, the line will depend upon the percentage of the reference income. The UN and OECD utilize 50 per cent of median. Atkinson et al. (2002) indicate that in European national anti-poverty action plans, 60 per cent of median is the most frequent measure used. However, in general, multiple measures are used, as results can be sensitive to the choice of measure. For example, in a comparison of poverty levels in Southern European countries, O'Donoghue et al. (2002), as outlined in Figure 3.5(b), finds that although the ordering of countries is robust to the measure used, the proportion of very poor (under 50 per cent of the median) is much less in France than in the other countries. This indicates the availability of social-protection instruments not found in the other countries. The same can be found in analyses of poverty reforms. One should, therefore, use multiple poverty lines when assessing the poverty impact of a reform.

In relation to the definition of living standards used, there are also a number of choices, such as:

- whether to uses a definition before or after housing costs are taken into consideration
- the choice of equivalence scale

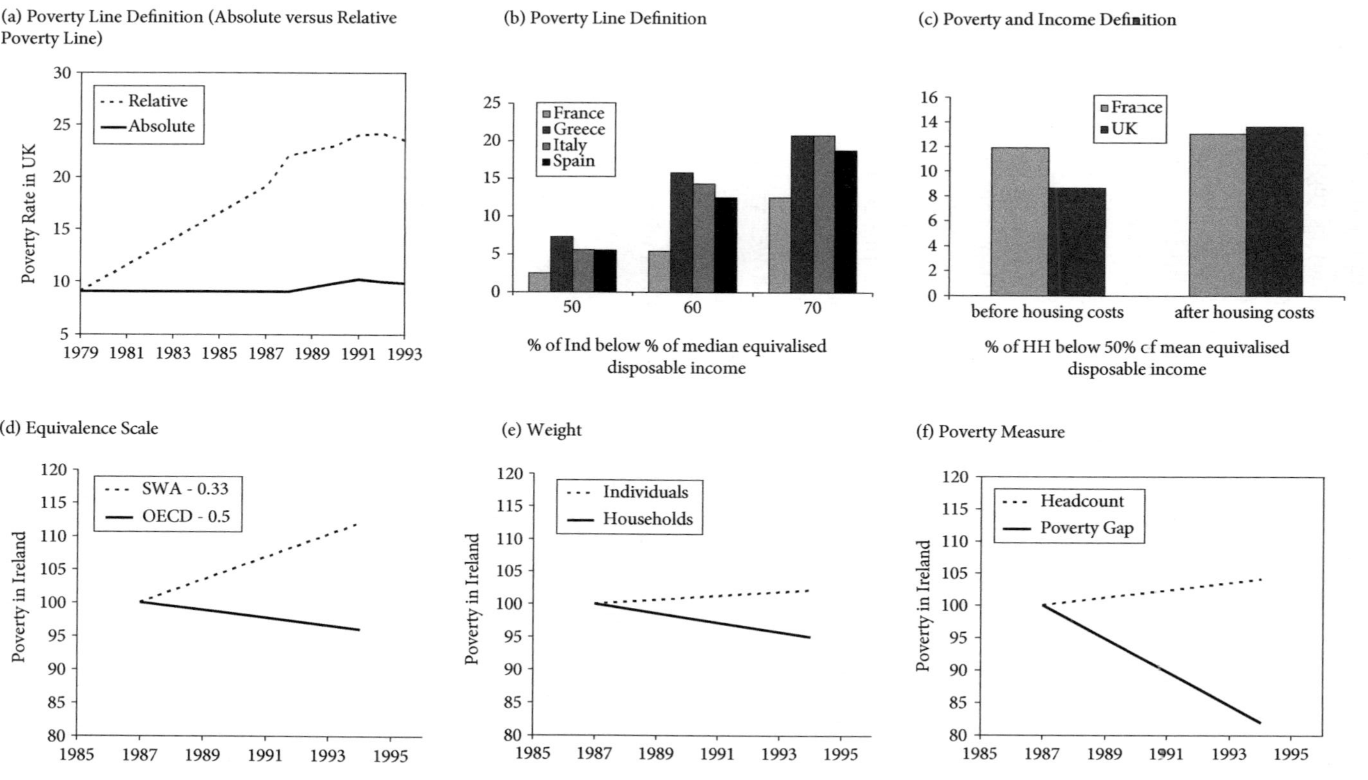


**Figure 3.5** Sensitivity of Poverty Line to Assumptions

Where there are substantial differences in housing costs, the presence of the same level of income in two locations within a country may imply different standards of living. Therefore, while a household may be regarded as poor in an area of high housing costs, they may not be regarded as poor in an area with low housing costs. For this reason, countries such as the UK calculate poverty statistics on the basis of both before and after housing costs. Atkinson (1998) highlights that the choice of method can result in alternative conclusions (Figure 3.5(c)). While the poverty rate at 50 per cent of mean income is higher in France before housing costs than in the UK, it is lower after housing costs.

Choice of equivalence scale as outlined above can also influence results such as the choice between the OECD (1/0.7/0.5) or the modified-OECD scale (1/0.5/0.3). The former scale places a greater weight on both adult and child dependants, so that larger families tend to appear to be poorer than under the latter scale. Thus, countries with larger families may tend to have higher poverty levels for a given income distribution. In Figure 3.5(d), the impact of alternative equivalence scales on poverty in 1987–94 in Ireland is seen, with poverty seeming to increase under the lower-valued state equivalence scale than under the modified-OECD scale. In this case, we see the impact of using an equivalence scale that gives a lower weight to households with children, indicating the poverty rates of families with children fell while those of families without children rose.

Historically, the household has been considered as the unit of analysis, with the poverty rate expressed sometimes as the proportion of households below the poverty line. This means that a household with four people below the poverty line contributes the same weight to poverty as a single-person household. However, countries are moving increasingly to individual weight-based poverty indices, so that it is the proportion of individuals below the poverty line that is used in determining the poverty level. In Figure 3.5(e), we highlight that the choice of weight can influence conclusions about poverty in Ireland in 1987–94. Here, poverty increased when the number of individuals in poverty were weighted, but decreased when weighting the number of households as the average size of poor households increased.

### 3.5.3 Measures of Poverty

So far, issues relating to the standard of living under which someone is regarded as being poor have been discussed. Now the degree of poverty within a country is quantified. We noticed above in the headcount measures of poverty, defined as the proportion below the poverty line, that conclusions varied depending upon the level of the poverty line in different countries. This related to the amount of bunching around the poverty line. So in France, those in poverty were in general just below the sixty-per-cent line, while in other Southern European countries they were below the fifty-per-cent line. Thus, the poor in Greece were relatively poorer.

The poverty-headcount measure consequently considers a household that is *just* below the poverty line to be the same as a household that is *substantially* below the poverty line. It is, therefore, a measure of the extent of poverty. Although it is easy to calculate, because it does not tell us how deep poverty is it does not give us an indication as to how much it would take to reduce poverty. The poverty gap, however, is a measure of the extent of poverty or the amount that would be required to lift all households out of poverty. This is often expressed as the poverty-gap ratio, which is the average poverty gap divided by the poverty headcount as a percentage of the poverty line.

In Figure 3.5(f), we see that choice of measure again can determine conclusions about the level of poverty in a country. In Ireland, while the headcount rate increased over time, the depth of their poverty decreased, concluding, therefore, that while the number of people living in households *just* below the poverty line increased, the number living in households *substantially* below the poverty line decreased.

While the poverty gap tells us how much it would take to eliminate poverty, it has the property that a transfer from a person who is *just* below the poverty line to someone *much* below the poverty line has no impact on the level of poverty. In other words, all income and individuals below the poverty line have the same importance. A euro given to someone just below the poverty line reduces the poverty gap to the same extent as a euro given to someone much below the line. A welfare-based measure of poverty places a greater weight on individuals who are more below the poverty line than those close to the poverty line. An example of this is the Foster–Greer–Thorbecke index:

Here, the greater the weight of the poverty-aversion parameter $\alpha$, the greater the weight placed on poor people. If $\alpha$ is 0, then it is the same as the headcount ratio. If $\alpha$ is the same as the product of the headcount and the poverty gap, and when $\alpha$ is greater than 1, a greater weight is placed on the poor. In other words, a transfer to a *very* poor person would reduce poverty by more than a transfer to a *moderately* poor person.

### 3.5.4 Poverty Targeting and Tax-Benefit Policy

The objective of poverty measures is to quantify the size and extent of poverty. However, in policy analyses we wish to assess the effectiveness of a policy or policy change in reducing poverty.

Beckerman (1979) proposed target-efficiency and poverty-reduction effectiveness indicators. Figure 3.6 describes the impact of transfers on disposable income, reporting pre- and post-transfer income. A number of indicators can be produced on the basis of this figure:

- The first measure is vertical-expenditure efficiency (VEE), meaning the share of total expenditure going to households who are poor before the transfer, and is equal to the area (A + B)/(A + B +C).
- The next indicator of poverty-reduction efficiency (PRE) is the fraction of total expenditure allowing poor households to reach the poverty line without overcoming it, and is defined as the area (A)/(A + B +C).
- The spillover index (S) is a measure of the excess of expenditure with respect to the amount strictly necessary to reach the poverty line, (B)/(A + B). Combining this, it can be seen that VEE (1 – S) = PRE.

These measures are not, however, sufficient to evaluate how good a transfer system is in fighting poverty. A transfer programme could be very efficient in reaching the poor, but if its resources are low it may not produce a significant

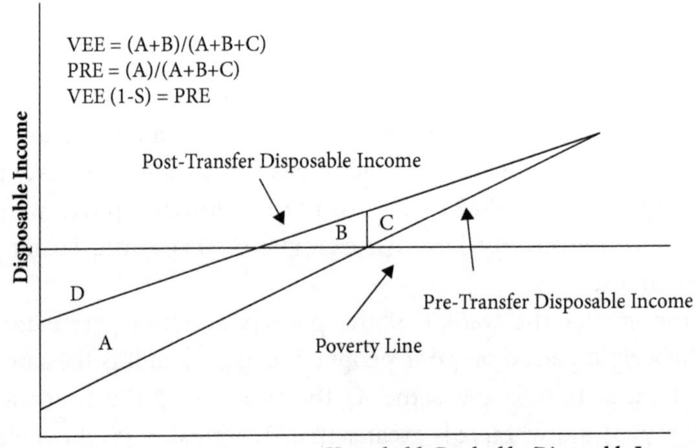


**Figure 3.6** The Efficiency of Social Transfers
*Source*: Beckerman (1979).

increase in the living standards of the beneficiaries. The poverty-gap efficiency (PGE) defined as (A)/(A + D) measures how effective a cash benefit is in filling the poverty gap.

## 3.6 Simulation: Introducing an Anti-Poverty Instrument

In this section, a number of social transfers are simulated. Utilizing the XLSIM model in Chapter 2, applied to Irish data, a number of working-age social benefits are introduced:

- CB
- means-tested unemployment assistance (UA)
- in-work means-tested cash transfer targeted at families with children, namely family income supplement (FIS)

### 3.6.1 Hypothetical Family Calculation

A hypothetical family calculation is first utilized to produce a budget-constraint diagram and to test the validity of our simulation. As in Section 3.2, we model in turn eligibility, means, and the maximum calculation for the instruments defined in Table 3.1. The value of the benefit is defined as:

$$benefit = Max\left(0,\left(es - r * Y\right)\right) if\ eligibility = 1$$

**Table 3.1** Benefit Rules

| Instrument | CB | UA | FIS |
|---|---|---|---|
| Eligibility | number of children > 0 | age >= 18 and age < 65 and unemployed = 1 and hours worked < 19 | age >= 18 and age < 65 and number of children > 0 and hours worked >= 19 |
| Means (Y) | 0 | Market income | Market income |
| Withdrawal Rate (r) | 0 | 1 | 0.6 |
| Maximum Calculation (es) | €166 per month for the first 2 children and €203 thereafter | €196 for claimant, €130 for partner, €30 per child (all per week) | FIS is calculated on the basis of 60 per cent of the difference between the income limit for the family size €506 per week for 1 child and €96 extra for each additional child up to 10 |

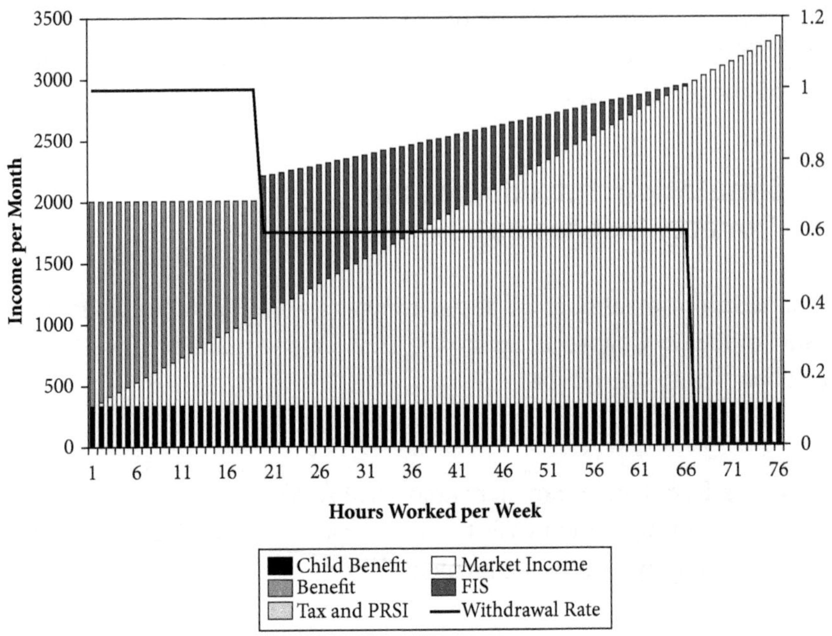


**Figure 3.7** Monthly Gross-Income Budget Constraint of Benefit Simulations on Couple with Two Children

*NB*: hourly wage–€10 per hour.

In Figure 3.7, the resultant budget constraint is reported. Note that taxes and contributions have not yet been modelled and thus the budget constraint is gross. We note the following:

- the universal CBs do not vary with income
- the budget constraint is flat over the period the UA is withdrawn
- that FIS operates to eliminate the unemployment trap by incentivizing work at nineteen hours or more

The black line reports the withdrawal rate. Over the course of the withdrawal of UA it is 100 per cent, while for FIS it is 60 per cent, and then zero once FIS is withdrawn.

### 3.6.2 Poverty Effectiveness

The next stage is to run a simulation on real data to assess the poverty effectiveness of the instruments. For the purpose of this analysis, the 2000 Living in Ireland survey is used, focusing only on households with working-age families that are either in work or unemployed. Pension-age families and more-complicated household structures are ignored.

**Table 3.2** Poverty-Efficiency Statistics

| | CB | UA | FIS |
|---|---|---|---|
| VEE | 0.199 | 0.999 | 0.661 |
| PRE | 0.061 | 0.863 | 0.049 |
| S | 0.692 | 0.136 | 0.926 |
| PGE | 0.241 | 0.824 | 0.191 |

Table 3.2 highlights some poverty-effectiveness instruments proposed by Beckerman (1979) in relation to target-efficiency and poverty-reduction effectiveness indicators. CBs have weak targeting, but greater poverty-gap efficiency than the more-targeted FIS as it spends more money, while UA has similar expenditure, but better PGE due to better targeting than CB.

### 3.6.3 Take-Up

In modelling these instruments, full take-up is assumed. In other words, all those who are eligible in the dataset receive the benefit. In reality, we observe both non-take-up in data where those who have simulated eligibility do not receive it in practice, and non-take-up in those who receive it in the data who are not simulated to have eligibility. While universal benefits such as CB typically have full take-up, means-tested benefits often have quite low take-up, varying in Europe from 40 to 80 per cent (Hernanz et al. 2004).

This can be due for a number of reasons (Matsaganis et al. 2009):

- high claiming costs
- administrative errors
- fear of stigma
- lack of information about entitlements

and implications:

- reduces anti-poverty effectiveness of benefits
- distorts the intended effects of social policy
- biases estimates of impact of policy change

# 4
# Redistribution and Income-Tax Reform

## 4.1 Introduction

One of the most significant determinants of the level of redistribution, or the capacity to change inequality within a tax-benefit system, is the structure of the taxation system (Creedy 2001). Countries use a variety of different tax instruments to finance public expenditure and to redistribute income. These include individual and corporate income taxes, social-insurance contributions, taxes on capital gains, taxes on capital, indirect taxes on consumption, etc. As a result, studies of the distributive nature of income taxation have been very important in the microsimulation literature (Verbist and Figari 2014; Figari and Paulus 2015).

The microsimulation models described in this book focus on the household sector. The system of income taxation modelled reflects this focus, with an emphasis on the taxation of the main income sources of households. As a result, the systems tend to be rather simpler than actual income-tax codes, e.g., ignoring detailed provisions for the taxation of capital income (Wood 2000), housing wealth (Di Nicola et al. 2015; Figari et al. 2017), or specific incentive schemes. The type of data contained in household surveys (which contain quite accurate employee incomes) is very suitable for personal taxes and contributions faced by households, as well as for social-insurance contributions and personal income-tax systems. However, they are less effective in modelling taxation that depends upon wealth or changes in wealth, such as capital, property, or capital-gains taxation. The models typically simulate annual tax liabilities, ignoring administrative arrangements such as withholding taxation.[1]

There is an extensive literature on tax structure and tax reform. Approaches that use microsimulation models to analyse the progressivity of income taxes include Verbist (2004) for EU countries, Bargain et al. (2015) for the US, and Palme (1996) for Sweden. Analyses that evaluated the impact of tax reform include Orsini (2005) for Belgium, Fuest et al. (2008) and Beznoska and

[1] See Levy and Mercador-Prats (2002) for a model of withholding taxes.

*Practical Microsimulation Modelling*. Cathal O'Donoghue. Oxford University Press. © Cathal O'Donoghue 2021.
DOI: 10.1093/oso/9780198852872.003.0004

Hentze (2017) for Germany, Berliant and Strauss (2007), Gale et al. (2004) for the US, Moisio et al. (2016) for Finland, Creedy and Mok (2018) for New Zealand, Wagenhals (2001, 2011) for Germany, Cozzolino and Di Marco (2015) for Italy, Ericson et al. (2009) for Sweden, Callan (1990) for Ireland, Castañer et al. (2004), Levy and Mercador-Prats (2002), Badenes-Plá and Buenaventura-Zabala (2017), and Bover et al. (2017) for Spain. Fiscal drag is addressed by Levy et al. (2010) for Brazil and Immervoll (2005) for European economies, while Beer (1998) analysed the Australian distribution of marginal tax rates. With greater availability of micro-data, and a greater interest in evidence-based policy making, the use of microsimulation models in middle-income countries has increased. Such studies include Jara and Varela (2017) for Ecuador, Wan (2018) for China, Higgins and Pereira (2014) and Jordaan and Schoeman (2018) for South Africa, and Higgins et al. (2016) for Brazil.

Other papers have looked at the functioning of components of the income-tax system, such as Matsaganis and Flevotomou (2007) in relation to mortgage interest, or Scholz (1996) in relation to the earned-income tax credit in the US. Brownstone et al. (1985) considered the impact of Swedish tax reform on the demand for housing, while O'Donoghue and Sutherland (1999) analysed the impact of alternative family-related components in income-tax systems in Europe.

In this chapter, the microsimulation model initiated in Chapter 3 is developed further, adding income taxation and social-insurance contributions to the analysis of social transfers. Methodologically, an issue which is common to the creation of base datasets, namely the inversion of data from net to gross, is explored. From a validation point of view, concepts associated with using external validation sources are introduced. From a measurement point of view, measures that aim to quantify the degree of progressivity and redistribution in tax systems are described. A redistributive analysis of a theoretical tax system is then undertaken.

## 4.2 Policy Context: Structure of Income-Tax Systems

Income taxation typically comprises a number of components: the income base on which taxes are levied, deductions from this income on which taxation is levied, the set of rates of taxes at different levels, and any reductions in the tax liability. The structure of these components influences the amount of taxation levied and the redistributive nature of the taxation.

Income taxation is defined as follows:

$$t_{net} = TaxSchedule\left(Y_{taxable} - Allowances - Deductions\right) - TaxCredits$$

The tax base is taxable income ($Y_{taxable}$) minus tax allowances minus tax deductions. The tax schedule is applied to this to get gross taxation ($t_{gross}$). Tax credits are subtracted to get net taxation ($t_{net}$). The tax unit is the unit (individual, couple, family) over which the taxation is calculated and can vary for all income types (employment, capital).

Taxable income refers to the income on which income taxation is based. Certain incomes may be exempt from taxation (e.g., some means-tested benefits or family benefits). Sometimes, there are specific types of income taxation levied on particular types of income, such as capital-income taxation. Certain exemptions may apply to incomes for various tax-incentive reasons, such as for specific types of property.

Tax allowances and deductions are subtracted from taxable income to get the tax base:

- Tax allowances are reductions in the tax base as a result of personal characteristics (such as age, marital status, child dependants, etc.).
- Deductions, meanwhile, are reductions in the tax base as a result of particular expenditures (such as private-pension contributions, mortgage-interest payments, health-insurance payments).

$$Y_{tax\ base} = max\left(Y_{taxable} - Allowance - Deduction, 0\right)$$

The tax schedule is the collection of tax bands and tax rates which principally determine the amount of tax levied and the progressivity of the tax system.[2] Tax allowances can be regarded also as zero-rate tax bands. As income-tax schedules are usually progressive, the purpose of generating a higher average tax rate for those on higher incomes is partially that of vertical redistribution in addition to revenue raising.

A tax schedule with three bands will take the following form:

$$t_{gross} = min\left(Y_{tax\ base}, band_1\right) \times rate_1 + min\left(max\left(Y_{tax\ base} - band_1, 0\right), band_2\right) \times rate_2 + max\left(Y_{tax\ base} - band_1 - band_2, 0\right) \times rate_3$$

[2] While most tax schedules are piece-wise linear, certain countries, such Germany, have a polynomial-based income-tax schedule.

Sometimes, particularly for social-insurance contributions, the taxable income may be limited to incomes that fall between a ceiling and/or a floor:

$$t_{net} = TaxSchedule\left(Y_{taxable} - Allowances - Deductions\right) - TaxCredits\, if\; Y_{taxable} > floor$$

The rationale for the ceiling is that, in general, there is a maximum value for social-insurance-related benefits. The floor, meanwhile, exists to keep those on low incomes outside of the contribution net.

Tax credits are amounts which are subtracted from gross taxation to produce net taxation. They have many similar characteristics to tax allowances, but, as is seen below, have a constant value and do not depend upon the marginal rate of tax. Tax credits are similar to tax allowances, but because their value does not depend on income, they are less regressive. Tax credits, however, have a similar disadvantage to allowances in that they depend on a tax unit actually paying tax.

Tax allowances are used for both vertical- and horizontal-equity purposes; they can be used to reduce the tax burden on those who have lower abilities to pay. For example, extra tax allowances may be given to families with children, single parents, families with single earners, or to help cover family-related expenditures, such as childcare and education. Some countries, in addition, allow unused allowances to be transferred to their spouse. These can be very beneficial to couples where there is a single earner, or where one spouse earns more than the other. However, transferable allowances mean that the lower-earning spouse may face higher marginal tax rates than if they were taxed individually. This may prove to be a disincentive to working or increasing hours worked. Yet, allowances used for horizontal redistribution still have the same regressive impacts as individual tax allowances, concentrating gains among those higher earners who qualify for the allowances.

There are a number of ways in which the structure of the tax schedule affects horizontal equity. First, as already described, the value of tax allowances depends on the marginal income-tax rate. Therefore, the amount of horizontal redistribution inherent in tax allowances directly depends on the shape of the tax schedule. Also indirectly, the tax schedule can have an impact on horizontal equity if families with children are concentrated at certain points on the tax schedule. In other words, if children tend to be concentrated in families in the lower part of the income distribution, then in a progressive tax schedule they will face lower average tax rates than families without children. This, however, relates more to vertical equity considerations rather than horizontal considerations. Finally, the tax schedule can be altered for particular family types. Transferable allowances come under this heading, as do widened tax bands in aggregate taxation and transferable tax bands.

### 4.2.1 Vertical Redistributive Nature of Income Taxation

The primary objective in this chapter is to model income taxation and assess its impact on inequality. In particular, the vertical redistributive nature of income taxation, i.e., the degree to which it alters the distribution of pre-tax incomes between rich and poor, is of interest. All of the sub-components of income taxation described above influence the redistributive nature of the instrument.

The tax schedule itself is one of the main redistributive drivers in the income-taxation system, typically through increasing marginal rates of income taxation. Figure 4.1 shows how other components influence income taxation. A tax allowance is equivalent to introducing a zero-tax band at the bottom of the distribution and lowering taxes at each income level. However, the value of tax allowances vary by income. Because they reduce the size of the total tax base, their value depends on the marginal rate of taxation. Thus, tax allowances are worth more for people on higher marginal tax rates. In a progressive taxation system, this means that the value of a tax allowance increases with income and is thus worth more to those with higher incomes. This can be seen in Figure 4.1, where the point at

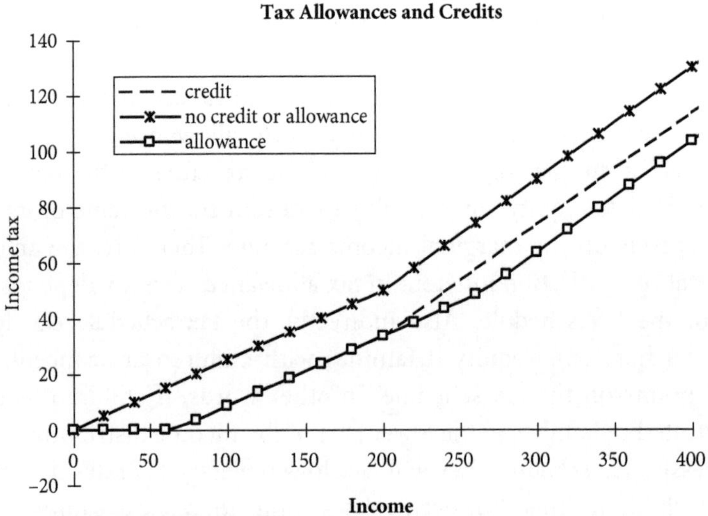


**Figure 4.1** Tax Allowances and Credits

which the high marginal tax rate starts is higher when there is a tax allowance. A tax credit, on the other hand, reduces income tax by the same amount for all levels of income. Tax allowances and credits, however, have the limitation that they are only of 'full' value to a tax unit if their income is more than the value of the allowance.

### 4.2.2 Horizontal Redistributive Measures

Income taxation also has horizontal redistributive objectives, reducing taxation for tax units who have a lower ability to pay (e.g., the tax burden of tax units with dependants may be reduced relative to tax units without dependants). O'Donoghue and Sutherland (1999) highlight how all components can influence horizontal redistribution.

A straightforward mechanism for horizontal redistribution is through the provision of tax allowances or credits that depend upon family status, such as the presence of dependant children or a spouse. Tax allowances and credits can also vary by family status, and can be transferable between spouses. Also, both can be given to sole-earner couples to reduce the taxation of families.

Taxation, in addition to being levied on an individual's income, can be based on a wider unit's income, as in the case of joint taxation. In this way, the scope of a tax is expanded from being reliant only on the individual to both spouses in Germany, or to spouses and their dependant children in France, or to encompassing other members of the household, such as non-dependant children, as in the case of some tax credits in Spain. In addition, joint taxation may be either compulsory, as in the case of Portugal, or optional, as in the case of Ireland. Tax units may opt for joint taxation, if, as a couple, they pay less taxation than they would if taxed individually.

Joint taxation, as a mechanism for horizontal redistribution, pools income allowances, bands, and credits, allowing for couples—where one spouse has a lower marginal tax rate than the other—to benefit by reducing the couple's average tax rate. Joint taxation will by itself, in fact, increase the overall average tax rate to cover the tax reduction for single-earner families. However, when joint taxation is combined with increased allowances, credits, and/or bands, total taxation may be reduced for the couple.

O'Donoghue and Sutherland (1999) describe a number of different mechanisms for joint taxation, namely aggregate, split, and quotient taxation. In aggregate taxation, the incomes of both spouses $Y_M$ and $Y_F$ are added, and the total is taxed as if the unit was a single individual. Aggregate taxation is usually accompanied by larger tax allowances, bands, and credits for couples than for single people.

$$Tax = T\left(Y_M + Y_F\right). \quad \text{(AggregateTaxation)}$$

Consider a couple with the husband in the top tax bracket ($Y_M$) per year and the spouse working part-time on a lower tax bracket ($Y_F$). Under individual taxation, they would pay taxes of $t(Y_M)$ and $t(Y_F)$ without aggregating allowances, etc. In aggregate taxation, the total tax would rise to $t(Y_M + Y_F) > t(Y_M) + t(Y_F)$, because all of the wife's income would be taxed at the husband's higher marginal rate of tax. However, most aggregated-tax systems involve some aggregation of tax allowances and bands, and, thus, under aggregate taxation, total taxation falls $t(Y_M + Y_F) < t(Y_M) + t(Y_F)$.

In split taxation and family-quotient taxation, incomes are aggregated but divided by a quotient which is dependent upon the structure of the family and then taxed in the same manner as a single person. Total tax-unit taxation is found by multiplying this tax amount by the family quotient. In the case of the splitting method, the tax unit is the couple and therefore the family quotient is two. Crucially, income splitting reduces the amount of income taxed at higher rates. Income splitting is, however, equivalent to an aggregate method, where all bands and allowances are doubled. In effect, splitting therefore enables a couple to effectively share unused allowances and bands between each other.

$$Tax = T\left(\frac{\left(Y_M + Y_F\right)}{2}\right) \times 2 \quad \text{(Split Taxation)}$$

Joint taxation and income splitting do not take account of the greater needs of larger families, however. The family-quotient method used in France encompasses a wider tax unit which includes other household members (such as children), thus allowing for reduced taxes for larger families. In this case, the quotient is dependent on the number of children. In family-quotient taxation, the income of both spouses is summed together with the income from D dependants. Dividing by the quotient Q, gives us the tax base, which is then applied to the individual tax schedule:

$$Tax = T\left(\frac{\left(Y_M + Y_F + \sum_1^D Y_i\right)}{Q}\right) \times Q \quad \text{(Family-QuotientTaxation)}$$

Joint taxation can have the advantage of single-earner couples (and some dual-earner couples) having a lower average tax rate than they would under individual taxation. However, joint taxation is cumbersome to administer and can have disincentive effects for the spouse to take up work, as they may face taxation at the couple's marginal rate. In addition, tax revenues from a joint system, if combined with multiples of the allowances and bands, will be lower than from an equivalent independent system, requiring higher average taxation than an independent system.

Independent taxation avoids this and also means more privacy in a couple's tax affairs, as incomes are legally separate. Although easier to administer, tax units which only apply to married couples apply the principle of horizontal equity differently. In this case, cohabiting and married couples with the same ability to pay may be taxed differently.

Joint taxation, however, can reduce horizontal equity. For example, a two-earner couple with the same income as a single-earner couple will pay the same tax, but incur greater work expenses in relation to childcare etc., and will thus be less well-off than a single-earner couple. Also, as joint taxation provides tax relief to the principal earner, it is likely to be less effective in directing assistance at children than a payment which is paid directly to the main carer. In addition, if, as a result of high marginal effective tax rates, a spouse is likely to reduce earnings, then they will have less control over financial resources and correspondingly less control over resources which could be directed towards children. Joint taxation adds to the complexity and administrative cost of a tax system, due to the need to cross-reference spouses' incomes, and due to the increased monitoring costs of this process.

With increased labour-force participation and labour-market opportunities for women, the implicit dependency assumed by the tax system must be questioned. The situation is different if there are dependants (such as children or elderly) to be cared for, as it is the dependants who create the case for favourable treatment and not the fact of being married.

## 4.3 Data Issues: Net to Gross Imputation

In order to model taxation, the income variables within the tax base need to be recorded before tax is deducted. However, survey data frequently only provide income data that are net of taxation. Thus, one of the data-preparation tasks for the base-data set may be to undertake a net-to-gross imputation.

There are a number of potential methods that can be used. Immervoll et al. (2001a) outline a statistical method used to produce 'net/gross ratios' in the

European Community Household Panel (ECHP).[3] Based on information where both net and gross income are provided within the data, a statistical model is formulated which yields estimates of net/gross ratios for those cases where survey respondents provide information on net incomes only. This 'statistical' approach raises several issues and it has been recognized by Eurostat[4] that 'the estimated net/gross ratios are a rather simplistic solution to a complex problem' and that 'some data users may wish to do their own conversion, using more sophisticated approaches based on country-specific modelling.' In fact, the estimation of a statistical model is not feasible if there are no observations with information on both net and gross income, or if the number of such observations is too small. In practice, statistical models of tax burdens are generally characterized by a poor fit, even for large samples. In general, the complexity of tax and benefit systems precludes the accurate statistical modelling of taxes and transfer payments. Tax burdens (and benefit entitlements) depend on a large number of individual and household characteristics. They are also highly non-linear, with numerous discontinuities or 'kink points', making it difficult to select an appropriate functional form, even when there are a large number of data points.

Another problem with the particular statistical approach used for deriving ECHP net-to-gross factors is the non-differential treatment of different recipients and different types of income within the household. Using one single household-wide conversion factor for all individuals and incomes in the household ignores the potentially very large differences in relative tax and contribution burdens faced by different individuals and income types. For instance, in many cases, individuals who are entirely exempt from taxation live together with high-income earners. Since, in the majority of cases, taxes and contributions depend on the incomes of units smaller than the household, these variations of net-to-gross ratios are highly relevant.

It is preferable to use a tax-benefit microsimulation model to impute gross incomes. In the case of a relatively simple tax system, or in the case of flat-tax systems, it may be possible to analytically invert the tax system and compute a direct value of the tax liability on the basis of the net income. Fiorio (2009) and D'Amuri and Fiorio (2009) describe a variant of this, incorporating a mixed analytical and iterative method to compute gross income. The main disadvantage relates to the effort required to build such a model.

Given these difficulties, an attractive route would be to exploit existing models of tax and contribution rules. Rather than analytically inverting the

[3] See Eurostat,ECHP UDB manual. https://ec.europa.eu/eurostat/documents/203647/203704/ECHP_variables/477f8adb-531e-4c7d-c071-de34ddc55765, accessed March 18th 2021.

[4] Eurostat (1999), 6.

tax and contribution system, the aim would be to exploit existing tax-benefit models and adapt them so that built-in fiscal algorithms can be used to 'reverse simulate' gross incomes. The basic idea is to adopt an iterative Monte Carlo approach.[5] For each observed net-income value, the algorithm would 'try' different levels of gross income, compute taxes using the tax-benefit model, and subtract them from the gross value to find a provisional measure of net income. This procedure is repeated for different values of gross income until the provisional measure of net income represents an acceptable approximation of the net value as recorded in the original data (Immervoll et al. 2001).[6]

The basic algorithm described in Immervoll et al. (2001) consists of the following steps:

a. In iteration $i = 0$, a suitable first estimate of imputed gross income $g_{i=0}$ has to be chosen. One possibility is to simply take net income $n_{ori}$ as supplied in the data. Hence, the first estimate of the net-to-gross factor is $k_i = 0$

$$k_i = 1 \qquad\qquad i = 0 \tag{1}$$

$$g_i = k_{i*}.n_{ori} \tag{2}$$

b. Applying the tax-benefit rules as implemented in the tax-benefit model to $g_i$, to obtain an estimate of net income (simulated net income, $n_{i=0}$). As long as the effective tax rate $t_i$ is positive, $n_i$ will be smaller than $n_{ori}$:

$$n_i = (1 - t_i).g_i \tag{3}$$

c. Compare $n_i$ with $n_{ori}$, to test if the correspondence between the two is sufficiently close. The exit condition is:

$$|(n_{ori} - n_i)/n_{ori}| \leq |\delta| \quad \text{exitcondition} \tag{4}$$

d. As long as the relative distance between $n_{ori}$ and $n_i$ exceeds $\delta$, the next estimate of gross income $g_i$ is generated in the next iteration. The new $g_{i+1}$ is obtained from Equation 2 using a revised estimate of the net-to-gross factor $k_{i+1}$ as follows:

[5] Monte Carlo simulation uses random sampling of error terms to generate statistical distributions around core-average results.

[6] Verbič et al. (2015) and Betti et al. (2011) utilize iterative models to impute gross incomes with varying degrees of estimation for Slovenia and Italy respectively.

$$k_{i+1} = k_i . n_{ori} / n_i \tag{5}$$

This ensures that $g_{i+1} > g_i$ if $n_i < n_{ori}$, and vice versa.

e. The algorithm continues with Step *b* above.

Several complications arise when implementing this approach in practice. First, in cases where a fiscal unit consists of more than one person (joint taxation), it can be difficult to produce separate net-to-gross factors for each member of the unit. Also, since different income components may be taxed at different rates, it is desirable to compute separate net-to-gross factors for each of these components. Finally, because the algorithm depends on convergence towards a solution, it is important to analyse whether the specific process of convergence gives rise to biased estimates.[7]

## 4.4 Validation: External Data

A critical part of the reliability of microsimulation models is the validity of the simulation results. This relates to not just comparing results against totals, but importantly also if there are differences, to understand the nature of these differences.

Although the policy rules may in fact be correctly coded in the model, simulated aggregates may not necessarily match official aggregates. Reasons why simulated data may differ from official aggregates include tax evasion—relating to the underpayment of income, differences between declared income in the dataset used for microsimulation, and the data used to calculate taxes and benefits by the authorities—and differences between the totals from survey weights and those for totals in the tax system.

Useful external sources of data for validation include official figures, other studies, other survey data, existing models, etc. What follows can be used as a checklist of potentially useful steps for the validation of aggregates. Immervoll and O'Donoghue (2009) report sources of external aggregates for validation that include:

Comparison of monetary aggregates:

[7] It is possible that the algorithm does not converge as a result of discontinuities in the (effective) tax schedule. If a solution is not found after a certain number of iterations, the algorithm starts over with a (randomly) different starting value $g_0$.

- for different components of instruments simulated (e.g., certain deductions)
- for each individual instrument simulated (e.g., employee insurance contributions)
- for groups of simulated instruments (e.g., employee contributions)

Comparison of monetary sub-aggregates (e.g., by quantile, by region, by type):

- for different components of instruments simulated (e.g., certain deductions)
- for each individual instrument simulated (e.g., employee insurance contributions)
- for groups of simulated instruments (e.g., employee contributions)

Numbers of taxpayers/benefit recipients:

- for different components of instruments simulated (e.g., certain deductions)
- for each individual instrument simulated (e.g., employee insurance contributions)
- for groups of simulated instruments (e.g., employee contributions)

There are a number of possible reasons for deviations of simulated results for each of the above. These should be quantified if possible—either as best estimates or quoting related studies if available. In drawing conclusions, it is important to look at the different instruments together. For example, can assumptions about the reasons for the deviation of one instrument be reconciled with the deviations of another instrument? If income taxes are 'too low', but contributions (which are subject to upper contribution limits) are 'OK', then this would be consistent with the explanation that the source of underestimating income taxes is the under-representation of high incomes in the underlying micro-data.

Known differences in the definition of simulated and reference aggregates are:

Data related:

- coverage of underlying micro-data (including attrition for panels)
- misrepresentation of certain types of units (e.g., high-income individuals)
- known bias of survey responses (e.g., self-employment incomes)
- imputation techniques
- missing variables in the data (e.g., mortgage interest, imputed rent)

- uprating techniques employed to carry the data forward to simulation year
- method used for net-to-gross conversion, etc.

Simulation related:

- simplifying assumptions regarding eligibility/liability conditions
- benefit take-up, tax evasion
- simplifying assumption regarding the computation of amounts of benefits/taxes

One of the most common problems in microsimulation is simulating the correct number of benefit recipients in non-universal systems. This is especially true if:

- The duration of entitlement for these instruments is limited, so that some of those units who appear to be eligible in the data (because they receive the benefit during the period covered by the survey) are in fact only eligible at any one point in time.
- The authorities can exercise some degree of discretion in determining who is eligible/liable for a certain instrument.

Myck and Najsztub (2014) describe a number of issues encountered in validating a static microsimulation model.[8] They find discrepancies between the data weighted using the baseline grossing-up weights and the official statistics for taxation. Correcting for these differences with new weights adjusted for economic status and tax characteristics, while improving the aggregate totals, significantly increases income inequality. Thus, while reweighting can improve the accuracy in terms of aggregates in the simulation, they argue that it should be used with caution.

## 4.5 Measurement Issues: The Distributional Impact of Taxation Analyses

In this section, some of the measurement issues relating to understanding the distributional impact of tax analyses are considered. Examples include

[8] Creedy (2003) describes the theory associated with a number of potential reweighting methods, using these to reweight the 2000–01 wave of the New Zealand Household Economic Survey (HES) data to 2003–04. See O'Donoghue and Loughrey (2014) for a survey of using reweighting for adjusting the sample to bring the characteristics from a historical sample to the present, a process known as 'now-casting'. Immervoll et al. (2005) describe the static-ageing technique known as 'reweighting' (altering the weights of different observations in the data) in order to meet control totals for the policy-simulation year.

changing the tax system to finance another policy change (such as the cost of a social transfer) or an analysis of the distributional incidence of all or part of the tax system. Two measures, 'gainers/losers' and those based upon the Gini inequality indicator, are used.

### 4.5.1 Gainers/Losers

Policy reform takes place within a political environment and therefore the design of a policy reform cannot take place independently of this dimension. It is not sufficient to merely consider costs and other measures, such as poverty reduction. One must also consider who gains and loses from the reform. Standard statistics of interest include:

- the number of gainers from the reform (including the revenue-raising component as well as the expenditure component)
- the numbers of gainers and losers by level of gain or loss
- the numbers of gainers and losers by type of household (e.g., family status, income decile, employment status, geographical concentration, pressure group such as farmers, etc.)

Those who lose out as a result of policy changes are more likely to complain about policies (in the media and in opinion polls) than gainers from the reforms are likely to praise reforms. Thus, politicians are reluctant to implement reforms that involve large-scale losers, who may be part of key constituent groups.

### 4.5.2 Redistribution

Redistribution can be classified as the mechanism by which the distribution of income is changed. There are a number of objectives of welfare states, including the provision of public goods, acting as a social safety net, providing insurance instruments for unexpected life events, for correcting for poor inter-temporal decision making, and for correcting market failures. Many of these objectives employ some element of redistribution, defined here as the transfer of resources between individuals at one point in time or across an individual's lifetime. Redistribution can broadly be classified under a number of headings, including income smoothing, insurance, vertical redistribution, and horizontal equity (see Barr 2012).

A common measure of inequality is the Gini coefficient, which is based on the Lorenz curve, a graph of the percentage of income versus the percentage of the population.[9] The Gini coefficient equals 0 when there is complete equality of incomes and 1 when one individual has all the income.

Descriptive measures of inequality such as the Gini coefficient have a number of problems. First, they lack generality in that the variance measures all use a squared difference and they all incorporate implicit and arbitrary weights. In addition, the Gini coefficient assumes rank-ordering weights, whereas the ordinary-variance measure assumes the same weights for all, and the logged-variance measure assumes logarithmic weights. Descriptive measures also only give a partial ordering, as arises when the Lorenz curves cross. They all also suffer from measurement errors encountered when quantifying standard of living. On the other hand, normative measures, such as the Atkinson or generalized-entropy inequality measures, take a social-welfare function as their starting point (Figures 4.2 and 4.3).

To measure the redistributive effect of the tax-benefit system, measures based on the Lorenz curve are used to examine the degree of these phenomena.[10] The Lorenz curve for pre-tax market income is simply a graph of the

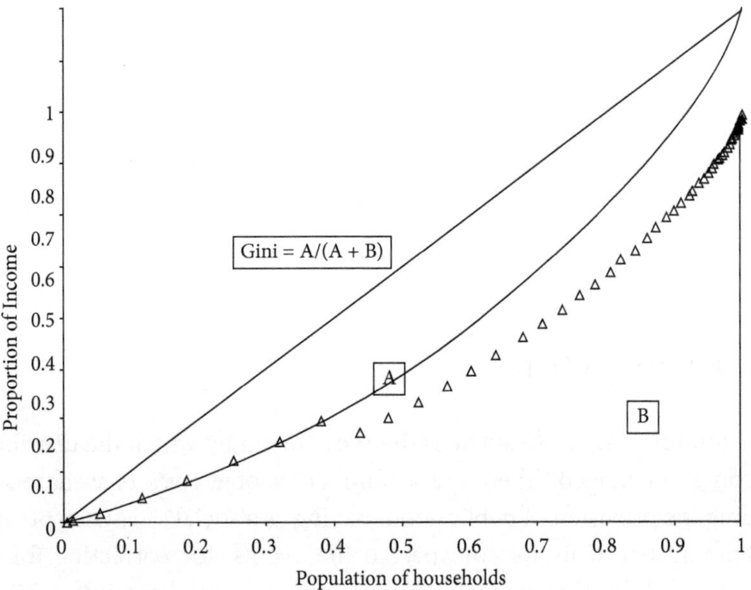


**Figure 4.2** Gini Coefficient

[9] See Barr (2012) for a good description of inequality measures.

[10] The methods described here are standard methods for examining the degree of redistribution and progressivity in a tax-benefit system (see Palme 1996 and Decoster et al. 2000).

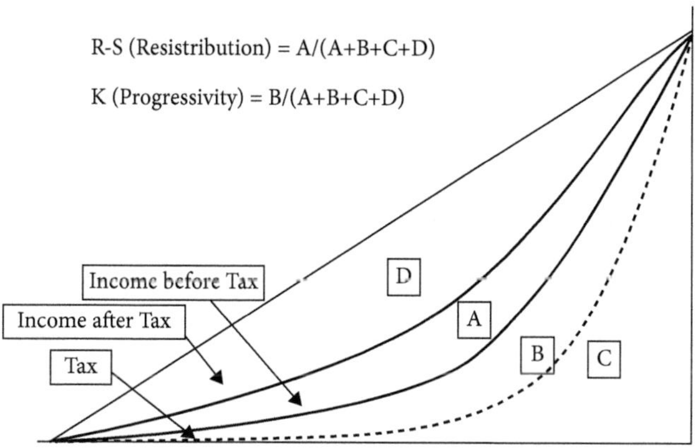


**Figure 4.3** Redistribution and Progressivity

cumulative population share versus the cumulative income for population ranked by order of their income. The Gini coefficient (Equation 6) is a standard index of inequality:

$$G_M = 1 - 2\int_0^1 L_M(p)dp \tag{6}$$

where $p$ is the cumulative population share and $L_M(p)$ is the Lorenz curve at point $p$. A population with no income inequality would have a Lorenz curve of 45° and, therefore, a Gini coefficient of 0. If Lorenz curve A lies completely inside Lorenz curve B, then it is possible to say that population A has greater inequality than population B, with $G_A > G_B$. However, if both Lorenz curves cross, it is not possible to make inequality comparisons without using value judgements. Palme (1996) points out that using the Gini coefficient will give highest weight to the area around the median, where the most observations occur and where, because of a higher density, re-ranking is more likely to occur. He suggests that using the generalized index allows one to place a higher weight on other areas of the income distribution.[11]

The generalized Gini coefficient due to Yitzhaki (1983), defined below, allows value judgements to be taken into account. In this case, higher values of $v$ indicate greater weight being placed on those in the lower end of the income distribution. If $v = 0$, then the social-welfare function is unconcerned about inequality, always taking a value of 1 regardless of the distribution. When $v = 2$, G(2) is the same as the standard Gini coefficient, while as $v \rightarrow \infty$, all the weight is placed on the lowest income, producing a Rawlsian social-welfare function:

[11] See Atkinson (1980) and Kaplow (2000) for further critiques of measures of horizontal equity.

$$G_M(v) = 1 - v(v-1)\int_0^1 (1-p)^{v-2} L_M(p)dp \tag{7}$$

To measure the redistributive impact of policy-change systems on inequality, the generalized Reynolds–Smolensky index (Reynolds and Smolensky 1977), which is the difference between the generalized Gini coefficients for market income and post-instrument income, is used. It is defined in Equation 8:

$$\prod_A^{RS}(v) = G_M(v) - G_{M+A}(v)$$
$$= v(v-1)\left(\int_0^1 (1-p)^{v-2}[L_M(p) - L_{m+A}(p)]dp\right) \tag{8}$$

The generalized Reynolds–Smolensky index of redistribution can be decomposed into the redistributive effect before re-ranking (the difference between the Lorenz curve for market income and the concentration curve for post-instrument income) and the re-ranking effect of the instrument (the difference between the concentration curve and the Lorenz curve), as highlighted in Equation 9. This equation can be further transformed in Equation 10 into three components: the progressivity (or departure from proportionality) ($\Pi^K(v)$), the relative size of the instrument in question ($a/(1+a)$), and the horizontal or re-ranking effect ($D(v)$) (see Kakwani 1984).

Progressivity is a measure of the difference between the level of redistribution of an instrument relative to an instrument with the same revenue effect, but where the effect is proportional to income. It is, therefore, a measure of the incidence of an instrument. If an instrument is disproportionally focused on the lower (upper) half of the distribution, then it is regressive (progressive). If an instrument is regressive (progressive), the concentration curve for the instrument will fall outside (inside) the Lorenz curve of market income. If the instrument is proportional to income, the concentration curve will be exactly the same as the Lorenz curve for market income.

In this section, the Kakwani index of progressivity, which is the difference between the Lorenz curve for income and the concentration curve for the instrument in question, is described. In addition, by using the generalized version of the index, the sensitivity of the results to different assumptions about value judgements can be examined:

$$\Pi_A^{RS}(v) = G_M(v) - G_{M+A}(v)$$
$$= (G_M(v) - C_{M+A}(v)) + (C_{M+A}(v) - G_{M+A}(v)) \tag{9}$$

$$\Pi_A^{RS}(v) = \frac{-a}{1+a}\Pi_A^K(v) + D(v) \tag{10}$$

If tax-benefit instruments are based on characteristics other than income, then income units may have a different order of incomes before and after the operation of the instrument. For example, if social benefits have extra components for dependants, then families will shift up the distribution relative to single people, after the payment of the benefit. Similarly, the existence of joint taxation may result in lower tax liabilities for married couples than single people with the same income. This type of redistribution is known as horizontal redistribution.

Changes in the order of income units in a distribution will result in the Lorenz curve of post-instrument income being different to its concentration curve. The Atkinson–Plotnick re-ranking index, the difference between the Lorenz and concentration curves, is a measure of horizontal equity. There have been a number of criticisms of this measure, however. For example, Kaplow (1989) argues that it does not adequately measure the degree of horizontal redistribution, as it ignores large changes in the distribution that do not affect the ordering of households, while small changes in income that result in re-ranking also result in a change in horizontal equity.

In order to explain the reasons for changes in the redistributivity of the system as a whole, it is necessary to look at what has been happening to sub-components. Equation 11 demonstrates how the redistributive effect of sub-components A and B, using the Reynolds–Smolensky index, can be aggregated to produce the redistributive effect for a broader instrument C. Similarly, the progressivity of different sub-components can be aggregated to produce an aggregated Kakwani index:

$$\Pi_C^{RS}(v) = \frac{-(1+a)\Pi_A^{RS}(v) - (1+b)\Pi_B^{RS}(v)}{1+a+b} - (G_{M+A+B} - C_{M+A+B}), a \neq -b \tag{11}$$

$$\Pi_C^K(v) = \frac{a\Pi_A^K(v) + b\Pi_B^K(v)}{a+b}, a \neq -b \tag*{(7) a}$$

where $a$ and $b$ are the average rates of instruments A and B (negative if they reduce income).

## 4.6 Simulation: Modelling Taxes and Contributions

In this section, social-insurance contributions and a personal income-tax system are simulated. Utilizing the XLSIM model in Chapter 2, and, as per Chapter 3, applied to Irish data for working-age households, the following instruments are introduced:

- employee social-insurance contributions (EESIC)
- self-employed social-insurance contributions (SESIC)
- employer social-insurance contributions (ERSIC)
- income taxation (IT)

### 4.6.1 Introduce New Contributions and Taxes

A hypothetical family calculation is first utilized to produce a budget-constraint diagram and to test the validity of the simulations. As in Section 2, we model in turn the taxable income, tax allowances, deductions' tax schedule, and tax credits, whose parameters are described in Table 4.1.

In Figure 4.4, each of these instruments are plotted against market income. Note that:

**Table 4.1** Contribution and Tax Rules

| Instrument | EESIC | SESIC | ERSIC | IT |
|---|---|---|---|---|
| Taxable Income | Employee earnings | Self-employed earnings | Employee earnings | Employee earnings+ self-employed earnings + capital income + pension income |
| Allowance | 127 per week | 0 | 38 per week | |
| Deduction | | | | Occupational pensions |
| Rates | 0.08 | 0.07 | 0.085 | 0.2<br>0.42 |
| Bands | | | | 36,400 per year |
| Tax Credit | | | | Personal: 1,830<br>Employee: 1,830<br>Lone parent: 1,830<br>Widow: 2,430<br>Aged 65+: 325<br>(all per year) |
| Floor | | 3,174 per year | | |
| Ceiling | 75,036 per year | n/a | n/a | n/a |

*Note* that the systems modelled here are simplified.

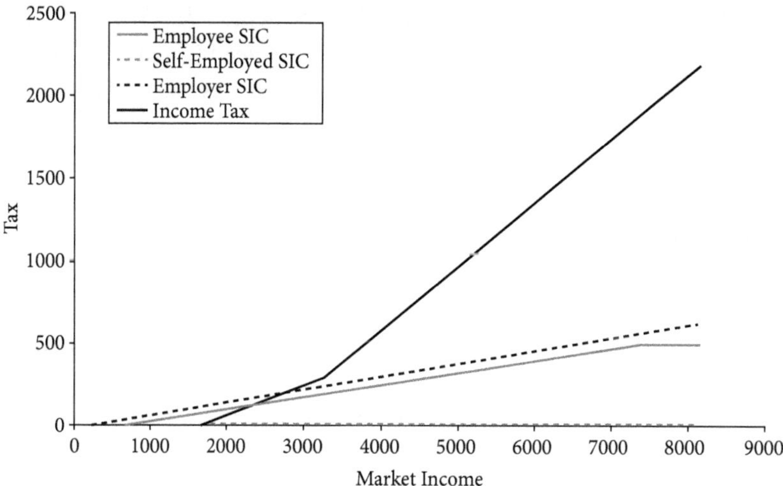


**Figure 4.4** Tax and Social-Insurance Contributions

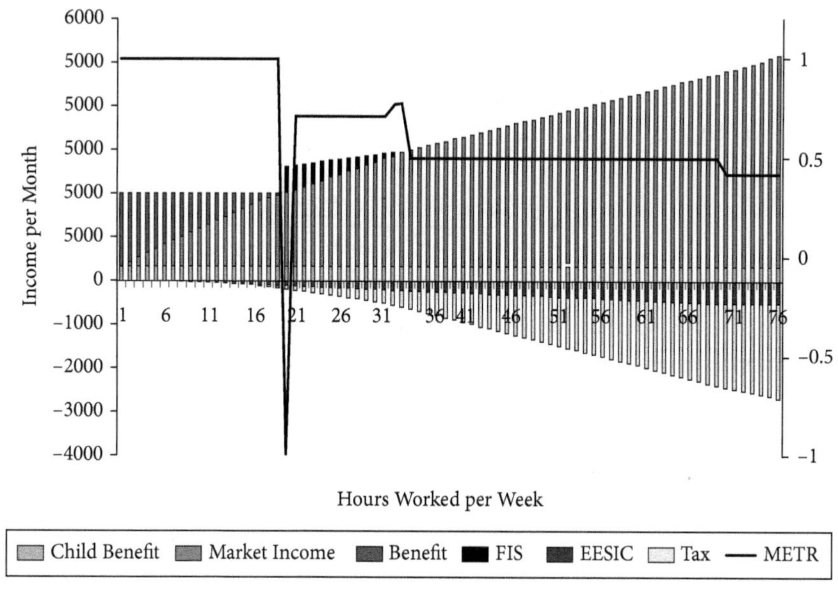


**Figure 4.5** Monthly Net-Income Budget Constraint of Benefit Simulations on Couple with Two Children

*NB*: hourly wage–€23 per hour.

- With a smaller allowance and slightly higher rate, the employer SIC calculation is higher at all levels than the employee SIC calculations.
- We see tax credits and a resulting zero income-tax rate, followed by two progressively increasing tax bands.

In Figure 4.5, the budget-constraint diagram (including taxation and social-insurance contributions) is reported, in addition to benefits calculated in Chapter 3. Note that:

- Social-insurance contributions and income taxation take negative values below the axis.
- ERSICs do not appear in the budget constraint, as they are subtracted from earnings before being paid to the worker.
- Earnings are net of taxes and contributions, so that the top of the graphic represents the budget constraint.

Combining benefit-withdrawal rate, social-insurance-contribution rate, and income-tax rate, the marginal effective tax rate (METR) is reported in the secondary axis.

The METR, were Δ is the change in a characteristic before a marginal change in income, can be defined as:

$$METR = \frac{\Delta Tax + \Delta SIC - \Delta Benefit}{\Delta Income}$$

where SIC is social-insurance contribution.

Note also:

- the one-hundred-per-cent METR at the start as unemployment assistance is withdrawn
- going negative as family income support (FIS) is introduced
- falling to 88 per cent as FIS is withdrawn
- falling to 28 per cent once the benefit has been withdrawn
- rising to 50 per cent once the higher tax band is paid
- falling to 42 per cent once income reaches the ceiling for EESIC

### 4.6.2 Measure Progressivity and Redistributive Effect

In order to measure the degree of redistribution, and the progressivity of the tax and social-insurance-contribution system, the system is simulated on the whole working-age population.

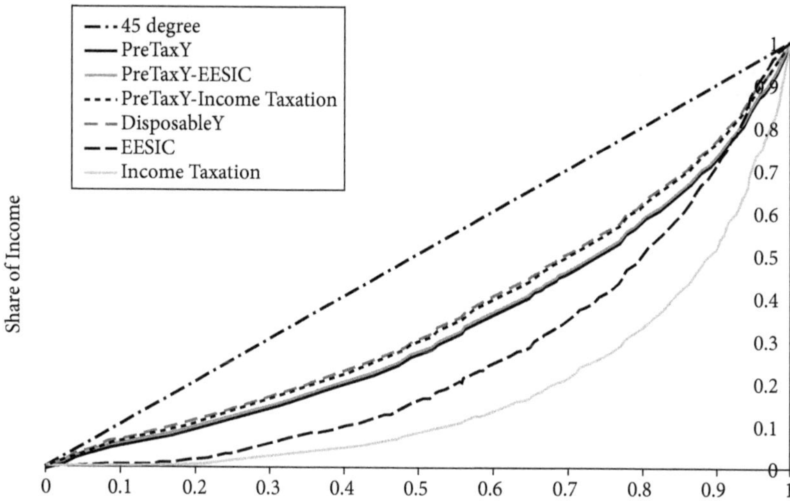


**Figure 4.6** Lorenz and Concentration Curves

In Figure 4.6, a series of Lorenz and concentration curves is graphed. Both the concentration curves for EESIC and income tax lie outside pre-tax income, indicating that they are progressive, with income taxation more progressive than pre-tax income. Although it is hard to discern the difference between the concentration curves for pre-tax income and pre-tax income less EESIC, we notice that the pre-tax income less income tax is visibly inside pre-tax income, indicating that inequality is lower, and that the progressive income tax is (note Table 4.2):

- the rate of the tax or contribution as a percentage of pre-tax income
- the Kakwani index as a measure of the progressivity of the instrument
- the Reynolds–Smolensky index as a measure of the redistributivity of the instrument

The concentration curve highlights that income taxation is more progressive than social-insurance contributions. As the rate is also higher, income

**Table 4.2** Progressivity and Redistribution

| | Rate | Progessivity (Kakwani) | Redistributive (Reynolds–Smolensky) |
|---|---|---|---|
| EESIC | 0.04 | −0.15 | 0.01 |
| SESIC | 0.010 | −0.150 | 0.001 |
| IT | 0.11 | −0.31 | 0.05 |
| All Taxes/Contributions | 0.153 | −0.26 | 0.06 |

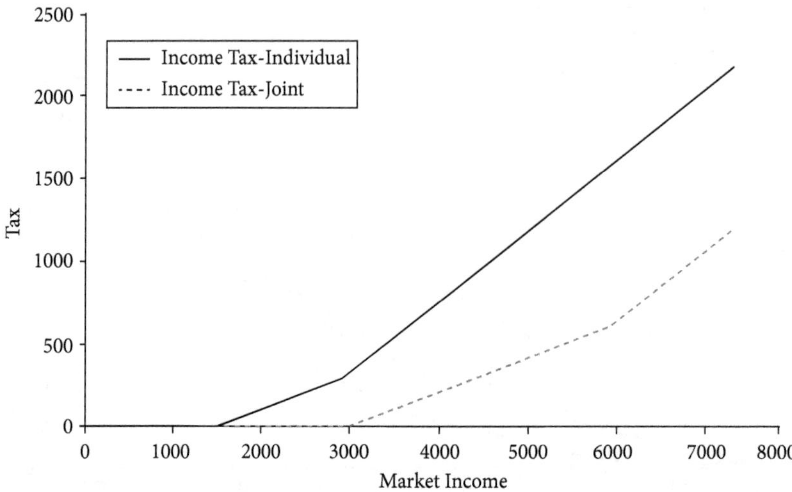


**Figure 4.7** Average Tax Liability for Joint and Individual Taxation for Single-Earning Married Couples

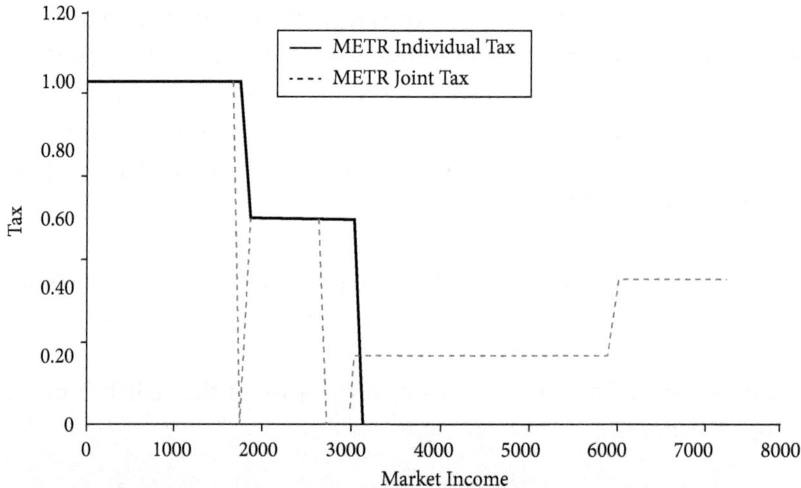


**Figure 4.8** Marginal Effective Tax Rates for Joint and Individual Taxation
*NB*: the marginal amount is earnings for the non-working spouse.

taxation is both more progressive and more redistributive. Conversely, although both EESIC and SESIC have similar progressivity, EESIC are more redistributive as they affect a greater number of people.

### 4.6.3 Undertake a Policy Reform

A policy reform, namely the introduction of joint taxation, is now analysed. Utilizing the terminology in Section 4.2, a split joint-taxation model is used, and it is assumed that joint-tax-return filing is compulsory and that all tax credits, allowances, deductions, and bands are transferable between spouses. Figure 4.7 reports the average tax liability for a single-earning married couple, under both joint and individual taxation. Joint taxation, by combining tax allowances, credits, and bands for couples, allows single-earning couples to reduce their tax burden. At every level of market income there is a lower tax liability.

However, the consequence, as described in Figure 4.8, is that the METR for a non-earning spouse is higher than under individual taxation. For lower-earning families, there is little difference between the two. This is because the means test for benefits (at a family unit of analysis) dominates. Nevertheless, once these benefits have been tapered, the non-working spouse moving into employment is bound by their spouse's METR. Thus, while joint taxation is horizontally redistributive, it generates negative work incentives.

# PART III

# BEHAVIOURAL MODELS

# 5 Labour-Supply Behaviour

## 5.1 Introduction

In the preceding chapters, the focus was on simulating policies that aim to reduce poverty, generate revenue, or redistribute resources. However, many public policies also try to incentivize behaviour, such as those to improve labour participation or supply, or to change behaviours in relation to savings or pollution.

Social- and fiscal-policy instruments face a fundamental trade-off. An instrument that performs well from an income-maintenance perspective may have unintended behavioural consequences. For example, a means-tested benefit may redistribute resources to the poor, thereby reducing poverty, but it may also reduce the incentive to work by diminishing the return to entering the labour market. In other words, if the tax-benefit instrument depends on characteristics that individuals can influence, then this may have a potential impact on their behaviour.

In many cases, changing individuals' behaviour is an intended consequence of policy and is, thus, desirable. Examples include taxes and fines on activities, which negatively affect others, the tax-deductibility of charitable donations, or unemployment benefits that enable jobseekers to undertake a more-thorough search process.[1] Frequently, however, the incentives for behavioural change that such instruments give rise to are unintended. Examples of behaviour of interest in microsimulation modelling include:

- labour-supply response (Aaberge and Colombino 2014)
- tax reform (Haan 2010)
- benefit take-up (Pudney et al. 2006; Matsaganis et al. 2010; Bhargava and Manoli 2015)
- consumption behaviour (Capéau et al. 2014)
- polluting behaviour (Hynes and O'Donoghue 2014)
- tertiary education participation (Flannery and O'Donoghue 2013)

[1] On the latter, see Acemoglu and Shimer (1999), who discuss under which conditions unemployment-insurance systems increase economic efficiency.

*Practical Microsimulation Modelling.* Cathal O'Donoghue. Oxford University Press. © Cathal O'Donoghue 2021.
DOI: 10.1093/oso/9780198852872.003.0005

- enterprise decisions (Buslei et al. 2014)
- recreational choice (Cullinan et al. 2011; Cullinan 2011)

However, in this chapter, we will focus mainly on labour-supply decisions (Blundell and MaCurdy 1999; Creedy and Duncan 2002; Creedy and Kalb 2006; Aaberge and Colombino 2014).

### 5.1.1 Theoretical Model

Thus far, the focus has been on analyses that measure the effectiveness of policy in the realm of poverty or inequality reduction. In addition to the revenue cost of introducing the instrument, there may also be a distortionary cost due to the fact that individuals may reduce their labour supply as a result of the increased tax required to pay for the anti-poverty policy, or as a result of the incentives that arise as part of the means test of the instrument.

This is illustrated in Figure 5.1, which draws upon the work of Atkinson (1996) in presenting an example of the impact of labour-supply responses on the relationship between the level of a lump-sum transfer or basic income (or flat benefit provided to all citizens) B and the tax rate $t$. It is assumed that a tax rate $t_0$ is required to pay for other government expenditures.

If the government chooses a higher tax rate than the minimum required for other expenditure, then the basic income becomes positive. In the absence of a labour-supply response, the value of the basic income would increase as the tax rate increases. However, if individuals reduce their labour

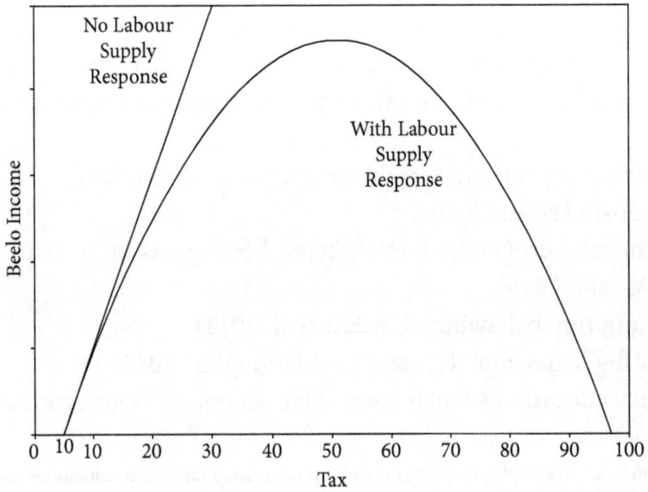


**Figure 5.1** Equity-Efficiency Trade-Off

supply as the tax rate rises (because the wage falls, and so the cost of leisure falls, resulting in a substitution away from work to leisure), then eventually as the tax rate rises, the total revenue falls at some point. Therefore, the amount available for redistribution falls as taxes increase. This trade-off between redistribution and behavioural distortions is known as the equity-efficiency trade-off.

In the EU, certain state transfers have been criticized as giving rise to adverse incentive effects and were—next to labour-market 'rigidities' and over-regulation—named as one of the main causes of slack economic growth and unemployment (Bean 1994). In particular, there was a concern that by intervening in the labour market, tax-benefit systems create incentives that negatively affect the behaviour of both employees and firms. On the demand side, high tax burdens increase the cost of labour, while on the supply side, high marginal tax rates reduce the reward for additional work efforts. In addition, generous out-of-work benefit payments are seen to lead people to reduce their efforts to seek employment (Snower and de La Dehesa 1997; Björklund 1991).

There is no consensus as to the quantitative significance of these effects[2] and, in any case, any negative implications of state interventions in the market have to be weighed against their success in achieving the economic- and social-policy goals for which they were originally designed (Atkinson et al. 2002). For example, in Southern Europe there have been concerns that the state does not provide protection against contingencies such as long-term unemployment. While excessively high supports may give rise to adverse incentive effects, low degrees of income maintenance will have negative consequences from both economic- and social-policy perspectives. In measuring and discussing the coverage (those with eligibility) and generosity (level of payment) of benefits, it is essential to take both into account.

From a social-policy point of view, the absolute level of out-of-work income is important, since it determines the minimum living standard that individuals are able to secure during periods of unemployment. Of course, the absolute benefit level also determines the public expenditure necessary to finance benefit payments. Because the burden of financing is, to a large extent, borne by employers and employees, generous benefits raise the cost of labour, which may in themselves lead to decreasing employment.[3] Moreover, generous benefits tend to improve the relative bargaining position of employees and may, therefore, lead to higher wages (Layard et al. 1991). On the other hand, the level of out-of-work income measured relative to

[2] Nickel and Layard (1999), Scarpetta (1996).

[3] Carey and Tchilinguirian (2000) provide estimates of taxes on labour and capital in OECD countries.

in-work income (the replacement rate) is a measure of the relative drop in living standards that individuals experience on becoming unemployed. This latter measure is also the relevant one for looking at work incentives. Looking at the same issue from a different and rather more-pointed perspective begs the question: is the hardship caused by being out of work 'sufficient' to ensure that employment and the efforts needed to secure employment become the more attractive alternative?

There are, of course, other dimensions to being unemployed that will be equally or more relevant in an individual's decision as to whether or not to seek or stay in employment. These other dimensions include non-financial rewards (for both being in work and out of work), the negative stigma of being unemployed (whether with or without benefits), individuals' perceptions as to the availability of benefits, and the likelihood of finding a suitable job, as well as other aspects of benefit systems, such as eligibility conditions or duration of entitlement (Atkinson and Micklewright 1991).

### 5.1.2 Stated Preferences and Revealed Preferences

There are a number of methods of estimating elasticities, or the proportional change in behaviour, relative to the proportional change in a driver, such as income. First, stated-preference techniques are based upon choice experiments that are carried out by collecting surveys and are frequently used for policy analysis in areas such as public services (Schläpfer 2017), transportation (Arencibia et al. 2015), or environment (Tu et al. 2016). Second, and the method considered here, is the use of revealed-preference techniques. These techniques look at observed behaviour in the data and consider the implications of making other choices, from which the structure of individuals' preferences is revealed by this information (see Tirachini et al. 2016).

In stated-preference models, individuals are asked about their preferences over alternatives, and a choice experiment is utilized to identify choice-specific attributes. These models have the advantage of having information over the full choice set presented, and allow for individual heterogeneity. However, they have the disadvantage of potentially misstating preferences for particular goods. The choices selected may also be context dependent. Solutions exist via external validation (revealed preferences, observed- versus simulated-market share) or internal validation, in relation to consistency of preferences (Boxall et al. 1996).

Revealed preferences, on the other hand, depend upon observed behaviour. There is an extensive literature of policy-impact evaluation using ex-post methods, where analysis focusing on the impact of a policy for a treatment group who participate in the policy is compared with a control group used as a comparator (Betcherman et al. 2004). Such ex-post analyses depend upon actual experiments with control versus treatment groups (Banerjee et al. 2015), or on natural experiments that utilize natural variation in populations (Rosenzweig and Wolpin 2000). Chetty (2009), Saez (2010), and Saez et al. (2012) review an extensive literature that looks at the tax responsiveness to changes in the marginal rate of tax, namely the new tax-responsiveness literature. However, these methods cannot assess the impact of policies that have not yet been implemented.

Ex-ante analyses, on the other hand, are based upon simulations utilizing natural variation among individual characteristics and choices in data (Aaberge and Colombino 2014). They have the advantage that the individuals have made choices in reality. However, they have the disadvantage that they only observe the actual choice, and that they cannot observe individual heterogeneity. In this chapter, the focus will be on ex-ante analysis.

### 5.1.3 Microsimulation Methods for Labour-Supply Analysis

This section deals with the consideration of how to use a microsimulation framework to design and evaluate policies that impact on behaviour. Examples can include policies that have an explicit focus on incentives, e.g., in-work family benefits, such as the US earned income-tax credit (EITC), or UK tax credits, or conditional cash transfers (CCT), such as Progressa, in Mexico, and Bolsa Família, in Brazil, which aim to reduce poverty and child labour and to increase education.

Microsimulation techniques have been used to assess behaviour since the early 1980s (see Blomquist 1983; Van Soest 1995; Klevmarken 1997), and are now mainstream components of tax-benefit models (Aaberge and Colombino 2014). Sometimes, models simply produce measures of potential behavioural incentives, such as replacement rates (Martin 1996; O'Donoghue 2011; Jahn 2018) and marginal effective tax rates (see Feldstein 1995; Immervoll 2005; Jara and Tumino 2013).

Alternatively, other techniques try to explicitly model the potential impact on behaviour of a policy change. In order to do this, and to assess the impact of a policy on behaviour within a microsimulation model, modellers need to have a quantifiable measure of the behavioural response or elasticity, which is the proportional rate of change of behaviour relative to a proportional change in (say) income.

In terms of methodology, a number of techniques have been used, including continuous-choice methods (Hausman 1985). While debate existed as to the robustness of these models throughout the 1980s (see the *Journal of Historical Research* special issue in 1990), the field has now evolved to the use of a discrete-choice methodology, due to Van Soest (1995), drawing upon the work of McFadden (1973).

There are a number of mechanisms for incorporating behavioural elasticities in microsimulation models. Some papers utilize either arbitrary values of elasticities or elasticities taken from the literature (Scholz 1996), while many estimate elasticities (Aaberge and Colombino 2014). Papers use microsimulation models to both develop micro-econometric estimates and simulate labour-supply responses.

Recent work has estimated the impact of policy-related labour-supply changes, respectively in New Zealand and Australia (Creedy and Mok 2017; Creedy and Hérault 2011), and consequentially looked at optimal tax reforms (Creedy et al. 2018). As in the case of other types of microsimulation modelling, labour-supply microsimulation has spread in recent years beyond traditional countries, such as the US, the UK, France, Italy, Sweden, and Australia, to new countries, such as Luxembourg (Berger et al. 2011), Spain (Oliver and Spadaro 2017), and Serbia (Ranđelović and Rakić 2013), and developing countries, such as Uruguay (Amarante et al. 2010) and Ecuador (Mideros and O'Donoghue 2015).

There is an increasing cross-national comparative literature that includes Bargain et al. (2014), who utilize a discrete-choice framework, and Jäntti et al. (2015), who use a continuous framework. While most models focus on work-related labour supply, Kabatek et al. (2014) extend labour supply to incorporate domestic labour, and utilize a microsimulation framework to assess the impact of moving from joint to individual taxation. In addition, although many analyses of labour supply within the microsimulation literature have utilized survey data, there are increasing opportunities to use administrative data (Mastrogiacomo et al. 2017). Yet, there have been relatively few validation estimates of the discrete labour-supply microsimulation literature. However, Thoresen et al. (2015) argue that some of the new tax-responsiveness ex-post literature can be used to validate discrete-choice estimates.

### 5.1.4 Chapter Outline

As mentioned earlier, this chapter first considers the structure of instruments, with an explicit goal to improve behavioural response, such as in-work benefits. Section 5.3 describes how to simulate the inputs required, and then estimate a revealed-preference-choice model. Section 5.4 describes a method used to calibrate choice models for simulation purposes. In terms of measurement issues related to the behavioural analysis, we describe the design and use of replacement rates. The chapter concludes by undertaking a simulation of the introduction of a change in in-work benefits.

## 5.2 Policy Context: In-Work Benefits

The focus of this section is on the design of a particular type of transfer payment that aims to both induce behavioural change and provide income maintenance, namely in-work benefits. In-work benefits are benefits that pay more when an individual works a particular number of hours. This type of payment has been developed by a number of countries to overcome poverty traps inherent in many transfer systems (Immervoll and Pearson 2009). The US introduced the EITC (Scholz 1996), where the benefit rate increases with hours worked (to a point). In the UK, family credit (Duncan and Giles 1996), and then a succession of refundable tax credits, paid extra amounts to families that had children and worked more than sixteen hours (Brewer et al. 2006). In Ireland, the family income supplement (FIS) was introduced for families that had children and worked more than twenty hours per week (Bargain and Doorley 2011).

In-work benefits are part of a wider series of benefits that combine cash payments with conditionality. In other cases, conditionality may instead of labour supply focus on health outcomes (Gertler 2004) or child-labour outcomes (Bourguignon et al. 2003). Ignoring taxation, Figure 5.1 describes the structure of the two CCT payments.

The child-focused cash payment is means tested in that it is only received by poorer families, with a fifty-per-cent taper above the payment threshold. CCTs, such as Brazil's Bolsa Escola and Mexico's Progressa programmes, do not taper, but rather have a strict cut-off. Typically, the unit of analysis is the family, while the period of analysis may vary. The refundable tax credit is typical of the types of systems internationally in which a payment is made, conditional on labour supply reaching a minimum level. These instruments are targeted at the working poor and thus contain an income taper, so that the instrument is withdrawn as incomes get higher.

### 5.2.1 Incentive Effects

While improving unemployment traps by increasing the return to work, in-work benefits can introduce a poverty trap. For example, FIS in Ireland (now the working-family payment) is a weekly tax-free payment available to employees with children. It gives extra financial support to people on low pay and where there is at least one child who is normally in residence or financially supported by the claimant. To qualify for FIS, net average-weekly family income must be below a certain limit for a specific family size $(L_F)$. The rate of FIS payable is 60 per cent of the difference between net family income and the relevant family-income limit that applies.

Of particular concern is the degree to which the taper depends upon net or gross data. For example, Callan et al. (1995) showed how the Irish FIS system, while reducing unemployment traps (a low incentive to enter work), induced a poverty trap due to the combination of a taper of 60 per cent based upon gross income, a marginal tax rate of 40 per cent, and a marginal social-insurance contribution rate of nearly 8 per cent, together producing a marginal effective tax rate of 108 per cent (0.6 + 0.4 + 0.08). In other words, for gross income $Y_G$ in this income range, the net income $Y_N$ is defined as:

$$Y_N = Y_G + 0.6 * Max\left(0, L_F - Y_G\right) - Y_G * \left(0.4 + 0.08\right)$$

The marginal effective tax rate, defined as $1 - \frac{\delta Y_N}{\delta Y_G}$, is therefore:

$$1 - \frac{\delta Y_N}{\delta Y_G} = 1 - \frac{\delta\left(Y_G + 0.6 * Max\left(0, L_F - Y_G\right) - Y_G * \left(0.4 + 0.08\right)\right)}{\delta Y_G}$$
$$= 1 - \left(1 - 0.6 - 0.48\right) = 1.08$$

Moving to a net income test:

$$Y_N = Y_G + 0.6 * Max\left(0, L_F - \left(Y_G - Y_G * \left(0.4 + 0.08\right)\right)\right) - Y_G * \left(0.4 + 0.08\right),$$

the marginal effective tax rate would reduce to:

$$1 - \frac{\delta Y_N}{\delta Y_G} = 1 - \left(1 + 0.6 * \left(-0.52\right) - 0.48\right) = 0.792$$

which although high is less than 100 per cent.

## 5.3 Data Issues: Preparation of Data for Labour-Supply-Choice Modelling

In this section, a methodology for estimating a simple discrete-choice behavioural model is described. Blundell and MaCurdy (1999), as is typical in the literature, describe the estimation of labour-supply models using a variant of the two good models of consumption, trading off leisure and consumption for alternative choices. Choices in this model thus depend upon the current attributes of the choices. More recently, Flannery and O'Donoghue (2013) utilized a life-cycle-choice model, trading off current costs, such as foregone earnings and fees, current household income, and future returns in terms of higher earnings.

Fundamental to this methodology is the fact that while the actual choice and some associated characteristics (age, school participation of the child, work participation of the adult, or university participation of the student) are observed in the data, information is also required about the alternative choices to extract a measure of preference function. For this, it is necessary to simulate characteristics of the counterfactual (alternative) choices using a microsimulation model. The characteristics required in the preference function will depend upon the nature of the preference function used, which in turn usually depends upon the economic theory used.

While the earlier literature due to Hausman (1985) allowed for continuous-hours choices, it posed challenges econometrically due to the convexity of preferences in non-linear budget constraints.

To understand the implications of the non-linear budget constraint, consider Figure 5.2, which describes a non-linear budget constraint or the income associated with different levels of leisure. To the right, with the highest leisure and correspondingly the least work, is the means-tested unemployment assistance. Lower levels of leisure lead to increasing marginal tax-rate bands (on the left). Between C and B, the dotted line is the standard-rate band. Using indifference curves to describe preferences, or the utility function of the decision maker, in part (a) of this system there is an unemployment trap. In other words, because of the flat part of the budget constraint that results from the means-tested unemployment assistance, where a euro of benefit is lost for every euro of income, there is no incentive to increase hours worked.

If an in-work benefit is introduced in BC, targeted at those who work (say twenty hours per week), the budget constraint becomes increasingly non-linear. It does, however, ensure that for someone with the same preferences, they will be more likely to overcome the unemployment trap if there is labour demand. However, this introduces a poverty trap in part (b). In this case, because the in-work benefit is not provided to all those in work, but rather tapers it away, once an individual has decided to work they may not have an incentive to work additional hours.

In labour-supply modelling, our aim is to estimate a utility function that describes the shape of the indifference curve, drawing the budget constraint

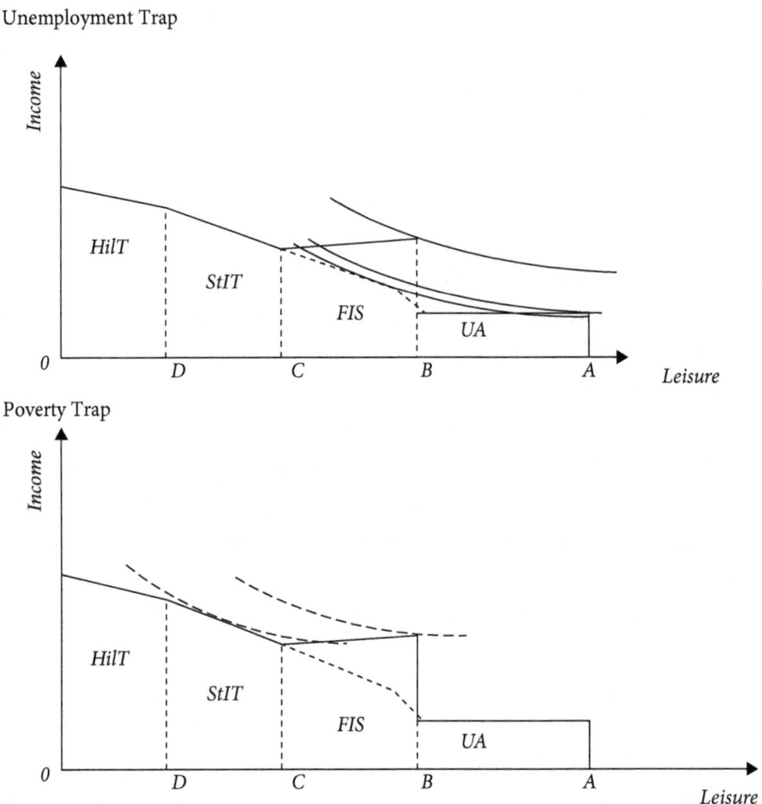


**Figure 5.2** Non-Linear Budget Constraint (Unemployment and Poverty Traps)

from a combination of market-income and tax-benefit instruments simulated in a static tax-benefit model.

The contemporary literature uses choice modelling, drawing upon the work of McFadden (1973). These methods are discrete-choice based, considering only a subset of hours rather than the entire hours set.

## 5.3.1 Modelling Choices

One of the first modelling choices required as part of the data preparation is the selection of the sample over which to estimate a labour-supply function. Typically, only a sub-sample is considered. For example, it is likely that only prime working-age adults, aged say twenty to sixty, will be considered. It can be argued that labour-supply choices at the start of the career are influenced more by life-cycle issues, such as education, which depend upon the income streams resulting from different education choices, rather than the specific tax-benefit system in a single year. At the other age extreme, the retirement choice is also a life-cycle choice, considering alternative expected values of retirement income rather than single-year values. The self-employed may also be excluded, as hours worked are often measured poorly, compared with employees. As civil servants cannot often easily be fired, and they may be disproportionally well rewarded in a negotiated wage-and-hours framework, they may not face the same choices in relation to hours of work as others, while individuals with disabilities may face different supply constraints. These groups can thus be excluded, along with couples where either member falls into one of these categories. Another choice that analysts face is whether to include the unemployed. It can be argued in a demand-constrained environment that this group is not making a voluntary choice, and so this group is also excluded in some analyses.

In developing an estimation of labour-supply choices, there are a number of modelling decisions to be made. Using the discrete-choice framework of Van Soest, where hours are banded, a decision needs to be made on the specific choices. For those who are in work in the data, it is necessary to decide how many hours-groups they can choose from. For those who are not in work, a decision needs to be made in relation to whether to focus only on those who are voluntarily out of work or inactive, or to also include those who are involuntarily out of work or unemployed.

As only the actual choices of individuals in the data are observed, not their potential choices, their counterfactual choices need to be simulated. To do this, the hours, employment status, and consequential market income associated with each hours-group choice, say 0, 8, 18, 24, 32, 40, 48+ or 0, part-time, full-time, etc., are altered. The wage rate is then applied to get the market income associated with that choice. For couples, if there are $m$ hours choices, $m \times m$ choices are simulated as each hours-group is allowable for all of the partner's hours-groups.

In a simulated-budget set, if there are ten hours choices plus two out-of-work states (inactive and unemployed), then for a couple there are twenty-four choices (2 (husband and wife) x 12 choices):

- inactive (not looking for work)
- unemployed (looking for work)
- in-work (1–8, 9–16, 17–24, . . . , 73–80 hours)

Within the hours groups, we typically sample (uniformly) from the eight hours in the hours band to select the counterfactual hours choice. However, the actual choice is always included in the estimation dataset and is one of the choices simulated in the budget set. So, if someone is actually working nineteen hours, rather than sampling from the seventeen-to-twenty-four-hours band, nineteen hours is chosen in this case. Other variables may then have to be adjusted deterministically and appropriately to the choice, e.g., in relation to occupation and industry assigned to workers.

A problem arises in relation to those in the data who are not in work, as their potential wages are not observed in the data. This information is necessary in order to simulate potential in-work income for those who are observed to be out of work in the data. In order to simulate counterfactual potential hourly wages for this group, an hourly earnings equation is estimated. Due to selection bias, a Heckman selection model is utilized, which combines a participation model with extra variables for identification and a Mincerian earnings equation:

$$ln(Y) = f(Z) + f\left(Years\ of\ Education,\ Experience,\ Experience^2,\ Region,\ IMR\right) + \varepsilon$$

$$IMR = g\begin{pmatrix} Z, \#\,children\,aged\,(0-5),\ \#\,children\,aged\,(6-10) \\ \#\,children\,aged\,(11-17), married, regional\,unemployment \end{pmatrix}$$

Another missing variable is the potential out-of-work incomes of those in work. It is possible to simulate these, but it generally requires information on previous income and contributory history. However, for labour supply, generally only short-term income-replacement measures, such as unemployment-insurance benefits, which have low insurance-eligibility requirements, or means-tested unemployment assistance, which have no insurance requirements, are considered.

Unless panel data are available, it is not generally possible to assess insurance requirements. However, for the group who move from employment in the survey to counterfactual unemployment, it is known that they were in work prior to becoming unemployed. It is reasonable to assume, therefore, that they have sufficient insurance payments to be in receipt of unemployment insurance. Similarly, as their in-work income is observed, this can be used as a proxy for previous earnings.

In cases where the benefit level depends upon the duration of receipt, it is not clear what level to set. One option is to select the level of benefit at the point of unemployment. An alternative is to select from the distribution of unemployment durations, if it is known. In the latter case, it is assumed that the employed face the same duration out of work if made unemployed. The entitlement and the level of the unemployment benefit can then be simulated.

Finally, while our survey may contain disposable income for the actual choice made, it doesn't contain data on the disposable income associated with counterfactual choices. A tax-benefit microsimulation model is used to simulate an estimate of the disposable income for each choice.

In order to recover the utility function associated with observed actual and potential labour-supply choices, a discrete-choice model is estimated. There are a number of different models that can be used where there are more than two choices (Hensher and Johnson 1981). In estimating choice based upon personal attributes, a multinomial logit (MNL) model is utilized:

$$Y_{ij} = B_j X_i + e_{ij}$$

In this case, the $X_i$ values are constant, but there are separate estimates of $B_j$ for each choice, where there are $m-1$ sets of estimates where $Y_i$ has $m$ choices. In the case of a policy example, such as the Bolsa Familia CCT, in Brazil, there are three choices described in Table 5.1, with associated incomes and costs. In this model, it is assumed that parental income is exogenous, that child income depends upon the earnings rate of a child, and that the transfer depends upon the choices made (Table 5.2).

The framework is similar to that of Bourguignon et al (2003), with $S_i$ representing the occupational choice of household $i$. This will take the value 0 if the child works, a value of 1 if the child goes to both work and school, while 2 will represent those that are in school and not in work. Bourguignon et al (2003) modelled this choice using the MNL model, where if an individual is

**Table 5.1** CCT or In-Work Transfer Payment

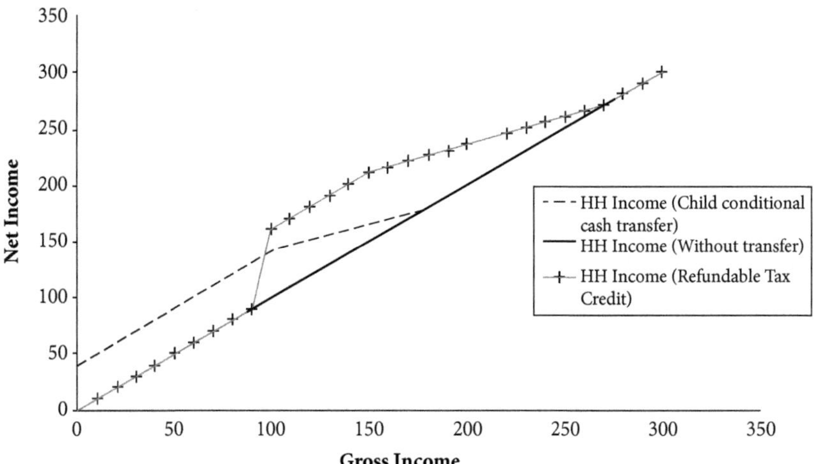

**Table 5.2** Choice Attributes for CCT

| Choice | Work | Work and School | School |
|---|---|---|---|
| Child Income | Full-time | Part-time | Zero |
| School Costs | No | Yes | Yes |
| Transfer | No | Yes | Yes |

choosing between $m$ alternatives, the probability individual $i$ chooses alternative $j$ is:

$$\Pr(i=j)=\frac{\exp(B_j X_i)}{\sum_{l=1}^{m}\exp(B_l X_j)}$$

where $X_i$ represents the observed characteristics of individual $i$. In the MNL approach, these characteristics are constant over the alternatives, with maximum likelihood estimates of $B$ providing the estimated effect of these characteristics on the probability that individual $i$ chooses alternative $j$.

Where the $X_i$ values vary by choice $m$, such as disposable income associated with hours choices, or work income and school costs associated with child labour-schooling decisions, a conditional logit (CL) model is used:

$$Y_j = B \quad X_j + e_j$$

In this case, the $X_i$ values vary by choice, but the estimates of $B$ are constant for each choice, and are equivalent to a utility function, drawing upon McFadden (1973). In this case, the probability that individual $i$ chooses alternative $j$ is:

$$\Pr(i=j)=\frac{\exp(BX_i)}{\sum_{l=1}^{m}\exp(BX_j)}$$

The CL model has fixed estimates for $B$, akin to a constant utility function, albeit allowing for observable-preference heterogeneity using taste shifters. However, choice-modelling frameworks increasingly utilize models where $B_i$ can vary randomly:

$$B_i \sim B + u_i, u_i \sim N(0,\theta)$$

known as the random parameters logit (RPL).

Haan (2006) has found that using an RPL relative to a CL does not make much difference in labour-supply econometrics. However, Pacifico (2013) shows that labour-supply elasticities can change significantly with respect to a model without unobserved heterogeneity, when the joint distribution of the varying tastes is left completely unspecified. It is also possible to extend the CL model to a latent-class CL specification, where the coefficients are allowed to be different across the population. In this chapter, a CL model is used as a demonstration, as it is both easier to estimate and to understand.

A modeller faces a choice in relation to the utility function. A convenient method often used in the literature is a quadratic utility function, which is a function of:

- disposable income
- disposable income x 2
- husband's leisure
- wife's leisure
- husband's leisure x 2
- wife's leisure x 2
- husband's leisure x wife's leisure
- coefficient of leisure interacted with age, number of children, number of young children, etc.

In a CL model, individual-specific attributes, such as age or number of children, drop out of the probability of an individual selecting a specific choice, as they do not vary across choice attributes. However, it is likely that the presence of children may influence labour-supply choices. To incorporate them in a model as a taste shifter, they are interacted with an alternative specific variable. To do this, new choice-specific variables are created by multiplying a choice-invariant variable by a choice-varying variable, such as disposable income or hours, and also restructuring our existing dataset to reflect the alternative-based independent variables required for the CL model. The taste shifters are interpreted as indicators of how preferences for income or leisure vary with the number of children.

In order to capture the extra fixed costs of working and looking for work, dummies are added to represent:

- individuals not looking for work
- individuals looking for work
- working individuals (potentially extended to part-time and full-time to reflect quantity constraints or utility of full-time work)
- a reference category: both spouses are inactive and not looking for work

Combining income and labour-supply measures, Creedy et al. (2011) present a useful social-welfare-based method to assess the non-money-metric welfare impact of policy changes, utilizing microeconomic concepts of compensating and equivalent variations.

### 5.3.2 Long-Term Decisions

In an education-labour-choice model, the objective is to assess the impact of policy reform on a university-participation decision relative to working part-time or full-time (see Flannery and O'Donoghue 2013).

Again microsimulation models are used to simulate counterfactual attributes associated with higher education as part of the process used to estimate university participation and part-time work. The model can then be used to simulate the impact of changed-support policies on the participation decision.

The education/labour decision is also estimated with a CL[4] model. It is assumed that the error terms are random and independently distributed, and when choosing across $m$ alternatives the probability that individual $i$ chooses labour/schooling choice $j$ is:

$$\Pr(\text{i chooses j}) = \frac{\exp(BZ_{ij})}{\sum_{l=1}^{m}\exp(BZ_{jl})}$$

Where Z is a vector of the choice-specific characteristics of each alternative, the impact of a variable on the choice probabilities derives from the difference of its values across the alternatives. Again, it is maximum-likelihood techniques that are used to provide estimates of $B$ in the CL model.

Another long-term decision of interest to policy makers is the retirement decision, e.g., in relation to:

- the design of polices, such as pension-tax credits
- the extension of the retirement age
- the decline in the effective retirement age

In order to model the impact of financial incentives on the retirement decision, similar methods are used to those used in working labour-supply models.

[4] This is also known as McFadden's choice model (McFadden 1973).

It is necessary to understand how the budget constraints of alternative choices affect the decision to participate in the labour market.

Modelling the retirement decision faces added difficulty as the budget constraint depends not only upon current characteristics, but on historical information in relation to pension rights accrued both publicly and privately. Retirement is also seen as a long-term choice, as the period of analysis is not merely a possibly temporary choice, because for most it leads to a permanent exit from the labour force. As a result, the present value of an income stream can be used instead of current income. The option-value model to postpone retirement (Stock and Wise 1990) expresses for each retirement age the trade-off between retiring now (resulting in a stream of retirement benefits that depends on this retirement age) and keeping all options open for some later retirement date (with associated streams of first labour, then retirement incomes, for all possible later-retirement ages) (Boersch-Supan 2001).

Estimating a model of this kind poses particular difficulties, as it requires information about the following issues:

- historical private- and occupational-pension membership
- historical national-insurance pension contributions
- (potentially) family circumstances of an individual

## 5.4 Validation: Derivation of Unobserved Residuals for Simulation

In a microsimulation model with the objective of assessing the impact of a policy change on, say, labour supply, the model estimated in the previous section can be used to imitate the impact using a Monte Carlo simulation.

In other words, a random number $u_i$ will be sampled and if $p_{n-1} < u_i \leq p_n$ (where $p_i$ is the probability of choice *i*, then individual *i* is simulated to have choice*n*). However, in doing this, as random numbers are drawn, there is no guarantee that in the baseline simulation the actual choices of individuals observed in the data will be replicated. Given the non-linear nature of the tax-benefit system, the result may show different aggregate values of cost, distribution, poverty, etc., than those that are actually observed.

Also, an issue is faced by individuals with low probabilities, such as lone parents, who have a low probability of working, even if some do actually work. In running a simulation with a CL model, it is necessary to produce residuals to avoid those with the highest probabilities always being chosen to be in a particular state, or vice versa. For example, lone parents would typically not be predicted to work without a residual. The residual thus allows for the model simulations to be 'shaken up', so that although people with higher risks will in general get the appropriate choice, it is not always the case.

In a CL model, there are $n$ choices $i$ per person, each with choice-specific variables that are a function of the disposable income for the choice and the hours for the husband and wife associated with the choice.

Chapter 9 describes a calibration method, known as alignment, where a binary-variable regression is calibrated to external exogenous totals. However, it is not possible to use the same method directly for categorical variables used in a CL model. This section introduces a different method of data alignment, which is primarily designed for CL analysis. It requires us to draw residuals such that the original choices are preserved in the baseline.

This alignment method utilizes the assumed distribution to derive the residuals of the observation while maintaining a consistent choice with the observations. The estimation of CL assumes that the error terms follow standard Gumbel (type 1, extreme value) distribution with a density function of:

$$f(\varepsilon) = \exp\left(-\varepsilon - \exp\left(-\varepsilon\right)\right)$$

To ensure the consistency between estimation and simulation, it is necessary to ensure the actual choices can be replicated based on the residuals drawn from the assumed distribution, while also following the theoretical framework developed.

According to our model, utility $U$ is maximized for the actual choice $i^*$ such that:

$$U_{i*} > U_i \forall i$$

which means that in the estimation of a residual, the following relationship should hold:

$$BZ_{i*} + \varepsilon_{i*} > BZ_i + \varepsilon_i \forall i$$

One method of generating the $\varepsilon_i$ s is to first sample $\varepsilon_i$ s for the counterfactual choices. $\varepsilon_i$ follows a truncated Gumbel distribution, with the minimum of $\max(\beta Z_{ij} + \varepsilon\_ij) - \beta Z_{ij}*$. In practice, the truncated distribution can be generated through the control of random number ranges. Both methods yield the same result, imposing extra distributional constraints on the random number. The second method is computationally faster, as it can guarantee the obtaining of the residuals in one iteration.

All $j \neq i$, where $j$ is the original choice, takes the extreme value distribution of the following shape:

$$\varepsilon_i = -\ln\left(-\ln\left(u_i\right)\right)$$

where $u_i$ is a uniform random number. There are a number of ways of deriving this residual.

It is necessary that:

$$\varepsilon_{i^*} > max\left(BZ_i - BZ_{i^*} + \varepsilon_i\right)\forall i$$

$\varepsilon_i$ can be found by drawing randomly; and maximizing the expression

$$\left[max\left(BZ_i - BZ_{i^*} + \varepsilon_i\right), \infty\right]$$

Transforming from an extreme value distribution, this is equivalent to:

$$u_i = exp\left(-exp\left(-\varepsilon_i\right)\right)$$

being in the following range:

$$\left[exp\left(-exp\left(-\left(max\left(BZ_i - BZ_{i^*} + \varepsilon_i\right)\right)_i\right)\right), 1\right]$$

Drawing a uniform random number will produce a residual with these properties. Thus, only one random number needs to be derived per residual, rather than many, making a large computational saving.

## 5.5 Measurement Issues: Replacement Rates

In trying to understand the drivers of behaviour, it is possible to estimate statistics such as the marginal effective tax rate described above, or the replacement rate.[5] The replacement rate is the ratio of disposable income from being out of work to disposable income in-work, which is a measure of both the degree of insurance provided and of the unemployment trap.

[5] In this section, we draw extensively upon the work of Immervoll and O'Donoghue (2001).

Replacement rates are a measure of the degree to which individuals' (and their households') standards of living while in work are maintained during periods of unemployment, and can be defined as the ratio of disposable income out of work to the disposable income while in work. The higher a household's replacement rate, the more protected they are from the impact of losing work income. At the same time, however, high replacement rates may reduce individual efforts to secure employment.

While disposable income is a better measure of welfare, early studies analysed the level of (gross) unemployment benefits as a fraction of employment income in isolation from the rest of the tax-benefit system (OECD 1994). However, the omission of taxes and benefits other than unemployment benefit can produce over-simplified, misleading results. Progressive income taxes on earnings, combined with a favourable or tax-free status of benefit payments, mean that replacement rates before taxes are markedly lower than the so-called net replacement rates, which are measured net of tax and contribution payments (OECD 1997). Equally important is the fact that the more-extreme values of replacement rates found for some people are frequently caused by very complex (and sometimes unintended) interdependencies between parts of the tax-benefit system, which have been introduced at different times, with different objectives, or are administered by different authorities or agencies. Unless all relevant parts of the tax-benefit system are taken into account, these 'anomalies', which can have very serious implications for work incentives, will not show up in the resulting replacement-rate calculations.

There are three different ways of calculating replacement rates:

- replacement rates of stylized households
- data-driven replacement rates
- simulation based replacement rates

Tax-benefit calculations for stylized households have been widely used in international comparisons of many different aspects of tax-benefit systems. Comparing situations of similar household types, they provide information about differences in national systems, and illustrate some of the effects of actual or hypothetical policy changes. The most common type of calculations assume a set of average characteristics (e.g., in-work income of an average production worker), and apply the relevant tax and benefit rules to find net in-work and out-of-work income (OECD 1999; Seven Countries Group 1996; Central Planning Bureau 1995; OECD 1994).[6] There are, however, problems

[6] There is also an 'empirical' version of the stylized approach, whereby a replacement rate is calculated by dividing the average receipt of unemployment insurance or unemployment assistance by average

with this approach because it attempts to reduce complex tax-benefit systems to single (or a few) point estimates. By using 'average household' characteristics, the analysis is likely to miss many of the important features of the tax-benefit system, which, although not applicable to the average household, may affect a significant part of the population.

Studies based on representative household micro-data do not run into the kinds of problems stated above. The most straightforward approach is to look at time-series information on individuals (panel data) and record their incomes in different employment states. The European Commission used the first wave of the European Community Household Panel (ECHP) (Salomäki and Munzi 1999), where the authors matched characteristics of the unemployed with those of similar employed individuals assuming that the income situation of the latter group is a good approximation of the potential in-work income of the former. A critical assumption is that the taxes and benefits of one group are representative of those that would apply to the other. Yet, the large number of characteristics relevant for determining taxes and benefits mean that many different characteristics need to be distinguished for the matching process. As the authors note, the replacement rates thus measured are, therefore, often based on very small sub-samples. Moreover, by comparing observed in-work and out-of-work individuals, the approach measures a mix of short-term and longer-term effects, which may not be appropriate if the replacement rates are to be interpreted as a measure of work incentives.

Tax-benefit models are computer programs that represent the rules governing a country's tax-and-benefit system. By applying these rules to a set of households that is representative of the population, it is possible to evaluate the effects of existing tax-benefit systems as well as policy changes in terms of income distribution and government revenue. For computing replacement rates, however, one also has to change other relevant characteristics (such as working hours, employment status) in addition to income, as these may also be relevant for determining taxes and benefits. Using this approach, one can avoid the main problem of stylized calculations: like the data-based approach described in the previous section, this method takes into account the actual structure of the population.

In addition, the simulation method allows us to explore replacement rates of the entire (working-age) population, rather than being restricted to looking at those individuals whose change of employment status can be

earnings per employee. As an indicator of income maintenance or labour-market incentives, this approach is even less satisfactory, since it does not take into account different family situations and other household characteristics, which may be important determinants of individual replacement rates.

observed in the data. Most data-based studies adopting the simulation approach have focused on individual countries (Callan et al. 1996; Atkinson and Micklewright 1985; O'Donoghue 2011), with a number of European anslyses using EUROMOD (Immervoll and O'Donoghue 2001).

Despite the advantages of the simulation approach, there are many problems to be addressed. The nature of simulation implies that important aspects of the scenarios to be explored are not actually observed in reality. For example, in terms of computing replacement rates, it is not clear whether people becoming unemployed will actually take up all the benefits to which they are entitled. There are numerous other uncertainties, including, for instance, the level of income an unemployed person could earn if they took up employment, the duration of unemployment, the level of detail people take into account when evaluating their incomes in the relevant employment states, or the take-up of in-work benefits. All these dimensions have important implications for the 'correct' way to measure replacement rates.

### 5.5.1 Conceptual Issues

Notwithstanding the fact that the replacement rate is a relatively simple concept in theory, it will become apparent that the number of issues, and the number of alternative approaches of dealing with them, make actual measurement quite difficult.

Every individual of working age faces a set of feasible labour-market states. Each of them is characterized by, among other things, a certain level of income, either actual or perceived (see below), that plays a part in determining the relative attractiveness of this state. Many studies of replacement rates have focused exclusively on the unemployed, and have computed their current income as a fraction of the prospective income they would earn if entering employment (e.g., Salomäki and Munzi 1999; European Commission 1998; Central Planning Bureau 1995). The initial impression is that this approach of focusing on what is termed the 'out-of-work replacement rate' is justified, if one considers the evidence suggesting that (a) EU rates of outflow from unemployment are low and that (b) most of the changes in European unemployment are caused by fluctuations in the outflow from unemployment (Burda 1988; Pissarides 1986). Clearly, to comprehensively measure the financial incentives related to these different transitions, it would be necessary to compute a replacement rate for each of the cells in a matrix representing all sources and destinations of feasible labour-market transitions.

### 5.5.2 Unit of Analysis

Although the transition from one labour-market state to another is a process at the individual level, the subsequent change in income potentially affects the well-being of other household members as well. Both from an income-maintenance and a work-incentive point of view, it is, therefore, not appropriate to only evaluate the alternative income situations of the person whose labour market status changes.

The choice of the household as the unit of analysis is mainly a result of three considerations. First, as asserted above, the level of resources available in the household as a whole will affect each household member's standard of living. Second, the employment status and incomes of individual household members can have important consequences for the amounts of taxes paid or benefits received by other household members (e.g., because of a joint income-tax system or the assessment of total household income for computing means-tested benefits). While we would ideally want to take into account how such joint taxes and benefits are actually shared within the household, we do not have the required information to identify such sharing arrangements. An analysis at the household level avoids having to specify arbitrary sharing mechanisms.

### 5.5.3 Definitional Issues in Using Replacement Rates

There are two main reasons why replacement rates are interesting:

- First, to measure the performance of tax-benefit systems in providing substitute income for those out of work.
- Second, to examine possible disincentive effects of high replacement rates.

The choice of the appropriate concept of replacement rate depends on the question to be addressed. The dimensions that are relevant in this context are:

- the selection of the incomes to include in the numerator and denominator of the replacement rate
- the direction of labour-market transition for which to compute the replacement rate

Depending upon the purpose of using a replacement rate, as a focus on work incentives, or with a focus on income maintenance, there are different choices. In measuring the degree of income maintenance, there are two main alternatives. If out-of-work benefits are looked on as an insurance system, then it could be interesting to measure the extent to which in-work incomes are insured. In this case, the numerator would be (net) out-of-work benefit income and the denominator would be (net) income from work. Only incomes of the person whose labour-market status changes would be taken into account, while all other household members' incomes would be disregarded. Alternatively, if the area of interest was the out-of-work living standard, as opposed to the in-work living standard, then both numerator and denominator would include all other incomes, such as investment income, benefits that are independent of work status, and the incomes of all other members of the household.

In addressing questions of income maintenance, we are only interested in the transition from in work to unemployment ($RR_{ab}$). It would also be interesting to consider which individuals should be included in the computation of $RR_{ab}$. To give an accurate picture of the level of income maintenance across the entire population, it is necessary to compute $RR_{ab}$ for both those currently in work and those currently out of work who have previously had a job. Limiting the analysis to those in work may potentially introduce a sample-selection bias, since individuals who have actually experienced job loss (and the income and lifestyle associated therewith) are not taken into account.

Because incentive effects are relevant for all types of labour-market transitions, the replacement rates that need to be computed under this heading are more varied. If we are interested in all three directions of labour-market transitions discussed, $RR_{ab}$, $RR_{ba}$, and $RR_{ca}$ are computed, respectively representing the work-unemployment, unemployment-work, and inactive-work transitions:

$$RR_{ab} = \frac{\Sigma\left(B_{UE} + B_{oth} + Y_{oth} - T_{UE}\right)}{\Sigma\left(Y_{w} + B_{oth} + Y_{oth} - T_{w}\right)}$$

$$RR_{ba} = \frac{\Sigma\left(B_{UE} + B_{oth} + Y_{oth} - T_{UE}\right)}{\Sigma\left(E_{w} + B_{oth} + Y_{oth} - T_{w}\right)}$$

$$RR_{ca} = \frac{\Sigma\left(B_{oth} + Y_{oth} - T_{OW}\right)}{\Sigma\left(E_{w} + B_{oth} + Y_{oth} - T_{w}\right)}$$

where the following are defined as:

$B_{UE}$: unemployment benefits
$B_{oth}$: other benefits
$Y_{oth}$: other income
$T_{UE}$: taxation (if unemployed)
$Y_w$: work income (if observed in data)
$E_w$: work income (if simulated)
$T_{IW}$: taxation (if in work)
$T_{OW}$: taxation (if out of work)
The same formula as for the income-maintenance replacement rates should be used, i.e., with total household income in both numerator and denominator. However, since transitions from out of work into work ($RR_{ba}$, $RR_{ca}$) are computed only for those who are currently out of work, it is necessary to estimate income from work $E_w$.

In calculating $E_w$, there are three approaches to choose from:

- using an arbitrary earnings level (such as the minimum wage, if it exists in the country under consideration)
- using actual previous in-work income
- estimating an earnings equation

In using previous in-work income, it would only be possible to compute $RR_{ba}$ and $RR_{ca}$ for those who have previously been in work rather than for all people for whom the decision whether or not to enter work is relevant. There is also a theoretical argument for using a general earnings equation. In terms of economic models explaining job-search behaviour, it is the distribution of job offers (characterized by the associated wage level) that is crucial in determining the probability of someone accepting a job.[7] This distribution is better represented by a statistically estimated earnings equation than by an arbitrary earnings level, or by actual previous in-work income, which, in terms of the distribution of offers, may be an outlier.

For these reasons, Immervoll and O'Donoghue (2001) use a standard earnings equation to estimate in-work income for those currently out of work. $RR_{ab}$ does not face these problems, since in-work replacement rates are only computed for those currently in work. The counterfactual out-of-work income can simply be computed by setting the in-work incomes to zero, altering all work-related variables to indicate that this person is now

[7] See Atkinson and Micklewright (1991) for a summary and critique of these and other popular economic models underlying theories of labour-market transitions.

unemployed, and then computing all taxes and benefits of the entire household on this basis.[8]

## 5.6 Simulation: Modelling the Behavioural Impact of Increasing an In-Work Cash Transfer

This section demonstrates a simple model of couple labour supply, with the aim of simulating some policy changes on CCT. The model follows the same theoretical framework as discussed in earlier sections.

### 5.6.1 Evaluate Simulation

Assume a couple is composed of two individuals, and they make decisions on their labour supplies together, with the goal of maximizing their joint utility. Mathematically, the joint utility can be expressed as:

$$U_{joint} = U_m + U_f = U(C, L_m) + U(C, L_f)$$

where $U_{joint}$ is the joint utility and $U_m$ and $U_f$ represent utility of each individual in the couple, which is a function of the total consumption and leisure that one can enjoy. As it is necessary to work for the money to spend, the total consumption is subject to the following constraint:

$$C = h_m \cdot w_m + h_f \cdot w_f - T + B - S$$

where $h$ is the number of hours that the couple work, $w$ is the wage rate, $T$ is the tax, $T$ $B$ is the benefit that the couple receives, and $S$ is the total saving, which could be either positive or negative. In case of a negative saving, the couple borrows money from future or existing savings.

Since there are only twenty-four hours per day, each individual is also subject to the following leisure constraint:

$$H = h_m + L_m = h_f + L_f$$

This simple model assumes pooling of the consumption, and equal weight in male and female utilities, in forming the joint-utility equation. This type of

[8] This chapter draws upon work with Jinjing Li and Herwig Immervoll.

method in modelling joint decisions is often termed a unitary framework. To relax some of the assumptions imposed by a unitary framework, it is also possible to introduce a Pareto parameter, which allows different couples to have different weight in the total utility function (van Klaveren and van Praag 2008; Michaud and Vermeulen 2011). Alternatively, one can also consider a household bargaining model. For simplicity purposes, this example uses a unitary model and assumes no savings or borrowing. A log-linear form of the utility function is used, which means that:

$$U_m = \alpha_1 \ln C + \beta_1 \ln L_m$$
$$U_f = \alpha_2 \ln C + \beta_2 \ln L_f$$

And, as the observed choices that a couple makes have the highest joint utility among all possible alternatives, this means:

$$U_{i^*,j^*} = Max(U_{i,j}) \qquad \forall i, j \in [0, H]$$

In practice, the number of hours worked may be subject to the institutional constraints, and, therefore, can only be chosen from limited options. This allows us to fit a discrete-choice model, described in an earlier section.

## 5.6.2 Simulating the Alternative Choices

Here, the methodology that describes the budget sets used in the models estimated in this chapter is presented. A tax-benefit model for Ireland is described in Chapters 8–10 that is used to simulate taxes and benefits for alternative choices. The standard instruments simulated are income taxes, social-insurance contributions, child benefits and other family benefits, and income-tested benefits. For the present study, unemployment benefits are simulated assuming that past unemployment-insurance contributions of individuals currently in work are 'sufficient' to be eligible for the (maximum duration of the) benefit, and that all transitions into unemployment are involuntary.[9]

Using data from the 2007 European Union Statistics on Income and Living Conditions (EU–SILC) for this chapter, and our tax-benefit microsimulation model, budget sets for couples are simulated. The sample that is simulated

[9] O'Donoghue (2011) describe in more detail the assumptions underlying the simulation of unemployment benefits.

includes all couples, except where a spouse is aged outside of the range [18,64], or where a spouse is in education, a civil servant, disabled, or primarily self-employed. For each couple, twelve times twelve choices are then simulated, comprising the following states:

- inactive—out of work and seeking work
- unemployed—out of work and seeking work
- in-work with hours groups

Table 5.3 describes the summary statistics of the labour-supply selection decision. Individuals in two adult households (the focus of this study) account for 47 per cent of the population. Given the tight eligibility conditions, only 25 per cent of this group were selected, while 58 per cent of those with self-employment income and 60 per cent of inactive individuals in two-person households were also chosen.

Figure 5.3 describes the distribution of hours for males and females in our selected sample. Notice modes of 0 and 40 for men, and modes of 0, 20, and 40 for women. The male distribution is slightly to the right of the female distribution. In order to capture these modes, and other hours groups of relevance to policy in this case, each individual can choose from seven different options (0—inactive; 1—unemployed; 2—one-to-fifteen hours; 3—sixteen-to-twenty-five hours; 4—twenty-six-to-thirty-five hours; 5—thirty-six-to-forty-five hours; 6—forty-six-and-more hours), resulting in forty-nine potential options for a couple.

For each couple, observe the actual hours worked. In order to estimate a labour-supply model, information is required in relation to the counterfactual choices. As the model is trying to maximize the utility within all possible alternatives, it is also necessary to generate all the counterfactuals. Essentially, an entry is created for each possible choice set in the data, and the potential total consumption is calculated using the estimated wage rate and tax-benefit rule.

For each hours choice, the simulated hours chosen is based on a uniform random number within the group. The actual choice is always simulated.

**Table 5.3** Data Selection for Labour Supply

| | |
|---|---|
| Individuals in two-adult household as share of total | 0.47 |
| Share of two-adult households selected | 0.25 |
| Share of self-employed selected | 0.58 |
| Share of inactive selected | 0.60 |

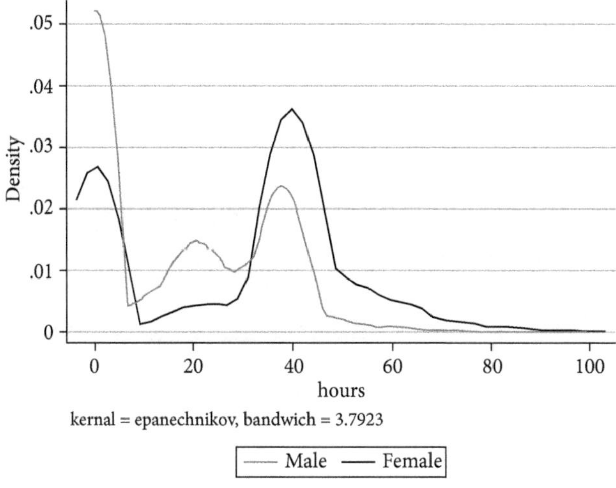


**Figure 5.3** Hours Distribution

Two out-of-work choices are made because the disposable income is different, depending upon the two choices. It may be argued that the unemployed state is an involuntary choice, and as such should not be included.

While most of the instruments simulated depend upon current income and characteristics, the income of an individual in the unemployed state depends upon unemployment benefit, which in turn depends upon contributions and the duration out of work.

Figure 5.4 describes the budget constraint for the baseline tax-benefit system for a single-earner couple with two children, varying their work from zero to eighty hours. As hours of work increase, earnings increase. Initially, the working-age jobseekers allowance is reduced as income increases. At twenty hours, the couple are eligibile for the in-work transfer, FIS. As income increases, so too do income taxation, income levies, and social insurance. Universal child benefit varies depending upon the number of children, but does not depend upon income.

Part (b) describes the impact of increasing FIS by 50 per cent. The initial payment increases, and, as the instrument is a means-tested income, it is tapered away.

Once this tax-benefit system is applied to the population under consideration, as described above, the distribution of marginal effective tax rates is described, with modes around 50 per cent and 25 per cent, reflecting the tax code, and a minor mode at 60 per cent, reflecting the share of population in receipt of means-tested benefits (Figure 5.5).

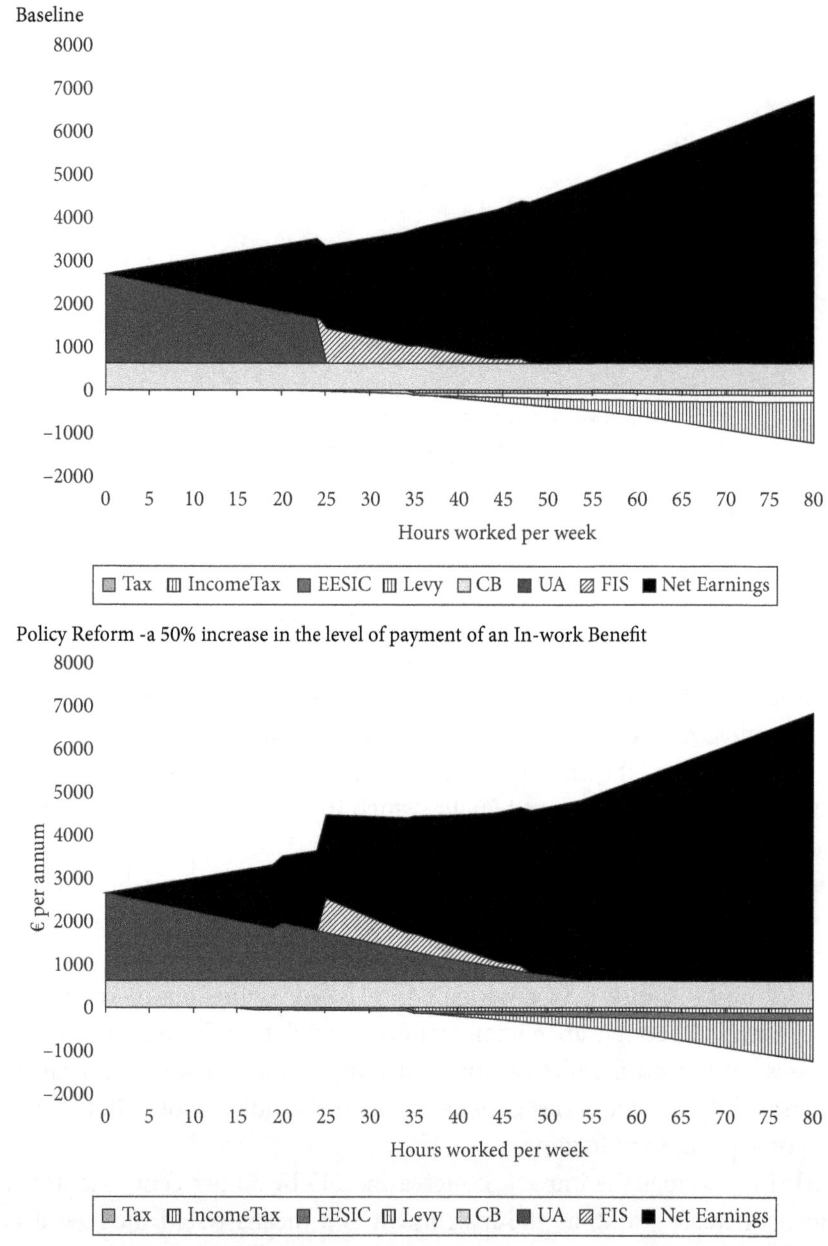


**Figure 5.4** Budget Constraint for Couple with Children

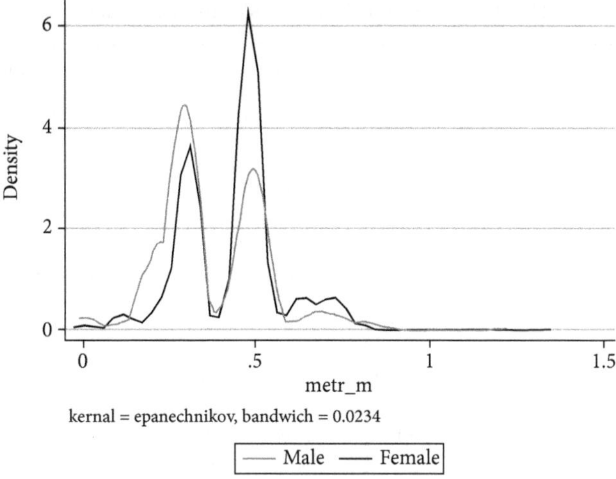


**Figure 5.5** Distribution of Marginal Effective Tax Rates

## 5.6.3 Estimating the Choice Model

In understanding the drivers of labour supply and participation, two models are estimated: a multinomial logit model in Table 5.4 and a CL in Table 5.5. The former is a reduced-form model, where the explanatory variables depend upon the characteristics of the couple, while the latter is a structural model, where the explanatory variables are a function of choice-specific variables.

The multinomial logit model in Table 5.4 is used to help us to decide on the set of taste shifters, which may reflect heterogeneous preferences. This model has three choices: out of work, part-time work, and full-time work of more than thirty hours per week. For males, the base state is full-time work, and for females it is not working. Each of the coefficients in the model are expressed relative to the base state.

In the case of the male model, age is not significant. The only characteristics of part-time work that are significantly different from full-time work are the presence of chronic illness and higher capital income, where otherwise full-time and part-time work have similar drivers. For the out-of-work state, married men and those with a mortgage are less likely to be out of work, and those with young children, who are renting social housing or have a chronic illness, are more likely to be out of work.

For women, the part-time model has more significant variables. Those with higher education are more likely to be working part-time, relative to not working. This rises at a declining rate with age. This is particularly true in urban areas, or for those with a mortgage. As in the case of men, those with young children, a mortgage, or chronic illness are less likely to be working

**Table 5.4** Multinomial Logit for Labour-Participation Supply Model

| | Male | | | Female | | |
|---|---|---|---|---|---|---|
| | Not Working | | | Part-Time | | |
| | Beta | SE | *p*-value | Beta | SE | *p*-value |
| Years of Education | - 0.039 | 0.028 | 0.166 | 0.093 | 0.026 | 0.000 |
| Age | 0.012 | 0.099 | 0.908 | 0.187 | 0.091 | 0.041 |
| Age$^2$ | 0.000 | 0.001 | 0.739 | - 0.003 | 0.001 | 0.013 |
| Married | - 0.919 | 0.404 | 0.023 | 0.340 | 0.420 | 0.418 |
| Town | - 0.174 | 0.245 | 0.478 | 0.503 | 0.208 | 0.016 |
| Peri-Urban | - 0.263 | 0.256 | 0.304 | 0.372 | 0.215 | 0.083 |
| Number of Children Aged 0–4 | 0.360 | 0.175 | 0.040 | - 0.654 | 0.172 | 0.000 |
| Number of Children Aged 5–11 | 0.326 | 0.127 | 0.010 | - 0.301 | 0.109 | 0.006 |
| Number of Children Aged 12–15 | - 0.326 | 0.216 | 0.130 | - 0.229 | 0.166 | 0.169 |
| Has a Mortgage | - 0.717 | 0.259 | 0.006 | 0.364 | 0.195 | 0.061 |
| Rents (Public Sector) | 1.304 | 0.319 | 0.000 | - 0.400 | 0.390 | 0.306 |
| Chronic Illness | 0.747 | 0.238 | 0.002 | −1.044 | 0.262 | 0.000 |
| Level of Capital Income | 0.000 | 0.000 | 0.573 | 0.000 | 0.000 | 0.915 |
| Constant | - 2.132 | 2.211 | 0.335 | - 5.033 | 1.975 | 0.011 |
| | Part-Time | | | Full-Time | | |
| | Beta | SE | *p*-value | Beta | SE | *p*-value |
| Years of Education | - 0.094 | 0.045 | 0.037 | 0.186 | 0.029 | 0.000 |
| Age | 0.131 | 0.197 | 0.505 | 0.017 | 0.085 | 0.843 |
| Age$^2$ | - 0.001 | 0.002 | 0.669 | - 0.001 | 0.001 | 0.228 |
| Married | - 0.139 | 0.782 | 0.858 | - 0.231 | 0.350 | 0.509 |
| Town | 0.058 | 0.374 | 0.877 | - 0.309 | 0.226 | 0.172 |
| Peri-Urban | - 0.108 | 0.403 | 0.789 | - 0.055 | 0.218 | 0.802 |
| Number of Children Aged 0–4 | - 0.260 | 0.387 | 0.502 | - 0.953 | 0.171 | 0.000 |
| Number of Children Aged 5–11 | 0.092 | 0.211 | 0.664 | - 0.865 | 0.127 | 0.000 |
| Number of Children Aged 12–15 | 0.102 | 0.299 | 0.733 | - 0.314 | 0.192 | 0.102 |
| Has a Mortgage | 0.366 | 0.370 | 0.323 | 0.623 | 0.205 | 0.002 |
| Rents (Public Sector) | 0.355 | 0.667 | 0.594 | - 0.513 | 0.456 | 0.260 |
| Chronic Illness | 0.741 | 0.348 | 0.033 | - 1.079 | 0.285 | 0.000 |
| Level of Capital Income | 0.000 | 0.000 | 0.059 | 0.000 | 0.000 | 0.423 |
| Constant | - 6.395 | 4.613 | 0.166 | - 0.097 | 1.760 | 0.956 |
| Pseudo $R^2$ | 0.093 | | | 0.140 | | |
| N | 981 | | | 981 | | |

part-time. The coefficients of full-time work for women take similar signs and significance as the part-time-work variable.

With the data generated from the above steps, it is possible to utilize a CL model to estimate the parameters specified in the early section. Since the couple pools their consumption, it is not possible to identify the consumption parameters separately. Instead, only the joint effect is estimated, which is $\alpha_1 + \alpha_2$. In this simple model, only three key variables are included in our estimation model, namely income, leisure for husband, and leisure for female, plus square terms and interaction effects. In addition, the model is

**Table 5.5** Conditional Logit for Labour-Supply Model

| | Model 1 | | | Model 2 | | |
|---|---|---|---|---|---|---|
| | Beta | SE | p-value | Beta | SE | p-value |
| Male Hours | - 0.028 | 0.031 | 0.373 | - 0.0663 | 0.0351 | 0.0590 |
| Female Hours | 0.042 | 0.033 | 0.204 | 0.1693 | 0.0428 | 0.0000 |
| Male In-Work Fixed Effect | | | | 0.9659 | 1.2488 | 0.4390 |
| Female In-Work Fixed Effect | | | | - 2.6881 | 1.2900 | 0.0370 |
| Disposable Income | 0.00001 | 0.000 | 0.000 | 0.0000052 | 0.0000 | 0.0240 |
| Disposable Income$^2$ | - 0.000 | 0.000 | 0.002 | | | |
| Male Hours$^2$ | 0.0008 | 0.000 | 0.003 | 0.0008 | 0.0003 | 0.0030 |
| Female Hours$^2$ | - 0.0004 | 0.001 | 0.476 | - 0.0008 | 0.0006 | 0.2150 |
| Male Hours x Female Hours | - 0.0000 | 0.000 | 0.949 | 0.0002 | 0.0004 | 0.5290 |
| Disposable Income x Male Hours | - 0.0000 | 0.000 | 0.745 | -0.0000001 | 0.0000 | 0.1670 |
| Disposable Income x Female Hours | 0.00000 | 0.000 | 0.174 | 0.0000001 | 0.0000 | 0.0470 |
| Male Hours x Number of Children Aged 0–4 | | | | 0.0049 | 0.0021 | 0.0200 |
| Male Hours x Number of Children Aged 5–13 | | | | 0.0043 | 0.0013 | 0.0010 |
| Male Hours x Has a Mortgage | | | | - 0.0014 | 0.0027 | 0.6120 |
| Male Hours x Rents (Public Sector) | | | | - 0.0069 | 0.0053 | 0.1920 |
| Male Hours x Chronic Illness | | | | 0.0012 | 0.0035 | 0.7410 |
| Male Hours x Town | | | | 0.0026 | 0.0029 | 0.3700 |
| Male Hours x Peri-Urban | | | | 0.0026 | 0.0030 | 0.3900 |
| Male Hours x Age | | | | - 0.0005 | 0.0003 | 0.1350 |
| Male Hours x Age$^2$ | | | | 0.0011 | 0.0003 | 0.0010 |
| Female Hours x Number of Children Aged 0–4 | | | | - 0.0178 | 0.0039 | 0.0000 |
| Female Hours x Number of Children Aged 5–13 | | | | - 0.0169 | 0.0027 | 0.0000 |
| Female Hours x Has a Mortgage | | | | 0.0110 | 0.0048 | 0.0230 |
| Female Hours x Rents (Public Sector) | | | | - 0.0083 | 0.0114 | 0.4640 |
| Female Hours x Chronic Illness | | | | - 0.0092 | 0.0070 | 0.1890 |
| Female Hours x Town | | | | - 0.0027 | 0.0053 | 0.6070 |
| Female Hours x Peri-Urban | | | | - 0.0025 | 0.0054 | 0.6490 |
| Female Hours x Age | | | | 0.0007 | 0.0006 | 0.2180 |
| Female Hours x Age$^2$ | | | | - 0.0028 | 0.0006 | 0.0000 |
| Pseudo $R^2$ | 0.0178 | | | 0.0386 | | |

extended using taste shifters, by interacting individual characteristics with male and female hours separately.

Table 5.6 provides an example of the estimation of a CL model using the EU–SILC dataset for 2007. It is difficult to interpret the model by directly reading the table, given the square and interaction terms. Figure 5.6 describes the marginal effects for income and labour at the values for the actual choice in the data. For the vast majority of cases, the marginal effect of income in

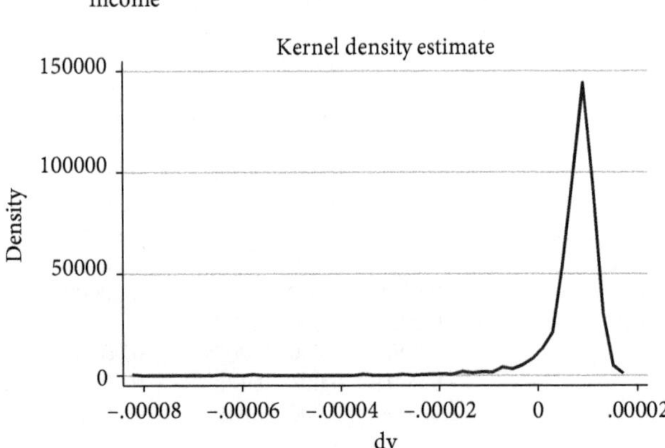


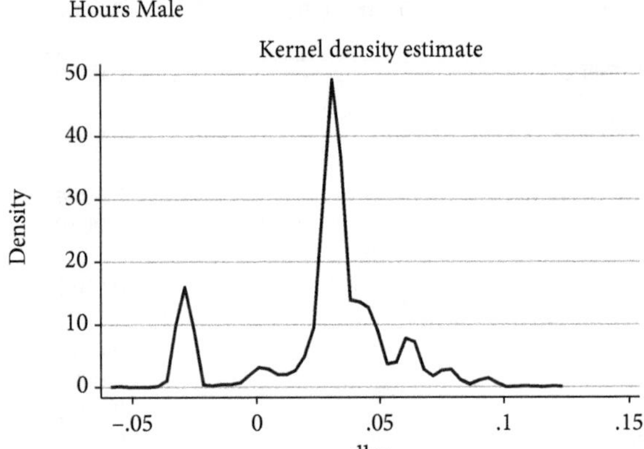


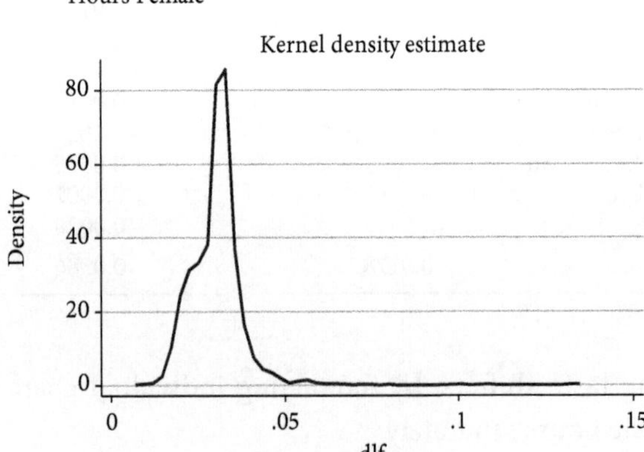


**Figure 5.6** Marginal Effects for Income and Hours for Model 1

**Table 5.6** Simulation of a 50-Per-Cent Increase in the Level of Payment of an In-Work Benefit

| | Baseline | Reform |
|---|---|---|
| Population of Those Affected | | |
| Percentage of Recipients who Change | 2.3 per cent | |
| Change in Utility | 0.032 | |
| Population of Movers | | |
| Average Hours Worked | 33.4 | 51.4 |

the utility function is positive. For male hours worked, it is mainly positive. For female hours, the marginal effect is negative.

Similar to the binary-model estimation and simulation, it is sometimes necessary to impose an external distributional constraint on the simulation output. This is useful for constructing a base scenario that matches with external benchmarks. To align the output of the labour-supply model with observed values, the method described earlier can be used, by drawing the residuals from a constrained Gumbel distribution. This method ensures consistency between the base scenarios with observed values.

Extending the model to incorporate preference heterogeneity, taste shifters for age, the presence of children, housing, location, etc., are added. These are interacted with both male and female hours. The presence of young children reduces the utility of female hours, while it increases that of male hours. Housing and location do not influence utility, as the coefficients are not statistically significant. The presence of a mortgage is the exception, increasing the utility of female hours. For both male and female hours, the square is significant and positive, increasing utility of work with age.

It is relatively straightforward to simulate a policy change using this model as long as the counterfactuals can be generated. For example, increasing FIS by 50 per cent ties the benefit to the income level of the household. If there is a reform that increases the amount of benefit, the new consumption level can be calculated for each potential labour-supply choice. With the estimated model parameters and the residuals from earlier steps, it is possible to calculate the new utility level for each potential choice, as well as the 'best' choice, given the new policy scenario. Table 5.6 compares the labour-supply patterns before and after the hypothetical reform. Only part of the population is affected by the reform, which increases utility, resulting in 2.3 per cent of the population changing their hours worked. For those who change their behaviour, a relatively large increase in hours worked is simulated. This analysis was relatively straightforward, utilizing a small sample. However, greater power can be incorporated in the model, utilizing more policy variation over time in the dataset.

# 6
# Indirect Taxation and Consumption Behaviour

## 6.1 Introduction

Indirect taxation refers to taxation that is levied on expenditure rather than on income and is one of the most important sources of revenue for governments, particularly in middle- and low-income countries.[1] As a result, indirect taxation is frequently included in microsimulation models. These models differ from those described thus far in that they involve the use of data that contains expenditures in addition to incomes.

Indirect taxation changes generate revenue and have consequential distributional implications, but also, like other sources of price change, such as inflation, change the price of goods consumed. Income can be spent on consumption or saved:

$$Y = C + S \tag{1}$$

Ignoring own-produced consumption, total consumption is valued as the price $p$ by the volume of $q$ consumed for the set of goods $i$:

$$C = \sum_i p_i q_i = QP = Y - S \tag{2}$$

Thus, volume of consumption can be related to income, savings, and price. An increase in price due to inflation or indirect tax will either reduce the volume of goods consumed or will require a change in the savings rate to maintain the level of consumption:

$$Q = \frac{(Y - S)}{P} \tag{3}$$

[1] This chapter draws upon work with Jason Loughrey.

*Practical Microsimulation Modelling.* Cathal O'Donoghue. Oxford University Press. © Cathal O'Donoghue 2021.
DOI: 10.1093/oso/9780198852872.003.0006

There is a relatively substantial literature using microsimulation models for indirect-taxation analysis in OECD countries, including in Australia (Creedy 2001), Belgium (Decoster and Van Camp 2001), Italy (Liberati 2001; Brunetti and Calza 2015; Gastaldi et al. 2017), Ireland (Leahy et al. 2011; Loughrey and O'Donoghue 2012), Greece (Tsakloglou and Mitrakos 1998; Kaplanoglou and Newbery 2003), the US (Toder et al. 2013), and Germany (Kaiser and Spahn 1989).

Indirect taxation, because it is easier to collect than income taxes, often forms a higher share of taxation in developing countries. Atkinson and Bourguignon (1991) found that much of the redistribution in the existing Brazilian system in the 1980s relied on instruments that were less important in OECD countries, where such indirect taxes, subsidies, and the provision of targeted non-cash benefits (such as public education and subsidized school meals) were found to be more important. Given the important share of total tax revenue provided by indirect taxes, and the availability of household-budget survey (HBS) data, the microsimulation modelling of indirect taxation is, and for a long time has been, a focus of developing and transition countries (Harris et al. 2018; Phillips et al. 2018), such as Pakistan (Ahmad and Stern 1991), Hungary (Newbery 1995), Romania (Cuceu 2016), Serbia (Arsić and Altiparmakov 2013), Uruguay (Amarante et al. 2011), Guatemala, (Castañón-Herrera and Romero 2012), Chile (Larrañaga et al. 2012), and China (Wei 2012).

While most papers have focused on single-country analyses, there is an increasing literature looking at indirect taxes in a comparative context (O'Donoghue et al. 2004; Decoster et al. 2009, 2010, 2011). Many of the papers in the literature focus on indirect taxes only, given the fact that income data in a HBS is not always of sufficient quality to model direct taxes. In some cases, as in the UK, it is possible to simulate both direct and indirect taxation (Redmond et al. 1998), but more often than not, as described below, there is a need to statistically match data from a budget survey into an income survey in order to model both direct and indirect taxes (Maitino et al. 2017). Picos-Sánchez and Thomas (2015) undertook comparative research looking at joint-direct and indirect-tax reform in a comparative context.

Indirect taxation is regarded as typically regressive, due primarily to the fact that lower-income households save less and thus spend a higher proportion of their income. They therefore face a higher rate of indirect taxation as a share of their income. The literature consequently focuses on measuring the redistributive nature of indirect taxation, using incidence methods described in Chapter 4.

There are a number of different types of indirect taxation. In Section 6.2, the structure of these instruments will be described briefly. A challenge to the simulation of indirect taxation arises in that the base datasets of microsimulation models typically do not include expenditure data. In Section 6.3, a relatively simple method for combining income and expenditure data is described.

As changes in indirect taxation affect the relative prices of goods, there will either be a change in consumption patterns or a change in savings. As a result, one needs to try to model behavioural response when modelling indirect taxation. Section 6.4 describes a number of methods for doing this. These methods are utilized to describe some descriptive measures for the distributional attributes of consumption and some directions for policy reform. In Section 6.5, the framework developed in this chapter will be used to model the welfare impact of changes to indirect taxation in an example simulation.

## 6.2 Policy Context: Indirect Taxation

Indirect taxes are levied on expenditure, and can take a number of forms, including:

- valued-added tax (VAT) ($t_i$)
- excise duty (ED) ($a_i$)
- *ad valorem* tax (AVT), applied on the consumer price ($v_i$)

These taxes principally differ in the way they are calculated. $p_{c,i}$ denotes the consumer or retail price for commodity $i$, and $p_{p,i}$ the producer price.

VAT is levied on pre-tax expenditure ($r_i$):

$$\text{Vat} = r_i * t_i s \tag{4}$$

ED, meanwhile, is levied on quantity of consumption $q_i$.

$$\text{ED} = q_i * a_i \tag{5}$$

AVT is an indirect tax on the consumer price of the good:

$$\text{AVT} = p_{c,i} * v_i \tag{6}$$

Redmond et al. (1998) describe a method for simulating indirect taxation. Using this notation, the linkage between the producer price and the consumer price for commodity $i$ can be written as follows:

$$p_{c,i} = (1+t_i)(p_{p,i} + a_i + v_i.p_{c,i}) \tag{7}$$

VAT is levied on pre-tax prices. However, the data on which our expenditure models are estimated are typically post-tax prices ($p_{c,i}$). Hence, the simulated expenditures are based on post-tax prices. To calculate VAT, we therefore need to first calculate the pre-tax expenditure $\frac{E_{retail,i}}{(1+t_i)}$ (where $E_{retail,i} = q_i \cdot p_{c,i}$), before applying the tax rate $vat$:

$$vat_i = t_i.\frac{p_{c,i}}{(1+t_i)} \tag{8}$$

ED is levied on the quantity of consumption. However, only the expenditures are known, not the quantities. To produce quantities, divide the price by the unit prices $p_{c,i}/q_i$ :

$$excise = q_i.a_i = p_{c,i}.\frac{q_i}{p_{c,i}}.a_i \tag{9}$$

The calculation of AVT is relatively straightforward as it is levied on the post-tax price:

$$advalorem = p_{c,i}.v_i \tag{10}$$

## 6.3 Data Issues: Linking Income and Expenditure Surveys

While some microsimulation models are built using an HBS, such as the POLIMOD model in the UK (Redmond et al. 1998), in most cases the quality of the income variables is not sufficient for modelling direct taxation or social transfers. As a result, income surveys, such as the European Union Statistics on Income and Living Conditions (EU–SILC), serve as the basis of these models. In order to model indirect taxation, a way of linking expenditure and income datasets has to be found.

To do this, statistical matching (D'Orazio et al. 2006) is used. Decoster et al. (2010) describe four different matching techniques that can be used for linking income and expenditure surveys. These can be divided into two categories.

- The first category contains the so-called explicit methods that use estimations of Engel curves to impute expenditure information into the income data set. Two techniques can be labelled as parametric regression (O'Donoghue et al. 2004) and non-parametric regression.
- The second category consists of implicit methods which match to each record in the income survey, a record with expenditure information coming from the budget survey. Two examples are the distance-function and grade-correspondence methods. For both techniques, there are many variations possible in their practical application (*Decoster and Van Camp 2001*; Sutherland et al. 2002).

In this section, the 'easiest' method, parametric-regression-based matching, will be described. Regardless of the method, the creation of a 'new' dataset, merging information from an income survey and a budget survey, requires the use of overlapping variables—variables that have common meaning in both datasets. The merging method designates this income dataset as the target dataset, in which expenditure data are to be imputed.

All matching techniques rely on the conditional-independence assumption. To understand this, let us label the variables in the income survey as (X, Y) and those ones in the budget survey as (X, Z). The overlapping variables are X, and the non-overlapping variables are Y and Z. The conditional-independence assumption then states that given X, Y, and Z should be independent, or equivalently, that all the correlation between Y and Z has to be explained by X. Note that this can be a heavy assumption in the case of budget and income data. Consider, for instance, two people with the same disposable income and the same socio-demographic profile (and so with the same values of X). Suppose they both have a car, but one of them has bought an energy-efficient car in order to avail of a tax reduction. In this case, there can be a positive correlation between the tax, which belongs to Y, and the private transportation costs, which belong to Z.

To make imputations from one dataset into another, it is important that both datasets cover the same population, and that the common characteristics are defined in the same way. The matching processes are based on the 'closeness' of the overlapping variables, which require that the variables used measure the same characteristics.

The resemblance of the two datasets can be tested using synthetic tests of distributional equality, such as the Kolmogorov–Smirnov and the

Kruskal–Wallis tests for quantitative variables, and the chi-square test for qualitative variables. However, these tests are often too strict, and may easily reject the null hypothesis of equality or independence. Moreover, they do not tell how strong a possible dependence on the sample is, and where (in which intervals or categories) the problem is situated. Therefore, another analysis of equalities and differences can be performed by looking at QQ-plots.[2]

As standard parametric-regression-based methods use Engel curves to impute for every household in the income survey, expenditure information, the presence of similar variables in both datasets, is required. Theoretically, this could reflect the disaggregation of expenditures from the budget survey, but in practice this is not possible, as it would result in very imprecise estimations of the Engel curves, whose quality is determined by the quality of their estimation. It is assumed that based on the explanatory variables (including disposable income, and some demographic characteristics such as household size and age of the household head), the behaviour of the dependent variable can be fully captured, and, moreover, that (standard) regression issues such as heteroscedasticity and multicollinearity can be dealt with adequately. For instance, a functional specification has to be determined a priori in the parametric case, and the explanatory variables are restricted to the appropriate set of overlapping variables.[3]

Another issue to consider in Engel-curve estimations is the issue of zero expenditures (e.g., Pudney 1989), which can be due to infrequent purchases, as well as abstention from consumption. This issue highlights that the reliability of the imputations relies upon a statistical model which may be (slightly) mis-specified in the presence of zero expenditures. The greater the level of disaggregation used, the greater the significance of zero expenditures. Besides these issues, which decrease the quality of the estimates, different definitions of the overlapping variables may also influence the quality of the imputation.

## 6.3.1 Total Expenditure

In practical terms, a model of total expenditure is first estimated utilizing for each country the corresponding national HBS $(B)$.[4] The functional form of the model to be estimated is:

[2] This draws upon the work Decoster et al. (2007).

[3] See Blundell (1988), Banks et al. (1997), and Blundell et al. (1998) for a description of the econometric issues.

[4] This section draws extensively upon O'Donoghue et al. (2004).

$$lnC_B = \alpha + \beta lnY_B + \gamma X_B + u \qquad (11)$$

where $C$ is consumption, $Y$ is income, and $X$ is the vector of socio-demographic characteristics, detailed below. The natural logarithm of consumption and income are used because both, typically, follow approximately a log-normal distribution. The estimated coefficients (indicated with a hat) are then applied to the model dataset ($Y$) so as to obtain an imputation of total consumption:

$$lnC_Y = \hat{\alpha} + \hat{\beta} lnY_Y + \hat{\gamma} X_Y + u^* \qquad (12)$$

In order to reproduce the same variance of consumption in the HBS, an error term ($u^*$) is generated that is normally distributed, with zero mean and a variance equal to the variance of the residual of the HBS regression. It is quite likely that the results are affected by heteroscedasticity; however, this problem only affects the standard errors of the coefficients, not their estimated value.

## 6.3.2 Imputation of Engel Functions

In order to introduce individual categories of expenditure, this expenditure needs to be simulated for disaggregated sub-groups, subject to the zero-expenditure biases highlighted above. Consumption on particular goods is estimated as budget shares of total consumption, utilizing Engel functions:

$$w_i = \alpha + \beta lnC_B + \gamma\left(lnC_B\right) + \delta X_B \qquad (13)$$

where $w_i$ is the $i^{th}$ budget share, $C$ is consumption as defined above, and $X$ is the same set of demographic characteristics used above.

In modelling aggregated-expenditure groups, certain categories of goods and services are grouped together, typically based upon standard COICOP[5] groupings, or for different indirect-tax rates to minimize the challenges associated with significant disaggregation. Grouping expenditures has the following advantages:

[5] The classification of individual consumption by purpose.

- It reduces the impact of the zero-expenditures problem, which could substantially undermine the results of ordinary least-squares (OLS) regressions.
- The estimates for smaller groups of goods could be unstable.

From these regressions carried out on the HBS, only the coefficients, not the residuals, are used. In order to take into account the problem of zero expenditures due to infrequent purchases, the simple use of estimated coefficients without residuals attributes to nearly all households a positive share for each good.

Using the OLS method guarantees that the sum of the imputed shares is one, but some of them may be negative (the sum in absolute value is greater than one), which is not acceptable. This problem can be solved by setting negative shares to zero, and correcting the other shares proportionally, so that the sum is still one for each household.

## 6.4 Measurement Issues: Modelling a Behavioural Response

In order to model behaviour, a demand system is required that relates the consumption of a particular good to the price of the good, the prices of other goods, the income of the household, and the characteristics of the household. See Deaton and Muellbauer (1980b) for an introduction to this field.

The objective of a demand system is to model households' expenditure patterns on a group of related items, in order to obtain estimates of price-and-income elasticities and to estimate consumer welfare. This has been popular since Stone's (1954) linear-expenditure system (LES). The dependent variable is typically the expenditure share. Two of the most popular methods are the trans-log system of Christensen et al. (1975) and the Deaton and Muellbauer (1980a) almost-ideal demand system (AIDS), with the latter extended by Banks et al. (1997) to include a quadratic-expenditure term (QUAIDS):

$$w_j = \frac{p_j c_j}{C} \text{ is defined as the budget share for good } j^6.$$

where $p_i$ is the price paid for good $i$, $c$ is the quantity of good $i$ consumed, and $m$ is the total expenditure on all goods in the demand system. The sum of the budget shares is constrained to be zero:

[6] See Creedy (1998) for more details.

$$\Sigma_i w_i = 1 \tag{14}$$

In the QUAIDS model, expenditure share equations have the form:

$$w_i = \Sigma_j \gamma_{ij} ln(p_j) + \beta_i ln\left(\frac{m}{P(p)}\right) + \frac{\lambda_i}{b(p)}\left[ln\left(\frac{m}{P(p)}\right)\right]^2 \tag{15}$$

where $p$ is the vector of all prices, and $b(p)$ is defined as:

$$b(p) = \prod_i p_i^{\beta_i} \tag{16}$$

and ln$P(p)$ is a price index defined as:

$$\ln P(p) = \alpha_0 + \sum_i \alpha_i \ln p_i + \frac{1}{2}\sum_i \sum_j \gamma_{ij} \ln p_i \ln p_j \tag{17}$$

However, there are a number of constraints imposed by economic theory, known as adding-up conditions, such as:

$$\sum_i \alpha_i = 1, \sum_i \beta_i = 0, \sum_i \lambda_i = 0, \sum_i \gamma_{ij} = 0, \forall j \text{ and} \sum_j \gamma_{ij} = 0, \forall i \tag{18}$$

## 6.4.1 LES-Based Estimates

Estimating a demand system such as QUAIDS requires sufficient price variability to be able to identify the parameters within the system. Frequently, however, there are not enough data, typically drawn from a number of different years of HBS, to be able to do this. Therefore, in this section, a simpler method is described, drawing upon Stone's LES.

Creedy (1998) describes an approximate method for producing price elasticities. Rather than estimating a system of demand equations, it relies on a method due to Frisch (1959) that describes own- and cross-price elasticities in terms of total-expenditure elasticities ($\eta_i$), budget shares ($w_i$), and the Frisch marginal-utility-of-income parameter ($\xi$) for directly-additive-utility functions.[7] This can be described as follows:

[7] Note an additive-utility function is utilized and does not allow for complements, and so one must exert a degree of caution in interpreting the results.

$$\eta_{ij} = -\eta_i w_j \left(1 + \frac{\eta_j}{\xi}\right) + \frac{\eta_i \delta_{ij}}{\xi}, \tag{20}$$

where $\delta_{ij} = 1$ if $i = j$, and 0 otherwise.
The total-expenditure elasticity ($\eta_i$) can be defined:

$$\eta_i = 1 + \frac{dw_i}{C}\frac{C}{w_i} = 1 + \left(\beta_i + 2\gamma_i \ln C\right)/w_i \tag{21}$$

The Frisch parameter ($\xi$) can be defined as the elasticity with respect to total per-capita nominal-consumption spending of the marginal utility of the last dollar optimally spent. Lluch et al. (1977) have empirically shown that $-\xi = 0.36.\{\text{real gross national product (GNP) per capita in 1970 US dollars}\}^{-0.36}$. This model produced a Frisch parameter for Australia of −1.82. Lahiri et al. (2000) have estimated a cross-country equation based on 1995 prices relating $-1/\xi = 0.485829 + 0.104019*\ln(\text{gross domestic product (GDP) per capita})$. Estimates for the US, Japan, the EU, and Australia are respectively −1.53, −1.41, −1.61, and −1.71. A method due to Creedy (1998), adapted using the exchange-rate parameter *ER*, elaborated on the Lluch et al. model as follows:

$$\ln(-\xi) = \phi - \alpha \ln(C/ER + \vartheta)$$

where the parameters $\phi$, $\alpha$, and $\vartheta$ are ad-hoc parameters (here respectively 9.2, 0.973, and 7,000) derived by trial and error—where the Frisch parameter for average EU income in euros is −1.61 and average income in Luxembourg (the richest state) is 0.93 higher than the EU figure. The maximum value of the Frisch parameter has been set at −1.3, which equates to about three-point-four times the EU average income. Note that consumption in this case is expressed as consumption per capita per month.

In order to produce equivalent income, a utility function is required. As in the case of Creedy (2001), a Stone–Geary LES direct-utility function is used:

$$U = \prod_i \left[x_i - \gamma_i\right]^{\phi_i} \tag{22}$$

where $\gamma_i$ are LES parameters known as committed consumption for each good $i$ and $0 \leq \phi_i \leq 1, \Sigma_i \phi_i = 1$. For convenience, ignore the subscripts indicating that different parameters are estimated for different demographic (and income) groups.

Maximizing utility subject to the budget constraint $C = \Sigma_i p_i \gamma_i$, the linear-expenditure function for good $i$ is:

$$p_i x_i = p_i \gamma_i + \phi_i \left( C - \sum_j p_j \gamma_j \right) \tag{23}$$

Differentiating with regard to $p_i$ and multiplying by $\frac{p_i}{p_i x_i}$ produce the own-price elasticity from which the $\gamma_i$ parameters can be derived:

$$\eta_{ii} = \frac{p_i \gamma_i}{p_i x_i} - \frac{p_i \phi_i}{p_i x_i}(\gamma_i) = \frac{\gamma_i (1-\phi_i)}{x_i} - 1 \tag{24}$$

$$\Rightarrow \gamma_i = \frac{(\eta_{ii} + 1) x_i}{(1-\phi_i)}$$

Differentiating (**) with regard to $C$ and multiplying by $\frac{C}{p_i x_i}$ produce the budget elasticity, from which the $\varphi_i$ parameters can be derived:

$$\eta_i = \frac{\phi_i C}{p_i x_i} \tag{25}$$

Implying:

$$\phi_i = \frac{\eta_i c_i}{C} = \eta_i w_i \tag{26}$$

## 6.4.2 Indirect-Tax Reform

This section utilizes the theory of marginal-tax reform to suggest the optimal direction for reform. It utilizes a methodology developed for the analysis of marginal-tax reform by Feldstein (1976), Ahmad and Stern (1984), and Newbery and Stern (1987), and utilized by Liberati (2001), Madden (1995a, 1995b), and Newbery (1995).

In this section, two measures of the impact of an indirect-tax reform on different expenditure category $i$ shall be considered:

- the distributional characteristic (DC) of expenditure $d_i$
- the marginal revenue cost (MRC) of indirect taxes $\rho_i$

The distributional impact is based upon a static analysis of the distribution of expenditure over the population and the welfare weights placed upon different groups. The MRC, however, incorporates the efficiency impact of marginal indirect tax changes.

This methodology is based on a social-welfare function (SWF) W = $(v^1,\ldots,v^H)$, where $v^h = v^h(c^h,p)$ is the indirect-utility function of household $h$ for expenditure c and prices $p$.[8]

Define the impact of change in price (or indirect taxation) as follows:

$$\frac{\delta W}{\delta p_i}=\sum_h \frac{\delta W}{v^h}\cdot\frac{\delta v^h}{\delta p_i}=\sum_h \frac{\delta W}{v^h}\cdot\frac{\delta v^h}{\delta c_i^h}\cdot\frac{\delta c_i^h}{\delta p_i}=-\sum_h \theta^h x_i^h, \tag{27}$$

where $\theta^h=\frac{\delta W}{\delta v^h}\cdot\frac{\delta v^h}{\delta c_i^h}$ and $c_i^h = p_i x_i^h$ is the social marginal utility of total expenditures for household $h$ and $x_i^h$ is the consumption of good $I$ by household $h$.

The DC of a marginal price reform of a good can be defined as the ratio of the marginal change in welfare due to a price change applying differential social-welfare weights to the marginal change with constant weights (equal to the average social-welfare weight).

$$d_i=\frac{\sum_h \theta^h x_i^h}{\bar{\theta}\sum_h x_i^h} \tag{28}$$

where $\bar{\theta}$ is the average social-welfare weight. The greater the consumption of a good by households with higher social-marginal utilities (social weight), the greater is the value of $d_i$. If, however, constant social-welfare weights are applied (i.e., indifferent between households of different income), then $d_i = 1, \forall i$.

The distributional impact of a marginal reform quantifies the distributional effect of a good, in the absence of demand effects. Consider now a measure that includes these effects (see Creedy 2001 for a discussion), with

[8] For a more detailed description of this method, see Liberati (2001).

the total revenue from indirect taxes, the product of the tax rate $t_k$, and consumption $x_k^h$:

$$R = \sum_h \sum_k t_k x_k^h,$$

The impact of a marginal tax reform on total revenue of a tax change for good $i$ can be found by differentiating with respect to $t_i$:[9]

$$\frac{\delta R}{\delta t_i} = \sum_h x_i^h + \sum_h \sum_k t_k \frac{\delta x_k^h}{\delta t_i} \tag{29}$$

The expression $\frac{\delta R}{\delta t_i}$ incorporates three effects of a marginal tax change:

- the effect due to the existing consumption of the good $\sum_h x_i^h$
- the direct effect due to the change in the consumption of the good, due to its own price elasticity of good $i$ $\sum_h t_k \frac{\delta x_k^h}{\delta t_i}, i = k$
- the indirect effect on other goods due to the change in their consumption, resulting from the cross-price elasticities $\sum_h \sum_k t_k \frac{\delta x_k^h}{\delta t_i}, i \neq k$

Marginal changes in tax changes revenue, according to Equation 29, and changes welfare, according to Equation 27. The ratio of these two measures, the MRC, $\rho_i$ gives the MRC of raising one unit of revenue from a change in tax on a good $i$.

$$\rho_i = -\frac{\delta R / \delta t_i}{\delta W / \delta t_i} \tag{30}$$

Ahmad and Stern (1984) point out that optimal tax requires that $\rho_i = \rho_j, \forall i, j$, i.e., that the MRC of all goods is the same. If this were not the case, then one could lower indirect taxes on a good with a low MRC and increase taxes on a good with a high MRC, and so increase welfare with reducing revenue. In order to move to an optimal tax design, one should alter tax rates until equality is achieved.

[9] We assume here that $\delta t_i = \delta p_i$, assuming that the impact of a tax would be passed on by producers to the consumer.

Assume as Ahmad and Stern do that incomes are fixed, accepting the weak separability of leisure and goods. Madden (1996) has derived an expression of MRC, where this assumption is relaxed where indirect-tax reform has an impact on the demand for leisure and thus labour supply.

Taking Equations 29 and 27, and multiplying numerator and denominator by $p_i$, an expression of the MRC can be derived:

$$\frac{\delta R}{\delta t_i} = \sum_h x_i^h + \sum_h \sum_k t_k \frac{\delta x_k^h}{\delta t_i} \tag{31}$$

$$\rho_i = \frac{\sum_h x_i^h p_i + \sum_h \sum_k \frac{t_k}{p_k} \frac{\delta x_k^h}{\delta p_i} \frac{p_i}{x_i^h} x_i^h p_k}{\sum_h \theta^h x_i^h p_i}, \tag{32}$$

$$= \frac{\sum_h x_i^h p_i + \sum_h \sum_k t^*_k \, x_i^h p_k \eta_{k,i}^h}{\sum_h \theta^h x_i^h p_i}$$

where $t^*_k$ is the ratio of the tax on good $k$ to the tax-inclusive price $p_k$, and $\eta_{k,i}^h$ is household $h$'s elasticity of demand for good $k$ with respect to the price of good $I$, $\frac{\delta x_k^h}{\delta p_i} \frac{p_i}{x_i^h}$.[10]

In order to construct the DC and MRC measures, the following components need to be to quantified:

- the welfare weight, $\theta^h = \frac{\delta W}{\delta v^h} \cdot \frac{\delta v^h}{\delta c^h}$
- the price elasticity of demand, $\eta_{k,i}^h = \frac{\delta x_k^h}{\delta p_i} \frac{p_i}{x_i^h}$

### 6.4.2.1 Welfare Weight

Compare the welfare impact of indirect taxation using a social-welfare function. As in the case of Creedy (2001), Liberati (2001), Newbery (1995), and Madden (1995b), utilize a variant of the Atkinson (1970) social-welfare function:

$$W = \frac{1}{H} \sum_h \frac{\left(v^h\right)^{1-e}}{1-e} \tag{33}$$

[10] Note $\delta p_i = \delta m_i + \delta t_i = 0 + \delta t_i = \delta t_i$.

where $H$ is the number of households and $e$ is the inequality-aversion parameter that relates to how much a transfer from rich to poor will improve social welfare; the higher the value of $e$ the more a transfer will improve welfare. When utility corresponds to consumption $v^h = c^h$, then $\theta^h = \frac{\delta W}{\delta c^h} = \frac{1}{H}\left(c^h\right)^{-e}$.

### 6.4.2.2 Equivalent Variation

The indirect-utility function of the LES can be produced by substituting into the direct-utility function (Equation 22), the Marshallian demand function:

$$V(p,y) = \prod_i \left[ \gamma_i + \frac{\phi_i}{p_i}\left( C - \sum_j p_j \gamma_j \right) - \gamma_i \right]^{\phi_i} \tag{34}$$

$$= \prod_i \left[ \frac{\phi_i}{p_i}\left( C - \sum_j p_j \gamma_j \right) \right]^{\phi_i} = \frac{\prod_i \left[ C - \sum_j p_j \gamma_j \right]^{\phi_i}}{\prod_i [p_i / \phi_i]^{\phi_i}}$$

$$= \frac{C - \sum_j p_j \gamma_j}{\prod_i [p_i / \phi_i]^{\phi_i}}$$

Cross-multiplying, the LES expenditure function for price $p_i$ is:

$$E(p, U, z) = C = \sum_i p_i \gamma_i + \prod_i (p_i / \phi_i)^{\phi_i} V(p, y)$$

while the expenditure function for price $p_{r,i}$ is:

$$E(p_r, U, z) = \sum_i p_{r,i} \gamma_i + \prod_i (p_{r,i} / \phi_i)^{\phi_i} U \tag{35}$$

where $U = V(p, y)$

Hence, from Equations 34 and 35 the equivalent income necessary to produce utility $U$ (based upon consumption $C$ and price $p_i$), when prices are $p_{r,i}$, can be produced:

$$y_e = \sum_i p_{r,i}\gamma_i + \prod_i (p_{r,i}/\phi_i)^{\phi_i} \cdot \frac{C - \sum_i p_i\gamma_i}{\prod_i (p_i/\phi_i)^{\phi_i}}$$
$$= \sum_i p_{r,i}\gamma_i + \left[\prod_i (p_{r,i}/p_i)^{\phi_i}\right] \cdot \left[C - \sum_i p_i\gamma_i\right] \tag{36}$$

Atkinson's measure of inequality is:

$$A(e) = 1 - \left[\frac{\left[\left(\frac{1}{H}\right) \cdot \sum_h \left(y_e^h\right)^{(1-e)}\right]^{1/(1-e)}}{\overline{y}_e}\right] = 1 - \left[\frac{y_{ede}}{\overline{y}_e}\right] \tag{37}$$

Combining Equation 37 with our SWF $W$ produces an SWF based upon equivalent income:

$$W = \frac{1}{H}\sum_h \frac{\left(y_e^h\right)^{1-e}}{1-e} = \frac{\left(y_{ede}\right)^{1-e}}{1-e}. \tag{38}$$

where $y_{ede} = \overline{y}_e\left(1 - A(e)\right)$ and $\overline{y}_e$ is the mean equivalent income and $A(e)$ is Atkinson's inequality of equivalent income. In this, $y_{ede}$ (the equally distributed equivalent value) can be interpreted as the income that, if distributed equally across the population, produces the same value of social welfare as the existing distribution of income. It captures the trade-off between equity and efficiency. The higher $y_{ede}$, the higher the product of mean equivalent income (efficiency) and equality, hence an increase in equality or efficiency can increase $y_{ede}$.

## 6.5 Simulation: Income and Indirect Taxation

In this section, a number of simulations using micro-consumption data in relation to indirect taxation are undertaken. Specifically, our analysis comprises of a number of steps:

- analyse the structure of expenditure in terms of budget elasticities and shares
- develop price elasticities
- analyse the structure of indirect taxes
- analyse the progressivity of these taxes
- assess the distributional characteristics of expenditure and the optimal direction for tax reform

This section will also describe the data requirements of the model estimation. The 2004 HBS for Ireland is utilized. The main requirement of the HBS is that there is sufficient detail among the consumption variables to model indirect taxation.

In order to undertake the proposed analysis, the following data were produced:

- a table indicating variable names and variable descriptions in English
- a matrix containing the COICOP code for each consumption variable
- a matrix containing the durable status for each consumption variable
- a matrix containing the indirect-tax parameters for each variable

The next step is the estimation of budget-share elasticities, and own- and cross-price elasticities, using the methodology described above for aggregated categories. The system for the COICOP aggregates is initially estimated. However, this may change depending on the quality of the model. Depending on the proportion of zero-expenditure categories, say for tobacco, we may estimate parallel models for different types of household. These issues are determined upon the analysis of the data.

The choice of grouped budget shares means:

- It reduces the impact of the zero-expenditures problem, which could substantially undermine the results of OLS regressions. The OLS regressions are not used for simulation purposes, but rather to produce price elasticities of demand.
- It achieves the objective of being able to distinguish between broad categories for which different rates of taxation apply.
- Estimates for smaller groups of goods could be unstable.

### 6.5.1 Modelling Budget Shares and Elasticities

Applying the methodology in earlier chapters, Table 6.1 describes the average budget share for each of the adjusted COICOP categories used in this

**Table 6.1** Budget Shares

| Expenditure Category | Average Budget Share |
|---|---|
| Food, non-alcoholic beverages | 0.22 |
| Alcoholic beverages | 0.03 |
| Tobacco | 0.03 |
| Clothing and footwear | 0.06 |
| Home fuels and electricity | 0.07 |
| Rents | 0.04 |
| Household services | 0.03 |
| Health | 0.08 |
| Private transport | 0.06 |
| Public Transport | 0.03 |
| Communication | 0.02 |
| Recreation and culture | 0.06 |
| Education | 0.01 |
| Restaurants and hotels | 0.07 |
| Other goods and services | 0.17 |

**Table 6.2** Budget Elasticities

| Expenditure Category | Budget Elasticity |
|---|---|
| Food, non-alcoholic beverages | 0.65 |
| Alcoholic beverages | 1.14 |
| Tobacco | 0.58 |
| Clothing and footwear | 1.37 |
| Home fuels and electricity | 0.43 |
| Rents | 0.78 |
| Household services | 1.22 |
| Health | 1.13 |
| Private transport | 0.92 |
| Public Transport | 1.30 |
| Communication | 0.63 |
| Recreation and culture | 1.25 |
| Education | 1.32 |
| Restaurants and hotels | 1.21 |
| Other goods and services | 1.16 |

model. As is the case in most countries, food has the highest average budget share, followed by home-energy use.

Table 6.2 defines the budget elasticities. All are positive, indicating that all expenditure types rise with income. However, the share of necessities such as food and fuel are less than 1, indicating the budget share declines with income.

The Frisch parameters ($\xi$) are then compared (Table 6.3), which is required to model price elasticities with other estimates for the US, Japan, the EU, and Australia, which have values respectively of −1.61, −1.60, −1.57, and −1.60. When applied to Irish data, we get an average of −1.60.

**Table 6.3** Frisch Parameters

| | Average Income | Frish |
|---|---|---|
| Hungary | 22,119 | −1.53 |
| Belgium | 39,788 | −1.59 |
| Finland | 38,655 | −1.58 |
| France | 36,104 | −1.58 |
| Greece | 25,331 | −1.54 |
| Ireland | 43,592 | −1.60 |
| Italy | 33,111 | −1.57 |
| Luxembourg | 91,388 | −1.67 |
| Netherlands | 43,198 | −1.60 |
| Portugal | 25,411 | −1.54 |
| Spain | 32,682 | −1.57 |
| UK | 36,901 | −1.58 |

**Table 6.4** Own-Price Elasticities

| Own-Price Elasticities | |
|---|---|
| Food, non-alcoholic beverages | −0.49 |
| Alcoholic beverages | −0.77 |
| Tobacco | −0.39 |
| Clothing and footwear | −0.92 |
| Home fuels and electricity | −0.30 |
| Rents | −0.53 |
| Household services | −0.82 |
| Health | −0.77 |
| Private transport | −0.63 |
| Public Transport | −0.87 |
| Communication | −0.43 |
| Recreation and culture | −0.84 |
| Education | −0.88 |
| Restaurants and hotels | −0.82 |
| Other goods and services | −0.81 |

Table 6.4 reports the average own-price elasticities for individual commodity groups. As outlined above, we group expenditure variables into adjusted COICOP categories to avoid issues associated with zero expenditures and to produce stable estimates. Elasticities are produced at the level of the group, which is a function of the presence of children, marital status, and retirement status. All coefficients are negative, with necessities being more price inelastic than other goods. These parameters are validated below.

## 6.5.2 Validation of Estimates

In this subsection, a validation of the process of estimation of the parameters used in the expenditure model is undertaken, and reported via the following steps:

- budget elasticities
- budget shares
- own-price elasticities

Each individual validation is reported via a validation against broadly comparable numbers from international estimates produced as part of the EUROMOD framework (O'Donoghue et al. 2004). It should be noted that the expenditure categories used in EUROMOD are slightly different, so that the comparison countries have higher GDP per capita, and that the estimates came from the 1990s.

Looking first at the budget elasticities in Figure 6.1, estimated via a series of equations in the HBS, the majority of elasticities are within the range of the EUROMOD countries. Except for public transport, the remainder typically fall within a few percentage points of the range found elsewhere.

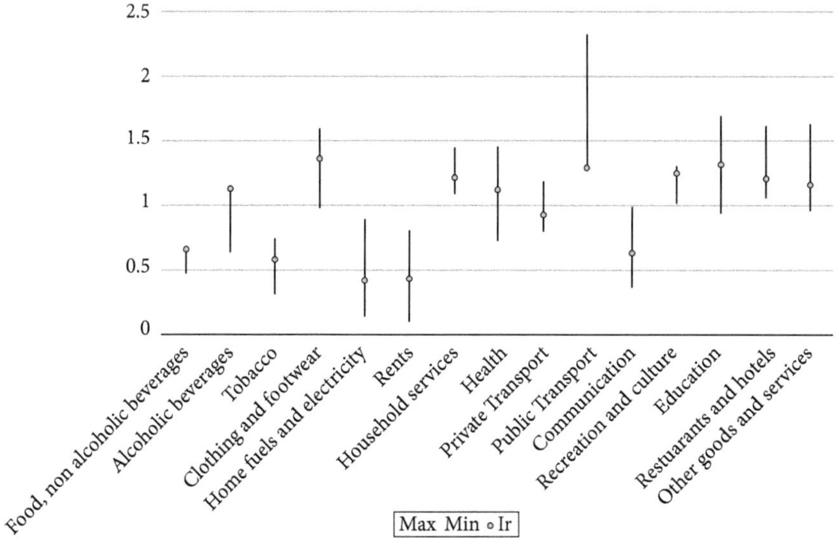


**Figure 6.1** Budget Elasticities

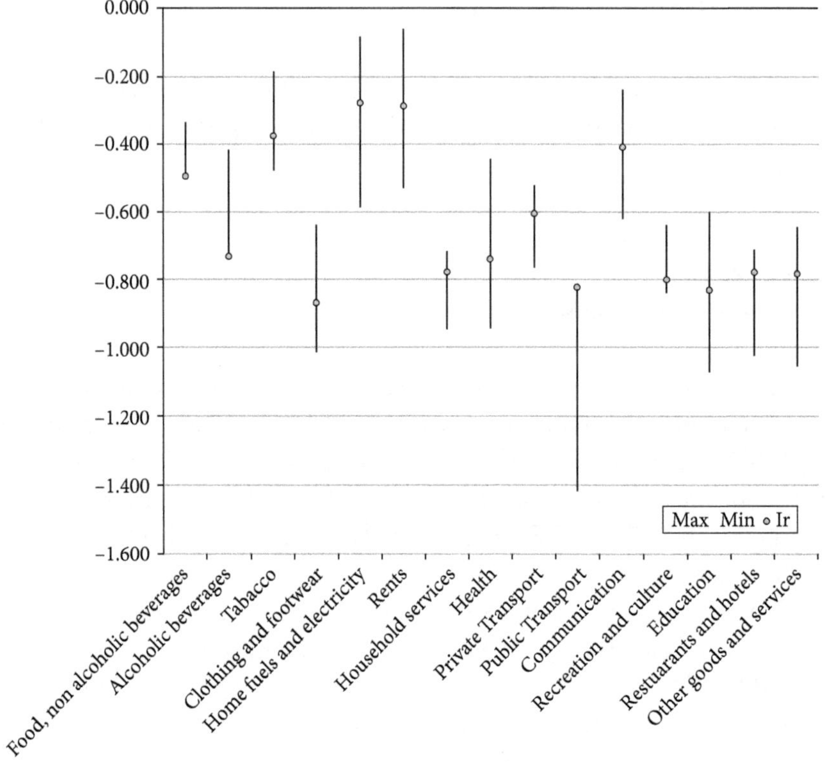


**Figure 6.2** Budget Shares

A similar profile is found among the budget shares in Figure 6.2, although, in this case, other goods have a budget share higher than the EUROMOD range, and household goods and services have a lower range. Given the similarity of the headings, as residual categories, the differences are likely to be due to different definitions.

Using our Frisch equation above, average price elasticities can be generated. Figure 6.3 reports the own-price elasticities that have the biggest contribution to behavioural response. Again, the elasticities are very close, and mostly within the range, or just outside the range, of existing estimates.

### 6.5.3 Distributional Statistic and MRC

The distribution characteristic explained above shows the desirability of tax reforms from a purely distributional perspective. The distributional statistics are presented in Table 6.5 for the 2004 HBS using an inequality-aversion parameter of 0.3. The higher distributional statistics imply that these goods

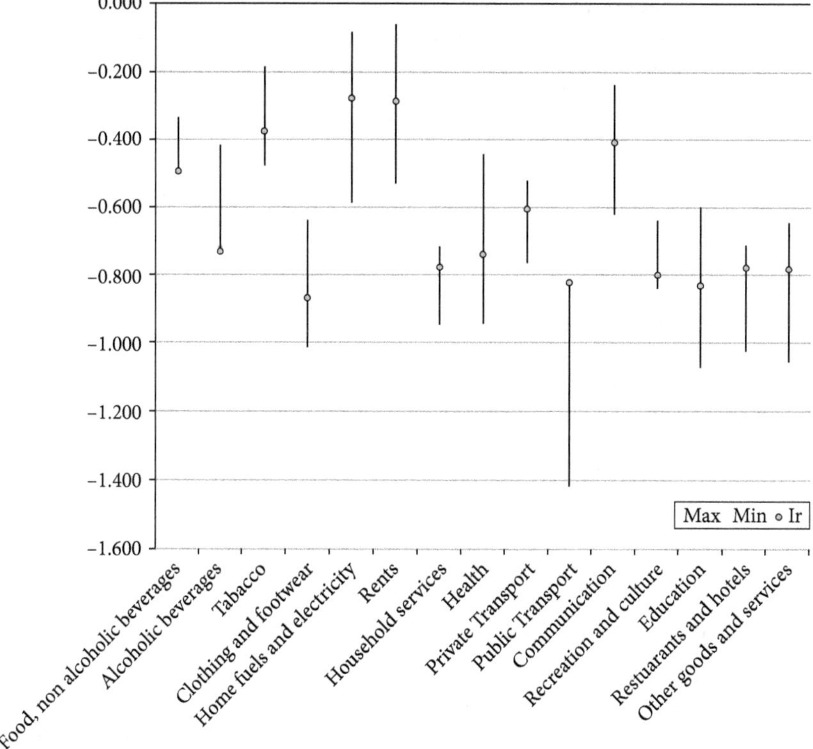


**Figure 6.3** Own-Price Elasticities

**Table 6.5** Distributional Statistics

| Expenditure Category | 2004 (E = 0.3) | Rank |
|---|---|---|
| Food, non-alcoholic beverages | 2.54 | 3 |
| Alcoholic beverages | 2.39 | 8 |
| Tobacco | 2.60 | 2 |
| Clothing and footwear | 2.35 | 11 |
| Home fuels and electricity | 2.61 | 1 |
| Rents | 2.53 | 4 |
| Household services | 2.38 | 9 |
| Health | 2.36 | 10 |
| Private transport | 2.40 | 7 |
| Public Transport | 2.33 | 13 |
| Communication | 2.53 | 5 |
| Recreation and culture | 2.42 | 6 |
| Education | 2.28 | 15 |
| Restaurants and hotels | 2.34 | 12 |
| Other goods and services | 2.32 | 14 |

**Table 6.6** MRC

| MRC | 2004 (E = 0.3) | Rank |
|---|---|---|
| Food, non-alcoholic beverages | 6.01 | 6 |
| Alcoholic beverages | 3.25 | 14 |
| Tobacco | 5.40 | 11 |
| Clothing and footwear | 5.78 | 8 |
| Home fuels and electricity | 6.23 | 3 |
| Rents | 4.55 | 13 |
| Household services | 6.61 | 2 |
| Health | 5.68 | 9 |
| Private transport | 6.76 | 1 |
| Public transport | 5.93 | 7 |
| Communication | 5.12 | 12 |
| Recreation and culture | 6.15 | 4 |
| Education | 5.54 | 10 |
| Restaurants and hotels | 6.11 | 5 |
| Other goods and services | 0.00 | 15 |

are purchased more intensively by poorer households. A higher ranking is given to those commodity groups. There are few changes in the rankings in response to different levels of inequality aversion in both years. The results for 2004 show that home fuels are consumed most intensively by poorer households, relative to richer households. Tobacco, food, rent, and communications are among the other commodities consumed most intensively by poorer households. Education expenses and other goods are the commodities consumed most intensively by richer households.

Table 6.6 reports the MRC for different goods with an inequality-aversion parameter of 0.3. As outlined above, under an optimal tax, the MRC would be equal for all goods. Goods with a higher MRC would have their tax rate increased under optimal taxation. Private transport, household services, and domestic fuels have the highest MRC, while other goods, alcohol, and rents have the lowest MRC, reflecting a combination of higher tax rate or lower-price elasticity for the former and the opposite for the latter.

# 7
# Environmental Taxation

## 7.1 Introduction

One of the basic concepts of environmental economics is that when individuals or firms do not face the marginal social cost of pollution, they may pollute more than is socially optimal. This is clear in relation to the debate on climate change, where society burns more fossil fuels, producing more greenhouse-gas emissions than the global environment can sustain, leading to increases in global temperatures and the resulting ecological consequences.

The environment as a policy issue has increased dramatically in importance in recent decades. The issues extend from global challenges, such as climate change, access to water and soils, ozone emissions, and biodiversity loss, to issues with a smaller geographical scope, such as water quality and congestion, to the impact of the environment on health (Orcutt et al. 1977). As the realization of the extent of these issues has increased, so too has the scope of public policy in relation to environmental regulations, carbon taxes, or emissions trading. In addition, strategies are being developed to increase both the market and non-market value of environmental and natural resources. Environmental policy measures, including environmental regulations, taxes, and emission trading schemes, have been proposed to reduce pollution. This chapter will focus on environmental taxes, as they are most amenable to simulation using a microsimulation model, requiring both the behavioural response to the policy to be measured and the distributional impact. In particular, the focus is on the modelling and design of Pigouvian taxes, such as a carbon tax, that aim to reduce environmental pollution.

Taxes on polluting goods can be similar to the indirect taxes described in Chapter 6, such as value-added tax or excise duties on fuels. However, pure environmental taxes are slightly different, as they are levied not in proportion to value or volume but in relation to the amount of pollution that is produced.

There is a relatively extensive literature on modelling the distributive impact of environmental taxes. Hynes and O'Donoghue (2014) provide a review of the wider literature of the use of microsimulation models for

*Practical Microsimulation Modelling*. Cathal O'Donoghue. Oxford University Press. © Cathal O'Donoghue 2021.
DOI:10.1093/oso/9780198852872.003.0007

environmental policy. The distributional implications of carbon taxes have been analysed by O'Donoghue (1997) and Callan et al. (2009) in Ireland, Hamilton and Cameron (1994) in Labandeira et al. (2009), and García-Muros et al. (2017) in Spain, Bureau (2010) and Berry (2019) in France, Casler and Rafiqui (1993) and Mathur and Morris (2014) in the US, Symons et al. (1994, 2002) in the UK, Yusuf and Resosudarmo (2015) in Indonesia, Kerkhof et al. (2008) in the Netherlands, Bach et al. (2002) and Bork (2006) in Germany, Poltimäe and Võrk (2009) in Estonia, Cornwell and Creedy (1996) in Australia, Rosas-Flores et al. (2017) in Mexico, and Vandyck and Van Regemorter (2014) in Belgium.

Microsimulation analyses have also been used to undertake distributional assessments of other environmental policies, such as tradable-emissions permits (Waduda 2008), taxes on methane emissions from cattle (Hynes et al. 2009), and taxes on nitrogen emissions (Berntsen et al. 2003). Doole et al. (2013) examined the distributional impact of a cap-and-trade strategy on dairy farms. Cervigni et al. (2013) have analysed the distributional impact of wider low-carbon economic development policies.

Other types of distributional-impact analysis include the simulation of 'what if' scenarios, such as the impact of an action on emissions if consumption patterns are changed. For example, Alfredsson (2002) utilized a microsimulation model to undertake a life-cycle analysis that incorporates energy use and carbon-dioxide ($CO_2$) emissions connected with the whole production process (up to the point of purchase) of alternative 'greener' consumption patterns. However, the impact is marginal.

The structure of these microsimulation models is described in Figure 7.1. It is similar to an indirect-tax model, containing input-expenditure data, a policy calculator, and the consumption-behavioural response. In addition, however, it has an additional component to model pollution, both directly in terms of the consumption of the households and indirectly, utilizing an

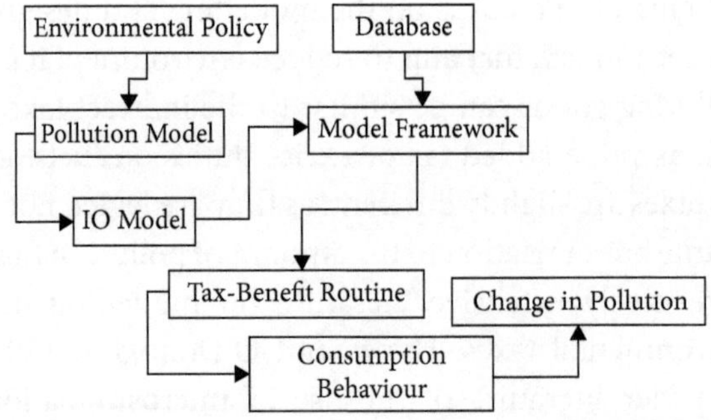


**Figure 7.1** Structure of an Environmental Microsimulation Model

input-output (IO) framework, through the polluting activity of the value chains of the goods consumed.

This chapter describes in more detail the development of an environmental taxation model, describing the policy context of environmental taxation in Section 7.2, methodological issues in terms of modelling pollution in Sections 7.3, and direct and indirect impact of taxation in Section 7.4. The welfare impact of an environmental tax is simulated in Section 7.5.

## 7.2 Policy Context: Environmental Taxation

Much environmental policy attempts to adjust behaviour so that the social costs of economic activity are incorporated in the decision space of private actors. Polluters will act, depending on their product mix, technological use, and production process, on the basis of their private costs and benefits, and not on the costs faced by society.

The rationale for the state to step in to control pollution arises from the existence of externalities, which are costs (or benefits) imposed by the polluter on others. For example, a household or firm burning fossil fuels faces only the private cost of purchasing the fuels, but does not face the social costs associated with the resulting emissions. Reducing the external cost of pollution control will require either regulation or some market mechanism such as a Pigouvian tax.

Figure 7.2 plots the marginal costs faced by society and the polluter (Y-axis) at different levels of pollution against the level of pollution on the X-axis. The marginal abatement cost (MAC) faced by the polluter rises with reducing levels of pollution, because it is assumed that cheaper methods of pollution abatement will be tried first. The marginal damage cost (MDC) of pollution faced by society will tend to rise with increasing pollution, as

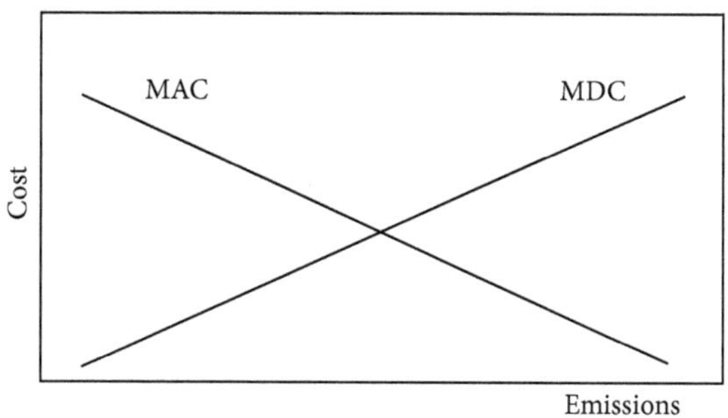


**Figure 7.2** Efficient Pollution Abatement for a Single Polluting Firm

higher pollution levels cause proportionately more damage. For theoretical reasons, society's optimal position will be the quantity of pollution where the marginal cost to the polluter of abatement is equal to the marginal cost to society of the damage.

In that they both require monitoring systems and administrative systems to be effective, regulations and market mechanisms are similar. Regulations can be designed to achieve the same level of pollution reduction as market measures. Regulations have the advantage that if they are adhered to, environmental standards are actually achieved. However, they are not dynamically efficient, in the sense that once these standards are achieved, there is no further incentive to improve on them. In addition, regulations are statically inefficient, as they make no allowance for the fact that the cost of compliance can vary across sectors of the economy, which means that the total cost to the economy would be higher if regulations were used.

Market-based instruments such as taxation can, by exploiting these cost differentials, lead to lower total compliance costs. They can also lead to continuous behavioural changes. An optimal tax would be set so as to reduce pollution to the point where the MDC and the MAC are equal.

However, it is difficult to determine the value of the external costs, or the cost to society of pollution not taken into account by the polluter. Incentive taxes are therefore used to achieve a certain target. In some studies, it has been found that a carbon tax has what is known as a double dividend; it can reduce carbon-dioxide emissions as well as financing the reduction of distortionary taxes such as income tax.

Nevertheless, there are a number of disadvantages in using taxation to regulate the environment (Symons et al. 1994; Pearce 1991; Smith 1995). Short-run energy elasticities are often lower than long-run elasticities, due to the time taken to switch to new technologies, which may slow down the achievement of targets. Simple environmental taxes may also not be appropriate where pollution is concentrated over time or in a certain location. More-complicated measures or regulation would thus be more effective here.

In addition to efficiency issues, environmental taxation has important distributional implications. Taxes placed on essential goods such as domestic fuels will hit those at the bottom of the income distribution most; however, fiscal measures such as increased transfer payments can be introduced to reduce the distributional impact[1]. Boccanfuso et al. (2011) survey the micro- and macro-micro-literature on the distributive impact of environmental taxes and find that carbon taxes in OECD countries are largely regressive;

[1] See Symons et al. (1994).

however, recycling revenue, through the double dividend, can reduce this regressivity. They found a relatively small literature in developing countries, but found a similar result in terms of the regressivity of tax; yet, they identified mechanisms for making the change less regressive, e.g., through counterbalancing changes in other indirect taxes.

Another problem with charging polluters is measuring how much they pollute. It is impossible to measure the quantity of greenhouse gasses emitted by each pollution source, as it would require the placing of measuring devices on every car exhaust and every chimney, etc. Instead, a tax could be levied at source, i.e., at the point of import or at the wholesaler level. Carbon-dioxide emissions are directly related to the volume of fuel used, which means that emissions can easily be taxed, by levying a tax proportional to the carbon component of the fuel. An environmental tax has an income effect, raising the price of energy, and also has a substitution effect, substituting expenditure away from fuels with a high carbon component, such as coal or peat, and towards fuels with lower carbon components, such as natural gas or wood fuel.

## 7.3 Data Issues: Modelling Pollution

When modelling the impact of policy changes that change the price of a good as a function of the pollution or pollution potential, the key difference with the types of models related to indirect taxation and consumption that were discussed in Chapter 6 is the ability to model pollution.

This chapter will focus on the objective of modelling carbon dioxide-related emissions. These emissions mainly affect global warming, which is an international issue. Other types of pollution, such as water quality degradation, which depends on locally concentrated emissions, are more difficult to model, as the impact and solutions are more diffuse.

There are three sources of carbon-dioxide emissions in household consumption:

- fuel consumption by households
- fuel consumption as part of the inputs to industrial production
- indirect carbon dioxide emitted in the production of imports

The primary focus of microsimulation models that are used to model greenhouse-gas emissions, and associated carbon-related taxation, is the distributional impact of the tax and the behavioural response to the tax.

As our microsimulation model is focused on the household sector, information is sourced on fuel consumption by households using data from a household-budget survey (HBS). Information on pollution produced in the production of other consumption goods can be generated using an IO table, as described below. O'Donoghue (1997) utilizes an IO table from the main source of imports.[2] However, unless there is an internationally organized environmental tax, it is reasonable to ignore the impact on imported goods in our analysis.

The first data requirement of an environmental-tax microsimulation model is to convert the tax per unit of pollutant into either a per-unit volume or per-unit-value amount, so that the tax can be applied as a rate to variables in the HBS. The first objective, therefore, will be to produce matrices C, which contain the quantities of carbon dioxide per € of fuel expenditure.

These need to be produced for each fuel type. This chapter utilizes 2010 data from Ireland for the example simulation below, thus carbon dioxide per unit-euro will be consistent with this data. These calculations are reported in Table 7.1. Expenditures are taken from the IO table for 2010, which is constructed in Section 7.5, while energy values in terrajoules (TJ) are taken from the national energy statistics, and carbon-dioxide emissions are imputed. Peat generates significantly more carbon dioxide at more than 15 tonnes of $CO_2$ per €1,000 of expenditure.

A carbon tax is defined per ton of carbon dioxide emitted. Thus, the rate of carbon tax per unit of fuel expenditure that can be applied in the microsimulation model can be calculated by multiplying by the rates '$tCO_2$ per €1,000 fuel expenditure' in Table 7.1.

## 7.4 Measurement Issues: Direct and Indirect Impacts of Environmental Taxation

Applying the carbon tax per unit of expenditure gives us the direct impact of the environmental tax. However, the environmental tax is also likely to impact the price of other goods consumed. It is also likely that the imposition of a carbon tax will have general equilibrium effects, as firms will also change their production structure. It may thus be suitable to conduct the analysis via a computable general-equilibrium (CGE) model, as in the case of Yusuf and Resosudarmo (2015). However, for the purpose of this analysis, the assumption

[2] For the carbon-dioxide emissions of imports, UK levels are assumed to be representative of average imported levels, and are found in Gay and Proops (1993).

**Table 7.1** Ratios of Carbon Dioxide and Energy to Expenditure by Fuel

| | Expenditure (€m) | TJ | t $CO_2$ (1,000s) | TJ per €1,000 Fuel Expenditure | t $CO_2$ per €1,000 Fuel Expenditure |
|---|---|---|---|---|---|
| Bituminous coal | 714 | 49,907 | 4,721 | 69.9 | 6.6 |
| Anthracite and manufactured | 17 | 1,172 | 115 | 69.9 | 6.9 |
| Milled peat | 171 | 25,414 | 2,966 | 148.8 | 17.4 |
| Sod peat | 46 | 6,908 | 718 | 148.8 | 15.5 |
| Crude oil | 2,094 | 124,390 | 9,118 | 59.4 | 4.4 |
| Gasoline | 795 | 43,836 | 3,069 | 55.1 | 3.9 |
| Kerosene | 378 | 21,813 | 1,557 | 57.7 | 4.1 |
| Jet kerosene | 778 | 44,882 | 3,205 | 57.7 | 4.1 |
| LPG | 95 | 3,894 | 248 | 41.1 | 2.6 |
| Gasoil/diesel/DERV | 1,754 | 85,160 | 6,242 | 48.6 | 3.6 |
| Petroleum | 78 | 4,647 | 468 | 59.4 | 6 |
| Natural gas | 1,362 | 196,863 | 11,241 | 144.6 | 8.3 |

is made that price changes due to a carbon tax are passed directly (by industry) to the consumer, without a behavioural response at the industry level.

In order to capture the indirect effect of the carbon tax, the transmission-of-price changes through the economy to the household sector is modelled using an IO table, developed initially by Leontief (1951). Similar analyses conducted internationally include O'Donoghue (1997) in Ireland, Gay and Proops (1993) in the UK, and Casler and Rafiqui (1993) in the US.

An IO table contains information about sectors of an economy, mapping the flows of inputs from one sector to another, or to final demand (that consumed by households or exported, etc.). Output in each sector has two possible uses: it can be used for final demand or as an intermediate input for other sectors. In an $n$ sector economy, final demand for sector $i$'s produce is denoted by $di$ and for the output of sector $i$ by $x_i$. Intermediate input from sector $i$ into sector $j$ is defined as $a_{ij}\ x_j$, where $a_{ij}$, the input coefficients, are fixed in value. In other words, $a_{ij}$ is the quantity of commodity $i$ that is required as an input to produce a unit of output $j$. Output can therefore be seen as the sum of intermediate inputs, and final demand as follows:

$$x_i = \sum_j a_{ij} x_j + d_i$$

or in matrix terminology:

$$x = A.x + d$$

Combining the output coefficients to produce an $(I - A)$ technology matrix and inverting it, the Leontief inverse matrix $(I - A)^{-1}$ is produced, which gives the direct and indirect inter-industry requirements for the economy:

$$x = d.(I - A)^{-1}$$

This can be expanded to produce the following:

$$x = d.\left(I + A + A^2 + A^3 + \ldots\right)$$

As $A$ is a non-negative matrix with all elements less than 1, $A^m$ approaches the null matrix as $m$ gets larger, enabling us to get a good approximation to the inverse matrix. It thus expands output per sector into its components of final demand $d$, $Ad$, the inputs needed to produce $d$, $A^2d$, and the inputs required to produce $Ad$, etc., to produce the number of units of each output used in the production of a unit of final demand for each good.

If tax $t$ is applied and is passed on in its entirety to consumers, then the tax on goods consumed in final demand is $td$, the tax on the inputs to these goods is $tAd$, the tax on inputs to these is $tA^2d$, and so on. Combining, total tax is:

$$x = t.d.\left(I + A + A^2 + A^3 + \ldots\right) = t.d\left(I - A\right)^{-1}$$

The original IO table contains information on only one fuel sector: petroleum and coal products. Because of the focus on the differential effect of price changes on individual fuels, such as petrol, diesel, kerosene, and other fuels, this component of the IO table is decomposed into its constituent parts. See O'Donoghue et al. (2019) for a description of the method.

Once the direct and indirect price changes in the economy as a whole are known, the effect on households can then be considered. The direct and indirect price changes per industrial sector give us the price changes that households will observe. In order to quantify the effect on households, a source of data is needed that contains household expenditures.

Again, as in the case of the IO table, it is necessary to make some adjustments to the data. First, as the data are out of date, the differential growth rate of fuels relative to other goods is applied. This differential growth is due both to changes in relative prices (prices of petrol and kerosene have grown more slowly than average, and diesel more quickly) and to the volumes consumed.

## 7.5 Simulation: Welfare Impact of a Carbon Taxation

In this section, the distributional impact of a carbon tax is modelled. One of the major criticisms of a carbon tax is that the distributional impact is quite regressive, with the burden of the tax falling proportionately more on poorer households. This is especially the case when a tax is placed only on household fuels (Smith 1992a, 1992b; Scott 1992). However, other studies have shown that incorporating the indirect impact of the tax on inputs reduces this distributional effect (Casler and Rafiqui 1993; Symons et al. 1994).

In order to measure the impact of policy reforms, the model applies the price change to the IO Leontief matrix, so that we get the net-price change in each sector. The sectoral headings in the IO table are different to the HBS, so the IO price changes can be applied to the IO-HBS transformation matrix, to get the net-price change in each expenditure category in the HBS.

Tables chronicling the average expenditure on each of 138 types of goods and services per gross-income-decile form the core of the model.

The carbon-dioxide component of each good and service purchased is modelled first. The indirect component is then simulated using the results of IO analyses. Once direct and indirect carbon-dioxide components have been modelled, the value of the carbon tax by consumption group and decile can be estimated.

The estimates of the direct carbon-dioxide component used here have been calculated above, using the fuel expenditures described in the HBS. An IO method described in O'Donoghue et al. (2019) produced figures for the indirect carbon-dioxide component of domestically produced goods and services. These indirect carbon-dioxide figures are at the level of industry (NACE), and have had to be transformed to the HBS categories to find the indirect carbon-dioxide production of each expenditure sector.

The distribution of fuel expenditure as a share of total expenditure per annum is outlined in Table 7.2 for each equivalized disposable-income decile. The bottom decile has two-point-three times the share of the top decile. Therefore, direct carbon-dioxide production forms a decreasing proportion of total carbon-dioxide production, going from poorer to richer households. This is not surprizing, due to the size of expenditure on household fuels as a proportion of total expenditure among the lower-income deciles.

Once the direct and indirect carbon dioxide produced per unit of expenditure is calculated, the level of the carbon tax can be imputed. Levying a carbon tax of €15 per ton of carbon dioxide, Table 7.3 reports the increase in prices per expenditure group as a result of this tax. The largest increase in prices arises in relation to fuels. Of other goods and services, clothing and

**Table 7.2** Fuel as a Share of Expenditure by Decile

| Equivalized Disposable Income Decile | Fuel as a Share of Expenditure | Carbon Dioxide per € of Expenditure |
|---|---|---|
| 1 | 7.2 | 0.6 |
| 2 | 7.8 | 0.65 |
| 3 | 7.2 | 0.61 |
| 4 | 5.7 | 0.49 |
| 5 | 5.2 | 0.46 |
| 6 | 4.9 | 0.41 |
| 7 | 4.7 | 0.4 |
| 8 | 4.1 | 0.36 |
| 9 | 3.8 | 0.34 |
| 10 | 3.1 | 0.26 |
| Total | 4.8 | 0.41 |
| Ratio Top/Bottom | 2.32 | 2.27 |

**Table 7.3** Percentage Direct and Indirect Increase in Prices of Consumption Goods Due to Carbon Tax

| Expenditure Group | Price Increase |
|---|---|
| Sod peat | 24.8 |
| Natural gas | 13.4 |
| Petrol | 10.3 |
| Coal | 9.4 |
| Diesel | 8.8 |
| Kerosene | 7.1 |
| Household services | 6.9 |
| LPG | 5.2 |
| Home fuels and electricity | 2.8 |
| Other goods and services | 1.5 |
| Clothing and footwear | 1.4 |
| Tobacco | 1.3 |
| Food, non-alcoholic beverages | 0.9 |
| Public transport | 0.8 |
| Private transport | 0.6 |
| Recreation and culture | 0.5 |
| Restaurants and hotels | 0.5 |
| Alcoholic beverages | 0.4 |
| Durables | 0.3 |
| Health | 0.2 |
| Communication | 0.2 |
| Education | 0.2 |
| Rents | 0.1 |

tobacco are the next in terms of magnitude, with increases of just over 1 per cent. All other sectors had increases of less than 1 per cent. Table 7.4 describes the share of individual fuel types across the income distribution. Poor households are more likely to have a higher share of coal, oil, petrol, and electricity, while richer households having a higher share of gas and diesel.

Table 7.5 outlines the first-round impact of a carbon tax before any adjustment in expenditure. The values represent carbon tax as a proportion of total expenditure by decile, and are split into a tax on direct expenditures on fuels and the indirect impact of carbon inputs. The direct impact of the tax is quite regressive, with the tax being two-point-three times as high as the proportion of expenditure in the bottom decile compared to the top decile. The indirect impact of the tax is flatter across the income distribution, with the bottom decile having a share of 45-per-cent-more expenditure. Combining the direct and indirect impacts produces a less regressive effect on the income distribution, in that the bottom decile now pays one-point-seven-eight times as much as the top decile.

**Table 7.4** Distribution of Share of Expenditure Type

| Decile | Electricity | Natural Gas | LPG | Coal | Peat | Kerosene and Oil | Diesel | Petrol |
|---|---|---|---|---|---|---|---|---|
| 1 | 2.9 | 32.1 | 5 | 15.6 | 18.2 | 2.6 | 0.2 | 0.2 |
| 2 | 2.2 | 32.5 | 5 | 17.4 | 24.1 | 4 | 0.2 | 0.3 |
| 3 | 2 | 32.7 | 11.7 | 12.1 | 23.7 | 3.5 | 0.2 | 0 |
| 4 | 1.5 | 37.5 | 13.7 | 10.9 | 22.3 | 2.7 | 0.3 | 0 |
| 5 | 2.1 | 42 | 13.3 | 8.8 | 23.5 | 1.9 | 0.3 | 0.3 |
| 6 | 2.1 | 45.4 | 15.6 | 6.5 | 21.5 | 2.4 | 0.2 | 0.2 |
| 7 | 2.1 | 43.8 | 18.6 | 5.9 | 24 | 2 | 0.3 | 0 |
| 8 | 2.2 | 49.2 | 18.3 | 5.8 | 20.5 | 1.8 | 0.4 | 0 |
| 9 | 1.5 | 44.8 | 22.7 | 4.7 | 22.8 | 1.5 | 0.4 | 0.2 |
| 10 | 1.7 | 48 | 24.7 | 3.3 | 19.8 | 1 | 0.3 | 0.1 |
| Total | 2 | 41.3 | 15.3 | 8.7 | 22 | 2.3 | 0.3 | 0.1 |
| 80/20 | 1.6 | 0.7 | 0.2 | 4.1 | 1 | 2.6 | 0.6 | 1.4 |

*Note*: Equivalized disposable income decile.

**Table 7.5** First-Round Impact of Carbon Tax (Carbon Tax as a Proportion of Expenditure)

| Equivalized Disposable Income Decile | Direct | Indirect | Direct and Indirect |
|---|---|---|---|
| 1 | 0.9 | 0.84 | 1.74 |
| 2 | 0.98 | 0.86 | 1.84 |
| 3 | 0.92 | 0.84 | 1.76 |
| 4 | 0.73 | 0.75 | 1.48 |
| 5 | 0.68 | 0.72 | 1.41 |
| 6 | 0.62 | 0.7 | 1.32 |
| 7 | 0.61 | 0.68 | 1.29 |
| 8 | 0.54 | 0.66 | 1.2 |
| 9 | 0.52 | 0.64 | 1.15 |
| 10 | 0.4 | 0.58 | 0.98 |
| Total | 0.62 | 0.69 | 1.31 |
| Ratio Bottom/Top | 2.27 | 1.45 | 1.78 |

### 7.5.1 Behavioural Change

The estimates for the tax levied above represent an upper bound. In the case of price increases, one would expect consumers to reduce their expenditures, and to substitute their expenditure towards goods with relatively lower price increases. This type of consumer behavioural change is one of the prime aims of a carbon tax. Essentially, goods with higher price increases will have generated higher proportions of carbon dioxide, and so have the biggest behavioural responses.

**Table 7.6** Own-Price Demand Elasticities

| Expenditure Group | Own-Price Elasticity |
|---|---|
| Food, non-alcoholic beverages | –49.5 |
| Alcoholic beverages | –75.6 |
| Tobacco | –46.6 |
| Clothing and footwear | –90.5 |
| Home fuels and electricity | –57.9 |
| Rents | 30.8 |
| Household services | –76.1 |
| Health | –77.4 |
| Private transport | –85.5 |
| Public transport | –100.8 |
| Communication | –58.9 |
| Recreation and culture | –67.5 |
| Education | –83.5 |
| Restaurants and hotels | –95.8 |
| Other goods and services | –74.1 |
| Natural gas | –39.8 |
| LPG | –105.4 |
| Coal | –15.3 |
| Sod peat | –24.5 |
| Kerosene | –36.1 |
| Diesel | –51.7 |
| Petrol | –52.8 |
| Durables | –69.8 |

In order to measure the behavioural responses to increases in prices due to a carbon tax, it is necessary to have a consumer-demand system, which includes values of own-price and cross-price elasticities. The method described in Chapter 6 is utilized here, using a linear expenditure to derive own-price, cross-price, and income elasticities for Ireland. An approach similar to Baker et al. (1990) is followed, using their microsimulation model for indirect taxation (SPIT) in producing estimates for own-price, cross-price, and budget elasticities of household expenditures on twenty-three types of goods. The results are presented in Table 7.6, which reports the own-price-demand elasticities, extending the method from Chapter 6 to incorporate a more disaggregated set of fuels. All goods have a plausible elasticity.

### 7.5.2 Policy Experiments

The model developed in previous sections is now used to simulate the impact of a carbon tax on the income distribution, total revenue, and the reduction in carbon dioxide as a result of behavioural response. The analysis examines

**Table 7.7** Tax as a Percentage of Total Expenditure and Disposable Income

| Equivalized Disposable Income Decile | Pre-Behavioural Response | | Post-Behavioural Response | |
|---|---|---|---|---|
| | As Percentage of Expenditure | As Percentage of Income | As Percentage of Expenditure | As Percentage of Income |
| 1 | 1.74 | 2.78 | 1.67 | 2.66 |
| 2 | 1.84 | 2.08 | 1.75 | 1.99 |
| 3 | 1.76 | 1.97 | 1.67 | 1.87 |
| 4 | 1.48 | 1.59 | 1.41 | 1.52 |
| 5 | 1.41 | 1.4 | 1.34 | 1.33 |
| 6 | 1.32 | 1.26 | 1.26 | 1.2 |
| 7 | 1.29 | 1.13 | 1.22 | 1.08 |
| 8 | 1.2 | 1.01 | 1.15 | 0.96 |
| 9 | 1.15 | 0.85 | 1.1 | 0.81 |
| 10 | 0.98 | 0.6 | 0.93 | 0.57 |
| Total | 1.31 | 1.12 | 1.25 | 1.07 |
| Ratio Bottom/Top | 1.78 | 4.65 | 1.78 | 4.65 |

**Table 7.8** Change in Expenditure on Goods as a Result of Indirect Carbon Tax (as Percentage)

| | Expenditure Group | Price Increase |
|---|---|---|
| 1 | Food, non-alcoholic beverages | –0.9 |
| 2 | Alcoholic beverages | –1.1 |
| 3 | Tobacco | –1.1 |
| 4 | Clothing and footwear | –2.2 |
| 5 | Home fuels and electricity | –2.2 |
| 6 | Rents | 0.3 |
| 7 | Household services | –5.9 |
| 8 | Health | –1 |
| 9 | Private transport | –1.4 |
| 10 | Public transport | –1.9 |
| 11 | Communication | –0.7 |
| 12 | Recreation and culture | –1 |
| 13 | Education | –1 |
| 14 | Restaurants and hotels | –1.5 |
| 15 | Other goods and services | –1.8 |
| 16 | Natural gas | –5.6 |
| 17 | LPG | –6.6 |
| 18 | Coal | –1.6 |
| 19 | Sod peat | –6.2 |
| 20 | Kerosene | –2.9 |
| 21 | Diesel | –5.1 |
| 22 | Petrol | –6 |
| 98 | Durables | –0.8 |
| 99 | Non expenditure | –1.3 |

**Table 7.9** Percentage Change in Carbon Emissions by Decile

| Equivalized Disposable Income Decile | Percentage Change in Carbon Emissions |
|---|---|
| 1 | −4.4 |
| 2 | −4.5 |
| 3 | −4.8 |
| 4 | −4.7 |
| 5 | −4.6 |
| 6 | −4.7 |
| 7 | −4.8 |
| 8 | −4.6 |
| 9 | −4.8 |
| 10 | −4.5 |
| Total | −4.6 |

the direct and indirect impact on the income distribution of a carbon tax. A carbon tax is modelled on all fuels that generate carbon dioxide. This will produce both the direct effect found, as above, and an indirect effect arising from the use of fuel, which is used as an input for household purchases.

Table 7.7 describes the impact of a carbon tax of €15 per ton of carbon dioxide as a share of expenditure, and of income before and after the behavioural response. The reform is of the order of about 1.3 per cent of expenditure and 1.1 per cent of income. Given the distribution of emissions, the impact is quite regressive. The impact is more pronounced for income, due to the structure of expenditure of households being less extreme than incomes, as many poorer households draw upon savings, while richer households save more. There is little behavioural difference pre and post behavioural response.

Table 7.8 describes the resulting change of behaviour for different groups, with fuels such as peat, petrol, and gas having the highest response at about 6 per cent. Household services have a high response, while food, durables, and communications have a low behavioural response. Applying these behavioural responses in Table 7.9, a change of about 4.6 per cent in total emissions is found. Relying on a relatively simple demand system, we do not find a significant difference between different deciles.

# PART IV

# DYNAMIC AND SPATIAL MODELS

# 8
# Decomposing Changes in Inequality Over Time

## 8.1 Introduction

Microsimulation models are often used to consider counterfactual situations and answering 'what if' questions. Chapter 7 used information about counterfactual incomes for those normally in work when out of work, and vice versa, to generate replacement rates. Similarly, information about simulated counterfactual incomes is used as input into an econometric model to estimate labour-supply behaviour.

The remaining chapters develop methodologies that explore the simulation of counterfactual income distributions. In this chapter, alternative income distributions are modelled to gauge the importance of individual income components. Later, Chapter 9 models alternative income distributions over time, incorporating intra-personal income mobility in simulating long-term economic processes and lifetime income distribution, and Chapter 10 utilizes simulation methods to develop spatial distributions of income.

There are a number of methodologies that can be used to understand the driving forces of inequality change. The seminal work of Shorrocks (1982, 1984) allowed for a non-parametric decomposition of inequality indices into income factors and population sub-groups, respectively. However, these methods decompose all changes that occur at a given time, but do not separately isolate the impact of individual components. Simulation-based methods have been developed that can be used to simulate counterfactual incomes if one or more component is changed. For example, using parametric-regression models, Oaxaca (1973) and Blinder (1973) tried to explain how much of the difference in mean outcomes is accounted for by group differences in the observed characteristics between two groups.

The literature based on Oaxaca's and Blinder's work is typically used to decompose differences in individual wages (Juhn et al. 1993). However, more complicated microsimulation models have been used to decompose the household income distribution. In the microsimulation literature, counterfactual

*Practical Microsimulation Modelling.* Cathal O'Donoghue. Oxford University Press. © Cathal O'Donoghue 2021.
DOI: 10.1093/oso/9780198852872.003.0008

income-generating processes (wages, employment, etc.) are simulated to assess the impact of alternative situations, such as the degree of inequality, using income-generating processes from another time period (Bourguignon et al. 2002) or country (Bourguignon et al. 2007).

The ground-breaking work of Oaxaca (1973) and Blinder (1973) set the stage for an extensive literature that uses the Oxaca–Blinder technique to decompose the differences in mean wages across population sub-groups with different characteristics. Juhn et al. (1993) and Blau and Khan (1996) utilized this method, combining data from one distribution with parameters from another, to simulate counterfactual distributions, in order to understand differences in earnings distributions. In a nut shell, the differences in mean wages reflect differences in the income-generation process (differences in the wage-regression parameters) and the differences in the joint distributions of observed characteristics between the sub-groups. Counterfactual wages are simulated to decompose wage differentials into an explained part due to group differences in productivity characteristics, (such as education or experience), and a residual 'unexplained' part. This unexplained part is often used as a measure for discrimination, although it includes all unobserved reasons.

Bourguignon et al. (2002) employed a broader set of equations or income-generation model to decompose changes in the distribution of market income over time into participation, occupational, and income-inequality components. DiNardo et al. (1996) used a semi-parametric method based upon kernel-density estimators, rather than regression parameters, to look at changing wage distributions over time, focusing on changing returns.

These papers, however, focus typically on the distribution of labour income or market income. Nevertheless, if one wants to consider the distribution of welfare, then the impact of taxes and benefits need to be considered. Bargain and Callan (2010) decompose changes in inequality into policy and other changes, utilizing tax-benefit microsimulation models to simulate counterfactual incomes. Bargain has built upon this work to develop an extensive literature of microsimulation-based decomposition papers in both OECD countries (Bargain 2012a; Bargain et al. 2017a) and developing countries (Bargain et al. 2017b).

This chapter utilizes, as a case study, Ireland, a developed country that experienced one of the highest sustained growth periods in recent decades, but also had one of the largest economic declines during the crisis period of 2007–12 (Jenkins et al. 2013). We will use the microsimulation framework to understand changes in inequality as the distribution of purchasing power associated with disposable income changed non-uniformly, using an

Oaxaca–Blinder–Bourguignon decomposition. This was in terms of income source, the composition of the population, the structure of the labour market, and the price growth.

## 8.2 Policy Context: Decomposition of Inequality

From a policy perspective, we are interested in understanding the process that generates the distribution of disposable income, so as to be able to make changes to the distribution. Inequality changes over time are examined to develop an understanding of the impact of demographic and education changes, their knock-on impact on market outcomes, and the consequential impact on tax liabilities and benefit entitlements. Differences across countries are also examined. Key to understanding these issues is the understanding of the underlying income-generation process. In this chapter, the concept of an income-generation model is introduced to help us to decompose the inequality into components.

The welfare derived from income depends upon the price paid and the amount of income available or disposable. Assuming that welfare is directly a function of income:

$$W = \frac{Y_D}{p}$$

Disposable income depends upon market income, benefits, and taxation, which are in turn dependent upon personal skills, family characteristics $Z$, and tax-benefit parameters $\theta$:

$$Y_D = Y_M(Z) - T(Z,\theta) + B(Z,\theta)$$

Market income is a function of income source $i$ $I_{M,i}$ and the amount $Y_{M,i}$. Each are a function of observable personal characteristics $Z$, unobservable characteristics $\varepsilon$, parameters $\theta$, and decomposition unit $t$, such as time period:

$$Y_M = \sum_i Y_{M,i}(Z,\theta_t,\varepsilon_t) \times I_{M,i}(Z,\theta_t,\varepsilon_t)$$

In order to understand the factors that influence inequality, and to design better policy, we would like to understand how the different influences on the components that affect income combine to generate the distribution of income.

### 8.2.1 Irish Case Study

After a very-high-growth period from the mid-1990s until the mid-2000s, growing from 115 per cent of EU gross domestic product (GDP) per capita in 1997 to a high point of 148 per cent in 2007[1], Ireland faced an unprecedented economic decline from late 2007, with a fall in real GDP/gross national product (GNP) per capita of 20.1 per cent/15.6 per cent from its peak in Q4 2007/Q4 2006 to Q4 2009/Q1 2012 (Figure 8.1a). The employment rate fell from a peak of 61.7 per cent, with 2.1 million in work in Q3 2007, to a low point of about 51 per cent in Q1 2012 (Figure 8.1b). Thus, in terms of national income per capita and employment, the decline occurred between a peak in 2007 and the lowest point in 2012. The main reasons for, and implications of, the economic crisis, were namely the response of a small, very open economy to the global economic and financial crisis, combined with the bursting of a property bubble, unsustainable construction sector, and banking-sector problems. The period saw large demographic changes, with high net immigration, followed by high net emigration, together with the largest birth cohorts in recent history.

Given these rapid economic changes, it is not surprizing that income growth from different sectors varied (Figure 8.1c), with a significant spread between sectors. For example, while the real-estate sector saw earnings decline by 29 per cent in 2007–12, industrial wages increased by 10 per cent. The consumer price index (CPI) grew 2.8 per cent during this period, with accommodation and restaurants, finance, administrative services and public administration, transportation, and education sectors seeing a growth rate of less than the CPI. While all sectors saw a decline in employment, construction saw a decline in employment of 40 per cent in 2007–12.

The impact of the decline in the labour market was felt in the household sector in a number of dimensions. Public-sector wages have been reduced via a number of policy changes.

## 8.3 Data Issues: Income-Generation Model

Cowell and Fiorio (2011) reviewed the two main strands of the inequality-decomposition methodology, utilizing a-priori approaches and explanatory models. A-priori approaches are essentially standard decompositions by population sub-groups (defined by different population characteristics) or

[1] See 'GDP Per Capita in Purchasing Power Standards (PPS) 1997–2008', Eurostat, Luxembourg.

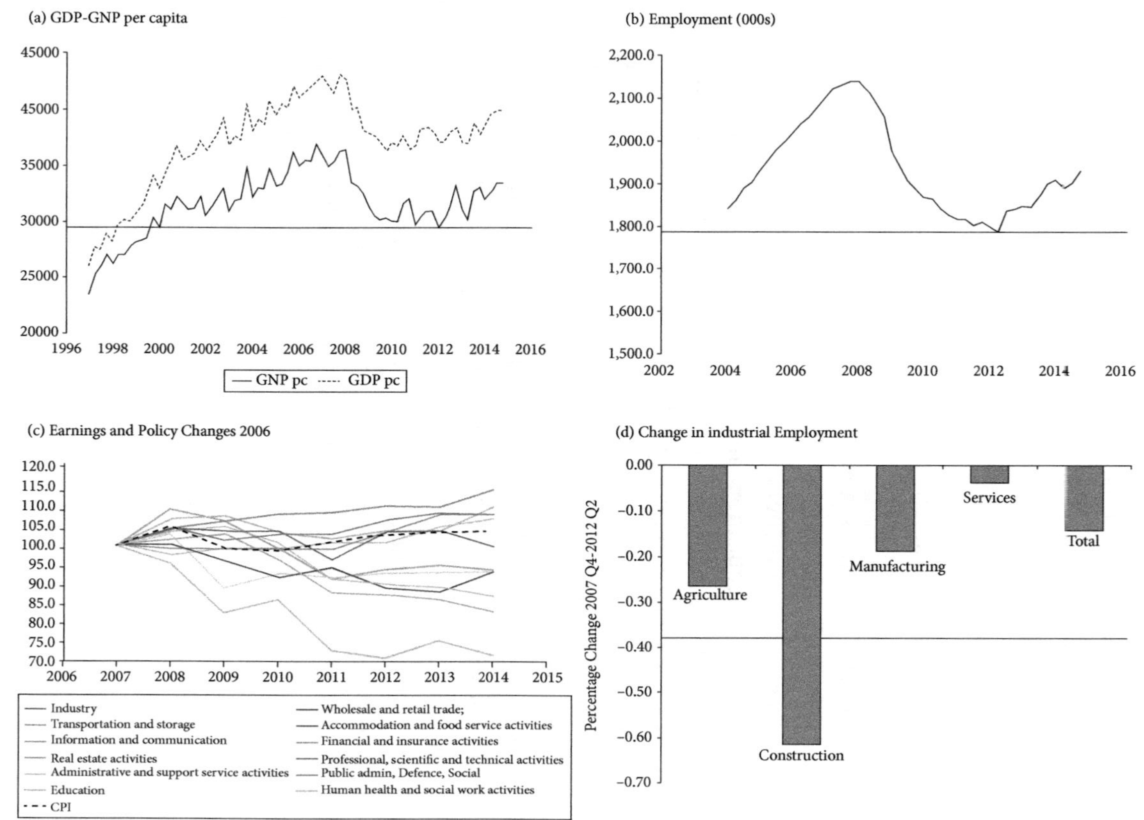


**Figure 8.1** National Accounts and Employment Rate 1996–2016

factor-source (Shorrocks 1982, 1984). A primary limitation of this approach lies in the difficulty in incorporating several explanatory factors, such as demographics and labour market. Other limitations include dependency on large sample sizes, as using many categories is not feasible in small samples, and there is considerable difficulty in assessing the influence of continuous variables such as age (Morduch and Sicular 2002). Using large numbers of categories also makes the calculations cumbersome. In addition, both subgroup- and factor-source-decomposition methods are also sometimes criticized as having poor explanatory power and as being irreconcilable one with another (Cowell and Fiorio 2011).

The regression-decomposition approach based on explanatory models was developed to address these limitations. The first step was taken by Fields (2003), and utilized by Fields and Yoo (2000), Redmond and Kattuman (2001), and Morduch and Sicular (2002), to investigate the contribution made by factors such as unemployment, labour-force participation, family status, age distribution, education, and inequality. This method can decompose the changes in inequality in a particular year into the contribution of characteristics (e.g., education composition, occupation composition), and returns to these characteristics. It is sometimes criticized on the basis that it is reliant on a single equation, typically based upon the relationship between disposable income and some explanatory variables.

One of the richest methods within this strand of microsimulation is the development of a structural model for inequality decomposition exemplified by Bourguignon et al. (2007), complemented with the semi-parametric reweighting techniques in the tradition of the DiNardo et al. (1996) approach to analysing the distribution of wages. This allows the comparison based on the means to be extended to comparing entire distributions. A similar approach is utilized in order to understand the differences in the distribution of household disposable income between two points in time $(f^t(Y_D)-f^{t-x}(Y_D))$.

Assuming that welfare is directly a function of income ($W$ = disposable income/price), disposable income $Y_D$ depends upon market income, benefits, and taxation, which are in turn dependent upon personal skills, individual and family characteristics ($Z$), and tax-benefit parameters ($\theta$):

$$Y_D = Y_M(Z) - T(Z,\theta) + B(Z,\theta).$$

Market income $Y_M$ is a function of the receipt of income source $i$, $I_{M,i}$, and the amount $Y_{M,i}$. Each are a function of the observable personal characteristics $Z$ that covariate with income, unobservable characteristics $\varepsilon$, parameters $\theta$, and the decomposition unit-time period $t$:

$$Y_M = \sum_i Y_{M,i}\left(Z, \theta_t, \varepsilon_t\right) \times I_{M,i}\left(Z, \theta_t, \varepsilon_t\right)$$

In order to understand the factors that influence the distribution of household disposable income, and to design better policies aimed at reducing poverty and inequality, it is necessary to understand how the different influences on the components that affect income combine to generate the distribution of income. Thus, in explaining the difference between the distribution of disposable income $f^t(Y_D) - f^{t-x}(Y_D)$, one needs to start from the joint distribution $\varphi^T\left(Y, Z\right)$ and its covariates. We follow the methodological exposition of the statistical decomposition in Bourguignon et al. (2007).

$Z$ is a set of variables which covariate with income, and are comprised of one set of exogenous demographics variables ($D$), such as age, education, marital status, number of children, and region, and another set composed of endogenous variables ($L$), which reflect the labour-market structure by occupation, sector, industry, and status in employment, which are modelled statistically depending also on $D$. The superscript $T$ reflects the time period.

The distribution of disposable income $f^T\left(Y\right)$ is the marginal distribution of $\varphi^T\left(Y, Z\right)$, which is the product of the conditional distribution of $Y$ on $L$ and $D$ ($g^T\left(Y \mid L, D\right)$) and the joint distribution of $Z$ ($h^T\left(L, D\right)$). By replacing $h^T\left(L, D\right)$ with the product of the conditional distributions for each element in $L$ and the joint distribution of demographic variables, $\psi^T\left(D\right)$, the distribution of disposable income in period $t$ and $t-x$ can be summarized by $f^t\left(Y\right) = f^t\left(Y, g^t, h^t, \psi^t\right)$ and $f^{t-x}\left(Y\right) = f^{t-x}\left(Y, g^{t-x}, h^{t-x}, \psi^{t-x}\right)$.

The difference between the two distributions can be investigated by replacing some of the observed conditional distributions ($g$, $h$), and/or the joint distribution of characteristics in $D$ in period $t$, with the corresponding conditional and/or joint distributions from period $t$–$s$. Each swapping generates a set of counterfactual distributions $f^s\left(Y, g^s, h^s, \psi^s\right)$ that would prevail in period $t$ had it had one (or more) conditional distributions and/or the joint distribution of $D$ from period $t$–$s$. The number of possible counterfactual distributions is the number of possible permutations in $\left(g, h, \psi\right)$. For each counterfactual distribution, the difference between the income distributions between periods can be decomposed:

$$f^t\left(Y\right) - f^{t-x}\left(Y\right) = [f^t\left(Y\right) - f^s\left(Y\right)] + [f^s\left(Y\right) - f^{t-x}\left(Y\right)].$$

The first term captures the distributional differences determined by the swapped factors, whereas the last term captures residual differences. These differences can be evaluated at any value of $Y$, and also for functions of these densities (Bourguignon et al. 2007). Thus, this approach can be used for comparing inequality indices and poverty measures, as well as measures of central tendency. This statistical decomposition can be applied to explore how inequality changes over time, the impact of demographic and education changes, their knock-on impact on market outcomes, and the consequential impact on tax liabilities and benefit entitlements. This chapter thus decomposes the changes in disposable household-income inequality.

In essence, this approach decomposes the differences in income distributions between two years using a sequence of counterfactual distributions that would prevail in year $t$, had it had one or more conditional distributions, and/or the joint distribution of exogenous factors from year $t{-}x$.

In practice, the challenge is to generate approximations to the true conditional distributions, and joint distributions of exogenous factors that would prevail under different 'what if' conditions. Several parametric and semi-parametric methods, or a combination of both methods, could be used to generate these approximations (Juhn et al. 1993; DiNardo et al. 1996; Hyslop and Maré 2005; Daly and Valletta 2006; Bourguignon et al. 2007; Fiorio 2011; Biewen and Juhasz 2012; Ferreira 2012).[2]

Most non-parametric and semi-parametric techniques, however, have been used for exploring wage differentials. More-complex income measures, such as household disposable income, which is determined by a high number of variables (human capital, labour-market and demographic characteristics, tax-benefit rules), require a parametric approach for generating counterfactual conditional distributions. Not only do the parameter estimates of the approximated statistical distributions have a direct economic interpretation, but also the income-generation process is more manageable when modelled fully parametrically (Bourguignon et al. 2007).

Going back to the definition of household disposable income (household market income – taxes + benefits), one has to model the complexity of each component. Household market income ($YM$) can be defined as the sum of income from employment, self-employment, capital, and other market sources:

$$Y_M = Y_{Emp} I_{Emp} + Y_{SE} I_{SE} + Y_{Cap} I_{Cap} + Y_{Other} I_{Other}$$

[2] Fiorio (2011) and Daly and Valletta (2006) use semi-parametric methods to decompose the changes in inequality in Italy and the US.

$Y_i$ is the income source $i$ and $I_i$ is the presence of this income. Both can be modelled as functions of $Y_i = f_i(Z, \theta_t, \varepsilon_{i,t})$ and $I_i = g_i(Z, \theta_t, \varepsilon_{i,t})$, where $Z$ is a set of personal characteristics, $\theta_t$ the parameters associated with the relevant model, and $t$ the time period. This method goes beyond the Oaxaca–Blinder-type models, in that the range of market incomes extends beyond employee income, as the distribution of household income depends not only on the returns and characteristics of its employed members but also on other income sources.

In addition, analysis at the household-unit level is more complicated than the Oaxaca–Blinder approach. The income-generation model requires, therefore, a system of equations capturing occupational/industry choices, the incomes associated with these choices, as well as the presence and level of other market-income sources. The system could also incorporate decisions such as fertility or education participation.

Another added value of the parametric approach is its greater flexibility to allow for the separation of the effect of labour-market factors (employment structure, returns, etc.) from the 'residual' population effect. Bourguignon et al. (2002) utilized this method to decompose changes in participation, wage rates, earnings-function residuals, and population trends associated with market income over time in Taiwan to understand changes in inequality. The parametric approach is also the basis of the analyses of Latin American countries in World Bank (2004).

Comparing differences in inequality across countries, Bourguignon et al. (2007) used a parametric method by simulating counterfactual distributions to understand differences in inequality across Brazil, Mexico, and the US. They expand the models, focusing solely on the wage distribution to incorporate labour-market participation, fertility behaviour, and educational choices. They use this decomposition to investigate the comparative roles of three factors: the distribution of population characteristics (or endowments), the structure of returns to these endowments, and the occupational structure of the population.

While market income in developing countries may approximate household welfare, the tax-benefit system in OECD countries substantially alters the distribution of income. A rapidly expanding number of studies (e.g., Bargain and Callan 2010; Creedy and Hérault 2011; Bargain 2012b) explore the extent to which the change in inequality can be explained by the tax-benefit system alone. Basically, these studies decompose the change in inequality into a policy effect and a 'residual' population effect using the counterfactual logic illustrated above. A parametric approach to the income-generation process allows one to separate out the effect of the labour market or some labour-market factors (e.g., occupational structure, market returns). The change in inequality can then be decomposed into a labour-market effect (where the employment-structure effect and wage-structure effect could also separated), a policy effect, and a residual population effect.

### 8.3.1 Parametric Income-Generation Model

The parametric income-generation model used to generate approximations of the true conditional distributions is composed of two modules: labour market and tax-benefit.

The labour-market module is a system of equations capturing:

- labour-market-status choices (in work/out of work)
- employee versus self-employed choices
- occupational and industry choices
- out-of-work status (inactive, unemployed, student, retired, disabled)
- incomes associated with these occupational choices, as well as the presence and level of other market-income sources

The model typically involves three types of models:

- binary model for binary choices and the presence of the income source
- multivariate-choice model
- Mincer-type-regression model for the level of income sources

In each case, the method involves estimating regression-model parameters $\beta$ and a measure of the error term $\varepsilon$.

Models of binary events, such as in work, use a logit model due to the computational ease of undertaking these simulations. In order to use the estimated probabilities from logistic models within a Monte Carlo simulation, a set of random numbers are drawn such that we predict the actual dependent variable in the raw data.

Once we have established whether an individual is in work or not, and their work status, such as employee, farmer, etc., multi-category choices such as occupation/industry are simulated using a reduced-form multinomial-logit model. In Bourguignon et al. (2007), the choices of inactivity, formal employment in industry, informal employment in industry, formal employment in services, or informal employment in services are modelled using a multinomial-logit model. Multinomial models may be used when the explanatory variables are not choice specific[3]:

$$P(Y = s) = \frac{e^{ZB_s}}{e^{ZB_s} + \sum_{j \neq s} e^{ZB_j}}$$

where $P(Y = s)$ is the probability of selecting choice $s$, and $Z$ are the set of personal characteristics. Disturbance terms for multi-category, dependent variables, such as occupation or industry, are derived from multinomial-logit models.

Once we have established the labour-force characteristics of each individual, the logged market-income variables may be modelled using an ordinary least-squares:[4]

$$Y_i = \exp\left(X^* B + \varepsilon\right),\ \varepsilon \sim N\left(0, \sigma^2_{\varepsilon,t}\right)$$

For each model, we require values of the disturbance terms for all individuals. We only recover $\varepsilon$ in an earnings equation for those that we observe to be in employment. However, it may be the case that an individual is simulated to be in employment in another period, and thus requires employee income to be simulated. In this case, we need a value for $\varepsilon$, thus a value is generated stochastically using a random draw from the distribution above. The same is true for the discrete choice (both binary and otherwise) described above.

As Mincer-type earnings models typically exhibit selection bias, it is common to estimate a Heckman-selection model (see Bourguignon et al. 2002).

In this section, the focus has been on models with an individual unit of analysis. However, the behaviour of individuals within a household, particularly between partners, is unlikely to be independent. One mechanism for incorporating this issue is to estimate the models jointly, where the error terms of spouses are correlated with each other. Yet, this can be difficult computationally. As a result, many models in this literature take the simultaneity between household member labour-supply decisions by estimating and simulating models sequentially. In addition, different models may be estimated depending on the position of a person in a family.

[3] There is a large literature on using choice-specific models for modelling multi-category choices, as in the case of structural labour-supply equations (Van Soest 1995; Callan et al. 2009). However, we use a calibration mechanism, described below, which dominates the behavioural operation of these models.

[4] Typically, the dependent variable is logged, as most market-income distributions are log-normal.

Having constructed the system of equations described above, the counterfactual distributions are simulated, swapping the parameters $\theta_t$, $\sigma^2_{\varepsilon,t}$ between time periods, while holding the residuals constant. The tax-benefit module is formed by a static microsimulation model, which models the tax-benefit rules in Ireland in both periods under analysis. A full validation of this model is described in O'Donoghue et al. (2013).

### 8.3.2 Data: Household Income Distribution in Ireland

The analysis in this chapter is based on the European Union Statistics on Income and Living Conditions (EU–SILC), a micro-dataset with detailed household and individual-level information on demographics, labour-market characteristics, incomes, and benefits. This survey has been carried out by Ireland's Central Statistics Office (CSO) since 2003. The EU–SILC is the successor to the earlier Living in Ireland Survey, which formed the Irish component of the European Community Household Panel (ECHP) Survey. The EU–SILC dataset is the primary source of analysis on poverty, inequality, and deprivation in Ireland.

The EU–SILC is collected at the national level, with a harmonized version supplied to Eurostat, which is then processed and provided to researchers as a user database (UDB). This analysis utilizes the Irish component of the EU–SILC UDB to model the income distribution. From 2004 to the present, each wave of the EU–SILC UDB contains between thirteen-and-fourteen-thousand individuals and more than four-thousand households. The EU–SILC contains a sizeable longitudinal component, and 75 per cent of households in each year are requested for interview in the following year. Savage et al (2015) show, however, that the retention rate is approximately 50–55 per cent due to attrition. The EU–SILC contains income data gross of taxes and contributions. The Irish component uses partial-survey and partial-register data, where 80 per cent of respondents allowed their national social-security number to be used to access administrative data in relation to their benefit entitlement (Callan et al. 2010).

A national weighting methodology is utilized, incorporating constraints (based upon gender, age-group, region, household composition) that in turn are based on population projections, using a combination of the census and the quarterly National Household Survey data (Callan et al. 2010). O'Donoghue et al. (2013) outline a number of challenges to utilizing the EU–SILC for microsimulation modelling. These include the treatment of policy instruments, which may require knowledge about inter-household units of analysis, e.g., higher-education grants and issues relating to the difference between the period of analysis for the income variables and the personal characteristics. The former typically refers to the year preceding the interview, while the latter typically refers to the time of the interview.

Thus, it is possible that there may be inconsistencies, as is the case of observing individuals who are classified as 'unemployed' in the interview year, but who have employment income in the data. Ireland has a slightly different definition, as the reference period spans two tax years: the income-reference period is 'twelve months prior to the date of the interview', while the end of the income-reference period is the date of the interview. As in the case of most tax-benefit microsimulation models, the definition of disposable income does not account for some missing variables, such as capital gains and wealth, or property values, and the taxes which may apply to these variables. This appears to be a reasonable assumption for an EU–SILC-based model.

Table 8.1 describes the change in equivalized disposable incomes over income distribution in Ireland in 2007–12. Disposable incomes fell on average by 10 per cent, with a narrowing of the income distribution during the crash, captured in a fall in the Gini coefficient by just over one point. As we will be modelling the change in the income distribution, these are simulated disposable incomes, using simulated market income, taxes, and benefits. However, the trend is consistent with those in the raw data, albeit given particular assumptions, such as full take-up of benefits.

Table 8.2 describes the changes to the employment structure in terms of industry and occupation. The industries with the largest fall in employment shares were agriculture and construction, while commerce and other sectors had the largest increase in share. The biggest fall in employment share by occupation was seen by managers, clerks, and craft workers. Associate professionals, sales workers, and skilled agricultural workers saw the highest rise in share.

In Table 8.3, we report the mean and distributional characteristics of sources of market income. The largest source of market income is income from employment, which fell over the period, reflecting the fall in

**Table 8.1** Changes in the Distribution of Equivalized Disposable Income 2007–12

| | 2007 | 2012 |
|---|---|---|
| Total | 25,169 | 22,581 |
| Gini coefficient (Simulated) | 0.304 | 0.292 |
| Gini coefficient (Raw) | 0.312 | 0.299 |

**Table 8.2** Occupation and Industry Share 2007–12

| Occupation Share | | | | | | | | | |
|---|---|---|---|---|---|---|---|---|---|
| | A | B | C | D | E | F | G | H | I |
| 2007 | 0.18 | 0.18 | 0.05 | 0.28 | 0 | 0 | 0.12 | 0.06 | 0.13 |
| 2012 | 0.08 | 0.18 | 0.11 | 0.25 | 0.01 | 0.08 | 0.09 | 0.08 | 0.13 |
| Industry Share | | | | | | | | | |
| | A | B | C | D | E | F | G | H | |
| 2007 | 0.06 | 0.10 | 0.12 | 0.17 | 0.05 | 0.28 | 0.15 | 0.05 | |
| 2012 | 0.04 | 0.07 | 0.12 | 0.21 | 0.05 | 0.28 | 0.16 | 0.07 | |

*Note*: Occupation: A—Managers; B—Professionals; C—Associated Professionals; D—Clerks; E—Service Workers; F—Skilled Agricultural Workers; G—Craft Workers; H—Plant Operators; I—Unskilled

Industry: A—Agriculture; B—Construction; C—Manufacturing; D—Commerce; E—Transport; F—Public Administration; G—Professional Services; H—Other

**Table 8.3** Distributional Characteristics of Market Income

| | 2007 | 2012 | 2007 | 2012 |
|---|---|---|---|---|
| | Mean | | Ratio Q5:Q3 | |
| Employment Income | 12,060 | 11,032 | 3.7 | 4.7 |
| Self-Employment Income | 1,891 | 1,058 | 5.1 | 3.4 |
| Capital Income | 954 | 266 | 4.8 | 5.2 |
| Other Income | 1,965 | 2,417 | 3.1 | 6.3 |
| Market Income | 16,871 | 14,774 | 3.5 | 3.8 |
| | 2007 | 2012 | 2007 | 2012 |
| | Mean | | Ratio Q5:Q1 | |
| In Work | 0.48 | 0.38 | 4.1 | 5.7 |
| University | 0.19 | 0.26 | 7.4 | 4.9 |
| Upper Secondary Educated | 0.26 | 0.24 | 1.3 | 1 |
| Age | 35 | 35.8 | 0.9 | 0.8 |
| Urban | 0.34 | 0.35 | 1.5 | 1.4 |
| Nch05 | 0.05 | 0.05 | 1.7 | 1.2 |
| Nch612 | 0.06 | 0.07 | 0.8 | 0.4 |
| Nch1317 | 0.07 | 0.06 | 0.5 | 0.3 |

employment. Self-employment and capital income also fell, with other income rising, due to an increase in recorded occupational-pension income in the data. We utilize the ratio of quintile 5 to quintile 3 as a measure of the distributional effect. We utilize quintile 3 as there is relatively little market income at the bottom of the distribution. In the case of employment income, capital, and other income, these income sources become more concentrated at the top of the distribution, while self-employment becomes less concentrated.

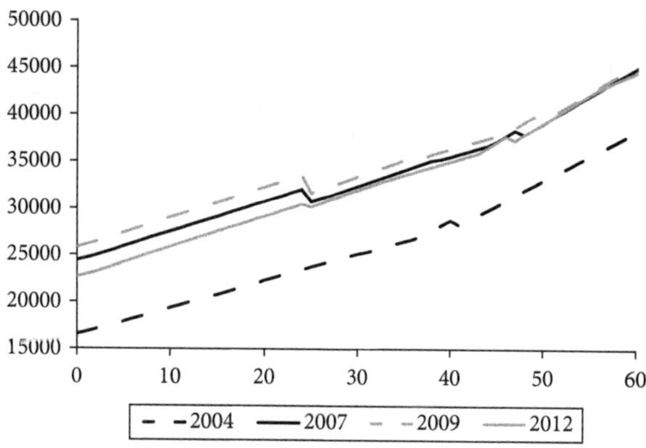


**Figure 8.2** Change in the Budget Constraint 2004–12

In Figure 8.2, trends in the overall budget constraint during the period 2004–12 are reported. In addition to the period after the crash, 2004 is included to highlight the change in purchasing power and redistribution in the period prior to the crash. These budget constraints reflect the disposable income associated with different hours worked at the averages, deflating by the CPI to account for changes to purchasing power. Wages are assumed to grow at the average rate for industrial employees. Most changes have been parametric, with some structural changes to 'income levies' or additional taxes, social-insurance contributions, and the introduction and abolition of a childcare supplement. Some of the changes applied to part-years. In order to incorporate this, looking at annual incomes, we apply a proportion of each set of policy parameters to the appropriate number of months.

In the period to 2007, the overall budget constraint flattens, with the ratio of disposable income for forty hours to zero hours decreasing from 1.74 in 2004 to 1.46 in 2007. It also continues to fall to 1.40 in 2009, before rising again to 1.55 in 2012. The period to 2007 also saw a steady rise in the level of the budget constraint, as the purchasing power for all parts of the budget constraint rose, as wage and benefit growth outstripped inflation. In 2009, the purchasing power of the bottom of the distribution rose, but fell at the top. In 2012, purchasing power fell for most groups, with the bottom group falling most.

## 8.4 Measurement Issues: Shapley-Value Decomposition

An issue that arises in the sequential decompositions based on (ordered) counterfactual distributions is path dependence (Bourguignon et al. 2001).

Effectively, the impacts of different characteristics, such as population, labour market, and earnings distribution, are simulated on alternative years, then the inequality measure is recalculated. The contribution made by each component depends, however, upon the order in which the component is replaced by a counterfactual.

Chantreuil and Trannoy (1999) and Shorrocks (1999) have proposed applications of the Shapley-value allocation method (Shapley 1953) to the decomposition of inequality by factor components that attempts to overcome the issue of path dependence. The Shapley-value decomposition defines an inequality measure as an aggregation (ideally a sum) of a set of contributory factors, whose marginal effects are accounted for by eliminating each of them in sequence and computing the average of the marginal contributions in all possible elimination sequences.[5] This technique considers the impact on overall inequality of eliminating each income source. However, we must average these impacts out over all possible sequences of elimination, as there is no natural order of elimination. Thus, in order to assess the effect of a given income source on overall inequality, we apply the before-after concept to the set of all possible combinations of income sources.

## 8.5 Simulation: Oaxaca–Blinder–Bourguignon Decomposition

We now consider an example simulation, where we estimate a system of equations or income-generation models and utilize the decomposition method described above—the Oaxaca–Blinder–Bourguignon method—to understand the driving forces of inequality change in Ireland over a period of economic crash in 2007–12. The change in inequality is decomposed into the effect of labour-market, market-income, and tax-benefit changes.

One of the potential drivers of inequality change is the change in the share of those with the highest levels of education observed. Ii is evident in Table 8.3 that the share of those with university education increased by 37 per cent. Table 8.4 reports the education coefficients for the main regression models used within the income-generation model, which, as described above, contains the presence and level of market-income sources, as well as the job characteristics of those in work.

[5] The Shapley-value decomposition, however, has some dilemmas that cannot be solved on purely theoretical grounds. Sastre and Trannoy (2002) propose a number of alternatives, including the nested-Shapley (Chantreuil and Trannoy 1999) and the Owen decomposition (Shorrocks 1999), based on defining a hierarchical structure of incomes which can overcome some of these issues.

Table [illegible].4 Regression Coefficients by Education 2007–12

| | Employment Income | | | Self-Employment Income | | | Capital Income | | | Other Income | | | Occupational Pension | | |
|---|---|---|---|---|---|---|---|---|---|---|---|---|---|---|---|
| | 2007 | 2012 | St. Diff. | 2007 | 2012 | St. Diff. | 2007 | 2012 | St. Diff. | 2007 | 2012 | St. Diff. | 2007 | 2012 | St. Diff. |
| Males | | | | | | | | | | | | | | | |
| $R^2$ | 0.38 | 0.31 | | 0.2 | 0.36 | | 0.08 | 0.08 | | 0.16 | 0.04 | | 0.26 | 0.25 | |
| rMSE | 0.84 | 0.87 | | 1.36 | 0.92 | | 1.29 | 2.13 | | 1.63 | 2 | | 1.7 | 1.26 | |
| Univ. | 0.64 *** | 0.61 *** | 0 | 0.67 *** | 0.89 *** | 0 | 0.57 *** | 0.59 * | 0 | 0.63 *** | 0.66 * | 0 | 1.79 *** | 1.02 *** | 1 |
| Up. Sec. Ed. | 0.32 *** | 0.16 *** | 1 | 0.28 ** | 0.52 *** | 1 | 0.26 ** | 0.2 | 0 | 0.43 *** | 0.48 | 0 | 1.03 *** | 0.25 *** | 1 |
| Females | | | | | | | | | | | | | | | |
| $R^2$ | 0.31 | 0.24 | | 0.203 | 0.355 | | 0.137 | 0.11 | | 0.064 | 0.064 | | 0.264 | 0.254 | |
| rMSE | 0.97 | 0.93 | | 1.363 | 0.92 | | 1.208 | 2.034 | | 1.349 | 1.349 | | 1.697 | 1.261 | |
| Univ. | 1.14 *** | 0.65 *** | 1 | 0.58 * | 0.18 | 0 | 0.61 *** | 1.38 | 1 | 0.01 *** | −0.16 *** | 1 | 1.73 *** | 1.74 *** | 0 |
| Up. Sec. Ed. | 0.53 *** | 0.13 ** | 1 | 0.23 | −0.2 | 0 | 0.36 *** | 0.96 | 1 | 0.28 *** | −0.1 *** | 1 | 1 *** | 1.07 *** | 0 |
| | Has In-Work Income | | | | | | Has Capital Income | | | Has Other Income | | | Has Occupational Pension | | |
| | 2007 | 2012 | St. Diff. | | | | 2007 | 2012 | St. Diff. | 2007 | 2012 | St. Diff. | 2007 | 2012 | St. Diff. |
| Males | | | | | | | | | | | | | | | |
| Pseudo $R^2$ | 0.31 | 0.23 | | | | | 0.12 | 0.03 | | 0.08 | −0.14 | | 0.27 | −0.48 | |
| Univ. | 1.2 *** | 1.08 *** | 0 | | | | 1.51 *** | 1.68 *** | 1 | −0.83 *** | −0.61 *** | 1 | 1.18 *** | 1.07 *** | 1 |
| Up. Sec. Ed. | 0.91 *** | 0.45 *** | 1 | | | | 0.99 *** | 0.83 *** | 1 | −0.48 *** | −0.1 | 0 | 0.8 *** | 0.77 *** | 1 |
| Females | Single | | | | | | | | | | | | | | |
| Pseudo $R^2$ | 0.40 | 0.30 | | | | | 0.10 | 0.22 | | 0.13 | −0.08 | | 0.34 | 0.33 | |
| Univ. | 1.89 *** | 1.46 *** | 1 | | | | 1.42 *** | 1.73 *** | 1 | −0.83 *** | −0.33 *** | 1 | 0.72 *** | 1.22 *** | 1 |
| Up. Sec. Ed. | 0.96 *** | 1.01 *** | 0 | | | | 0.96 *** | 1.01 *** | 0 | −0.34 *** | 0.16 | 1 | 0.28 ** | 0.24 * | 1 |
| Females | Couple | | | | | | | | | | | | | | |
| Pseudo $R^2$ | 0.32 | 0.25 | | | | | | | | | | | | | |
| Univ. | 1.85 *** | 1.56 *** | 1 | | | | | | | | | | | | |
| Up. Sec. Ed. | 0.88 *** | 0.77 *** | 0 | | | | | | | | | | | | |

The employment rate is higher for the higher educated; however, the coefficients in relation to the presence of employment declined over the period, although this was only significant for males with upper-secondary education and females (both single and in couples) with tertiary education. The relationship between education and employment income increased for males, but significantly decreased for females.

The coefficients for self-employment income rose (but not significantly) for university-educated individuals. Among the other income-presence equations, the return to education widened for capital incomes for women and for occupational pensions for women, but narrowed for men, while the coefficients increased for other income. Among income-level equations, the only significant changes were increases in capital incomes for women, falls in occupational pensions for men, and decreases for other income for women.

### 8.5.1 Decomposing Changes in Inequality

In order to decompose the change in inequality, we simulate the labour-market, market-income, and tax-benefit models on each data set, altering one component at a time, and comparing each of the two years 2007 and 2012. There are sixteen possible combinations of the components.

Averaging the change in the Gini coefficient associated with each individual change as per the Shapely transformation, Table 8.5 reports the average contribution change to inequality of each of the components. The sum of the contributions equals the total change in the Gini coefficient year on year.

The falling employment rate saw the labour-market changes result in increased inequality during the crisis. Meanwhile, the changes in market incomes were inequality reducing. Among the components of market income, the changes in employment earnings were inequality increasing, albeit counterbalanced by other income sources, such as self-employment income and

**Table 8.5** Decomposing Change in Gini Coefficient of Equivalized Disposable Income

| Average | Demographic and Data | Labour Market | Market Income | Tax-Benefit | Total Change |
|---|---|---|---|---|---|
| 2007–12 | 0.010 | 0.016 | −0.010 | 0.002 | 0.018 |

*Note*: Changes represent the Shapley values or average across each of sixteen possible transitions between each of two years.

Equivalence scale used: square root of number of persons in the households.

*Source*: European Union Statistics on Income and Living Conditions (EU–SILC), author's simulations.

other income with inequality-reducing effect. The change in population, particularly the increase in education, as well as sampling error, had an increasing effect on inequality.

In Table 8.6, the average and distributional characteristic of market, gross (market plus benefits), and disposable (gross minus taxes and charges) incomes are reported for each of the sixteen combinations in the transition of 2007–12. In relation to market income, moving from 2007–12, data increases market income by 29 per cent when we have 2007 labour markets and 2007 market-income distributions, by 10 per cent when we have 2007 labour markets and 2012 market-income distributions, by 24 per cent when we have 2012 labour markets and 2007 market-income distributions, and by 18 per cent when we have 2012 labour markets and 2012 market-income distributions. Thus, the first effect is the result of the higher education levels, which is unambiguously average-income increasing. However, the lower rate of growth in market income, when 2012 data are used (containing higher-education levels), results from a decline in non-work income when 2012 data are applied, while the increase in education levels increases work income.

**Table 8.6** Equivalized Household Income Under Different Pathways

| | | | | Market Income | | Gross Income | | Disposable Income | |
|---|---|---|---|---|---|---|---|---|---|
| D | L | M | TB | Average | Ratio Q5:Q3 | Average | Ratio Q5:Q1 | Average | Ratio Q5:Q1 |
| 2007 | 2007 | 2007 | 2007 | 27,454 | 3.3 | 31,757 | 7 | 49,959 | 5.4 |
| 2012 | 2007 | 2007 | 2007 | 35,478 | 3.8 | 40,253 | 8.5 | 62,757 | 6.3 |
| 2007 | 2007 | 2012 | 2007 | 26,094 | 3.3 | 30,091 | 7.3 | 48,059 | 5.7 |
| 2012 | 2007 | 2012 | 2007 | 28,802 | 3.6 | 33,411 | 7.6 | 52,831 | 5.9 |
| 2007 | 2012 | 2007 | 2007 | 22,830 | 4 | 27,358 | 8.6 | 46,079 | 6.6 |
| 2012 | 2012 | 2007 | 2007 | 28,278 | 3.8 | 33,594 | 8.4 | 53,150 | 6.2 |
| 2007 | 2012 | 2012 | 2007 | 19,856 | 3.8 | 24,101 | 8.9 | 42,078 | 7 |
| 2012 | 2012 | 2012 | 2007 | 23,430 | 3.6 | 28,464 | 7.5 | 45,439 | 5.8 |
| 2007 | 2007 | 2007 | 2012 | 27,449 | 3.2 | 31,767 | 6.5 | 50,050 | 5.2 |
| 2012 | 2007 | 2007 | 2012 | 35,478 | 3.8 | 40,168 | 8.4 | 63,895 | 6.4 |
| 2007 | 2007 | 2012 | 2012 | 23,594 | 3.2 | 27,634 | 6.5 | 45,145 | 5.3 |
| 2012 | 2007 | 2012 | 2012 | 28,802 | 3.6 | 33,297 | 7.6 | 53,952 | 6 |
| 2007 | 2012 | 2007 | 2012 | 22,830 | 4 | 27,385 | 8.4 | 46,869 | 6.5 |
| 2012 | 2012 | 2007 | 2012 | 28,278 | 3.8 | 33,541 | 8.3 | 53,494 | 6.2 |
| 2007 | 2012 | 2012 | 2012 | 19,856 | 3.8 | 24,168 | 9 | 42,580 | 7.1 |
| 2012 | 2012 | 2012 | 2012 | 23,430 | 3.7 | 28,414 | 7.5 | 45,894 | 5.9 |

Utilizing 2012 data increases market-income inequality, as measured by the quintile ratio when we utilize 2012 markets, but it reduces when 2012 labour markets are used.

The introduction of 2012 labour-market characteristics unambiguously reduces incomes due to the large fall in employment. The 2012 labour market is inequality increasing. The introduction of 2012 market incomes also reduces incomes, with the effect slightly lower when 2012 data are used, and lower when 2012 labour markets are used. While reducing incomes, inequality is also slightly reduced in moving from 2007 market incomes to 2012 market incomes. As there is no policy endogeneity in the model, market income remains unchanged when alternative tax-benefit systems are modelled.

## 8.6 Validation Issues

### 8.6.1 Shapely Transformation

We are interested in the variability of these routes, and to understand the sources of variability. Figure 8.3 presents the average change across the sixteen potential routes from 2007–12 of the four different drivers considered under the Shapely transformation. The potential impact of each component can vary quite substantially, by as much as 6 percentage points. The population (demographic and data) component has the widest range, from a reduction of 2 percentage points to an increase of 4.2 percentage points. Changes to the labour market have the next biggest change, varying from an

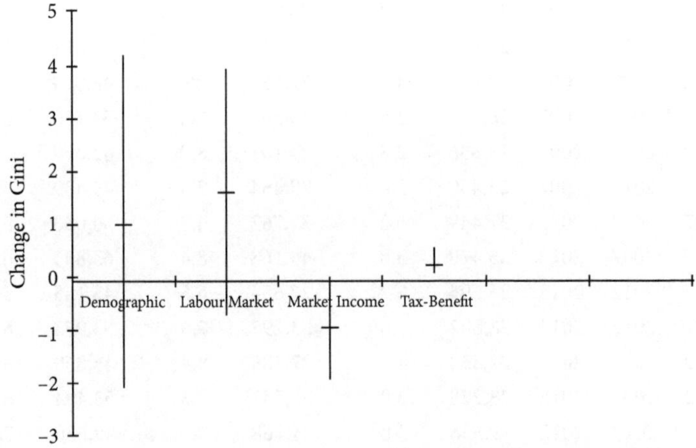


**Figure 8.3** Sensitivity of Order of Simulation on Change in Gini Coefficient 2007–12

inequality reduction of 0.7 percentage points to an increase of 3.9 percentage points, with a range of 4.6 percentage points. Market-income variability sees a range of 1.9 percentage points from an increase of 0.02 percentage points to a reduction of −1.9 percentage points. Each of these components span zero, so that the change in each component can be inequality increasing or inequality decreasing, depending upon the order of simulation. Last, the inequality-reducing effect of the tax-benefit system has the smallest variability, varying from 0.08–0.54 percentage points, depending upon the order.

Thus, the order of simulation can be very important, with hugely different conclusions, depending upon the order taken. While we have sixteen possible combinations of the components, we have twenty-four (four by three by two by one) possible pathways from inequality in year *t*–1 to inequality in year *t*. For example, starting in 2007, it is possible to have four initial possible moves to 2012 first: demography and data, labour market, earnings variability, or tax-benefit system. In the second transition, there are three potential changes, excluding the first change, then two, excluding the first two, and finally one change.

Figure 8.4 plots each of the twenty-four routes between inequality levels in the two years. The impact of the first change has the biggest variability in effect. This plot raises a number of questions in relation to what drives the extremes. Of the twenty-four pathways, twelve of the demography-data and the labour-market components are negative, and twelve are positive, with the

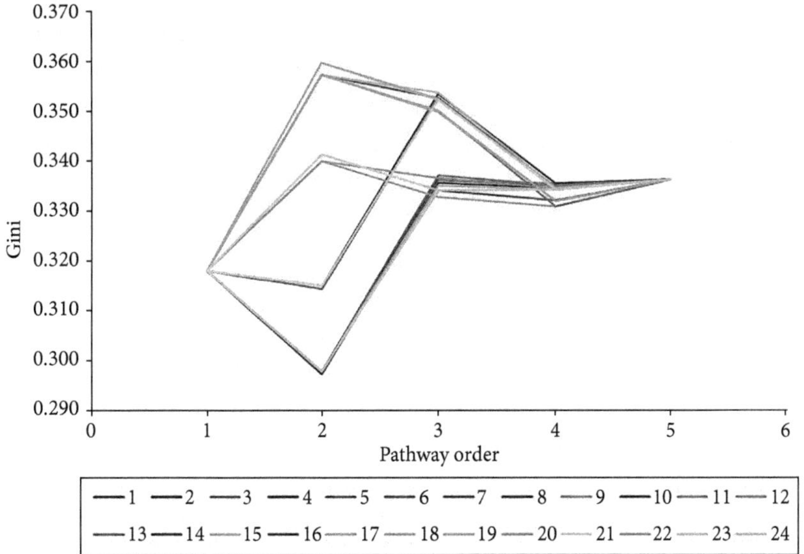


**Figure 8.4** Inequality Pathways 2007–12

*Note*: 1–inequality in 2007; 2–change due to demography and data; 3–change due to labour market; 4–change due to market income; 5–inequality in 2010 resulting from change in tax-benefit system.

**Table 8.7** Decomposing Change in Gini Coefficient of Equivalized Disposable Income

| Average | Demographic and Data | Labour Market | Market Income | Tax-Benefit | Total Change (ex-Data) | Total Change |
|---|---|---|---|---|---|---|
| Mean | | | | | | |
| Transition | | | | | | |
| 2007–12 | 0.010 | 0.016 | –0.010 | 0.002 | 0.008 | 0.018 |
| 2007 Data | | 0.038 | –0.001 | 0.002 | 0.038 | |
| 2012 Data | | –0.006 | –0.018 | 0.003 | –0.021 | |
| Number of Inequality-Increasing Transition | | | | | | |
| 2007–12 | 12 | 12 | 2 | 24 | | |
| 2007 Data | | 6 | 1 | 6 | | |
| 2012 Data | | 0 | 0 | 6 | | |

*Note*: While there are twenty-four potential pathways when both 2007 and 2012 data are used, there are only six when one data point is used.

positive higher than the negative, resulting in a positive average. For the market-income component, in twenty-two pathways the impact is inequality reducing, and for eight the market impact is inequality reducing, while in all twenty-four of the pathways, the impact of the tax-benefit system is inequality increasing.

To help us to understand these transitions further, consider separately the decomposition when we use either the 2007 or the 2012 transition in Table 8.7. Utilizing 2007 data results in the labour market increases inequality in all six transitions, with an average of a 0.038 percentage points increase. Meanwhile, with 2012 data, none of the transitions increase inequality, with an average of –0.006 percentage points decrease. For market income, the average increase is negative at –0.01, but with a similar number of pathways with increasing inequality of 1 percentage point using 2007 data and 0 percentage points using 2012 data. In either dataset, the tax-benefit system increases inequality in each pathway in a similar way.

The main difference in the main explanatory variables between the two datasets is education, with the share of those with tertiary education increasing by 40 per cent in 2007–12. This is likely to be due to cohort shifts in education levels and differential migration. There are only marginal differences to other age, spatial, or family characteristics data. Because of the greater number of third-level educated individuals, and the lower impact of education on being in work, there is a greater spread of this group across the income distribution. Thus, with a transition from a 2007 labour market to a 2012 labour market, we see an increase in inequality using 2007 data with a lower-education level, but with the higher-education levels in 2012, we see a very marginal change in inequality.

# 9

# Pension Reform and Life-Course Distributions

## 9.1 Introduction

In order to carry out micro-level analyses of economic behavior, and of the influence of public policy over time, such as examining the redistributive impact of the tax-benefit system over the life course, it is necessary to utilize a panel dataset with many years of data.[1] In general, such datasets are not available, either because the analysis relates to the future, as in the case of pension projections, or because existing datasets do not cover sufficiently-long time horizons. Instead, therefore, dynamic microsimulation models are used to synthetically generate a hypothetical panel. In this chapter, we discuss some of the methodological issues related to the construction of a dynamic microsimulation model, surveying current practice in the field across the world (for surveys of dynamic microsimulation, see Zaidi and Rake 2001; O'Donoghue 2001a; Li and O'Donoghue 2012).

Building upon the work in Chapter 8, we develop the concept of income-generation models to model changing income distributions over time. We also introduce the concept of alignment, which allows us to calibrate the aggregate results of income-generation models to external control totals. There have been a number of survey articles written over time (including O'Donoghue 2001; Li and O'Donoghue 2013; Li et al. 2014; Dekkers and Van den Bosch 2016; O'Donoghue and Dekkers 2018) that have described the progress of the field and reviewed the modelling choices made by different dynamic microsimulation models.

The principal uses of dynamic microsimulation models can be classified into a number of headings (Li and O'Donoghue 2012). Dynamic microsimulation models project samples of the population over time. If a full cross-section of the population is projected, then one can examine future income distributions under different economic and demographic scenarios

[1] This chapter draws upon work co-authored with Jinjing Li.

*Practical Microsimulation Modelling.* Cathal O'Donoghue. Oxford University Press. © Cathal O'Donoghue 2021.
DOI: 10.1093/oso/9780198852872.003.0009

(Wertheimer et al. 1986; Favreault and Smith 2004; Harding 2007b). These projected cross-sections can then be used to evaluate the future performance of various governmental long-term programmes, such as pensions, health and long-term care, and educational financing.

In addition, the existence of baseline projections also allows one to design new public policy by simulating the effect of potential reforms, such as pension reform (O'Donoghue 2009; Kennell and Sheils 1990; Galler and Wagner 1986; Falkingham and Johnson 1995), or education finance (Hain and Helberger 1986; Harding 1993; Flannery and O'Donoghue 2011), or social-insurance reforms (Fölster 1997). As inter-temporal models, they can be used to study inter-temporal processes and behavioural issues, such as wealth accumulation (Keister 2000; Baekgaard 1998; Stroombergen et al. 1995), intergenerational transfers (O'Donoghue 2009; Baroni et al. 2009), demographic behaviour of women (Lutz 1997), or the impact of tax-benefit systems on labour-market mobility (Klevmarken and Olovsson 1996).

Single-cohort models have been used to investigate life-course redistribution in tax-benefit systems, and the degree of redistribution between life-rich and life-poor versus redistribution over one's life course (see Harding 1993; O'Donoghue 2001b; Baldini 1997; Falkingham and Hills 1995), or inter-cohort redistribution issues such as the redistributive impact of the social-security system on different cohorts (Nelissen 1996; Caldwell et al. 1998), or intergenerational transfers (Rowe and Wolfson 2000; Bonnet and Mahieu 2000; Blanchet et. al. 2009), or issues associated with health status over the life course (Propper 1995; Will et. al 2001).

The chapter is divided into sections as follows. First, Section 9.2 discusses the model components. Next, Section 9.3 discusses methodological issues related to dynamic modelling, such as static versus dynamic ageing, behavioural versus statistical simulation, discrete versus continuous time, open versus closed models, steady state versus forecasted projections, cohort versus population models, and validation. Then, Section 9.4 discusses the calibration method known as alignment, and in Section 9.5, we describe how to quantify inter-temporal redistribution, between and within life trajectories. Finally, Section 9.6 describes the distribution of income over a lifetime using a Chilean case study.

## 9.2 Policy Context: Pensions and Ageing

The analysis of ageing and related pensions policy is one of the main uses of dynamic microsimulation models. Pension eligibility typically depends upon the accumulation of entitlement over time, and as such it requires the inter-temporal component of dynamic microsimulation models.

Pensions policy has become of increasing relevance for policy makers, particularly in OECD countries, as it interacts with the process of demographic ageing, due to a combination of both falling birth and mortality rates resulting in longer life expectancy (Falkingham and Johnson 1992; OECD 1996; European Commission 2007; Börsch-Supan et al. 2018). Changes in retirement ages and eligibility for pensions has not kept pace with the ageing of the population, and thus an increasing proportion of the population will be inactive due to retirement and in receipt of pensions, subsequently increasing the dependency ratio. In the OECD countries, for instance, the old-age dependency ratio is expected to double by 2050 to around 40 per cent, compared to an average 18 per cent in the 1990s (OECD 1996). This has negative economic consequences, such as higher pension and health-care costs, lower private and national savings, lower growth, and, eventually, higher poverty and inequality.

Ageing poses sustainability challenges for public policy in terms of the cost of funding pensions and other old-age-related programmes, accompanied by a smaller share of working-age populations and income, with consequential negative imbalances for public finances.

The flip side of this pressure on public finances is the distributional impact that policy changes will have. The elderly in many countries have higher poverty rates than the working-age population (see Tsakloglou 1996; Pacolet et al. 2018). Dynamic microsimulation models are particularly well suited to analysing distributional impacts of policy issues such as this.

Addressing these challenges involves not only parametric changes to pensions policies, such as the relative generosity, but also may involve structural changes to policy, such as moves to a more or less redistributive system. It may also be accompanied by changes that involve addressing micro-behaviour, such as raising labour-market participation among the elderly, or incentivizing higher fertility rates. Understanding these issues may require methodologies that incorporate behavioural feedbacks from policy, thus requiring an inter-temporal-choice framework analogous to the short-term frameworks discussed in Chapter 5.

The interplay of micro-level processes and policies, ageing, and pensions, have macroeconomic consequences. These create challenges for models, requiring ideally a macroeconomic interaction to address issues associated with the public-finance imbalance identified above. These processes also present a political challenge. As the population ages, the balance of political power may change, which may in turn have an impact on the public choice-making mechanisms. Ageing may, therefore, have an impact in relation to increasing costs, and thus, from an economic perspective, may result in a pressure to reduce costs, while at the same time having a higher population share, resulting in a pressure to increase costs (see Abid-Fourati and O'Donoghue 2010).

Another socio-economic perspective that influences the interplay between population structure and pension outcomes is the life cycle. Later life-cycle cohorts are likely to be more educated, to have spent less time in the labour market earlier in their lives (having spent time at university), to have experienced more uncertain labour-market and different working patterns (e.g., more part-time and fixed-term employment), and to have encountered marriage dissolution, etc. (Falkingham and Hill 1995). These changes may happen in tandem with population ageing, and so the effects may interact, changing the potential impact of ageing. Thus, a life-cycle-change perspective is important in understanding how 'ageing' will affect the living standards of future elderly, and consequently of an 'aged' population. For instance, dependency ratios might not look as bad as current projections show, if future generations have different (longer) work histories relative to current cohorts. Indeed, as ageing takes place, Rowntree's (1902) traditional life cycle theory of 'want and plenty' associated with different stages of life (Falkingham and Hills 1995) might no longer hold.

## 9.3 Data and Modelling Issues

A dynamic microsimulation model essentially consists of two components:[2]

- a data-generation process that produces a panel dataset under alternative scenarios
- a policy analysis applied to the generated dataset

In this section, we consider the mechanism by which the data-generation process can produce a panel dataset.

The potential uses of a dynamic microsimulation model are influenced by a number of factors, including:

- the initial base dataset
- the types of processes simulated
- the types of policy instruments incorporated in the model

[2] In preparing the literature review, I have drawn extensively on the work of Li and O'Donoghue (2012).

In this section, we also consider a number of methodological issues relating to dynamic microsimulation models. These affect choices we make in relation to:

- static versus dynamic ageing models
- behavioural versus probabilistic models
- competing risks: discrete versus continuous time
- steady state versus forecasted projections
- cohort versus population models
- link between micro-models and macro-models
- validation

### 9.3.1 Static Versus Dynamic Ageing

If the objective is to generate cross-sections of the population, consistent with scenarios associated with projections of the future, and then to analyse policy impacts on this population, either static or dynamic ageing models can be used.

Static ageing takes macro-aggregates and then adjusts the underlying distribution using reweighting to produce projections of the population distribution over time (see Creedy 2003; Immervoll et al. 2005; O'Donoghue and Loughrey 2014). It is an ageing procedure that takes a sample whose underlying characteristics are held constant, while the weights given to different parts of the sample are changed through the use of a dynamic reweighting mechanism to produce different weighted distributions, corresponding to expected characteristics in the future.

While a relatively simple method to apply, static ageing has a number of theoretical objections (Klevmarken 1997). The most obvious issue is that static ageing does not capture longitudinal change at the individual level. In a steady-state world, this may not be much of a problem; however, given the relatively frequent policy reforms that occur in the area of pensions, the pattern of life-cycle contributions at one time may not be consistent with those from another period. Where there are low or no individuals of a particular type, static ageing will require high weights, with resulting unstable results. Changing demographic and economic trends over time may mean that increasing weight is placed on population types, with very few cases in the sample. In addition, static ageing assumes that the characteristics within a weighted group do not change over time.

Static-ageing procedures are relatively well suited to short-to-medium-term forecasts, of approximately three to five years, where it can be expected that large changes have not occurred in the underlying population. However, over longer periods of time, it may be more difficult to use static ageing, due to changing characteristics of the population.

Dynamic ageing involves the estimation of a system of equations that can project individual characteristics at the micro-level. An income-generation model, as described in Chapter 8, takes the following form:

$$Y_M = Y_{Emp} I_{Emp} + Y_{SE} I_{SE} + Y_{Cap} I_{Cap} + Y_{Other} I_{Other}$$

where $Y_i$ is income source $i$, and $I_i$ is the presence of this income, and where $Y_i = f_i\left(Z, \theta_t, \varepsilon_{i,t}\right)$ and $I_i = g_i\left(Z, \theta_t, \varepsilon_{i,t}\right)$ for all income sources $i$.

The income-generating process in a dynamic model is slightly different. Estimating on historical data and simulating into the future means that the parameters are to some extent time-invariant. We will, however, discuss later how we can calibrate the system using alignment, to be able to run alternative and time-specific scenarios, which might be regarded as altering the intercept. Thus the models will take the form:

$$Y_i = f_i\left(Z, \theta, \varepsilon_{i,t}\right)$$

and

$$I_i = g_i\left(Z, \theta, \varepsilon_{i,t}\right)$$

Typically, as the models are inter-temporal, we will usually use a panel-data specification, where the error term $\varepsilon_{i,t}$ will be a function of an individual fixed effect $u_i$ and a residual noise term $v_{i,t}$, which may itself have a more-complicated structure, incorporating an ARMA[3] process:

$$\varepsilon_{i,t} = u_i + v_{i,t}$$

In a dynamic microsimulation model, the number of observations is not constant, as there are, typically, new births and deaths, and also, potentially, migrants. In addition, many of the variables of interest are time-invariant, such as gender, parental characteristics, and date of birth, etc. Therefore, it is not possible to utilize a fixed-effects, panel-data model, rather, a random-effects model is necessary. Nevertheless, random-effects-model coefficients are only unbiased if:

[3] Auto-regressive moving average (ARMA).

$$Cov(Z, u_i) = 0$$

However, often this assumption is broken. In this case, it is possible to utilize a Mundlak approximation. Splitting $Z$ into $Z1$ and $Z2$, respectively time-variant and time-invariant explanatory variables, produces:

$$u_i = \gamma \bar{Z}_{1,i} + \eta_i$$

In a cross-sectional model, it may be reasonable to assume that demographic characteristics are exogenous, as in the case of income-inequality decomposition. However, in a dynamic microsimulation model, it should be noted that nearly all the variables are endogenous. As a result, we also require models of these variables, including fertility, mortality, partnership formation and dissolution, and education outcomes, etc., such that:

$$Z_i = h_i(X, \theta, \varepsilon_{i,t})$$

where $X$ represents explanatory variables.

Equations in a dynamic microsimulation model are typically estimated individually, with error terms assumed to be independent between individuals in the same households. Inter-personal correlations are captured via sequential estimation. It may be more appropriate to jointly estimate the entire system, but due to data limitations this is generally infeasible.

## 9.3.2 Behavioural Versus Probabilistic Models

The equations described above can be either behavioural or probabilistic. Klevmarken (1997) categorizes three types of behavioural adjustments in a dynamic microsimulation model: imputation of missing data, updating of simulation population, and behavioural adjustments to policy changes. We concentrate here on the latter two. Behavioural models are grounded in economic theory, in the sense that changes to institutional or market characteristics result in a change in the behaviour of agents within the model. A probabilistic model, on the other hand, attempts to reproduce observed distributional characteristics in sample surveys without necessarily a theoretical underpinning, and so they may or may not be able to dynamically respond to external market and institutional characteristics.

Updating of the simulation population, also known as probabilistic modelling, is a process used to age a sample. This method refers to the functions used to simulate mortality, fertility, family formation, and labour-market transitions, etc. They are not necessarily grounded in microeconomic theory, but are a probability-based method, and do not depend on the policy parameters in the model. In practice, many transitions are based on only a small number of factors, such as age and sex. Methods that can be used include regression models, Markov processes, and survival functions. This is an example of a probabilistic dynamic model. The marginal distribution of $Y_1$ after tax-labour income, $f_{Y_1/Y_2,X_1}$ depends on the marginal distribution of hours worked $f_{Y_2/X_2}$. In this model, hours worked does not depend on the tax system, and, therefore, fits our example of a probabilistic model:

$$f_{YX}(Y,X/P)=f_{Y_1/Y_2,X_1}(Y_1/Y_2,X_1,P)\cdot f_{Y_2/X_2}(Y_2/X_2)\cdot f_X(X)$$

This is thus an example of a non-behavioural income-generation model.

It might, however, be expected that changing economic and social policies would have an impact on behaviour. Klevmarken's third approach relates to models of this kind. In a behavioural model, where individual behaviour changes as a result of changing policies, the policy parameters must have a direct or indirect impact on the model. An example includes the models of labour supply that respond to changes in the tax-benefit system, as described in Chapter 5. This equation can be expanded to introduce a new decomposition of $Y$. These include:

- $Y_1$, the alignment targets of the simulation, endogenous variables, which impact on $Y_1$
- $Y_2$ endogenous variables, which do not depend on policy parameters
- $Y_3$ endogenous variables, which depend upon policy parameters

In our example, $Y_3$ might still be hours worked, but now takes the form of a Hausman-type labour-supply model (Hausman 1981):

$$f_{YX}(Y,X/P)=f_{Y_1/Y_2,Y_3,X_1}(Y_1/Y_2,Y_3,X_1,P_{11})\cdot f_{Y_2/X_2}(Y_2/X_2)\cdot$$
$$f_{Y_3/X_2}(Y_3/X_3,P_{13})\cdot f_X(X)$$

Stability of the parameters is a requirement of behavioural models. The parameters of the behavioural model must not change as a result of a policy change. One of the problems encountered with behavioural models is how to cope with individual heterogeneity. For example, a reduction in taxes may increase the labour supply of a low-income worker, but reduce the labour supply of a high-income worker. A potential way around this problem is to make the behavioural response state-dependent:

$$f_{YX}(Y,X/P) = f_{Y_1/Y_2,Y_3,X_1}(Y_1/Y_2,Y_3,X_1,P_{11}) \cdot f_{Y_2/X_2}(Y_2/X_2) \cdot$$
$$f_{Y_3/X_3}(Y_3/X_3,P_{13},P_0,Y_0,Y_{30}) \cdot f_X(X)$$

The behavioural part of this equation accounts for state dependence by making the marginal distribution of the behavioural variable $Y_3$ dependent on not only the policy, but also the type of policy system $P_0$, and the original states, $Y_3$ and $Y_{30}$.

Pudney and Sutherland (1996) have found that predictions based on behavioural models have very wide confidence intervals. Also, the addition of feedback loops from tax-benefit algorithms can substantially increase the time of simulation. For these reasons, builders of microsimulation models have often opted not to include behavioural responses in their models. Most dynamic microsimulation models are thus primarily probabilistic, with the behavioural response limited to labour-market simulation and retirement decisions (see Li and O'Donoghue 2011). Incorporating behavioural responses into microsimulation models has been found to be very difficult, as the estimates of the value of the relevant elasticities have varied a great deal in econometric studies (Citro and Hanushek 1991c).

### 9.3.3 Classifying Models: Cohort Versus Population Models

Harding (1993) and others have categorized inter-temporal dynamic models into two types: cohort/longitudinal models, which model a single cohort over their lifetime, and population/cross-section models, which model a population cross-section over a period of time.

From a model-design viewpoint, the distinction between cohort and population models is less significant than the use to which the model is put. The distinction in the literature has more to do with computing power and data constraints rather than any major methodological differences. Cohort models have been typically used because the computing costs to simulate whole lifetimes for cross-sections (with sufficient sample sizes to be able to examine specific cohorts) are high. Both types of model can be simulated in the same modelling environment. A cohort model is simply a model that ages a sample of unrelated individuals aged zero, while a population model ages a sample of individuals of different ages, some of whom are related.

### 9.3.4 Base Data

As a state-dependent model, the structure of the initial or base dataset is an important driver of future distributions. Several papers (Cassells et al. 2006; Zaidi and Scott 2001) have discussed the choice of base dataset. Household surveys, although typically having small sample sizes, have extensive contextual information. However, they suffer from the drawback of differential non-response, and so have to use non-response weights.

The larger the sample size, the more one can consider smaller groups. Sample sizes are more important for inter-temporal analysis, because the number of dimensions increases. This is because similar individuals in a cross-section may in fact be very different, due to perhaps having taken different paths to reach that state. Sample size also has an impact on the run time of the model.

Base data can also be divided into historical and current data. A number of models (CORSIM, DYNAMOD, and DYNACAN) start with historic data, such as census files from the earlier decades. These models start their simulation at a point in the past, building up a sufficiently long work history to the present day. Some models, such as MOSART or PENSIM, have base datasets that include work histories, so the early start date is not necessary, while other models, such as DESTINIE or LIAM, simulate forward as other models do, but also backward to create work histories (See Li and O'Donoghue 2012).

Data can also be categorized as administrative, census, survey-sample, and synthetic data. Administrative data often contains the most accurate data for benefit or pension calculations. As the data are often collected for the whole population, sample sizes are often much larger than survey samples. However, administrative data typically have limited contextual information, such as education levels or household information. For this reason, countries that use administrative data often supplement information contained in administration data with extra survey data.

Some models use census data, which although having better coverage than household surveys, often have less contextual information, and so often have to be supplemented with imputed information from other sources. The use of weights in a dynamic model adds complexity in many areas, and can result in individuals having different weights at different points of their lives. One solution for this issue is the replication of households according to their non-response weights, so that each household then has the same weight.

### 9.3.5 Competing Risks: Discrete Versus Continuous Time

The period of analysis considered influences, whether a discrete-time period or continuous-time period is used. At any point in time, a number of mutually exclusive transitions are possible for individuals in a dynamic model. Different outcomes may be regarded, as different events can be competing with each other in order to be observed. Whichever event comes first will influence the other. This is the notion of competing risks. Galler (1997) discusses some of the issues relating to the modelling of simultaneous risks in dynamic microsimulation models.

Ageing modules in dynamic models are often constructed using annual transition-probability matrices or discrete-choice models. Individuals are passed through a collection of discrete processes in each time period of the simulation (usually a year) to determine their simulated life paths. This method assumes that life events are independent of each other, while in reality they can be interdependent. Therefore, the order in which the transition matrices are applied is very important. Galler (1997) discussed a number of options for this situation, including the procedure of random ordering.

There are a number of other problems with this type of approach. First, transitions are assumed to take place at a single point in each time period, and the duration of the event must last at least one time period. For example, if the time period is a year, then this approach rules out transitions in and out of unemployment over the course of the year, which may be unrealistic for seasonal workers. Therefore, the discrete time transitions simulate net transitions at discrete points in time.

Some dynamic models, such as DYNAMOD in Australia, and the demographic microsimulation model SOCSIM (Hammel 1990), used survival-analysis techniques to model life-event transitions, modelling the length of time that an individual will face in this current state (Antcliff 1993; Antcliff et al. 1996).

The use of survival functions in microsimulation models poses some problems, however. One of the assumptions of using hazard-function continuous-time models is that the probability of two events occurring at one point in time is zero (see Galler 1997). This, however, is unrealistic in a dynamic model, where a number of labour-market processes may happen at the same time. Thus, a number of processes need to be determined simultaneously. Galler argues that it is preferable to regard these types of simultaneous events as a single composite event.

Another problem relating to the use of continuous-time models is that incorporating explanatory variables, which vary continuously over time, may result in very complex econometric models, which are difficult to solve (Galler 1997). A potential solution holds these explanatory variables constant for finite periods, so that they can be considered within the model as discrete-time explanatory variables.

Galler also points out that macro-aggregates, which are typically discrete-time variables, can be accommodated easily as explanatory variables in a continuous model. In many respects, the incorporation of macro-variables is easier in the continuous-time framework. This is the case if the time period of the micro-process is less than that of the macro-process in a discrete-time framework, in which case some interpolation may be necessary. However, another use of macro-aggregates lies in the alignment of aggregates from the model. Here, the problem of combining the continuous-time-predicted variables into discrete periods to make them compatible with macro-aggregates is again encountered, where it is necessary to try to force the number of transitions within the discrete interval to match the aggregate totals.

### 9.3.6 Open Versus Closed Models

One of the decisions that a dynamic-microsimulation-model builder has to consider is whether the model should be open, closed, or a mixture of both. A model is defined as closed if, except in the case of newly-born children and new migrants, the model only uses a fixed set of individuals. Thus, if an individual is selected to be married, their spouse is selected from within the existing population of the model. An open model, on the other hand, would start with a base population, and if spouses are required, new individuals are generated (Rowe and Wolfson 2000). This has the advantage that simulations for individuals (and their immediate families) can be run independently of other individuals. It thus allows the model to be run in parallel on different computer processors, allowing overall run times to be reduced.

However, sometimes it is necessary to interact (in a modelling sense) with individuals outside of the immediate family. This is particularly true in the alignment process. Although possible, it is a non-trivial task to align a varying population with macro-aggregates, as the weights would necessarily have to be dynamically reweighted constantly. In any case, if this is done, most of the benefits of running the model in parallel will be lost. As a result, most dynamic models utilize a closed-model method (Li and O'Donoghue 2012). Despite this, most models have to incorporate some degree of openness, due to migration.

## 9.4 Validation: Alignment

One of the major perceived problems of dynamic models is the fact that insufficient effort has been placed on validation matters, and there is no international consensus on the validation procedure. Morrison (2008) published the steps of validation in a DYNACAN model, while the National Research Council (1997) argues that projection models of all types, including dynamic microsimulation models, ought to have a number of validation goals and should:

- first, provide accurate estimates of policy outcomes
- second, provide estimates of the uncertainty associated with projections
- third, incorporate the most up-to-date information about underlying behaviour

The National Research Council (1997) advocates that one should use ex-post analyses of previous periods to assess the reliability of models. It is for this reason that a number of the major microsimulation projects have taken historic datasets as the starting population base for their simulations. For example, the CORSIM model takes as its base a sub-sample of the 1971 US census, while the DYNACAN model takes as its base a sample of the 1970 Canadian census. By running the model forward to the present, model forecasts can be compared against what actually happened (e.g., see Morrison 2000; Caldwell and Morrison 2000).

Another method described in Caldwell (1996) uses an indirect approach, known as a multiple-module approach, an example of which involves validating the numbers of married persons with health insurance, when the directly-simulated processes are marriage and medical-insurance membership.

### 9.4.1 Binary Discrete-Choice-Variable Alignment

Projections over time at the micro-level are particularly susceptible to mis-specification error, as modelling at this level involves more detail than in macro-models. In addition, our knowledge about micro-behaviour is not good enough to specify a fully dynamic model. Therefore, what is more commonly used is a combination of dynamic ageing with an alignment (calibration) mechanism to keep aggregate outputs in line with projections that are either based upon scenarios or predictions from macro-models.

This procedure combines both static and dynamic ageing, and allows for individual transitions to be simulated, as well as ensuring that aggregate outputs track macro-forecasts (e.g., see Chénard 2000a, 2000b).

Baekgaard (2002) lists a number of reasons for the use of alignment in microsimulation models:

- Alignment may be used to 'repair' the unfortunate consequences of insufficient estimation data by incorporating additional information in the simulations.
- Alignment provides a facility for producing scenarios based on different assumptions.
- Alignment is instrumental in establishing links between microsimulation models of the household sector and economy-wide models.
- Alignment can be used to reduce Monte Carlo variability.

Although very important within the dynamic-microsimulation-modelling literature, the literature on alignment is relatively sparse, with Caldwell et al. (1998), Neufeld (2000), Chénard (2000a, 2000b), Baekgaard (2002), Morrison (2006), and Kelly and Percival (2009) being obvious exceptions. Morrison (2006) provides a comprehensive history of the development of alignment in dynamic microsimulation models.

This section describes a method to calibrate binary variables. Models of binary events (e.g., in work) may be modelled using a logit model, due to the computational ease of undertaking these simulations.[4] In order to use the estimated probabilities from logistic models within a Monte Carlo simulation, a set of random numbers is drawn, such that the actual dependent variable is predicted in the base year. The relevant logit model is defined as follows:

$$y_i^* = \text{logit}(p_i) = \ln\frac{P_i}{(1-P_i)} = B_o + \sum_k \beta X_i^k + \varepsilon_i$$

such that:

$$y = 1 \text{ if } y_i^* > 0$$

In order to create the stochastic term $\varepsilon_i$, we use the following relationship:

[4] Alignment or calibration techniques are described in Caldwell (1996), Morrison (2006), and Li and O'Donoghue (2014b).

$$\varepsilon_i = \ln\left(\frac{u_i}{1-u_i}\right)$$

such that:

$$y = 1 \text{ if } u_i < \log it^{-1}\left(B_o + \sum_k \beta X_i^k\right) = p_i$$

A value of $u_i$ that satisfies this is:

$$u_i = (Y=1)*(r*p_i) + (Y=0)*(p_i + (r*(1-p_i)))$$

where $r$ is a uniform random number.

The objective of calibrating a microsimulation model is to ensure that the simulated output matches exogenous totals (Baekgaard 2002).

Binary-choice models are calibrated by ranking $y^*$, as defined in the above equation, and selecting the highest $N$ cases from our external control totals. In multiple-choice models, a similar method is developed, ranking $y_j^*$ for each choice $j$ in turn, to be consistent with externally defined $Nj$. Income variables are adjusted by uprating, using group-specific income-growth rates.

### 9.4.2 Behavioural Response

Alignment faces a difficulty if there is a behavioural response to a policy change. The existence of an alignment mechanism may constrain model outputs to always hit aggregate targets, even if there has been an underlying behavioural or structural change. This is evident in the case where education levels rise. One would expect this to reduce mortality rates and increase female labour-force participation. If the alignment mechanism for each process does not incorporate the impact of educational achievement, then an increase in the education level would have no effect on these aggregates.

A potential solution may be provided by the examination of the average (pre-alignment) event value, such as the average transition rate or average earnings in the baseline scenario, against the alternative scenario, and then increasing alignment values by the proportional difference between them. This is a method utilized in some dynamic models; however, it assumes that all processes are unconstrained. For example, this may be the case with the mortality rate. One may expect that an exogenous increase in human capital will reduce total mortality rates, and thus one can reduce the alignment totals as appropriate.

## 9.5 Measurement Issues: Inter-Temporal Redistribution

The measurement indicators we utilize with dynamic microsimulation models reflect the welfare-state objectives that policies simulated using these models are trying to achieve. They are also influenced by the longer period of analysis over which the simulation occurs.

The replacement rate is the ratio of out-of-work income to in-work income. Replacement rates can be used as a measure of incentives to work; however, from the perspective of pensions analysis, the measure is used to describe the income-smoothing nature of the pension. For example, the OECD's 2011 document *Pensions at a Glance* reports the ratio of retirement income to the average wage for hypothetical families. As in the case of the working-age replacement rates, the measure can be based upon gross-income components:

$$RR_{Gross} = \frac{Y_{Pension}}{Y_{In-Work}}$$

or net-income components:

$$RR_{Net} = \frac{Y_{Pension} - t_{Pension}}{Y_{In-Work} - t_{In-Work}}$$

The denominator can either utilize the income at the point of retirement, to reflect short-term income smoothing, or the average career income, reflecting longer-term smoothing.

### 9.5.1 Insurance

As an insurance mechanism, analysts are often interested in how the rate of return an individual may receive from a social-security pension compares to a private-sector pension. For this, an internal rate of return is used. This is the interest rate *i* such that the accumulated pension contributions saved at a compound-interest rate is equal to the discounted stream of benefits:

$$\sum_{t=1}^{r-1} c_t \cdot \left( \sum_{r=t}^{r-1} i^r \right) = \sum_{t=r}^{T1} \frac{p_t}{1+i^r}$$

### 9.5.2 Redistribution

Redistribution can be classified as the mechanism by which the distribution of income is changed. Generally, redistribution $R(P)$ due to a policy $P$ is the difference between income inequality before the policy has been implemented $D_{pre}(P)$ and after the policy has been implemented $D_{post}(P)$:

$$R(P) = D_{pre}(P) - D_{post}(P)$$

However, income inequality and the resulting redistribution differ, depending upon the accounting period or period of analysis utilized.

The accounting period used can influence the degree of redistribution measured. Shorter accounting periods will tend to increase the degree of income inequality measured within a population. This arises due to the nature of short-term mobility and life-cycle effects.

In focusing on the redistributive nature of the pensions system over the lifetime, one needs to consider transfers over the lifetime, from periods when an individual is rich to when they are poor, analogous to the income smoothing highlighted above, and analogous to vertical redistribution. Higher mobility over the lifetime will result in lower vertical redistribution over a lifetime than in a single year. For example, pensioners are one of the largest net beneficiaries from the tax-benefit system in any one period, as their incomes are typically below average. However, when viewed from a lifetime perspective, as most pensioners receive contributory benefits, receipt of benefit represents a return on contributions made during the lifetime, rather than as a pure distribution from rich to poor over the lifetime. The existence of intra-personal redistribution in tax-benefit systems implies that such objectives could be achieved through private savings mechanisms.

To examine the variability of incomes between individuals, and the variability of incomes over their lifetime, we utilize a method to examine the decomposition of inequality or variability between and within population sub-groups. If one regards the set of all annual incomes as the total population, where the groups are individuals, then total variability of incomes can be decomposed into a factor attributed to between individuals (between group variability) and variability across the life course (within group variability). Utilizing the $I2$ index, total variability can be broken up into within-group variability (or intra-personal variability over the life course) and between-group variability (or inter-person variability).[5] The between-person inequality is in fact the inequality of mean lifetime income:

$$I_b(y) = \frac{1}{2}\left[\sum_j f_j\left(\frac{\mu_j}{\mu}\right)^2 - 1\right] = \frac{1}{2}\left[\frac{1}{n}\sum_j\left(\frac{\mu_j}{\mu}\right)^2 - 1\right] = I(\mu) = \overline{I}$$

where $\mu_j$ is the mean lifetime income for person $j$, the population share is $\left(\frac{1}{n}\right)$, and $\mu$ is the mean population-lifetime income. Intra-personal redistribution, or within-person inequality, can be defined as follows:

$$I_w = \sum_j w_j I_j$$

where $w_j = v_j^2 f_j^{-1}, v_j$ is the income share of each person $j$, and $f_j$ is the population share of each person, in this case $\left(\frac{1}{n}\right)$.

## 9.6 Simulation: Distribution of Income Over the Life Course

### 9.6.1 Constructing a Simple Dynamic Microsimulation Model

This section describes the development of a simplified dynamic microsimulation model. In modelling the income-smoothing effect of a pension system, it is necessary to have an income stream up until the point of retirement, and a stream of pensions post-retirement until the point of death. The income stream depends upon the existence of being in work, and the level of income when in work.

For the purpose of this simple analysis, we will abstract from household-formation characteristics, focusing solely on the individual unit of analysis. Family formation will more than likely influence the employment pattern of females, where their welfare often depends upon the incomes of the household in which they live, in addition to public policies related to maternity and/or the presence of a child. Abstracting from these issues here, the focus is on employment patterns and interaction with the pension system.

[5] Björklund and Palme (2002) use a similar decomposition method, but instead use the $I_0$, Theil L, and $I_1$ Theil T indices.

During the working years (assumed here to be between the ages of eighteen and sixty-five), the model therefore will be comprised of:

- an employment module
- a wage module
- a simple private-savings model and wealth-accumulation function

To account for social insurance during periods out of work (within working age), a simple unemployment-assistance module is modelled. Social-insurance contributions are made towards a pension in retirement. Income taxation pays for general government expenditures.

In pension age, we model:

- pension entitlement
- pension level
- conversion of working-age private savings into an annuity
- income taxation

## 9.6.2 Labour-Market Characteristics

This model utilizes social-security data for a case-study country, Chile, to model employment and employment income. The objectives are to model these variables, which reflect both cross-sectional distribution and inter-temporal volatility.

The first stage of analysis is to undertake some data cleaning and assessment of the quality and structure of the data. As the data are gross data, it is not vital to run a net-to-gross algorithm.

Before utilizing the data, it is first necessary to attempt to understand the quality and structure of the data, by undertaking an initial data analysis. The age profile of those in employment is examined in Figure 9.1. If the data represented a steady-state population, then the graphics would be in parallel. However, the rising and often sharply rising number in each age group reflects both an increasing population and the fact that older age groups entered the workforce more slowly. Surprisingly, however, there is also a fall in the numbers of those aged between twenty and twenty-nine years, perhaps reflecting sample-selection issues with effectively almost no individuals born from 1984 onward in the sample.

Figure 9.2 illustrates a decomposition of the data by cohort, presenting a relatively different perspective. For the older cohorts (1930s and 1940s),

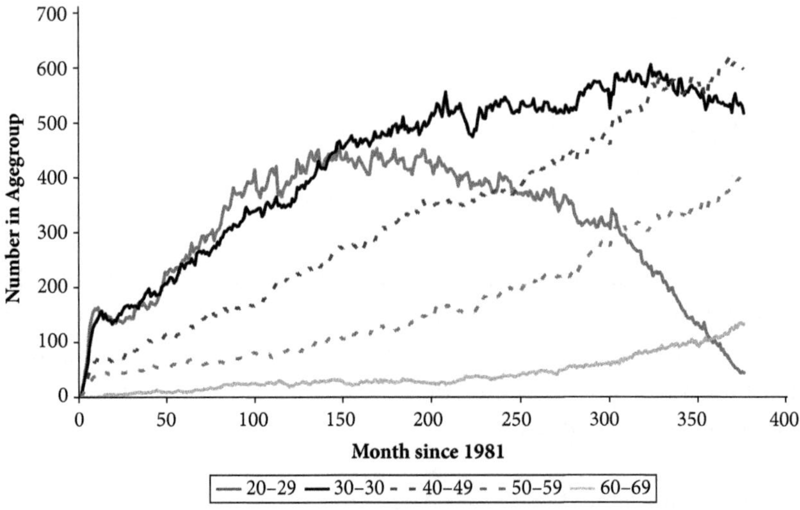


**Figure 9.1** Age-Group-Profile Structure of Those in Employment

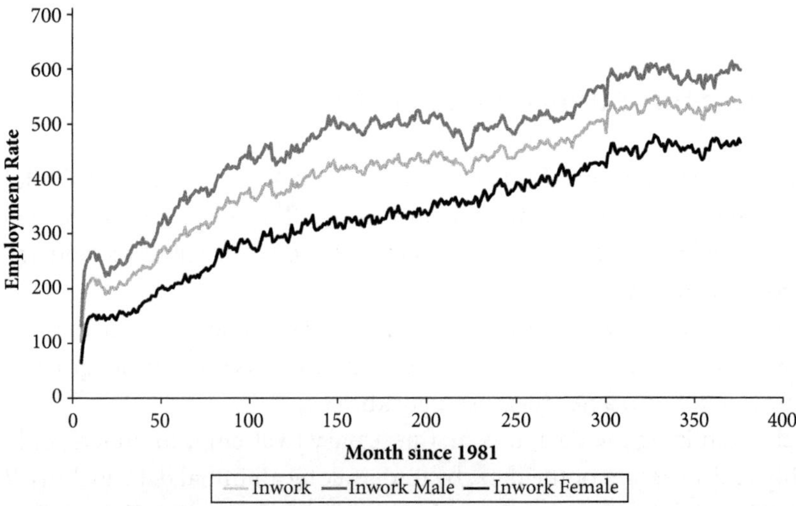


**Figure 9.2** Employment Rate of Those Aged 16–65

relatively small numbers became members of the social-insurance scheme; however, they reached a steady state relatively quickly. The 1950s cohort reached higher numbers of participants in the scheme, but it took until they were aged between thirty and forty years until they reached a steady state. Later cohorts reached a steady state aged between twenty and thirty years.

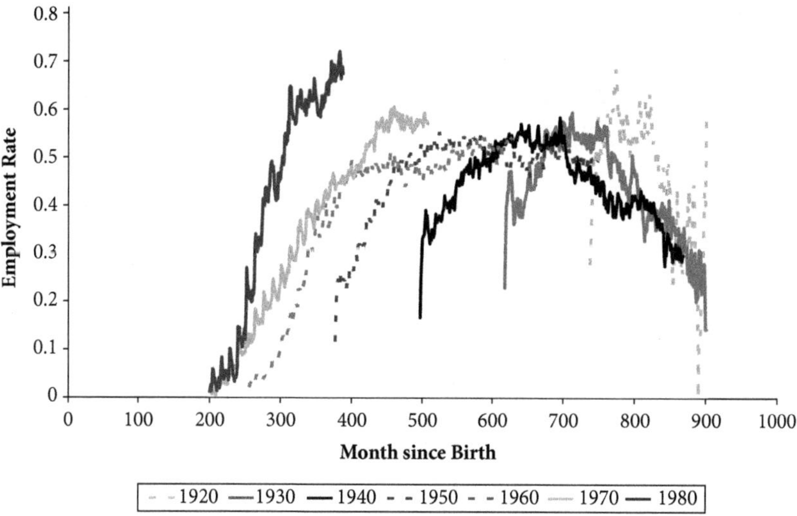


**Figure 9.3** Cohort Employment Rate

The small numbers in the 1980s cohort reflect the sampling issue identified above.

As there is both age and time variation, it is possible to estimate equations reflecting the population. However, given the relatively-low participation rate among older cohorts, one needs to be careful of bias, as these cohorts are more likely to be in higher-status professions and occupations. Similarly, one needs to be careful of the data in the period to 1990 (time = 100), when the system was maturing and participation was increasing.

In Figure 9.3, the employment rate by cohort is plotted against age (in months). Note the consistency of the younger cohorts (1960–80) at the start of their working career, and the consistency of the older cohorts (particularly 1930–50) later in their career. However, in early career, there is a lower employment rate, reflecting the slow take-up rate earlier in their career.

### 9.6.3 Simulation Properties

A critical test for a module in a dynamic microsimulation model is to test not only the estimation results, but also to test the simulation properties of the model. For a binary-dependent variable such as employment, we test in three dimensions:

- level (the employment rate)
- duration (the duration in the current state)
- transition (the probability of staying in employment, conditional on being in employment)

We are therefore interested not only in the cross-sectional distribution, but also in longitudinal characteristics, such as the duration and the rate of flow. The methodology for calibrating the model is described above, and can be useful for scenario analysis and for correcting simulation failures. However, for initial-testing purposes, it is important to test the simulation performance of each module without calibration.

These simulation properties are reported in Figure 9.4, comparing, in each case, the actual and simulated data. While the level is reasonably OK, bouncing around the same trend as the original data, the simulation properties of both the duration and the rate of flow are poor. Both of these are related, and result from a lack of longitudinal information in the model.

Therefore, in Figure 9.5, a lag term and a duration-in-current-state term are introduced into the model, resulting in a much-improved performance for both duration and flow, but a slightly worsened performance for the level. A calibration mechanism described above is employed to correct for this, and to allow for scenarios of different future employment trends. These results are reported in Figure 9.6. Annually-smoothed average employment rates for men and women by age group are utilized as the calibration data. This dramatically improves the level, while the flow is very good. The only remaining concern is the performance of the duration in current state, which is slightly diverging from the actual data. There is not yet a solution to remedy this remaining issue.

The model is simulated until everyone in the 1980s cohort dies in 2090. In Figure 9.7, the cohort-specific employment profile from 1981–2090 is reported, illustrating the similar life-cycle profile of employment across cohorts, with later cohorts having higher employment rates.

The distribution of disposable income over the life course for different cohorts is reported in Figure 9.8, illustrating the rising age-market income profile that falls in retirement at sixty-five years, where relatively small market-based pensions are received. In gross income where benefits and social pensions are received, the gap between retirement and earnings reduces. However, when taxes and contributions are subtracted, the distribution flattens out.

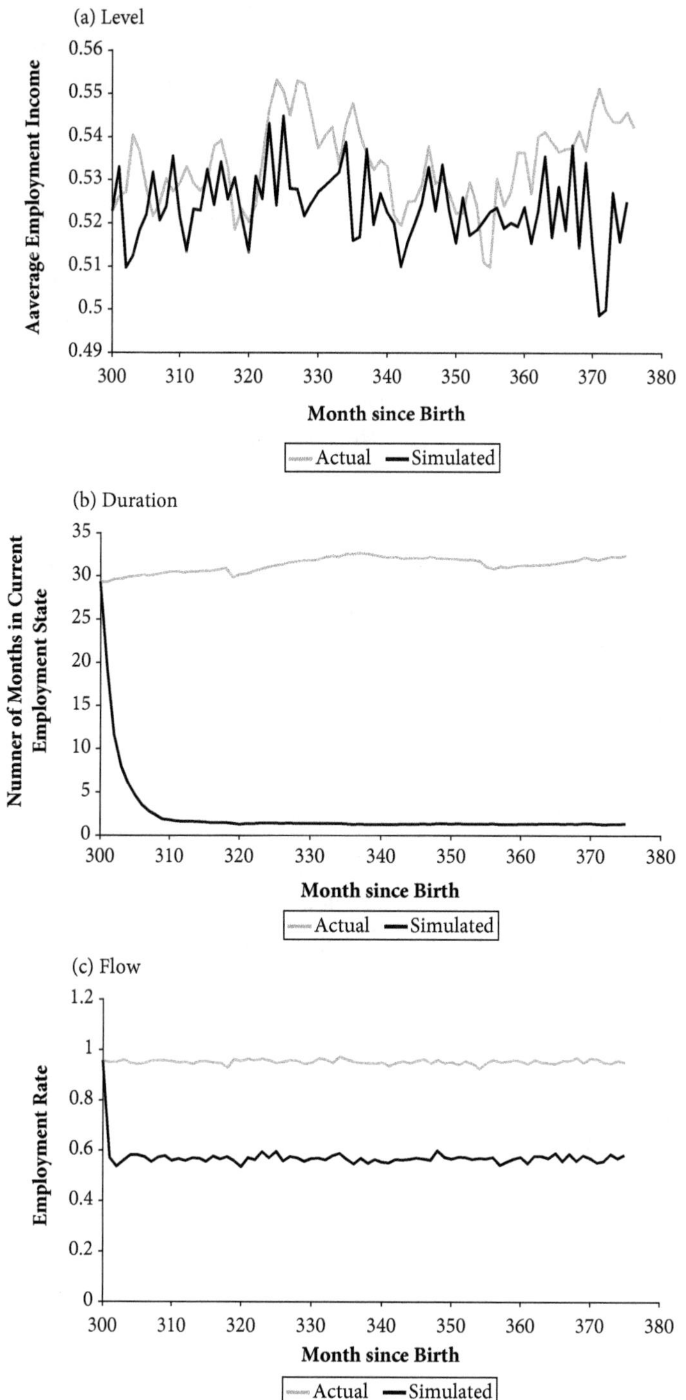


**Figure 9.4** Simulation Properties of Employment

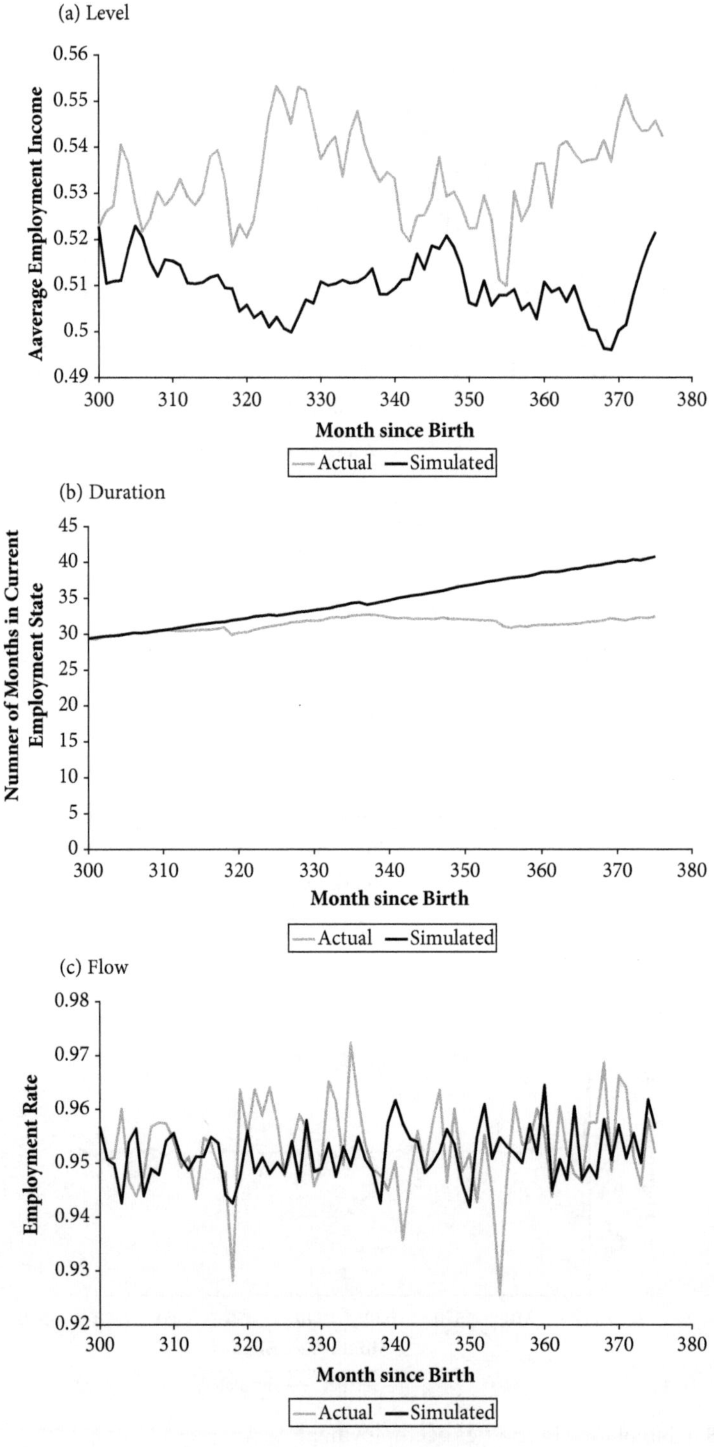

(a) Level

Aaverage Employment Income

0.56
0.55
0.54
0.53
0.52
0.51
0.5
0.49

300 310 320 330 340 350 360 370 380

Month since Birth

Actual —Simulated

(b) Duration

Numner of Months in Current Employment State

45
40
35
30
25
20
15
10
5
0

300 310 320 330 340 350 360 370 380

Month since Birth

Actual —Simulated

(c) Flow

Employment Rate

0.98
0.97
0.96
0.95
0.94
0.93
0.92

300 310 320 330 340 350 360 370 380

Month since Birth

Actual —Simulated

**Figure 9.5** Simulation Properties of Employment Model 3

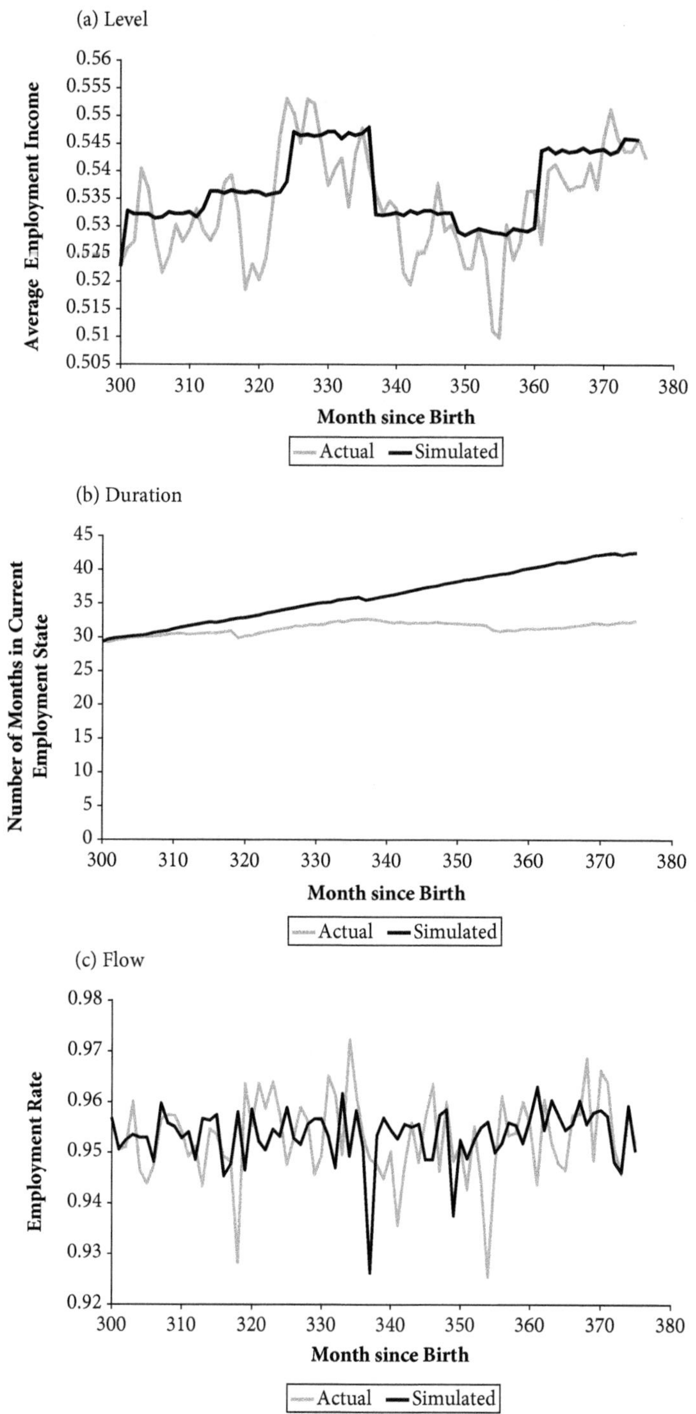


**Figure 9.6** Simulation Properties of Employment

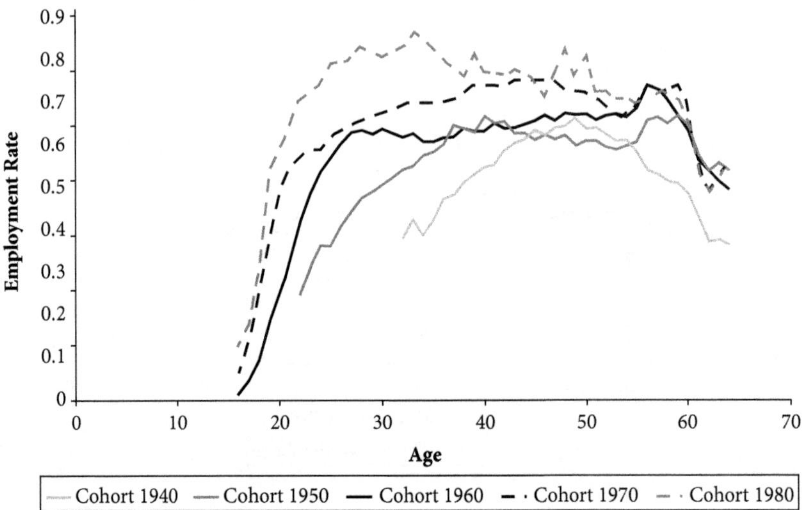


**Figure 9.7** Employment Profile

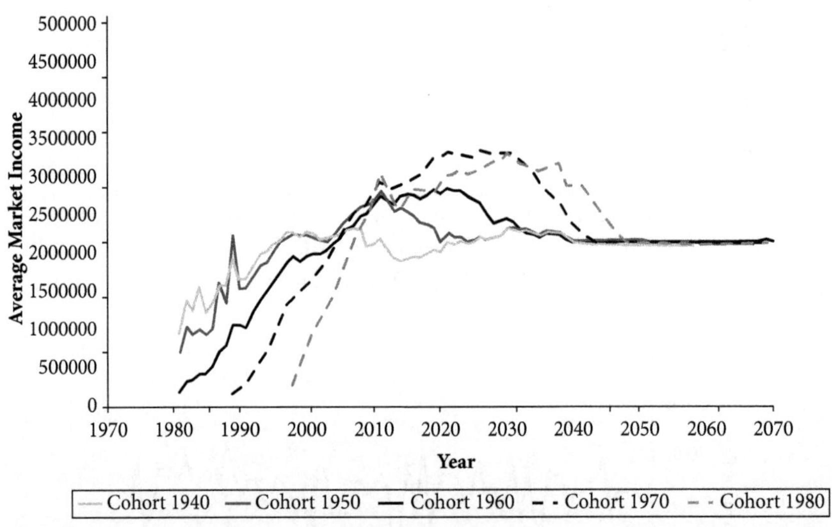


**Figure 9.8** Lifetime Distribution of Disposable Income

# 10
# Spatial Inequality

## 10.1 Introduction

There has been a growing emphasis on the spatial targeting of policy options in the area of poverty and social exclusion.[1] The importance of this type of spatial policy has been emphasized by findings that poor households tend to group together in specific areas (Jencks and Mayer 1990; Hajnal 1995; Ravallion and Jalan 1997). On foot of this, policy makers are keen to identify the spatial context of poverty and/or target resources towards individuals/areas that need them the most (Watson et al. 2005). The benefit of such a regional approach to welfare policy has been illustrated by Elbers et al. (2007).

Spatial microsimulation models have developed to consider spatially defined policy in many areas, including transport (Hollander and Liu 2008), urban development and planning (Waddell 2002), and other types of spatially focused public policy. In this chapter, following the focus of the other areas of policy already simulated, the focus will be on using microsimulation to look at policies related to inequality and poverty.

When researchers have access to spatially defined micro-data, then the challenge becomes relatively trivial. The methods developed in earlier chapters could be applied, and data could be decomposed by spatial location. This is typically possible for high-level spatial aggregates, such as region (see Lloyd et al. 2000), but less-frequently possible for sub-regional areas (Lindgren 1999). Spatial data typically exist in national-census datasets, but very frequently these data do not contain information on incomes. The challenge, therefore, is to generate datasets that are spatially consistent, in order to facilitate the linkage of spatially defined data, such as local-area census data, with nationally representative surveys that contain labour, demographic, and income information.

As spatial microsimulation modelling has been developing into a mainstream analytical tool within the social-science community (Birkin and Clarke 2012), there have been a number of surveys of spatial microsimulation models, including recent reviews (Ballas and Clarke 2009; Tanton and

[1] This chapter draws upon work co-authored with Karyn Morrissey and Niall Farrell.

*Practical Microsimulation Modelling.* Cathal O'Donoghue. Oxford University Press. © Cathal O'Donoghue 2021.
DOI:10.1093/oso/9780198852872.003.0010

Edwards 2013; Hermes and Poulsen 2012; O'Donoghue et al. 2014; Tanton 2014; Clarke and Tanton 2014). In particular, Tanton and Edwards (2016) provide an in-depth review of the methodological approaches to what may be referred to as 'mainstream' spatial microsimulation models, i.e., models that link micro-level data containing more-detailed individual-level data, typically income data, to spatially representative constraints.

In recent years, the field has developed extensively in many areas, as described elsewhere in this book, but additionally bringing a spatial dimension. There is also a significant and growing field looking at spatial health inequalities (Koh et al. 2015; Deetjen and Powell 2016; Campbell et al. 2017; Markham et al. 2017; Hakim and Rahman 2018; Koh et al. 2018). Demographic analyses in a spatial setting have too been undertaken (Rees et al. 2017; Lomax and Smith 2017).

Reflecting the importance of place and spatial location in terms of the environment, it is logical that policy studies of environmental, natural-resource, and agricultural policy have utilized spatial microsimulation modelling. O'Donoghue (2017a, 2017b) and Morrissey et al. (2014) utilize the method for agricultural and marine spatial-income-incidence studies respectively. In cities, the method has been used to look at energy demand, use, and emissions (Ma et al. 2014; Muñoz and Esteban 2016; Dochev et al. 2016). Looking at the environment in terms of its impact on incomes, Kilgarriff et al. (2018) modelled the impact of flooding events on incomes. Philips et al. (2017) extended the literature on recreation.

The geographical scope of income-distribution studies has extended beyond North West Europe and Australia to analysis from Greece (Panori et al. 2017). In addition, Vega et al. (2017) considered the impact of commuting, and Kilgarriff et al. (2018) has considered the impact of housing consumption on the spatial distribution of incomes.

Given the methodological challenges in undertaking spatial microsimulation analyses, a burgeoning sub-field has developed, focusing on technical issues in a range of topics identified by Tanton (2018). Lovelace and Dumont (2016) published a book on using the programming language R for spatial microsimulation. As in other areas of microsimulation, there has been a move beyond point estimates to create confidence intervals around results (Whitworth et al. 2017; Rahman 2017). Other papers have focused on the performance of individual reweighting methods (Tanton et al. 2014; Lovelace et al. 2015; Burden and Steel 2016), or on validation (Timmins and Edwards 2016). Extensions have also been created with other types of models, such as agent-based models (Ballas et al. 2019) or macro-micro analyses (Rao et al. 2015; van Leeuwen et al. 2016).

### 10.1.1 Chapter Structure

The purpose of this chapter is to provide an insight into the rationale, development, and application of the spatial microsimulation method for analysing the spatial distribution of inequality. The policy context for spatial inequality analysis is discussed initially, before considering the statistical method for synthetically generating spatially consistent household-income-distribution data. Approaches to validating these methods are then discussed, before applying quantitative methods to measuring spatial inequality.

## 10.2 Policy Context: Spatial Inequality and Poverty

Jalan and Ravaillon (2002) define the notion of a spatial poverty trap as one that 'exist(s) if a household living in a better endowed area sees its standard of living rising over time, while the other does not'. Bird et al. (2010) define spatial poverty traps as: 'where "geographic capital" (the physical, natural, social, political, and human capital of an area) is low and poverty is high, partly as a result of geographic disadvantage. Spatial poverty traps may be geographically remote (areas that are far from the centres of political and economic activity), "low potential" or marginal (ecologically disadvantaged areas that have low agricultural or natural resources), "less favoured" (politically disadvantaged areas), or "weakly integrated" (areas that are poorly linked both physically and in terms of communication and markets).'

There is an extensive literature on spatial poverty traps. Bird and Shepherd (2003) and Escobal and Torero (2005) find links between peripherality, low levels of public and private investment, and spatial poverty and inequality in Zimbabwe and Peru respectively.

The need to spatially identify pockets of poverty exists for a number of reasons. The most straightforward justification is that research has found that poor households are grouped together in specific areas (Jencks and Mayer 1990). Thus, in identifying areas with the highest levels of social exclusion, policy makers would like to be able to identify the spatial context of poverty and/or target resources towards individuals/areas that need them the most (Watson et al. 2005). Spatial inequality and poverty traps relate to situations where spatial factors, including quality of public services and remoteness, are strongly related to local poverty rates (Minot et al. 2003).

Why do spatial inequality and poverty traps deserve policy attention? Bird et al. (2010) outline a number of points:

- Spatial factors can partially explain the poverty experienced by a large number of people in the world. These factors may be more responsive to policy interventions than household- or individual-targeted policy.
- Spatial poverty traps are characterized by compound disadvantage, such as low returns on all forms of investment, partial integration into fragmented markets, social and political exclusion, and inadequate access to public services.
- The 'bad-neighbourhood effect' constrains the opportunities of people living in spatial poverty traps and limits poverty exit.
- Finally, there is a significant regional dimension to the incidence of poverty, with spatial poverty traps found even in richer countries.

The World Bank has developed a poverty-mapping methodology (Hentschel et al. 1998; Elbers et al. 2003). The method involves parametric statistical matching of micro-household data (such as a budget survey) with spatial census data to develop poverty maps. The Food and Agriculture Organization (FAO) (Davis 2003) and the International Food Policy Research Institute (IFPRI) (Benson 2006) have also used this method to explore food-security-related issues.

These methods have been utilized in parallel in developed countries to consider similar issues. For example, the National Centre for Social and Economic Modelling (NATSEM), at the University of Canberra, has developed a suite of spatial microsimulation models. Their modelling framework was initially built around a regional income model (Lloyd et al. 2000), and the Marketinfo model, of local expenditure and incomes focusing on market clients. There have been a number of models built in the UK for spatial-poverty and inequality analysis. SimLeeds (Ballas and Clarke 2001a) was developed to examine the labour market in and around the Leeds metropolitan area. Ballas (2004) used the SimLeeds framework to look at changes in poverty and inequality in Leeds and Sheffield between the 1991 and 2001 censuses. Anderson (2007) has also developed a spatial microsimulation model for studying deprivation in England. Similarly, Morrissey and O'Donoghue (2011) use a multi-stage method to simulate the spatial distribution of incomes in Ireland.

Although developing spatial indicators of income inequality is in itself a useful tool to facilitate spatial planning, the addition of tax-benefit microsimulation-modelling techniques allows for the spatial impact of policy in reducing poverty and inequality to be assessed. In Australia, NATSEM's model SYNAGI (Synthetic Australian Geo-Demographic Information), later called SpatialMSM, has been extended to simulate taxes and benefits (Chin et al. 2005), and has been developed to study issues related to differential spatial poverty and inequality rates (Harding et al. 2009). In Europe, the Leeds team extended their modelling framework to York and Wales (Ballas et al. 2005c), and later to cover the whole country in the SimBritain model (Ballas et al. 2005b), looking at income and spatial-distribution issues.

To date, much of the literature in this area has focused on spatial income inequality (O'Donoghue et al. 2013a), with only a few papers taking advantage of the capacity of microsimulation models to simulate the impact of policy reform in relation to the income distribution. Harding et al. (2009) simulated the impact of a national family-tax-benefit reform, while the SimLeeds team used a partial tax-benefit model to simulate a number of tax and pension changes on income (see Ballas et al. 2003).

## 10.3 Data Issues: Matching Spatial Data and Micro-Data

In this section, methods to link spatial data to micro-income data to generate small-area income-distribution estimates are considered. The starting point in undertaking spatial microsimulation, or the simulation of welfare-changing policy, or activities on micro-units within a spatial context, is a dataset of the population of interest, containing spatial attributes at the micro-level. This could be based on a micro-file of a national census with attached spatial attributes (e.g., Pratschke and Haase 2005), administrative-based micro-data with spatial attributes (e.g., Rephann at al. 2005), or spatially disaggregated micro-survey analysis (Nolan et al. 1998). However, this issue becomes more complicated when spatial-micro data do not exist or where the spatial scale is relatively aggregated (Watson et al., 2005). This may be the case either because the data do not include a spatial identifier, or where the dataset is not of sufficient size to be representative at the spatial level, or frequently where spatial data exist (as in the case of administrative data or census data), but are not not available for research purposes for confidentiality reasons.

This is the case in many countries, such as in Australia (Chin and Harding 2006), the UK (Ballas et al. 2005a), and Ireland (O'Donoghue et al. 2013). In Ireland, while census micro-data are available, there are a number of reasons why these data are not suitable for our purposes:

- A national census micro-data file, the Sample of Anonymized Records (SARS), of the Irish Census of Population, has been released to the Irish

Social Science Data Archive. However, these data have been released only with an individual unit of analysis, which is not sufficient for welfare analysis.

- These data contain only very aggregated spatial units, and so are not suitable for local-area analysis.
- Even if the data contained spatial attributes, and were of the required unit of analysis (household), they still would not be sufficient for welfare analysis, as they do not contain income variables.

In order to undertake a spatial micro-based analysis, it is necessary to turn to alternative means, through the use of statistical data-fusion techniques to combine the contextual information of aspatial (or limited spatial) micro-data with spatial attributes of a calibration dataset, such as a small area census file.

There are a number of objectives that a data-fusion algorithm must have, namely:

- To link both types of data, either through sampling or simulation.
- To have the capacity to handle units of analyses of the datasets used, at the individual or household level, or a combination of the two, in the case of household micro-data and individual-level spatial-calibration data.
- To be computationally efficient.
- To minimize validation error.

Spatial microsimulation has three main advantages over more-traditional micro-models:

- First, it allows data from various sources to be linked if datasets contain at least one attribute in common.
- Second, the models are flexible in terms of spatial scale, as data can be re-aggregated or disaggregated. For example, the results can be aggregated to higher levels, such as county or region.
- Third, spatial microsimulation models store data efficiently as lists. These lists generally consist of unidentifiable units with associated characteristics, obtained, as mentioned above, from a survey or census.

There are a number of alternate ways to do this, and they depend upon the type of data available. These methods (referred to in Ballas et al. 2005b) can be divided into:

- Monte Carlo
- reweighting
- sampling

Where spatial micro-data exist, but do not contain income information, e.g., in the case of anonymized census data with spatial coordinates, then a statistical-matching technique similar to those described in Chapter 6 would be required. In this chapter, however, the focus is on methods that are applicable where the modeller has access only to spatially aggregated data, without access to spatially representative micro-data, i.e., where only tabulations of population characteristics are available, such as when it is only possible to identify the numbers of people by age, gender, education, and employment status, etc., at a relatively-detailed spatial scale.

### 10.3.1 Monte Carlo

The main Monte Carlo-based method utilizes iterative proportional fitting (IPF), which is a probabilistic methodology for constructing spatially disaggregated tables from aggregate spatial totals, in the absence of pre-existing micro-data. This method takes tables of marginal totals, such as age times gender, and education times gender, and creates an approximation of an age-times-gender-times-education table. This is achieved by adjusting the marginal tables iteratively until row sums and column sums equal some predefined aggregate values. In a geographical context, this method can be used to generate disaggregated spatial data from spatially aggregated data (Wong 1992). The population is then generated by using Monte Carlo simulation, based upon the probabilities in the resulting table. The method, thus, simulates synthetic micro-data using spatial tabulations, rather than utilizing actual micro-data-constrained spatial tabulations. Monte Carlo techniques are then used to simulate a population by drawing random numbers and randomly selecting characteristics reflecting the structure of the joint table generated by the IPF method. The method is flexible and computationally relatively efficient, and can be extended to more than two dimensions.

However, while it is a relatively straightforward method of generating spatial data, it has a number of drawbacks:

- The method assumes independence between marginal totals. This may be unrealistic (Norman 1999), and could potentially be avoided through the use of reweighting or sampling methods.

- Another difficulty is that both the constraints and the resulting micro-data need to have the same unit of analysis. This may be inconsistent with the objectives of spatial welfare analysis.

As a result, we will focus on methods that allow us to generate spatial data with individuals grouped into households, but where the data-generation process is constrained to individual totals.

### 10.3.2 Generalized Reweighting

An alternative method is to generate weights for micro-data that are consistent with spatially defined weights. Generalized-regression weights (GREGWT), an algorithm written by the Australian Bureau of Statistics, has been developed to reweight survey data to spatial constraints. Similarly to the generation of non-response correcting weights used in nationally representative surveys, this method generates a set of weights for each spatial unit. The method has been used by NATSEM in many of their spatial microsimulation projects as a means of creating household weights for small areas (see Tanton et al. 2011).

GREGWT is a constrained distance-minimization function which uses a generalized-regression technique (Bell, unpublished) to get an initial weight, and iterates the regression until an optimal set of household or individual weights for each small area is derived. GREGWT is a deterministic reweighting algorithm, in that it generates the same result each time it is run. Optimization is achieved when the difference between the estimated count and the known census count for each of the constraint variables is minimized, or a predefined number of iterations is made, at which stage the iteration stops.

### 10.3.3 Deterministic Reweighting

An alternative method used to generate spatial micro-data is deterministic reweighting. The deterministic approach to reweighting national sample survey data is an attempt to fit small-area statistics tables or benchmarks for each small area, but without using random-sampling procedures (Ballas et al. 2005a).

A number of spatial microsimulation models have incorporated a deterministic reweighting approach. In SimBritain, Ballas et al. (2005b) use a deterministic approach to reweighting the survey households so that they fit small-area statistics tables, with the aim of dynamically simulating urban and regional populations in Britain. Anderson (2007) uses a deterministic reweighting approach for the estimation of the incidence of income poverty for each district in Wales. SimObesity is a spatial microsimulation model that combines individual micro-data from two national surveys with lower-level geographic data from the 2001 UK census, using a deterministic reweighting algorithm. Edwards and Clarke (2009) use the model to create micro-level estimates of obesogenic variables in Leeds (see Appendix in Edwards and Clarke 2009 for a worked example of the algorithm). Smith and Clarke (2009) also use a deterministic reweighting method in creating a synthetic population.

The objective of deterministic reweighting is to reweight a survey population or household dataset to best fit the individual or household characteristics that are known at the small-area level by using census variables. However, a particular characteristic of this approach is that it does not use random sampling at any stage (hence the term 'deterministic'), and, therefore, the estimated population distributions will be the same each time the model is run (Ballas et al. 2005b). This allows any number of changes to the data in the model to be made, until an optimal reweighting methodology is reached (Smith et al. 2007).

Ballas et al (2005) note that after implementing the above algorithm, there were, in some cases, comparatively high overestimates and underestimates of some variables that were not used as constraint variables when they compared the weighted data with their census counterparts. In reducing this error further, and producing a better fit, a swapping algorithm was developed to swap suitable simulated units between small areas.

It should be noted that in the Ballas et al. (2005) model, the survey-selection pool is less than a thousand individuals, and these are being used to estimate area populations which contain thousands of individuals. However, in many cases, the population sizes in these datasets would be the reverse, in the sense that the model would be selecting from thousands of individuals to estimate a small-area-level population with a magnitude of hundreds. This reweighting process produces weights which are very small, as the initial reweighting process is repeated a number of times for convergence purposes. In order to alleviate this situation, Smith et al (2009) apply a scaling factor on the weights, to adjust them back to numbers which equate more to actual population values. They also take a very unique approach in spatial microsimulation modelling, where they develop a model which can be adjusted for area-specific characteristics.

### 10.3.4 Sampling

An alternative to reweighting methods is the use of sampling methods. Instead of assigning spatial weights, units are sampled from the micro-dataset so as to replicate the observed tabular distribution. The resulting population thus has unit weights.

Combinatorial optimization (CO) techniques overcome the synthesis issues of IPF by reweighting existing survey micro-data, at either the individual or household level. Simulated annealing (SA) is an example of a CO method. SA allows the survey data and constraints to have different units of analysis. Unlike IPF, SA contains mechanisms to avoid becoming trapped at local minima (Wu and Wang 1998). It is also less sensitive to convergence issues. Williamson (2009) found that in an Australian simulation, SA performed slightly better at matching than GREGWT, for both constrained and unconstrained variables. This was particularly the case in districts where there was no convergence.

The main disadvantage of SA is the high computational intensity, which is due to the degree to which new household combinations are tested for an improvement in fit during simulation. To illustrate, Hynes et al. (2009) found that it took two days to generate almost one-hundred-and-forty-thousand individual farm records from twelve-hundred survey-data points on a 2G Dell workstation. If it was desirable to carry out repeated simulations for sensitivity analyses, and simulations of future population projections, then this would incur even greater costs. Thus, practical restrictions imposed by computational intensity may limit the use of CO methods. This has motivated the development of a more-efficient algorithm, through a reduction in the number of required computations called 'quota sampling'.

### 10.3.5 Quota Sampling

Quota sampling (QS) is a probabilistic reweighting methodology developed by Farrell et al. (2011). This procedure operates in a similar fashion to SA, whereby survey data are reweighted according to key constraining totals for each small area, with amendments made in the sampling procedure in order to improve computational efficiency. The basic sampling procedure, and its implementation in the overall simulation process, is outlined.

QS analyses individuals that are grouped into households against constraints at either the individual or household level. Similar to SA, QS selects observations at random, until what we term 'quotas' are reached. Unlike SA, however, QS only assigns households that conform to aggregate constraint totals, and once a household is deemed selected it is not replaced. To accommodate this, small-area aggregate totals for each constraining variable are designated as the initial values for quotas. These quotas may be considered as running totals for each constrained variable, which are recalculated once a household is admitted to a small-area population.

The basic procedure is best explained in the context of allocating one household at a time, in the presence of a single age constraint. If the household sum of each constraining characteristic (e.g., two persons aged between twenty and twenty-five years) is less than or equal to each small-area total (e.g., ten persons aged between twenty and twenty-five years), the household is assigned to the small-area population. Upon deeming a household appropriate for a given small area, quota counts are amended, reduced by the sum of the characteristics of the assigned household(s). For individual-level constraints, the running totals per constraint are incremented by the number of people in the household with that particular constraint. For household-level constraints, we increment by one (for the example used in this chapter, the electoral district (ED) quota is amended to eight persons remaining to be assigned). This procedure continues until the total number of simulated individuals is equal to the small-area population aggregates (i.e., all quotas have been filled).

Thus, it can be seen that the intra-household variation of admitted households cumulates in a random sort, which is consistent with aggregate constraint totals. This mechanism of sampling without replacement avoids the repeated sampling procedure of SA, and is fundamental to the efficiency gains of the QS procedure. The process is analogous to the type of QS undertaken by market researchers, whereby only individuals considered relevant to concurrent quota counts are admitted to a sample. This method of improving efficiency presents a number of convergence issues, however. A process analogous to the 'swapping' of SA (Morrissey et al. 2008; Hynes et al. 2009) is undertaken when constraint quotas approach capacity.

## 10.3.6 Selection of Constraint Totals

A key choice in the data-generation process is the decision of what variables should be used as constraints or matching variables (Smith et al. 2009). One potential choice, described in O'Donoghue et al. (2013), regresses the main variables of interest (such as market income), against a range of potential constraint variables. However, as data fusion using spatial microsimulation can be computationally costly, it is likely that only a subset of variables will be chosen. The choice will depend upon a variety of factors, including the sample size, available computer hardware, and the data available.

Disparities in population distributions between census and survey totals may create a number of problems for household-based microsimulation procedures. This is because survey micro-data are representative at the national level, whereas census data are representative at the district level. This poses little difficulty in simulating small areas that have a population distribution similar to that of the national distribution, but regions that differ from the national distribution may lead to some demographic groups consistently being under-represented in a given district. Such deviations may be further increased if a district contains individuals who live in institutions, such as nursing homes, religious orders, and psychiatric units, etc. (i.e., non-household members), as survey data generally do not cover individuals that are not part of a household. In the case of institutions such as boarding schools, children's hospitals, or young offender institutions, a situation could arise where there are many children in an area relative to the number of adults. These differences may cause some districts to consistently fail in reaching adequate convergence.

Finally, the use of sampling without replacement in QS results in quota counts becoming increasingly more restrictive as the simulation progresses. As quota counts reach their targets, the search space is continuously refined in accordance with concurrent quotas, whereby all households no longer eligible (given updated quota totals) are removed from the subset and the procedure is repeated[2]. When each constraint allocation reaches its target quota, all individuals of that characteristic are removed from the candidate search space. These mechanisms accumulate to offer a continuously diminishing search space, and may prohibit convergence, whereby no household is able to satisfy all concurrent quota counts.

The problems identified above can be corrected by a number of steps. Some households tend to be under-represented using random sampling (such as households with children or large households). As children must in general be in households with adults, a random selection of a disproportionate amount of adults early in a sample may result in an under-representation of children. This can be corrected by first sampling those groups that are more likely to be under-represented.

As the sample proceeds, there will be diminishing quotas, which may make it more difficult to find a set of appropriate households in a reasonable

[2] For example, with a remaining quota count of $n$ individuals of class $k$ to be filled, the search space is refined to exclude households containing $n+1$ individuals of class $k$.

time. One solution is to reduce the number of constraints by broadening the categories. If the algorithm fails to assign any further households, due to overly-restrictive quotas, one constraint is removed. This increases the search space, allowing households to be considered that were once excluded. This is repeated (one constraint at a time) until either all remaining quota counts are filled or all constraints have been removed. If the algorithm fails to assign an adequate number of individuals during this procedure, individuals are assigned at random to meet the required population. Constraints are removed in reverse order of the degree to which they influence household income, determined by pre-synthesis-regression analysis (for detail of this procedure, see Farrell et al. 2011). This design minimizes subjectivity, whereby the broadening of constraints is only introduced when absolutely necessary, and in a fashion which ensures that those variables that explain the greatest level of variability are retained to the greatest extent. Sometimes, all quotas are filled and this stage is skipped.

Thus, the synthesis procedure begins by allocating under-represented large households. A household-size constraint is applied, and a random allocation of large households is carried out using the selection process. Subsequent to this, under-represented households are assigned in a similar fashion. Households containing children are considered first, and this is followed by a weighted random sort, to determine demographic characteristics of greatest proportional disparity. This is carried out by measuring concurrent quota counts relative to micro-data totals for each constraint. A prioritization of simulation based on those constraint classes of greatest proportional disparity is then created. Finally, to overcome prohibitively-restrictive quota counts, a process similar to the swapping of households in SA is required (see Morrissey et al. 2008). This is done by broadening the constraints to allow the final few households to be allocated.

It could be considered that broadening the constraints in such a manner may cause validation issues to arise, in that the distribution for larger households or under-represented groups may be less robust. To ensure that this does not occur, the validation of the QS output is an integral component of the model's construction.

## 10.4 Validation: Conditional Independence and Spatial Calibration

Once the base dataset has been synthesized, validation is carried out to ensure the simulated populations are consistent with empirical benchmarks, both internal and external to the simulation process. This is difficult, as the creation of synthetic micro-data is motivated by the non-existence of such data for small geographic areas. However, as Oketch and Carrick (2005) point out, it is only through validation that the creditability and reliability of a microsimulation model, and thus the regional welfare distributions in spatial microsimulation, can be assured. Key to any statistical matching method, such as data synthesis using spatial microsimulation, is the notion of conditional independence. Conditional independence, in the context of spatial microsimulation, relates to the assumption that all spatial variability of the unconstrained variables is accounted for by the constrained or overlapping variables.

More formally, consider two datasets, say A and B, with sets of variables $(X,Y)$ and $(X, Z)$ respectively. Statistical matching involves matching two datasets together by finding units in sample B with similar values of the $X$ variables in sample A, to produce new datasets $(X, Y, Z)$. Implicit in this method is finding a distance function $\mathrm{D}(X_A, X_B)$, where the match is found when the distance is minimized for the set of overlapping variables $X$.

In terms of spatial microsimulation, A is the spatial dataset where $X$ represents the overlapping variables used for matching and $Z$ are the spatial attributes, while sample B is the attribute-rich dataset, such as an income survey.

The assumption outlined in Rodgers and DeVol is that the conditional distribution of $Z$ given $X$ is independent of the conditional distribution of $Y$ given $X$. This assumption is known as conditional independence. The variance-covariance matrix for these datasets can be defined:

$$C = \begin{pmatrix} Cov(X,X) & Cov(X,Y) & Cov(X,Z) \\ Cov(Y,X) & Cov(Y,Y) & Cov(Y,Z) \\ Cov(Z,X) & Cov(Z,Y) & Cov(Z,Z) \end{pmatrix}$$

Each of these covariances can be measured using either dataset, except for $Cov(Y,Z)$ and $Cov(Z,Y)$. It is assumed that these covariances are zero. In a spatial microsimulation model, the relationship between our non-overlapping variables $Y$ and our spatial variables $Z$ are uncorrelated, once we condition on the matching variables. Thus, it is assumed that the spatial incidence of $Y$ is fully accounted for by the spatial distribution of our $X$ variables. However, this assumption does not always hold, so essentially there is spatial heterogeneity of the variables of interest, independent of the correlation with the overlapping or matching variables $X$. This assumption is key to the analysis in this chapter.

### 10.4.1 Validation

In undertaking the validation, there are two primary tasks:

- The maintenance of the relationship between *X* and *Z*, taken from our spatial microsimulation, must be tested. This is essentially a confirmation that the spatial relationship of overlapping variables is maintained, and that the core functioning of the match has been successful.
- The second validation is essentially a confirmation of the conditional independence outlined above.

However, validation presents a clear challenge in spatial microsimulation frameworks, due to the difficulty in validating the model outputs, since microsimulation models estimate distributions of variables which were previously unknown. There is an extensive validation literature on this subject.

Caldwell (1996) suggests several methods that may be used to validate the outputs from a microsimulation model. These methods include:

- in-sample validation
- out-of-sample validation
- multiple-module validation

This is consistent with Voas and Williamson's (2000) division of validation into the fit of the synthetic data to known constraints, equivalent to in-sample validation, the fit of unconstrained interactions between constrained variables, which is related to multiple-module validation, and the fit of unconstrained variables and the interactions between them (out-of-sample validation).

In-sample validation assesses the predictive power of the model in describing the data on which it was estimated, akin to testing the $Cov(X,Y)$ and $Cov(X,Z)$ in the new spatial dataset. The process is based on statistical methods, such as $\chi^2$ tests, z-scores, $z^2$-scores, and total absolute-error statistics (Hynes et al. forthcoming; Ballas and Clarke 2001). In-sample validation may be used when the variables that are synthetically created previously co-existed or 'overlapped' each other in a dataset.

Out-of-sample validation attempts to measure the predictive power of the model in explaining data of a similar type, which were not used in the estimation of the model. A weakness of in-sample validation is that it fails to compare the newly-created data with external data (Caldwell 1996). Out-of-sample validation involves comparing the synthetically created micro-data with new, external data. Comparing synthetic micro-data with exogenous data provides an effective measure of the model's accuracy. However, comparable exogenous data at the same level of aggregation is not always available. This is especially problematic for aspatial microsimulation models. However, with regard to spatial microsimulation modelling, model outputs may be aggregated or disaggregated to levels where exogenous data is available.

Multiple-module validation refers to a technique whereby the interaction between two or more synthetically created variables is validated against pre-existing data on the interaction of these processes (Caldwell 1996). An example of this is comparing generated-poverty statistics with external sources.

While most validation analyses focus on the validation of constrained or overlapping variables, there is relatively little focus on non-overlapping variables. In their three-stage validation procedure (constrained variables, unconstrained labour-market and income variables, and tax variables), Chin and Harding (2006) undertake (particularly in the second and third stages) a significant degree of validation on primarily non-overlapping variables, and so implicitly test for conditional independence. Smith et al. (2009) discuss their validation process in detail, and provide a very useful appendix in relation to the validation they have undertaken. In particular, the validation analysis they undertake focuses on a non-overlapping variable: marital status.

In the literature, there is perhaps a disproportionate emphasis on 'success stories', and there is relatively little focus on validation difficulties. There are exceptions to this, where Chin and Harding (2006) highlight some of the issues associated with non-converging districts. It is perhaps the latter tests that are most useful to other analysts in evaluating which methodologies to use, however.

Key to having confidence in a microsimulation model is undertaking adequate validation, and evaluation of the matching or data-generation process. Cohen (1991), in a discussion of the validation of US microsimulation models, highlighted the limited extent of validation within the field. In more recent years, validation and evaluation has increased, although it is nevertheless often difficult to achieve successfully. This section discusses various options undertaken by different modelling teams.

Although most analyses undertake in-sample validation of constraint variables, Melhuish et al. (2002) describe a number of methods for undertaking validation, such as:

- a comparison of the numbers of individuals with simulated values of target variables versus target values
- assessment of the proportion of districts with more than a one-household difference in target value
- the distribution of maximum residuals
- non-convergent districts
- multi-dimensional percentage residuals

Within demographic projection models, Wachter et al. (1997) undertook out-of-sample validation, comparing model simulations with survey data collected subsequently. They found relatively small validation errors, but that the errors followed particular patterns. Out-of-sample validation like this is often difficult in spatial microsimulation, as frequently there is no single source of external data.

Edwards et al. (2009) described a number of methods for testing the validation of a spatial microsimulation relating to the spatial characteristics of obesity in the UK. One of the methods involved regressing actual versus simulated variables, a method also used by Holm et al. (2004).[3] In a second method, similar to Birkin and Clarke (1988), they recommend re-aggregating estimated-data sets to levels at which observed-data sets already existed, and comparing the estimated distributions with the observed. Melhuish et al. (2002) graphed the proportion of districts close to their targets in the capital territory in Canberra, producing a very good match in most cases, focusing on convergent districts. They also, however, undertook a statistical analysis of non-convergent districts.

Voas and *Williamson* (2001a) describe a methodology, based upon the random nature of the match process, to evaluate outcomes from spatial microsimulation methods utilizing $Z$-scores. $Z$-scores are based on the difference between the relative size of the category in the synthetic and actual populations (Voas and Williamson 2001a). A $Z$-score can be summed and squared to provide a measure of tabular fit similar to a chi-squared statistic. If a cell's $Z$-score exceeds the critical value, the cell is deemed not to fit. $Z^2$-score is the second statistic that may be used to validate overlapping variables. The critical value for the $Z^2$-score is 1.64 (95 per cent), and like the $Z$-scores it is chi-squared-distributed. If a $Z^2$–score exceeds the critical value, then the

[3] Most of the validation in this chapter focuses on inter-temporal validation, as a major component of the model is inter-temporal. Base-data production is less onerous, being able to use spatial micro-data.

dataset is deemed not to fit (i.e., $|Z| > 1.96$). The $Z$-score calculation is given by:

$$Z = \frac{\dfrac{T_{ij} - O_{ij}}{\sum_{ij} O_{ij}} \pm \dfrac{1}{2 \times \sum_{ij} O_{ij}}}{\sqrt{\dfrac{\left(\dfrac{O_{ij}}{\sum_{ij} O_{ij}}\right)\left(1 - \dfrac{O_{ij}}{\sum_{ij} O_{ij}}\right)}{\sum_{ij} O_{ij}}}}$$

where $T_{ij}$ is the estimated data, column $i$, row $j$, $O_{ij}$ is the census data, column $i$, row $j$, and $\sum_{ij} O_{ij}$ is the sum of all the elements in the table. The $\frac{1}{2 \times \sum_{ij} O_{ij}}$ stochastic component is added or subtracted, because in some large tables it is possible to have 0 values, and then one would have division by zero. A stochastic component is added if $T_{ij} < O_{ij}$ and subtracted if $T_{ij} > O_{ij}$. Of course, if the observed and the expected are the same, then $Z$ is 0.

The third statistic that may be used to assess internally the model's goodness of fit is the relative error, using an $\chi^2$ test of independence:

$$\chi^2 = \sum_{i=1}^{n} \frac{(O_i - E_i)^2}{E_i}$$

where:
$\chi^2$ = Pearson's cumulative-test statistic, which asymptotically approaches a $\chi^2$ distribution with $n$-1 degrees of freedom
$O_i$ = an observed frequency, resulting from the data-synthesis procedure
$E_i$ = an expected frequency, as defined by the control totals
$n$ = the number of cells in the table

To undertake in-sample validation, $O_i$ and $E_i$ are compared for variables used to constrain the simulation. To complement our validation of constrained variables, we also perform out-of-sample validation. This may also use the $\chi^2$ test. Because of computational constraints, we are unlikely to use all potential constraint variables. We can perform the $\chi^2$ test as a test of conditional independence.

Multi-module validation can be undertaken by comparing the result of a number of processes, such as the calculation of poverty, that result from the data-synthesis procedure, as well as the non-linear relationship with disposable income and resulting poverty calculation, with an external source of local-area poverty that might be generated from another dataset. For example, O'Donoghue et al. (2013) compared county-level poverty statistics, generated by the SMILE model, and poverty statistics from a spatially representative survey, the National Survey of Household Quality (NSHQ) of 2001–02, as reported in Watson et al. (2005).

## 10.4.2 Income-Generation Models

Where validation problems exist, a number of suggested solutions include the use of alternative or additional constraints, namely: the sampling of micro-units from the same (aggregated) spatial area (Voas and Williamson 2000); separate matching methods for different spatial clusters (Smith et al. 2009); or alternative sets of constraints depending on the purpose (Chin and Harding 2006). However, given the heavy computational cost of employing additional constraints identified in Miller (2001), along with the desire to have a single-model configuration for all uses, an alternative calibration procedure is next reported.

The objective of the calibration mechanism is to 'correct' problems in non-constraint variables. A similar method is used to the calibration method used within the dynamic microsimulation models discussed in Chapter 9. The first task is, as in Chapter 8, is to estimate a system of equations, or income-generation models, on the national data set:

$$Y_M = Y_{Emp} I_{Emp} + Y_{SE} I_{SE} + Y_{Cap} I_{Cap} + Y_{Other} I_{Other}$$

where $Y_i$ is income source $i$, and $I_i$ is the presence of this income, and where $Y_i = f_i\left(Z, \theta_i, \varepsilon_i\right)$ and $I_i = g_i\left(Z, \theta_i, \varepsilon_i\right)$ for all income sources $i$.

As in the case of the dynamic model, we estimate only a single set of estimates; however, the error-component structure is simpler, not having an inter-temporal component. In the same way as in the dynamic model, the simulations are constrained to be consistent with external control totals at a sub-national level. For example, in the case of an in-work model, we constrain the local employment rate to be consistent with local-level employment data.

### 10.4.3 Implementation

Chapter 9 describes the practical detail of how to do this for binary-choice models. The process for two other types of model, multiple-choice models and log-income regress models, is described here. Each model requires a set of parameters, relating to the explained or deterministic part of the equation, and an error component reflecting stochastic variability. The models are estimated on the original micro-data, and then simulated consecutively for each district.

Multi-category choices, such as occupation, are simulated using a reduced-form multinomial logit model, in other words the explanatory variables are not choice-specific. isturbance terms for multi-category-dependent variables, such as occupation or industry, are derived from multinomial logit models using the following method. First, a set of random variables is generated for counterfactual choices using the extreme-value distribution:

$$v_j = -\ln\left(-\ln\left(u\right)\right)$$

where $u$ is a uniform random number and $j$ is choice $j$, and not the actual choice chosen by the individual in the original data. Our objective now is to choose a random variable from the extreme-value distribution $v_i$ for the actual choice $i$ such that:

$$xb + v_i > xb + v_j \forall j \neq i$$

### 10.4.4 Alignment

However, even with a detailed system of equations with many explanatory variables, there is still unexplained spatial heterogeneity, due to the failure of conditional independence. This may be due to a number of reasons:

- Where unconstrained variables have a poor relationship with the constrained variables, Voas and Williamson (2000) identified that when using substantial numbers of constraint variables, the resulting explained spatial heterogeneity is still poor. This is the case even for unconstrained variables with the greatest explanatory association with the constraint variables. For unconstrained variables, with a limited association with the constraint variables, their distribution tended to that of the national distribution.

- The estimated equations used for Monte Carlo simulation may have poor predictive power (Alderman et al. 2002), particularly where some states are either relatively densely or sparsely represented in the data. Thus, the further from 50 per cent the probability of an event occurring, the less effective these decision rules are at producing the desired result. In this case, a logit model used on its own may under- or over-predict the number of events.

In order to capture spatial heterogeneity, we draw again from the dynamic-microsimulation-modelling literature, where simulated variables are constrained to match external alignment totals (for a description of the methodology, see O'Donoghue and Morrissey 2011; for an example applied to health data, see Morrissey et al. 2008).

Using alignment, the Monte Carlo-simulated variables are calibrated, via the system of equations in the example model, to exogenous alignment constraints. The general objective of this methodology in calibrating a spatial microsimulation model is to ensure that the simulated output matches exogenous totals at varying levels of spatial disaggregation.

There are a number of different alignment processes that may be used, and the choice of process depends on the type of data outputted from the microsimulation model and the data type of the exogenous 'target' data. In the example model, three types of alignment for binary-discrete data, discrete data with more than two choices, and continuous data are utilized.

Fundamentally, the structure of our generalized linear models is estimated on external micro-data for binary-choice, multiple-choice, and logged-income-regression models, which take the general form:

$$y_i = g\left(BX_i\right) + \varepsilon_i$$

Simulation is then undertaken according to the distribution of characteristics $X_i^{\bullet}$ of units in the synthetic spatial dataset:

$$y_i^{\bullet} = g\left(BX_i^{\bullet}\right) + \varepsilon_i (*)$$

The external totals used for calibration are based upon small-area census data. For binary variables, our calibration routine operates where $N$ cases of a particular unconstrained variable are required in the relevant district; we thus rank our predicted variable $y_i^*$ defined in (*) such that we select the $N$ cases with the highest value of $y_i^*$.

In multiple-choice models, a similar method is developed, ranking $y_j^*$ for each choice *j* in turn to be consistent with externally defined $N_j$. Income variables are adjusted by uprating, using group-specific income-growth rates.

This method is undertaken for each of the simulated processes, so that the aggregate number of cases of each variable *y* is consistent with the control total from the census small-area statistic.

The use of alignment or calibration is not without criticism. Winder (2000) argues that the reason for the use of alignment is: 'that microsimulation models usually fail to simulate known time-series data. By aligning the model, goodness of fit to an observed time series can be guaranteed. Opinions vary as to the admissibility of this procedure. Most microsimulation modellers accept alignment as an unfortunate, but unavoidable necessity, while other thermodynamic modellers (the author among them) consider it to be an "indefensible fiddle" which, to use Popper's celebrated phrase, effectively immunizes the model against empirical refutation.' He also argues that 'the only way microsimulation modellers can predict the future is by persuading someone who knows more than they do to tell them what's going to happen', and goes on to contend that thermodynamic models are non-alignment microsimulation models and that aligned microsimulation models are irreconcilable.

## 10.5 Measurement Issues: Spatial Inequality

In addition to identifying the distributional impact of different tax-benefit policy instruments described in earlier chapters, it is also useful to understand how much redistribution there is within and between spatial entities. To do this, examining the variability of incomes between individuals within and across regions, inequality is decomposed into population sub-groups, where groups are districts or other spatial entities (WanShorrocks and Wan 2005).

The objective of this method is to decompose inequality into two categories: between group or district, and within group or district. There are a number of inequality indicators that are decomposable, of which the most common is the family of generalized entropy indices, such as the mean logarithmic deviation, the Theil coefficient, and the half of the squared coefficient of variation (Theil 1972; Bourguignon 1979; Shorrocks 1984; Cowell 1980). It should be noted that sub-group consistency is also satisfied by the Atkinson class of inequality measures, but the Gini coefficient is not sub-group-consistent, and therefore not decomposable (Wan and Shorrocks 2005).

In modelling the distribution of welfare, it is assumed (as elsewhere in this book) that disposable income is a proxy for a household's standard of living. It should be noted that in doing this, home production and non-pecuniary income are ignored, along with the advantages and disadvantages systematically associated with geographical location, including climate, regional price variations, local public-good provision, and environmental quality (Brereton et al., 2008). In other words, the analysis assumes that individuals with the same income at different locations are equally well-off.

One can then decompose total variability of incomes into a factor attributed to between group variability across space and variability within a district (within group variability). Utilizing the Theil index:

$$T = \frac{1}{n}\sum_{i=1}^{n}\frac{y_i}{\bar{y}}\ln\left(\frac{y_i}{\bar{y}}\right)$$

where $y_i$ can be defined as the equivalized income of household $i$, and $\bar{y}$ the average income per capita, and $n$ is the population size. Spatially decomposing into $k$ districts or regions, we can decompose $T$ into between-group and within-group inequality:

$$T = \left(\sum_{j=1}^{k}\frac{n_j}{n}\frac{y_i}{\bar{y}}\ln\left(\frac{\bar{y}_j}{\bar{y}}\right)\right) + \sum_{j=1}^{k}\left[\frac{1}{n}\frac{\bar{y}_j}{\bar{y}}\sum_{i=1}^{n_j}\frac{y_{ij}}{\bar{y}_j}\ln\left(\frac{y_{ij}}{\bar{y}_j}\right)\right] = B + W$$

where $n_j$ is the population size of district $j$, $\bar{y}_j$ is the average income of district $j$, and $y_{ij}$ is the income of the $i$th individual in the $j$th district.

## 10.6 Simulation: Modelling the Spatial Distribution of Income in Ireland

In this section, the methodology is applied to Irish datasets to model the spatial distribution of income. Spatial-control totals are derived from the 2006 census, while income data is drawn from the 2007 European Union Statistics on Income and Living Conditions (EU–SILC). Utilizing calibration variables of age, gender, education, and employment, the SILC is sampled to be consistent with about three-thousand-four-hundred small-area districts in Ireland, with a population of about four million, using the QS methodology described earlier. Utilizing the calibration-based alignment methodology, also described earlier, additional variables relating to employment status, occupation, and industry, as well as all the key market incomes, are derived. Applying the tax-benefit algorithm to the market incomes of our population within the districts, disposable income, i.e., market income plus benefits minus taxes, is calculated.

In a validation exercise, comparing the ratio of county income against national income for simulated SMILE data, and actual data taken from the Central Statistics Office (CSO) county data, a high correlation of 97 per cent between actual and simulated disposable income per capita between the two sources is evident. This gives confidence that the tax-benefit model is a good representation of the structure of taxes and benefits within Ireland.

Equivalizing by the square root of household size, and taking the average per district, a map of average disposable income by district is produced and presented in Figure 10.1. For ease of exposition, districts are grouped into four quartiles. As one can see, the east of the country, particularly the Greater Dublin Area, has much higher levels of the disposable income compared to the rest of the country. The four other main urban centres, Cork, Limerick, Galway, and Waterford, also have higher than average disposable income. These results are consistent with CSO statistics, which found that at the NUTS-3 level the Dublin region had the highest disposable income per person of the eight NUTS-3 regions. Furthermore, the CSO reported that at the county level, only Dublin, Limerick, Kildare, and Wicklow had average disposable incomes greater than the state average (€16,625). Again, as can be seen from Figure 10.1, the spatial pattern of the simulated data created by SMILE is representative of this county distribution, with the EDs that constitute Dublin city and county displaying above-average disposable-income levels. Furthermore, Kildare (just west of Dublin),Wicklow (just south of Dublin), and Limerick (in the Mid-West) also exhibit average disposable-income levels greater than the state average.

In Table 10.1, the map is aggregated into twelve classifications of districts as a function of the urban-rural nature of the district. It is evident that rural areas and small villages have the highest ratio of disposable income to market income, with the Dublin counties and Galway city having the lowest.

### 10.6.1 Between and Within Spatial-Area Inequality

Next, the inequality-reducing effect of tax and benefit policy is assessed, both across families and districts using the methodology described in Section 10.4. Table 10.2 displays the between- and within-group inequality by income at the ED level. Income is divided into three components; market income, gross

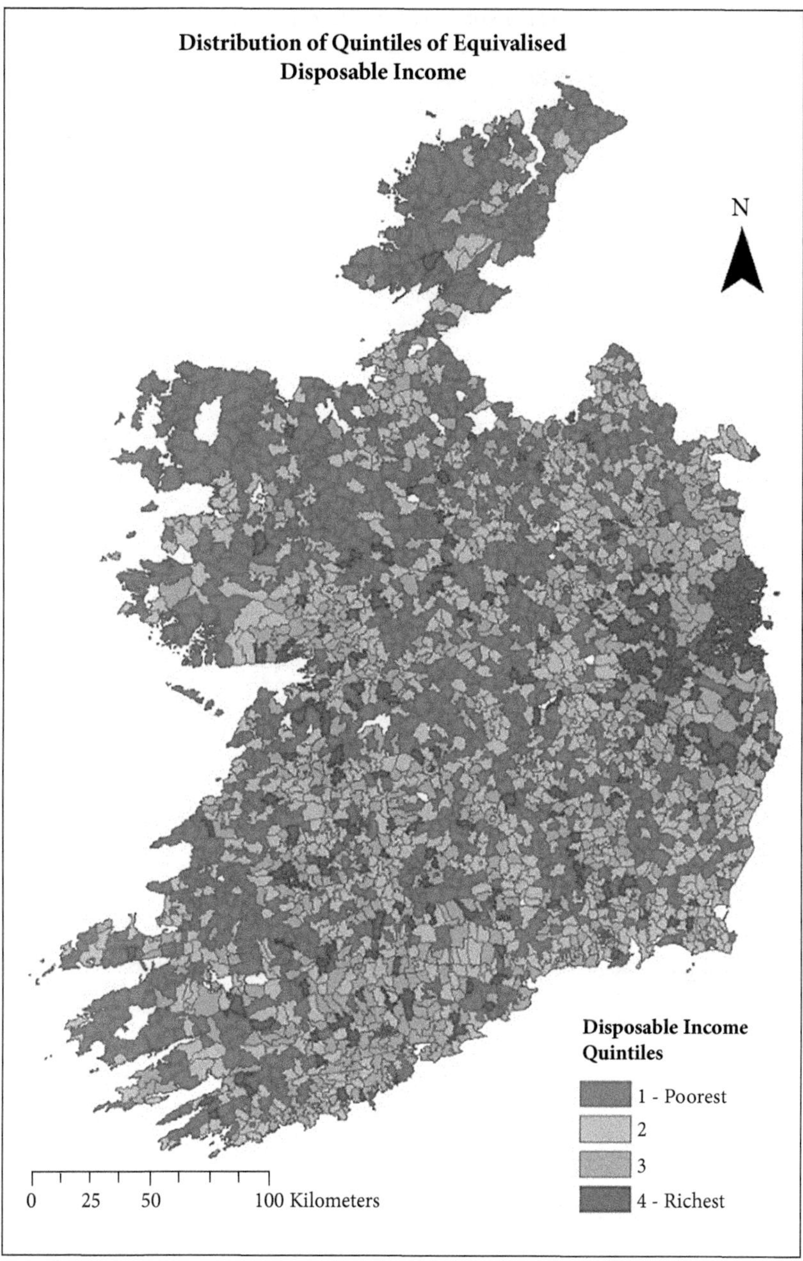


**Figure 10.1** Simulated Average-Equivalized Household Disposable Income at the District Level
*Source*: author's calculations.

**Table 10.1** Urban Versus Rural Market and Disposable Income

| | Market Income | Disposable Income | Ratio |
|---|---|---|---|
| Rural | 87 | 91 | 105 |
| Village (200–1,499) | 85 | 91 | 107 |
| Town (1,500–2,999) | 99 | 99 | 100 |
| Town (3,000–4,999) | 97 | 99 | 101 |
| Town (5,000–9,999) | 103 | 102 | 99 |
| Town (10,000+) | 104 | 102 | 98 |
| Waterford City | 100 | 100 | 101 |
| Galway City | 110 | 106 | 96 |
| Limerick City | 93 | 93 | 100 |
| Cork City | 95 | 97 | 102 |
| Dublin City | 117 | 113 | 97 |
| Dublin County | 123 | 115 | 94 |
| Total | 100 | 100 | 100 |

*Source*: SMILE.

**Table 10.2** Between- and Within-Group Inequality by Income Component

| | Grouping Variable | | | | |
|---|---|---|---|---|---|
| | District | County | Density | Distance to Hub | Population Change |
| Market Income | | | | | |
| I2 | 0.46 | 0.46 | 0.46 | 0.46 | 0.46 |
| Between % | 5.3 | 3.1 | 1.6 | 0.8 | 0.7 |
| Within % | 94.7 | 96.9 | 98.4 | 99.2 | 99.3 |
| Gross Income | | | | | |
| I2 | 0.31 | 0.31 | 0.31 | 0.31 | 0.31 |
| Between % | 5.3 | 3.2 | 1.7 | 0.8 | 0.6 |
| Within % | 94.8 | 96.8 | 98.3 | 99.2 | 99.4 |
| Disposable Income | | | | | |
| I2 | 0.21 | 0.21 | 0.21 | 0.21 | 0.21 |
| Between % | 5.6 | 3.3 | 1.8 | 0.9 | 0.6 |
| Within % | 94.5 | 96.7 | 98.2 | 99.1 | 99.4 |

income, and disposable income. Examined here also is the impact on income inequality on five different grouping variables, such as district, county level, density, the distance to hub, and population change.

In examining inequality between groups from Table 10.2, it can be seen that between-district inequality accounts for a very small percentage of overall inequality (at most, 5 per cent of the total), with most inequality existing within districts (between families). We also note that the more aggregated the spatial concept, the greater the share of within-group inequality.

However, the level of inequality reduces as one adds benefits and subtracts taxes to get gross income and disposable income respectively, the proportion accounted for by between-group inequality remaining roughly the same. Thus, tax-benefit policy does not act to reduce spatial inequality; rather, it acts more to reduce between-family inequalities.

Over the last thirty years, attempts to map the distribution of income, both within Ireland and internationally, have been hindered by the use of aggregate data for large spatial units. The use of aggregate data, although interesting with regard to international income comparisons, is limited for within-country analysis, as it does not allow for in-depth, sub-national/sub-population analysis. This, in turn, tends to conceal poverty at the local level. This research provides an insight into the distribution of income in Ireland at the national, district, and urban/rural level, by mapping disposable income at local level using data produced by a spatial microsimulation model.

Using the aligned income data from SMILE, and the SMILE tax-benefit component, this chapter provides an urban/rural comparison of the distribution of income, and the impact that the tax-benefit system has on changing this distribution. It was found that disposable income is on average lower in rural than urban areas, with transfers from urban to rural areas. These results correspond to those of Morgenroth (2010), who developed an analysis of the regional transfers across the country. Morgenroth's analysis shows that there is a transfer of resources from the Greater Dublin Area and the South West to the rest of the country.

As such, this analysis demonstrated that a spatial profile of disposable income in Ireland can be achieved through the use of spatial microsimulation techniques. Integrating this data within a geographic information system (GIS) provides policy makers with small-area-level maps of income. These maps in turn can deepen our understanding of the determinants of inequality and poverty, and lead to improvements in the design of policies tailored to local conditions.

# References


Aaberge, R., and Colombino, U. (2014), 'Labour Supply Models', in C. O'Donoghue, ed., *Handbook of Microsimulation Modelling* (Bingley: Emerald Group Publishing), 167–221.

Abello, A., Lymer, S., Brown, L., Harding, A., and Phillips, B. (2008), 'Enhancing the Australian National Health Survey Data for Use in a Microsimulation Model of Pharmaceutical Drug Usage and Cost', *Journal of Artificial Societies and Social Simulation*, 11/3, 2.

Abid-Fourati, Y., and O'Donoghue, C. (2010), 'Simulating the Political Sustainability of Pension Systems', in Cathal O'Donoghue, ed., *Life-Cycle Income Analysis Modelling* (Saarbrücken: Lambert Academic Publishing).

Acemoglu, D., and Shimer, R. (1999), 'Efficient Unemployment Insurance', *Journal of Political Economy*, 107/5, 893–928.

Ahmad, E., and Stern, N. (1984), 'The Theory of Reform and Indian Indirect Taxes', *Journal of Public Economics*, 33, 357–62.

Ahmad, E., and Stern, N. (1991), *The Theory and Practice of Tax Reform in Developing Countries* (Cambridge: Cambridge University Press).

Ahmed, V., and O'Donoghue, C. (2007), 'CGE-Microsimulation Modelling: A Survey', MPRA Working Paper No. 9307.

Ahmed, V., and O'Donoghue, C. (2009), 'Redistributive Effect of Personal Income Taxation in Pakistan'. *Pakistan Economic and Social Review*, Vol. 47, No. 1 1–17.

Alfredsson, E. (2002), 'Green Consumption Energy Use and Carbon Dioxide Emission', Ph.D. dissertation, Kulturgeografi. Umea University.

Alderman, H., Babita, M., Demombynes, G., Makhatha, N., and Ozler, B. (2002), 'How Low Can You Go? Combining Census and Survey Data for Mapping Poverty in South Africa', *Journal of African Economics*, 11, 169–200.

Amarante, V., Arim, R., de Melo, G., and Vigorito, A. (2010), 'Family Allowances and Child School Attendance: An Ex-Ante Evaluation of Alternative Schemes in Uruguay', in *Child Welfare in Developing Countries* (New York: Springer), 211–45.

Amarante, V., Bucheli, M., Olivieri, C., and Perazzo, I. (2011), 'Redistributive Effects of Indirect Taxes: Comparing Arithmetical and Behavioral Simulations in Uruguay', *Documento de Trabajo/FCS-DE*, 23/11, 1–11.

Anderson, B. (2007), Creating Small Area Income Estimates for England: spatial microsimulation modelling. University of Essex Chimera Working Paper Number: 2007-07.

Anderson, R. E., and Hicks, C. (2011), 'Highlights of Contemporary Microsimulation', *Social Science Computer Review*, 29/1, 3–8.

Antcliff, S. (1993), 'An Introduction to DYNAMOD: A Dynamic Microsimulation Model', DYNAMOD Technical Paper No. 1, National Centre for Social and Economic Modelling (NATSEM), University of Canberra, Australia.

Antcliff, S., Bracher, M., Gruskin, A., Hardin, A., and Kapuscinski, C. (1996), 'Development of DYNAMOD 1993 and 1994', DYNAMOD Working Paper No. 1, National Centre for Social and Economic Modelling (NATSEM), University of Canberra, Australia.

Arencibia, A. I., Feo-Valero, M., García-Menéndez, L., and Román, C. (2015), 'Modelling Mode Choice for Freight Transport Using Advanced Choice Experiments', *Transportation Research Part A: Policy and Practice*, 75, 252–67.

Arsić, M., and Altiparmakov, N. (2013), 'Equity Aspects of VAT in Emerging European Countries: A Case Study of Serbia', *Economic Systems*, 37/2, 171–86.

Atkinson, A. B. (1970), 'On the Measurement of Inequality'. *Journal of Economic Theory*, 2/3, 244–263.

Atkinson, A. B. (1980), 'Horizontal Equity and the Distribution of the Tax Burden', in H. Aaron and M. Boskin, eds., *The Economics of Taxation* (Washington, DC: Brookings Institution).

Atkinson, A. B. (1983), *Social Justice and Public Policy*. Cambridge MA: MIT Press.

Atkinson A. B., and Bourguignon, F. (1991), 'Tax-Benefit Models for Developing Countries: Lessons from Developed Countries', DELTA Working Paper No. 90–15, École Normale Supérieure, Paris.

Atkinson, A. B., and Bourguignon, F. (1991), 'Tax-Benefit Models for Developing Countries: Lessons from Developed Countries'. *Tax Policy in Developing Countries* (Washington, DC: The World Bank), 216–226.

Atkinson, A. B. (1995), *Incomes and the Welfare State: Essays on Britain and Europe.* (Cambridge: Cambridge University Press).

Atkinson, A. B. (1996), 'Public Economics in Action: The Basic Income/Flat Tax Proposal', *Oxford University Press.*

Atkinson, A. B. (1998), *Poverty in Europe* (Oxford: Blackwell).

Atkinson, A. B., Bourguignon, F., O'Donoghue, C., Sutherland, H., and Utili, F. (2002), 'Microsimulation of Social Policy in the European Union: Case Study of a European Minimum Pension', *Economica*, 69/274, 229–43.

Atkinson, A. B., and Micklewright, J. (1985), *Unemployment benefits and unemployment duration: A study of men in the United Kingdom in the 1970s* (Vol. 6). Suntory-Toyota International centre for Economics and Related Disciplines, London School of Economics and Political Science.

Atkinson, A. B., and Micklewright, J. (1991), 'Unemployment Compensation and Labor Market Transitions: A Critical Review', *Journal of Economic Literature*, 29/4, 1679–1727.

Badenes-Plá, N., and Buenaventura-Zabala, J. M. (2017), 'The Spanish Income Tax Reform of 2015: Analysis of the Effects on Poverty and Redistribution Using Microsimulation Tools', *Public Sector Economics*, 41/3, 315–33.

Bach, S., Kohlhaas, M., Meyer, B., Praetorius, B., and Welsch, H. (2002), 'The Effects of Environmental Fiscal Reform in Germany: A Simulation Study', *Energy Policy*, 30/9, 803–11.

Baekgaard, H. (1998), 'Simulating the Distribution of Household Wealth in Australia: New Estimates for 1986 and 1993', Technical Paper No. 14—June, National Centre for Social and Economic Modelling (NATSEM), University of Canberra, Australia.

Baekgaard, H. (2002), 'Micro-Macro Linkage and the Alignment of Transition Processes: Some Issues, Techniques and Examples', Technical Paper No. 25, National Centre for Social and Economic Modelling (NATSEM), University of Canberra, Australia.

Baker, P., McKay, S., and Symons, E. (1990), 'The Simulation of Indirect Tax Reforms: The IFS Simulation Program for Indirect Taxation', Working Paper Series No. W90/11, Institute for Fiscal Studies.

Baldini, M. (1997), *Diseguaglianza e Redistribuzione nel Ciclo di Vita* (Bologna: Il Mulino).

Ballas, D., Broomhead, T., and Jones, P. M. (2019), 'Spatial Microsimulation and Agent-Based Modelling', in *The Practice of Spatial Analysis* (Cham: Springer), 69–84.

Ballas, D. (2004), 'Simulating Trends in Poverty and Income Inequality on the Basis of 1991 and 2001 Census Data: A Tale of Two Cities. *Area*, 36/2, 146–163.

Ballas, D., and Clarke, G. P. (2001), 'Modelling the Local Impacts of National Social Policies: A Spatial Microsimulation Approach'. *Environment and Planning C: Government and Policy*, 19/4, 587–606.

Ballas, D., and Clarke, G. P. (2009), 'Spatial Microsimulation'. *Handbook of Spatial Analysis* (London: Sage), 277–298.

Ballas, D., Clarke, G., Dorling, D., Eyre, H., Thomas, B., and Rossiter, D. (2005), 'SimBritain: A Spatial Microsimulation Approach to Population Dynamics'. *Population, Space and Place*, 11/1, 13–34.

Ballas D, Clarke G.P., and Turton I. (2003), 'A Spatial Microsimulation Model for Social Policy Evaluation'. In Boots B., and Thomas R. eds., *Modelling Geographical Systems* (The Netherlands: Kluwer), 143–168.

Ballas, D., Clarke, G. P., and Wiemers, E. (2005), 'Building a Dynamic Spatial Microsimulation Model for Ireland', *Population, Space and Place*, 11/3, 157–72.

Ballas, D., Clarke, G. P., and Wiemers, E. (2006), 'Spatial Microsimulation for Rural Policy Analysis in Ireland: The Implications of CAP Reforms for the National Spatial Strategy', *Journal of Rural Studies*, 22/3, 367–78.

Ballas, D., Rossiter, D., Thomas, B., Clarke, G., and Dorling, D. (2005), *Geography Matters: Simulating the Local Impacts of National Social Policies*, Joseph Rowntree Foundation Contemporary Research Issues (York: Joseph Rowntree Foundation).

Banerjee, A., Duflo, E., Glennerster, R., and Kinnan, C. (2015), 'The Miracle of Microfinance? Evidence from a Randomized Evaluation', *American Economic Journal: Applied Economics*, 7/1, 22–53.

Banks, J., Blundell, R., and Lewbel, A. (1997), 'Quadratic Engel Curves and Consumer Demand', *Review of Economics and Statistics*, 69, 527–39.

Bargain, O. (2012a), 'The Distributional Effects of Tax-Benefit Policies Under New Labour: A Decomposition Approach', *Oxford Bulletin of Economics and Statistics*, 74/6, 856–74.

Bargain, O. (2012b), 'Back to the Future: Decomposition Analysis of Distributive Policies Using Behavioural Simulations', *International Tax and Public Finance*, 19/5, 708–31.

Bargain, O., and Callan, T. (2010), 'Analysing the Effects of Tax-Benefit Reforms on Income Distribution: A Decomposition Approach', *Journal of Economic Inequality*, 8/1, 1–21.

Bargain, O., Callan, T., Doorley, K., and Keane, C. (2017a), 'Changes in Income Distributions and the Role of Tax-Benefit Policy During the Great Recession: An International Perspective', *Fiscal Studies*, 38/4, 559–85.

Bargain, O., Dolls, M., Immervoll, H., Neumann, D., Peichl, A., Pestel, N., et al. (2015), 'Tax Policy and Income Inequality in the United States, 1979–2007', *Economic Inquiry*, 53/2, 1061–85.

Bargain, O., and Doorley, K. (2011), 'In-Work Transfers in Good Times and Bad: Simulations for Ireland', in *Research in Labor Economics* (Bingley: Emerald Group Publishing), 307–39.

Bargain, O., Jara, H. X., and Rodriguez, D. (2017), 'Learning From Your Neighbor: Tax-Benefit Systems Swaps in Latin America', *The Journal of Economic Inequality*, 15/4, 369–92.

Bargain, O., Orsini, K., and Peichl, A. (2012), 'Comparing Labor Supply Elasticities in Europe and the US: New Results', Discussion Paper No. 6735, Institute for the Study of Labour (IZA).

Bargain, O., Orsini, K., and Peichl, A. (2014), 'Comparing Labor Supply Elasticities in Europe and the United States New Results', *Journal of Human Resources*, 49/3, 723–838.

Bargain, O., and Peichl, A. (2013), Steady-State Labor Supply Elasticities: A Survey. *ZEW-Centre for European Economic Research Discussion Paper*, 13–084.

Baroni, E., Žamac, J., and Öberg, G. (2009), *IFSIM Handbook* (Stockholm: Arbetsrapport).

Barr, N. (2012), *Economics of the Welfare State* (Oxford: Oxford University Press).

Barten, A. P. (1969), 'Maximum Likelihood Estimation of a Complete System of Demand Equations'. *European Economic Review*, 1(1), 7–73.

Bastagli, F. (2015), 'Bringing Taxation into Social Protection Analysis and Planning', Working Papers, Overseas Development Institute, London.

Bean, C. R. (1994), 'European Unemployment: A Survey', *Journal of Economic Literature*, 32/2, 573–619.

Beckerman, W. (1979), 'The Impact of Income Maintenance Payments on Poverty in Britain, 1975', *The Economic Journal*, 89/354, 261–79.

Beer, G. (1998), 'The State of Play of Effective Marginal Tax Rates in Australia in 1997', *Australian Economic Review*, 31/3, 263–20.

Bell, P. (unpublished), *GREGWT and TABLE Macros—Users Guide* (Australian Bureau of Statistics, Canberra), 2000.

Benhassine, N., Devoto, F., Duflo, E., Dupas, P., and Pouliquen, V. (2015), 'Turning a Shove into a Nudge? A "Labeled Cash Transfer" for Education', *American Economic Journal: Economic Policy*, 7/3, 86–125.

Benson, T. (2006), 'Insights from Poverty Maps for Development and Food Relief Program Targeting', Discussion Paper No. 205, Food Consumption and Nutrition Division, International Food Policy Research Institute, Washington, DC.

Berger, F., Borsenberger, M., Immervoll, H., Lumen, J., Scholtus, B., and De Vos, K. (2001), *The Impact of Tax-Benefit Systems on Low-Income Households in the Benelux Countries: A Simulation Approach Using Synthetic Datasets* (No. EM3/01). Euromod Working Paper.

Berger, F., Islam, N., and Liégeois, P. (2011), 'Behavioural Microsimulation and Female Labour Supply in Luxembourg', *Brussels Economic Review*, 54/4, 389–420.

Berliant, M. C., and Strauss, R. P. (2007), 'State and Federal Tax Equity: Estimates Before and After the Tax Reform Act of 1986', *Journal of Policy Analysis and Management*, 12/1, 9–43.

Berliant, M. C., Strauss, R. P., and Hiser, S. M. (2008), 'Distributional Analysis of Prospective 2009 US Individual Income Taxes: Current Law and the Candidates' Tax Plans', Paper No. 11221, MPRA.

Berntsen, J., Petersen, B. M., Jacobsen, B. H., Olesen, J. E., and Hutchings, N. J. (2003), 'Evaluating Nitrogen Taxation Scenarios Using the Dynamic Whole Farm Simulation Model FASSET'. *Agricultural Systems*, 76/3, 817–839.

Berry, A. (2019), 'The Distributional Effects of a Carbon Tax and its Impact on Fuel Poverty: A Microsimulation Study in the French Context', *Energy Policy*, 124, Jan 81–94.

Betcherman, G., Dar, A., and Olivas, K. (2004), 'Impacts of Active Labor Market Programs: New Evidence from Evaluations with Particular Attention to Developing and Transition Countries', Social Protection, World Bank, Washington, DC.

Betti, G., Donatiello, G., and Verma, V. (2011), 'The Siena Micro Simulation Model (SM2) for Netgross Conversion of EU-SILC Income Variables'. *International Journal of Microsimulation*, 4/1, 35–53.

Beznoska, M., and Hentze, T. (2017), 'Demographic Change and Income Tax Revenue in Germany: A Microsimulation Approach', *Public Sector Economics*, 41/1, 71–84.

Bhargava, S., and Manoli, D. (2015), 'Psychological Frictions and the Incomplete Take-Up of Social Benefits: Evidence from an IRS Field Experiment', *The American Economic Review*, 105/11, 3489–529.

Biewen, M., and Juhasz, A. (2012), 'Understanding Rising Income Inequality in Germany, 1999/2000–2005/2006'. *Review of Income and Wealth*, 58/4, 622–647.

Bird, K., Higgins, K., and Harris, D. (2010), 'Spatial Poverty Traps: An Overview', ODI/CPRC Working Paper Series Nos. WP321 and WP161, Overseas Development Institute, London, and CPRC, University of Manchester.

Bird, K., and Shepherd, A. (2003), 'Livelihoods and Chronic Poverty in Semi-Arid Zimbabwe', *World Development*, 31/3, 591–610.

Birkin, M., and Clarke, M. (1985), 'Comprehensive Dynamic Urban Models: Integrating Macro- and Micro-Approaches', in D. A. Griffith and R. P. Haining, eds., *Transformations Through Space and Time: An Analysis of Nonlinear Structures, Bifurcation Points and Autoregressive Dependencies* (Dordrecht: Martinus Nijhoff), 165–292.

Birkin, M., and Clarke, M. (1988), 'SYNTHESIS—A Synthetic Spatial Information System for Urban and Regional Analysis: Methods and Examples', *Environment and Planning A*, 20, 1645–71.

Birkin, M., and Clarke, G. (2012), 'The Enhancement of Spatial Microsimulation Models Using Geodemographics'. *The Annals of Regional Science*, 49/2, 515–532.

Björklund, A. (1991), *Labour Market Policy and Unemployment Insurance*, ii (US: Oxford University Press).

Björklund, A., and Palme, M. (2002), 'The Life Cycle Versus Between Individuals: Empirical Evidence Using Swedish Panel Data', *The Economics of Rising Inequalities*, 205.

Blanchet, D., Crenner, E., and Minez, S. (2009), 'The Destinie 2 Microsimulation Model: Increased Flexibility and Adaptation to Users' Needs', Conference Paper, International Microsimulation Association.

Blau, F., and Khan, L. (1996), 'Flowage Structure and Earnings Differentials: An International Comparison'. *Economica*, 63, 250.

Blinder, A. S. (1973), 'Wage Discrimination: Reduced Form and Structural Estimates', *Journal of Human Resources*, 8, Oct 436–55.

Blundell, R., Duncan, A., McCrae, J., and Meghir, C. (2000), 'The Labour Market Impact of the Working Families' Tax Credit', *Fiscal Studies*, 21/1, 75–104.

Blomquist, N. S. (1983), 'The Effect of Income Taxation on the Labor Supply of Married Men in Sweden', *Journal of Public Economics*, 22/2, 169–97.

Blundell, R. (1988), 'Consumer Behaviour: Theory and Empirical Evidence—A Survey', *The Economic Journal*, 98 (389), 16–65.

Blundell, R., Duncan, A., and Pendakur, K. (1998), 'Semiparametric Estimation and Consumer Demand'. *Journal of applied econometrics*, 13(5), 435–461.

Blundell, R., and MaCurdy, T. (1999), 'Labor Supply: A Review of Alternative Approaches', in O. C. Ashenfelter and D. Card, eds., *Handbook of Labor Economics*, iii (Amsterdam: North-Holland), 1559–1695.

Boccanfuso, D., Estache, A., and Savard, L. (2011), 'The Intra-Country Distributional Impact of Policies to Fight Climate Change: A Survey', *The Journal of Development Studies*, 47/1, 97–117.

Boersch-Supan, A. H. (2001), 'Incentive Effects of Social Security under an Uncertain Disability Option', in D. A. Wise (ed.), *Themes in the Economics of Aging* (Chicago: University of Chicago Press), 281–310.

Boeters, S., Böhringer, C., Büttner, T., and Kraus, M. (2010), 'Economic Effects of VAT Reforms in Germany', *Applied Economics*, 42/17, 2165–82.

Bommier, A., and Lee, R. D. (2003), 'Overlapping Generations Models with Realistic Demography', *Journal of Population Economics*, 16/1, 135–60.

Bonnet, C., and Mahieu, R. (2000), 'Public Pensions in a Dynamic Microanalytic Framework: The Case of France', in L. Mitton et al., eds., *Microsimulation in the New Millennium* (Cambridge: Cambridge University Press).

Bork, C. (2006), 'Distributional Effects of the Ecological Tax Reform in Germany: An Evaluation with a Microsimulation Model', in Y. Serret and N. Johnstone, eds., *The Distributional Effects of Environmental Policy* (Cheltenham: Edward Elgar Publishing/ OECD), 139–70.

Börsch-Supan, A., Kneip, T., Litwin, H., Myck, M., and Weber, G., eds. (2015), *Ageing in Europe-Supporting Policies for an Inclusive Society* (Berlin: Walter de Gruyter GmbH).

Börsch-Supan, A., Bucher-Koenen, T., Kutlu-Koc, V., and Goll, N. (2018), 'Dangerous Flexibility–Retirement Reforms Reconsidered'. *Economic Policy*, 33/94, 315–355.

Bourguignon, F. (1979), 'Decomposable Income Inequality Measures'. *Econometrica: Journal of the Econometric Society*, Vol. 47, No. 4 July 901–920.

Bourguignon, F., Bussolo, M., and Cockburn, J. (2010), 'GUEST EDITORIAL Macro-Micro Analytics: Background, Motivation, Advantages and Remaining Challenges', *International Journal of Microsimulation*, 3/1, 1–7.

Bourguignon, F., Ferreira, F. H., and Leite, P. G. (2002), *Beyond Oaxaca-Blinder: Accounting for Differences in Household Income Distributions Across Countries*, Vol. 478 (World Bank Publications).

Bourguignon, F., Ferreira, F. H., and Leite, P. G. (2003), 'Conditional Cash Transfers, Schooling, and Child Labor: Micro-Simulating Brazil's Bolsa Escola Program', *The World Bank Economic Review*, 17/2, 229–54.

Bourguignon, F., Ferreira, F. H., and Leite, P. G. (2008), 'Beyond Oaxaca–Blinder: Accounting for Differences in Household Income Distributions'. *The Journal of Economic Inequality*, 6(2), 117–148.

Bourguignon, F., O'Donoghue, C., Sastre-Descals, J., Spadaro, A., and Utili, F. (1997), 'Eur3: A Prototype European Tax-Benefit Model', Working Paper No. MU9703, Microsimulation Unit, Faculty of Economics, University of Cambridge.

Bourguignon, F., O'Donoghue, C., Sastre-Descals, J., Spadaro, A., and Utili, F. (1998), 'Eur3: A Prototype European Tax-Benefit Model: A Technical Description', Research Note No. R25, Microsimulation Unit, Faculty of Economics, University of Cambridge.

Bourguignon, F., O'Donoghue, C., Sastre-Descals, J., Spadaro, A., and Utili, F. (2000), 'Eur3: A Prototype European Tax-Benefit Model: Issues and Initial Experiments', in A. Gupta and V. Kaipur, eds., *Microsimulation in Government Policy and Forecasting* (Amsterdam: North-Holland).

Bourguignon, F., and Spadaro, A. (2006), 'Microsimulation as a Tool for Evaluating Redistribution Policies', *The Journal of Economic Inequality*, 4/1, 77–106.

Bover, O., Casado, J. M., García-Miralles, E., Labeaga Azcona, J. M., and Ramos Magdaleno, R. (2017). 'Microsimulation Tools for the Evaluation of Fiscal Policy Reforms at the Banco de España'. *Banco de Espana Occasional Paper*, 1707.

Boxall, P. C., Adamowicz, W. L., Swait, J., Williams, M., and Louviere, J. (1996), 'A Comparison of Stated Preference Methods for Environmental Valuation', *Ecological Economics*, 18/3, 243–53.

Brereton, F., Clinch, J. P., and Ferreira, S. (2008), 'Happiness, Geography and the Environment'. *Ecological Economics*, 65/2, 386–396.

Brewer, M., Browne, J., Joyce, R., and Payne, J. (2011), *Child and Working-Age Poverty from 2010 to 2020* (London: Institute for Fiscal Studies).

Brewer, M., Duncan, A., Shephard, A., and Suarez, M. J. (2006), 'Did Working Families' Tax Credit Work? The Impact of In-Work Support on Labour Supply in Great Britain', *Labour Economics*, 13/6, 699–720.

Brown, R. J., Caldwell, S. B., and Eklund, S. A. (1992), 'Microsimulation of Dental Conditions and Dental Service Utilisation', in J. G. Anderson, ed., *Proceedings of the Simulation in Health Care and Social Services Conference*, Society for Computer Simulation, San Diego.

Browne, J., and Immervoll, H. (2017), 'Mechanics of Replacing Benefit Systems with a Basic Income: Comparative Results from a Microsimulation Approach'. *The Journal of Economic Inequality*, 15/4, 325–344.

Brownstone, D., Englund, P., and Persson, M. (1985), 'Effects of the Swedish 1983–85 Tax Reform on the Demand for Owner-Occupied Housing: A Microsimulation Approach', *The Scandinavian Journal of Economics*, 87/4, 625–46.

Brunetti, A., and Calza, M. G. (2015), 'Redistributive Effects of Changes in Indirect Taxation', *Rivista di Statistica Ufficiale*, 17/2, 67–75.

Buddelmeyer, H., Hérault, N., Kalb, G., and de Jong, M. V. Z. (2012), 'Linking a Microsimulation Model to a Dynamic CGE Model: Climate Change Mitigation Policies and Income Distribution in Australia', *International Journal of Microsimulation*, 5/2, 40–58.

Burda, M. (1988), 'Wait Unemployment'in Europe'. *Economic Policy*, 3/7, 391–425.

Burden, S., and Steel, D. (2016), 'Constraint Choice for Spatial Microsimulation', *Population, Space and Place*, 22/6, 568–83.

Bureau, B. (2010), 'Distributional Effects of a Carbon Tax on Car Fuels in France', *Energy Economics*, 33/1, 121–30.

Burlacu, I., O'Donoghue, C., and Sologon, D. M. (2014), 'Hypothetical Models', in C. O'Donoghue, ed., *Handbook of Microsimulation Modelling* (Bingley: Emerald Group Publishing), 23–46.

Burtless, G. (1995), 'The Case for Randomized Field Trials in Economic and Policy Research'. *Journal of Economic Perspectives*, 9/2, 63–84.

Burtless, G. (1996), 'A Framework for Analyzing Future Retirement Income Security'. *Assessing Knowledge of Retirement Behavior*, 244.

Buslei, H., Bach, S., and Simmler, M. (2014), 'Firm Level Models Specifically Firm Models Based upon Large Data Sets', in C. O'Donoghue, ed., *Handbook of Microsimulation Modelling* (Bingley: Emerald Group Publishing), 479–503.

Cai, L., Creedy, J., and Kalb, G. (2006), 'Accounting for Population Ageing in Tax Microsimulation Modelling by Survey Reweighting', *Australian Economic Papers*, 45/1, 18–37.

Caldwell, S. B. (1996), 'Health, Wealth, Pensions and Life Paths: The CORSIM Dynamic Microsimulation Model', in A. Harding, ed., *Microsimulation and Public Policy* (Amsterdam: Elsevier/North-Holland).

Caldwell, S. B., Clarke, G. P., and Keister, L. A. (1998), 'Modelling Regional Changes in US Household Income and Wealth: A Research Agenda'. *Environment and Planning C: Government and Policy*, 16/6, 707–722.

Caldwell, S. B., and Morrison, R. (2000), 'Validation of Longitudinal Microsimulation Models: Experience with CORSIM and DYNACAN', in L. Mitton et al., eds., *Microsimulation in the New Millennium* (Cambridge: Cambridge University Press).

Callan, T. (1990), *Income Tax Reform: A Microsimulation Approach* (Dublin: Economic and Social Research Institute).

Callan, T., and Keane, C. (2009), 'Non-Cash Benefits and the Distribution of Economic Welfare', *The Economic and Social Review*, 40/1, 49–71.

Callan, T., Keane, C., Walsh, J. R., and Lane, M. (2010), 'From Data to Policy Analysis: Tax-Benefit Modelling Using SILC 2008'. *Journal of the Statistical and Social Inquiry Society of Ireland*, 40, 1.

Callan, T., Leventi, C., Levy, H., Matsaganis, M., Paulus, A., and Sutherland, H. (2011), 'The Distributional Effects of Austerity Measures: A Comparison of Six EU Countries', Working Paper Series No. EM6/11, EUROMOD at the Institute for Social and Economic Research, Essex.

Callan, T., Lyons, S., Scott, S., Tol, R. S. J., and Verde, S. (2009), 'The Distributional Implications of a Carbon Tax in Ireland', *Energy Policy*, 37/2, 407–12.

Callan, T., Nolan, B., and O'Donoghue, C. (1996), 'What Has Happened to Replacement Rates? *Economic and Social Review*, 27/5, 439.

Callan T., O'Donoghue, C., and O'Neill, C. (1996), 'Simulating Welfare and Income Tax Changes: The ESRI Tax-Benefit Model', The Economic and Social Research Institute, Dublin.

Callan, T., O'Neill, C., and O'Donoghue, C. (1995), 'Supplementing Family Income', Policy Research Series Paper No. 23, Economic and Social Research Institute, Dublin.

Callan, T., Van Soest, A., and Walsh, J. R. (2009), 'Tax Structure and Female Labour Supply: Evidence from Ireland'. *Labour*, 23/1, 1–35.

Campbell M and Ballas D (2017), SimAlba: A Spatial Microsimulation Approach to the Analysis of Health Inequalities. *Front. Public Health* 5:340, 1–9. doi: 10.3389/fpubh.2017.00340

Capacci, S., Mazzocchi, M., Shankar, B., Macias, J. B., Verbeke, W., Pérez-Cueto, F. J., et al. (2012), 'Policies to Promote Healthy Eating in Europe: A Structured Review of Policies and Their Effectiveness', *Nutrition Reviews*, 70/3, 188–200.

Capéau, B., Decoster, A., and Phillips, D. (2014), 'Consumption and Indirect Tax Models', in C. O'Donoghue, ed., *Handbook of Microsimulation Modelling* (Bingley: Emerald Group Publishing), 223–73.

Carey, D., and Tchilinguirian, H. (2000), 'Average Effective Tax Rates on Capital, Labour and Consumption', Working Paper No. 258, Economic Department, OECD, Paris.

Casler, S. D., and Rafiqui, A. (1993), 'Evaluating Fuel Tax Equity: Direct and Indirect Distributional Effects', *National Tax Journal*, 46/2, 197–205.

Cassells, R., Harding, A., and Kelly, S. (2006), 'Problems and Prospects for Dynamic Microsimulation: A Review and Lessons for APPSIM', Discussion Papers No. 63, National Centre for Social and Economic Modelling (NATSEM), University of Canberra, Australia.

Castañer, J. M., Onrubia, J., and Paredes, R. (2004), 'Evaluating Social Welfare and Redistributive Effects of Spanish Personal Income Tax Reform', *Applied Economics*, 36/14, 1561–8.

Castañón-Herrera, A., and Romero, W. (2012), 'A Microsimulation Model for Guatemala: The Case of Direct and Indirect Taxes'. In Urzúa, C.M. (ed) *Fiscal Inclusive Development: Microsimulation Models for Latin America*, 87, 87–100.

Central Planning Bureau (1995), 'Replacement Rates—A Transatlantic View', Working Paper No. 80, Central Planning Bureau.

Central Statistics Office (2000), *Household Incomes: Regions and Counties 1991–1997*, Government Publication (Dublin: Stationery Office).

Cervigni, R., Dvorak, I., and Rogers, J. A., eds. (2013), *Assessing Low-Carbon Development in Nigeria: An Analysis of Four Sectors* (Washington, DC: World Bank Publications).

Chantreuil, F., and Trannoy, A. (1999), *Inequality decomposition values: the trade-off between marginality and consistency* (Doctoral dissertation, auto-saisine).

Chantreuil, F., and Trannoy, A. (2013), 'Inequality Decomposition Values: The Trade-Off Between Marginality and Efficiency', *The Journal of Economic Inequality*, 11/1, 83–98.

Chénard, D. (2000a), 'Earnings in DYNACAN: Distribution Alignment Methodology', Paper Presented to the Sixth Nordic Workshop on Microsimulation, Copenhagen, June 2000.

Chénard, D. (2000b), 'Individual Alignment and Group Processing: An Application to Migration Processes in DYNACAN D', in L. Mitton et al., eds., *Microsimulation Modelling for Policy Analysis: Challenges and Innovations* (Cambridge: Cambridge University Press).

Chetty, R. (2009), 'Is the Taxable Income Elasticity Sufficient to Calculate Deadweight Loss? The Implications of Evasion and Avoidance'. *American Economic Journal: Economic Policy*, 1/2, 31–52.

Chin, S.-F., and Harding, A. (2006), 'Regional Dimensions: Creating Synthetic Small-Area Microdata and Spatial Microsimulation Models', Technical Paper No. 33, National Centre for Social and Economic Modelling (NATSEM), University of Canberra, Australia.

Chin, S. F., Harding, A., Lloyd, R., McNamara, J., Phillips, B., and Vu, Q. N. (2005), 'Spatial Microsimulation Using Synthetic Small-Area Estimates of Income, Tax and Social Security Benefits'. *Australasian Journal of Regional Studies*, 11/3, 303–335.

Christensen, L. R., Jorgenson, D. W., and Lau, L. J. (1975), 'Transcendental Logarithmic Utility Functions'. *The American Economic Review*, 65/3, 367–383.

Citro, C. F., and Hanushek, E. A., eds. (1991a), *The Uses of Microsimulation Modelling*, i: *Review and Recommendations* (Washington, DC: National Academies Press).

Citro, C. F., and Hanushek, E. A., eds. (1991b), *The Uses of Microsimulation Modelling*, ii: *Technical Papers* (Washington, DC: National Academies Press).

Citro, C. F., and Hanushek, E. A. (Eds.). (1991c), *Improving Information for Social Policy Decisions: The Uses of Microsimulation Modeling Volume 1 Review and Recommendations* (Washington, DC: National Academy Press).

Cockburn, J., Corong, E., and Cororaton, C. (2010), 'Integrated Computable General Equilibrium (CGE) Micro-Simulation Approach', *International Journal of Microsimulation*, 3/1, 60–71.

Cohen, M. L. (1991), 'Evaluations of Microsimulation Models: Literature Review'. *Improving Information for Social Policy Decisions: The Uses of Microsimulation Modeling*, 2, 255–275.

Colombino, U., Locatelli, M., Narazani, E., and O'Donoghue, C. (2010), 'Alternative Basic Income Mechanisms: An Evaluation Exercise with a Microeconometric Model'. *Basic Income Studies*, 5(1), 1–31.

Cornwell, A., and Creedy, J. (1996), 'Carbon Taxation, Prices and Inequality in Australia'. *Fiscal Studies*, 17(3), 21–38.

Cowell, F. A. (1980), 'On the Structure of Additive Inequality Measures'. *The Review of Economic Studies*, 47/3, 521–531.

Cowell, F. A., and Fiorio, C. V. (2011), 'Inequality Decompositions—A Reconciliation', *The Journal of Economic Inequality*, 9/4, 509–28.

Cowell, F. A., and Mercader-Prats, M. (1999), 'Equivalence Scales and Inequality', in J. Silber (ed). *Handbook of Income Inequality Measurement* (Dordrecht: Springer), 405–35.

Cozzolino, M., and Di Marco, M. (2015), 'Micromodelling Italian Taxes and Social Policies', *Rivista di Statistica Ufficiale*, 17/2, 17–26.

Cramton, P., and Kerr, S. (1999), 'The Distributional Effects of Carbon Regulation: Why Auctioned Carbon Permits are Attractive and Feasible', in T. Sterner, ed., *The Market and the Environment* (Cheltenham: Edward Elgar Publishing).

Crawford, R., and Johnson, P. (2015), 'The UK Coalition Government's Record, and Challenges for the Future', *Fiscal Studies*, 36/3, 275–82.

Creedy, J. (1998), *Measuring Welfare Changes and Tax Burdens* (Cheltenham: Edward Elgar Publishing).

Creedy, J. (2001a), 'Indirect Tax Reform and the Role of Exemptions'. *Fiscal Studies*, 22/4, 457–486.

Creedy, J. (2001), 'Tax Modelling'. *Economic Record*, 77/237, 189–202.

Creedy, J. (2003), 'Survey Reweighting for Tax Microsimulation Modelling', Treasury Working Paper Series No. 03/17.

Creedy, J. (2004), 'Survey Reweighting for Tax Microsimulation Modelling', in John A. Bishop and Yoram Amiel, eds., *Studies on Economic Well-Being: Essays in the Honor of John P. Formby* (Bingley: Emerald Group Publishing), 229–49.

Creedy, J., and Duncan, A. (2002), 'Behavioural Microsimulation with Labour Supply Responses', *Journal of Economic Surveys*, 16/1, 1–39.

Creedy, J., Gemmell, N., Hérault, N., and Mok, P. (2018), 'Microsimulation Analysis of Optimal Income Tax Reforms: An Application to New Zealand', GLO Discussion Paper No. 213.

Creedy, J., and Hérault, N. (2011a), 'Welfare-Improving Income Tax Reforms: A Microsimulation Analysis', *Oxford Economic Papers*, 64/1, 128–50.

Creedy, J., and Hérault, N. (2011b), 'Decomposing Inequality and Social Welfare Changes: The Use of Alternative Welfare Metrics', Working Paper Series No. 8/11, Melbourne Institute.

Creedy, J., Hérault, N., and Kalb, G. (2011), 'Measuring Welfare Changes in Behavioural Microsimulation Modelling: Accounting for the Random Utility Component', *Journal of Applied Economics*, 14/1, 5–34.

Creedy, J., and Kalb, G. (2005), 'Discrete Hours Labour Supply Modelling: Specification, Estimation and Simulation', *Journal of Economic Surveys*, 19/5, 697–734.

Creedy, J., and Kalb, G. (2006), *Labour Supply and Microsimulation* (Cheltenham: Edward Elgar Publishing).

Creedy, J., and Mok, P. (2017), 'Labour Supply in New Zealand and the 2010 Tax and Transfer Changes', *New Zealand Economic Papers*, 51/1, 60–78.

Creedy, J., and Mok, P. (2018), 'The Marginal Welfare Cost of Personal Income Taxation in New Zealand', *New Zealand Economic Papers*, 52/3, 323–38.

Cuceu, I. C. (2016), 'The Distributional Effects of Value Added Tax', *Ovidius University Annals, Economic Sciences Series*, 16/2, 450–54.

Cullinan, J. (2011), 'A Spatial Microsimulation Approach to Estimating the Total Number and Economic Value of Site Visits in Travel Cost Modelling', *Environmental and Resource Economics*, 50/1, 27–47.

Cullinan, J., Hynes, S., and O'Donoghue, C. (2011), 'Using Spatial Microsimulation to Account for Demographic and Spatial Factors in Environmental Benefit Transfer', *Ecological Economics*, 70/4, 813–24.

Cury, S., Pedrozo, E., and Coelho, A. M. (2016), 'Cash Transfer Policies, Taxation and the Fall in Inequality in Brazil: An Integrated Microsimulation-CGE Analysis', *International Journal of Microsimulation*, 9/1, 55–85.

Daly, M. C., and Valletta, R. G. (2006), 'Inequality and Poverty in United States: The Effects of Rising Dispersion of Men's Earnings and Changing Family Behaviour'. *Economica*, 73/289, 75–98.

D'Amuri, F., and Fiorio, C. V. (2009), 'Grossing-Up and Validation Issues in an Italian Tax-Benefit Microsimulation Model', Economia Pubblica Working Paper No. 117, University of Milan.

Davis, B. (2003), *Choosing a Method for Poverty Mapping* (Rome: Food and Agriculture Organization of the United Nations).

De Agostini, P., Hills, J., and Sutherland, H. (2018), 'Were We Really All in it Together? The Distributional Effects of the 2010–15 UK Coalition Government's Tax-Benefit Policy Changes,' *Social Policy & Administration*, 52/5, 929–49.

Deaton, A., and Muellbauer, J. (1980), 'An Almost Ideal Demand System'. *The American Economic Review*, 70(3), 312–326.

Deaton, A. S., and Muellbauer, J. (1980b), *Economics and Consumer Behavior* (Cambridge: Cambridge University Press).

Decoster, A., de Rock, B., de Swerdt, K., Loughrey, J., O'Donoghue, C., and Verwerft, D. (2007), 'Comparative Analysis of Different Techniques to Impute Expenditures into an Income Data Set', Accurate Income Measurement for the Assessment of Public Policies Deliverable 3.4, KU Leuven, Leuven, Belgium.

Decoster, A., Loughrey, J., O'Donoghue, C., and Verwerft, D. (2009), 'Incidence and Welfare Effects of Indirect Taxes', European Measures of Income and Poverty: Lessons for the US International Policy Exchange Series.

Decoster, A., Loughrey, J., O'Donoghue, C., and Verwerft, D. (2010), 'How Regressive Are Indirect Taxes? A Microsimulation Analysis for Five European Countries'. *Journal of Policy analysis and Management*, 29(2), 326–350.

Decoster, A., Loughrey, J., O'Donoghue, C., and Verwerft, D. (2011), 'Microsimulation of Indirect Taxes', *International Journal of Microsimulation*, 4/2, 41–56.

Decoster, A., Schokkaert, E., and Van Camp, G. (1997), 'Is Redistribution Through Indirect Taxes Equitable?', *European Economic Review*, 41/3–5, 599–608.

Decoster, A., Standaert, I., Valenduc, C., and Van Camp, G. (2000), What makes personal income tax progressive? The case of Belgium. *Discussion Paper Series (DPS) 00.08*, 1–29.

Decoster, A., Sutherland, H., Pirttilä, J., and Wright, G. (2019), 'SOUTHMOD: Modelling Tax-benefit Systems in Developing Countries,' *International Journal of Microsimulation, International Microsimulation Association*, 12/1, 1–12.

Decoster, A., and Van Camp, G. (2001), 'Redistributive Effects of the Shift from Personal Income Taxes to Indirect Taxes: Belgium 1988–93'. *Fiscal studies*, 22(1), 79–106.

Deetjen, U., and Powell, J. A. (2016). 'Internet Use and Health: Connecting Secondary Data through Spatial Microsimulation'. *Digital health*, 2, 2055207616666588.

Dekkers, G., Buslei, H., Cozzolino, M., Desmet, R., Geyer, J., Hofmann, D., et al. (2010), 'What Are the Consequences of the European AWG-Projections on the Adequacy of Pensions?

An Application of the Dynamic Microsimulation Model MIDAS for Belgium, Germany and Italy', in C. O'Donoghue, ed., *Life-Cycle Income Analysis Modelling* (Saarbrücken Lambert Academic Publishing).

Dekkers, G., Inagaki, S., and Desmet, R. (2012), 'Dynamic Microsimulation Modeling for Policy Support: An Application to Belgium and Possibilities for Japan', *The Review of Socionetwork Strategies*, 6/2, 31–47.

Dekkers, G., and Van den Bosch, K. (2016), 'Prospective Microsimulation of Pensions in European Member States', in G. Dekkers and J. Mészáros, eds., *Applications of Microsimulation Modelling g: A Selection of Papers Presented during the 2016 European Meeting of the 25 International Microsimulation Association in Budapest. Budapest: Társadalombiztosítási könyvtár.*

Dekkers, G., and van Leeuwen, E. (2010), 'Guest Editorial-Special Issue on "Methodological Issues in Microsimulation"', *International Journal of Microsimulation*, 3/2, 1–2.

De Lathouwer, L. (1996), 'Microsimulation in Comparative Social Policy Analysis: A Case-Study of Unemployment Schemes for Belgium and the Netherlands', in A. Harding, ed., *Microsimulation and Public Policy: Selected Papers from the IARIW Special Conference, Canberra, 5–9 December 1993*, 69–91.

De Lathouwer, L. (2017), 'Reforming the Passive Welfare State: Belgium's New Income Arrangements to Make Work Pay in International Perspective', in Saudenrs, Peter (ed) *Welfare to Work in Practice: Social Security and Participation in Economic and Social Life*, 129.

De Melo, J. (1988), 'Computable General Equilibrium Models for Trade Policy Analysis in Developing Countries: A Survey', *Journal of Policy Modeling*, 10/4, 469–503.

De Menten, G., Dekkers, G., Bryon, G., Liégeois, P., and O'Donoghue, C. (2014), 'LIAM2: A New Open Source Development Tool for Discrete-Time Dynamic Microsimulation Models', *Journal of Artificial Societies and Social Simulation*, 17/3, 1–9.

Department of the Environment, Heritage and Local Government (2010), *Implementing the National Spatial Strategy: 2010 Update and Outlook* (Dublin: Stationery Office).

DiNardo, J., Fortin, N., and Lemieux, T. (1996), 'Labor Market Institutions and the Distribution of Wages, 1973–1992: A Semi-Parametric Approach', *Econometrica*, 64/5, 1001–44.

Di Nicola, F., Mongelli, G., and Pellegrino, S. (2015), 'The Static Microsimulation Model of the Italian Department of Finance: Structure and First Results Regarding Income and Housing Taxation,' *Economia Pubblica*, 2, 125–157.

Dochev, I., Seller, H., and Peters, I. (2016), 'Constructing a Synthetic City for Estimating Spatially Disaggregated Heat Demand', *International Journal of Microsimulation*, 9/3, 66–88.

Doole, G. J., Marsh, D., and Ramilan, T. (2013), 'Evaluation of Agri-Environmental Policies for Reducing Nitrate Pollution from New Zealand Dairy Farms Accounting for Firm Heterogeneity', *Land Use Policy*, 30/1, 57–66.

D'Orazio, M., Di Zio, M., and Scanu, M. (2006), *Statistical Matching: Theory and Practice* (New York: John Wiley & Sons).

Duncan, A., and Giles, C. (1996), 'Labour Supply Incentives and Recent Family Credit Reforms', *The Economic Journal*, 106/434, 142–55.

Eardley, T., Bradshaw, J., Ditch, J., and Gough, I. (1996), *Social Assistance in OECD Countries: Synthesis Report* (Paris: OECD).

Edwards, K. L., and Clarke, G. P. (2009), 'The Design and Validation of a Spatial Microsimulation Model of Obesogenic Environments for Children in Leeds: SimObesity', *Social Science and Medicine*, 69/7, 1127–34.

Edwards, K. L., Clarke, G. P., Thomas, J., and Forman, D. (2011), 'Internal and External Validation of Spatial Microsimulation Models: Small Area Estimates of Adult Obesity', *Applied Spatial Analysis and Policy*, 4/4, 281–300.

Edwards, S. (2010), 'Techniques for Managing Changes to Existing Simulation Models', *International Journal of Microsimulation*, 3/2, 80–89.

Elbers, C., Fujii, T., Lanjouw, P., Özler, B., and Yin, W. (2007), 'Poverty Alleviation Through Geographic Targeting: How Much Does Disaggregation Help?', *Journal of Development Economics*, 83/1, 198–213.

Elbers, C., Lanjouw, O. J., and Lanjouw, P. (2003), 'Micro-Level Estimation of Poverty and Inequality', *Econometrica*, 71/1, 355–64.

Eliasson, G. (1991), 'Modelling the Experimentally Organized Economy—Complex Dynamics in an Empirical Micro-Macro Model of Endogenous Economic Growth,' *Journal of Economic Behaviour and Organization*, 16/1–2, 153–82.

Ericson, P., Flood, L., and Wahlberg, R. (2009), 'SWEtaxben: A Swedish Tax/Benefit Micro Simulation Model and an Evaluation of a Swedish Tax Reform', Working Papers in Economics No. 346, Department of Economics, Göteborg University.

Escobal, J., and Torero, M. (2005), 'Measuring the Impact of Asset Complementarities: The Case of Rural Peru', *Latin American Journal of Economics*, 42/125, 137–64.

Esping-Andersen, G. (2013), *The Three Worlds of Welfare Capitalism* (New York: John Wiley & Sons).

European Commission (1998), *Social Protection in Europe 1997* (Brussels: European Commission).

European Commission Directorate-General (2007), 'Pensions Schemes and Projection Models in EU-25 Member States', European Economy Occasional Papers No. 35 European Commission Directorate-General.

Evans, M., and Lewis, W. (1999), 'A Generation of Change, a Lifetime of Differences? Model Lifetime Analysis of Changes in the British Welfare State Since 1979' (Oxford: Policy Press).

Falkingham, J., and Hills, J., eds. (1995), *The Dynamic of Welfare: The Welfare State and the Life Cycle* (New York: Prentice Hall).

Falkingham, J., and Johnson, P. (1995), 'A Unified Funded Pension Scheme (UFPS) for Britain', in J. Falkingham and J. Hills, eds., *The Dynamic of Welfare: The Welfare State and the Life Cycle* (New York: Prentice Hall).

Falkingham, J., and Lessof, C. (1991), 'LIFEMOD: The Formative Years', Research Note No. 24, London School of Economics, London.

Farrell, N., O'Donoghue, C., and Morrissey, K. (2011), 'Spatial Microsimulation Using Quota Sampling', Working Paper, Teagasc Rural Economy Development Programme, Ireland.

Favreault, M., and Smith, K. (2004), 'A Primer on the Dynamic Simulation of Income Model (DYNASIM3)', Urban Institute Discussion Paper, Washington, DC.

Feldstein, M. (1976), 'On the Theory of Tax Reform', *Journal of Public Economics*, 6/1–2, 77–104.

Feldstein, M. (1995), 'The Effect of Marginal Tax Rates on Taxable Income: A Panel Study of the 1986 Tax Reform Act', *Journal of Political Economy*, 103/3, 551–72.

Fernald, L. C., Gertler, P. J., and Neufeld, L. M. (2008), 'Role of Cash in Conditional Cash Transfer Programmes for Child Health, Growth, and Development: An Analysis of Mexico's Oportunidades', *The Lancet*, 371/9615, 828–37.

Ferreira, F. H. G. (2012), 'Distributions in Motion: Economic Growth, Inequality, and Poverty Dynamics', in P. Jefferson, ed., *Oxford Handbook of the Economics of Poverty* (Oxford: Oxford University Press).

Ferrera, M. (1996), 'The "Southern Model" of Welfare in Social Europe', *Journal of European Social Policy*, 6/1, 17–37.

Fields, G. S. (2003), 'Accounting for Income Inequality and its Change: A New Method, with Application to the Distribution of Earnings in the United States', *Research in Labor Economics*, 22/3, 1–38.

Fields, G. S., and Yoo, G. (2000), 'Falling Labor Income Inequality in Korea's Economic Growth: Patterns and Underlying Causes', *Review of Income and Wealth*, 46/2, 139–59.

Figari, F., and Paulus, A. (2015), 'The Distributional Effects of Taxes and Transfers Under Alternative Income Concepts: The Importance of Three "I"s', *Public Finance Review*, 43/3, 347–72.

Figari, F., Paulus, A., and Sutherland, H. (2015), 'Microsimulation and Policy Analysis', in A.B. Atkinson and F. Bourguignon, eds., *Handbook of Income Distribution*, ii (Amsterdam: Elsevier), 2141–221.

Figari, F., Paulus, A., Sutherland, H., Tsakloglou, P., Verbist, G., and Zantomio, F. (2017), 'Removing Homeownership Bias in Taxation: The Distributional Effects of Including Net Imputed Rent in Taxable Income', *Fiscal Studies*, 38/4, 525–57.

Figari, F., and Tasseva, I. V. (2013), 'Editorial Special Issue on EUROMOD', *International Journal of Microsimulation*, 1/6, 1–3.

Fiorio, C. V. (2009), *Microsimulation and Analysis of Income Distribution* (Dordrecht: VDM Publishing).

Fiorio, C. V. (2011), 'Understanding Italian inequality trends'. *Oxford Bulletin of Economics and Statistics*, 73/2, 255–275.

Flannery, D., and O'donoghue, C. (2011), 'The Life-Cycle Impact of Alternative Higher Education Finance Systems in Ireland'. *Economic & Social Review*, 42/3.

Flannery, D., and O'Donoghue, C. (2013), 'The Demand for Higher Education: A Static Structural Approach Accounting for Individual Heterogeneity and Nesting Patterns', *Economics of Education Review*, 34, June 243–57.

Fölster, S. (1997), 'Social Insurance Based on Personal Savings Accounts', European Economy Occasional Papers No. 1997/4 (Brussels: European Commission).

Frick, J. R., Büchel, F., and Krause, P. (2000), 'Public Transfers, Income Distribution, and Poverty in Germany and in the United States', in R. Hauser and ⊠I. Becker, eds., *The Personal Distribution of Income in an International Perspective* (Berlin and Heidelberg: Springer), 176–204.

Frisch, R. (1959), 'A Complete Scheme for Computing All Direct and Cross Demand Elasticities in a Model with Many Sectors'. *Econometrica: Journal of the Econometric Society*, Vol. 27 No. 2 177–196.

Fuest, C., Peichl, A., and Schaefer, T. (2008), 'Is a Flat Tax Reform Feasible in a Grown-Up Democracy of Western Europe? A Simulation Study for Germany', *International Tax and Public Finance*, 15/5, 620–36.

Gay, P. W., and Proops, J. L. (1993), 'Carbon dioxide Production by the UK Economy: An Input-Output Assessment'. *Applied Energy*, 44/2, 113–130.

Gago, A., Labandeira, X., and López-Otero, X. (2014), 'A Panorama on Energy Taxes and Green Tax Reforms', *Hacienda Pública Española*, 208/1, 145–90.

Gale, W. G., Orszag, P. R., and Shapiro, I. (2004), 'Distributional Effects of the 2001 and 2003 Tax Cuts and Their Financing', *Tax Notes*, 103/12, 1539–48.

Galler, H. P. (1997), 'Discrete-Time and Continuous-Time Approaches to Dynamic Microsimulation Reconsidered', Discussion Paper, National Centre for Social and Economic Modelling (NATSEM), University of Canberra, Australia.

Galler, H. P., and Wagner, G. (1986), 'The Microsimulations Model of the Sfb3 for the Analysis of Economic and Social Policies', in G. H. Orcutt et al., eds., *Microanalytic Simulation Models to Support Social and Financial Policy* (Amsterdam: North-Holland), 227–44.

García-Muros, X., Burguillo, M., González-Eguino, M., and Romero-Jordán, D. (2017), 'Local Air Pollution and Global Climate Change Taxes: A Distributional Analysis for the Case of Spain', *Journal of Environmental Planning and Management*, 60/3, 419–36.

Gastaldi, F., Liberati, P., Pisano, E., and Tedeschi, S. (2017), 'Regressivity-Reducing VAT Reforms', *International Journal of Microsimulation*, 10/1, 39–72.

Gatti, D. D., Fagiolo, G., Gallegati, M., Richiardi, M., and Russo, A., eds. (2018), *Agent-Based Models: A Toolkit* (Cambridge: Cambridge University Press).

Gertler, P. (2004), 'Do Conditional Cash Transfers Improve Child Health? Evidence from PROGRESA's Control Randomized Experiment', *The American Economic Review*, 94/2, 336–41.

Gough, I., Bradshaw, J., Ditch, J., Eardley, T., and Whiteford, P. (1997), 'Social Assistance in OECD Countries', *Journal of European Social Policy*, 7/1, 17–43.

Haan, P. (2006), 'Much Ado about Nothing: Conditional Logit vs. Random Coefficient Models for Estimating Labour Supply Elasticities', *Applied Economics Letters*, 13/4, 251–6.

Haan, P. (2010), 'A Multi-State Model of State Dependence in Labor Supply: Intertemporal Labor Supply Effects of a Shift from Joint to Individual Taxation', *Labour Economics*, 17/2, 323–35.

Haase, T., and Pratschke, J. (2005), *Deprivation and Its Spatial Articulation in the Republic of Ireland* (Dublin: Area Development Management).

Haase, T., and Foley, R. (2009), *Feasibility Study for a Local Poverty Index* (Dublin: Combat Poverty Agency).

Hain, W., and Helberger, C. (1986), 'Longitudinal Simulation of Lifetime Income', in G. H. Orcutt et al., eds., *Microanalytic Simulation Models to Support Social and Financial Policy* (New York: North-Holland).

Hajnal, Z. L. (1995), 'The Nature of Concentrated Urban Poverty in Canada and the United States'. *The Canadian Journal of Sociology*, 20/4, 497–528.

Hakim, M. A., and Rahman, A. (2018), 'Simulating the Nutritional Traits of Populations at the Small Area Level Using Spatial Microsimulation Modelling Approach', *Computational Biology and Bioinformatics*, 6/1, 25.

Hamilton, K., and Cameron, G. (1994), 'Simulating the Distributional Effects of a Canadian Carbon Tax', *Canadian Public Policy*, 20/4, 385–99.

Hammel, E. A. (1990), 'SOCSIM II', Working Paper No. 29, Graduate Group in Demography, University of California at Berkeley.

Hancock R. (1997), 'Computing Strategy for a European Tax-Benefit Model', Discussion Paper No. MU9704, Microsimulation Unit, Faculty of Economics, University of Cambridge.

Harding, A. (1993), 'Lifetime Income Distribution and Redistribution: Applications of a Microsimulation Model', *Contributions to Economic Analysis* (Amsterdam: North Holland), 221.

Harding, A. (2007a), *Challenges and Opportunities of Dynamic Microsimulation Modelling*.

Harding, A. (2007b), *APPSIM: The Australian Dynamic Population and Policy Microsimulation Model* (Canberra: NATSEM).

Harding, A., Vu, N. Q., Tanton, R., and Vidyattama, V. (2009), 'Improving Work Incentives and Incomes for Parents: The National and Geographic Impact of Liberalising the Family Tax Benefit Income Test', *Economic Record*, 85/September, S48–S58.

Harding, A., and Warren, N. (1998), *An Introduction to Microsimulation Models of Tax Reform* Canberra: NATSEM, http://www.canberra.edu.au/centres/natsem/publications?sq_content_src=per cent2BdXJsPWh0dHAlM0ElMkYlMkZ6aWJvLndpbi5jYW5iZXJyYS5lZHUuYXUlMkZuYXRzZW0lMkZpbmRleC5waHAlM0Ztb2RlJTNEcHVibGljYXRpb24lMjZwdWJsaWNhdGlvbiUzRDEwMzkmYWxsPTEper cent3D, accessed 2 Jan. 2012.

Harris, T., Phillips, D., Warwick, R., Goldman, M., Jellema, J., Goraus, K., et al. (2018), 'Redistribution via VAT and Cash Transfers: An Assessment in Four Low and Middle Income Countries', Paper No. W18/11, Institute for Fiscal Studies, London.

Haskins, R., and Margolis, G. (2014), *Show Me the Evidence: Obama's Fight for Rigor and Results in Social Policy* (Washington, DC: Brookings Institution Press).

Hausman, J. A. (1981), 'Exact Consumer's Surplus and Deadweight Loss'. *The American Economic Review*, 71/4, 662–676.

Hausman. J., (1985), 'The Econometrics of Nonlinear Budget Sets'. *Econometrica* 53/6, 1255–1283.

Heckman, J. J., Lalonde, R. J., and Smith, J. A. (1999), 'The Economics and Econometrics of Active Labor Market Programs', in O. C. Ashenfelter and D. Card, eds., *Handbook of Labor Economics*, iii/A (Amsterdam: North-Holland).

Hensher, D. A., and Johnson, L. W. (1981), *Applied Discrete-Choice Model* (Andover: Croom Helm).

Hentschel, J., Lanjouw, O. J., and Lanjouw, P. (1998), 'Combining Census and Survey Data to Study Spatial Dimensions of Poverty', Working Paper Series No. 1928, World Bank Policy Research, Washington, DC.

Hentschel, J., Lanjouw, J. O., Lanjouw, P., and Poggi, J. (2000), 'Combining Census and Survey Data to Trace the Spatial Dimensions of Poverty: A Case Study of Ecuador'. *The World Bank Economic Review*, 14/1, 147–165.

Hermes, K., and Poulsen, M. (2012), 'A Review of Current Methods to Generate Synthetic Spatial Micro Data Using Reweighting and Future Directions', *Computers, Environment and Urban Systems*, 36/4, 281–90.

Hernanz, V., Malherbet, F., and Pellizzari, M. (2004), Take-up of welfare benefits in OECD countries: A review of the evidence. Social Employment and Migration Working Papers 17, OECD.

Hertin, J., Jordan, A., Turnpenny, J., Nilsson, M., Russel, D., and Björn, N. (2009), 'Rationalising the Policy Mess? Ex Ante Policy Assessment and the Utilisation of Knowledge in the Policy Process', *Environment and Planning A: Economy and Space*, 41/5, 1185–1200.

Higgins, S., Lustig, N., Ruble, W., and Smeeding, T. M. (2016), 'Comparing the Incidence of Taxes and Social Spending in Brazil and the United States', *Review of Income and Wealth*, 62, Aug S22–S46.

Higgins, S., and Pereira, C. (2014), 'The Effects of Brazil's Taxation and Social Spending on the Distribution of Household Income', *Public Finance Review*, 42/3, 346–67.

Hollander, Y., and Liu, R. (2008), 'The Principles of Calibrating Traffic Microsimulation Models', *Transportation*, 35/3, 347–62.

Holm, E., Lindgren, U., Mäkilä, K., and Malmberg, G. (1996), 'Simulating an Entire Nation', in G. Clarke, ed., *Microsimulation for Urban and Regional Policy Analysis* (London: Pion), 64–87.

Hufkens, T., Goedemé, T., Gasior, K., Leventi, C., Manios, K., Rastrigina, O., . . . Verbist, G. (2019), *The Hypothetical Household Tool (HHoT) in EUROMOD: A New Instrument for Comparative Research on Tax-Benefit Policies in Europe* (No. 05/2019). JRC Working Papers on Taxation and Structural Reforms.

Hynes, S., Morrissey, K., O'Donoghue, C., and Clarke, G. (2009a), 'Building a Static Farm Level Spatial Microsimulation Model for Rural Development and Agricultural Policy Analysis in Ireland', *International Journal of Agricultural Resources, Governance and Ecology*, 8/2, 282–99.

Hynes, S., Morrissey, K., O'Donoghue, C., and Clarke, G. (2009b), 'A Spatial Microsimulation Analysis of Methane Emissions from Irish Agriculture', *Journal of Ecological Complexity*, 6/2, 135–46.

Hynes, S., and O'Donoghue, C. (2014), 'Environmental Models', in C. O'Donoghue, ed., *Handbook of Microsimulation Modelling* (Bingley: Emerald Group Publishing), 449–77.

Hyslop, D. R., and Maré, D. C. (2005), 'Understanding New Zealand's Changing Income Distribution 1983–98: A Semiparametric Analysis', *Economica*, 72/3, 469–95.

Immervoll, H. (2002), 'The Distribution of Average and Marginal Effective Tax Rates in European Union Member States', Working Paper Series No. EM2/02, EUROMOD at the Institute for Social and Economic Research, Essex.

Immervoll, H. (2005), 'Falling Up the Stairs: The Effects of "Bracket Creep" on Household Incomes', *Review of Income and Wealth*, 51/1, 37–62.

Immervoll, H., Levy, H., Nogueira, J. R., O Donoghue, C., and Siqueira, R. B. D. (2006), 'Simulating Brazil's Tax-Benefit System Using Brahms, the Brazilian Household Microsimulation Model', *Economia Aplicada*, 10/2, 203–23.

Immervoll, H., Lindström, K., Mustonen, E., Riihelä, M., and Viitamäki, H. (2005), 'Static Data Ageing Techniques. Accounting for Population Changes in Tax-Benefit Microsimulation', EUROMOD Working Paper Series No. EM7/05, EUROMOD at the Institute for Social and Economic Research, Essex.

Immervoll, H., and O'Donoghue, C. (2001a), 'Imputation of Gross Amounts from Net Incomes in Household Surveys: An Application Using EUROMOD', Working Paper Series No. EM1/01, EUROMOD at the Institute for Social and Economic Research, Essex.

Immervoll H., and O'Donoghue, C. (2001b), 'Towards a Multi-Purpose Framework for Tax-Benefit Microsimulation', Working Paper Series No. 2/01, EUROMOD at the Institute for Social and Economic Research, Essex.

Immervoll, H., and O'Donoghue, C. (2001c), 'Welfare Benefits and Work Incentives: An Analysis of the Distribution of Net Replacement Rates in Europe Using EUROMOD, a Multi-Country Microsimulation Model', Working Paper Series No. EM4/01, EUROMOD at the Institute for Social and Economic Research, Essex.

Immervoll, H., and O'Donoghue, C. (2009), 'Towards a Multi-purpose Framework for Tax-Benefit Microsimulation: Lessons from EUROMOD'. *International Journal of Micro Simulation*, 2/2, 43–54.

Immervoll, H., O'Donoghue, C., and Sutherland, H. (1999), 'An Introduction to EUROMOD', Working Paper, Microsimulation Unit, Faculty of Economics, University of Cambridge.

Immervoll, H., and Pearson, M. (2009), 'A Good Time for Making Work Pay? Taking Stock of In-Work Benefits and Related Measures Across the OECD', *OECD Social, Employment, and Migration Working Papers*, 81/1.

Jahn, D. (2018), 'Distribution Regimes and Redistribution Effects During Retrenchment and Crisis: A Cui Bono Analysis of Unemployment Replacement Rates of Various Income Categories in 31 Welfare States', *Journal of European Social Policy*, 28/5, 433–51.

Jalan, J., and Ravallion, M. (2002), 'Geographic Poverty Traps? A Micro Model of Consumption Growth in Rural China,' *Journal of Applied Econometrics*, 17/4, 329–46.

Jäntti, M., Pirttilä, J., and Selin, H. (2015), 'Estimating Labour Supply Elasticities Based on Cross-Country Micro Data: A Bridge Between Micro and Macro Estimates?', *Journal of Public Economics*, 127, Jul 87–99.

Jara, H. X., and Tumino, A. (2013), 'Tax-Benefit Systems, Income Distribution and Work Incentives in the European Union', *The International Journal of Microsimulation*, 6/1, 27–62.

Jara, H. X., and Varela, M. (2017), 'Tax-Benefit Microsimulation and Income Redistribution in Ecuador (No. 177)', World Institute for Development Economic Research (UNU-WIDER), United Nations University, Tokyo.

Jencks, C., and Mayer, S. E. (1990), 'The Social Consequences of Growing Up in a Poor Neighborhood', in L. Lynn and M. McGeary, eds., *Inner-City Poverty in the United States* (Washington, DC: National Academy Press), 111–86.

Jenkins, S., Brandolini, A., Micklewright, J., and Nolan, B., eds. (2013), *The Great Recession and the Distribution of Household Income* (Oxford: Oxford University Press).

Johnson, T. (2001), 'Nonlinear Alignment by Sorting', CORSIM Working Paper. Cornell University.

Johnson, P. A., and Falkingham, J. (1992), *Ageing and Economic Eelfare* (Sage Publications).

Jordaan, Y., and Schoeman, N. J. (2018), 'The Benefit of Aligning South Africa's Personal Income Tax Thresholds and Brackets with That of its Peers Using a Micro-Simulation Tax Model', *South African Journal of Economic and Management Sciences*, 21/1, 1–9.

Joust, M., and Rattenhuber, P. (2018), 'A Role for Universal Pension? Simulating Universal Pensions in Ecuador, Ghana, Tanzania, and South Africa', WIDER Working Paper No. 2018/23 (Helsinki: UNU-WIDER).

Juhn, C., Murphy, K., and Pierce, B. (1993), 'Wage Inequality and the Rise in Returns to Skill', *Journal of Political Economy*, 101/3, 410–42.

Kabatek, J., Van Soest, A., and Stancanelli, E. (2014), 'Income Taxation, Labour Supply and Housework: A Discrete Choice Model for French Couples', *Labour Economics*, 27, Apr 30–43.

Kaiser, H., and Spahn, P. B. (1989), 'On the Efficiency and Distributive Justice of Consumption Taxes: A Study of VAT in West Germany', *Journal of Economics*, 49/2, 199–218.

Kakwani, N. C. (1977). 'Measurement of Tax Progressivity: An International Comparison', *The Economic Journal*, 87/345, 71–80.

Kaplanoglou, G., and Newbery, D. M. (2003), Indirect taxation in Greece: evaluation and possible reform. *International Tax and Public Finance*, 10/5, 511–533.

Kakwani, N. (1984), 'The Relative Deprivation Curve and Its Applications'. *Journal of Business & Economic Statistics*, 2/4, 384–394.

Kaplow, L. (1989), 'Horizontal Equity: Measures in Search of a Principle', *National Tax Journal*, 42/2, 139–54.

Kaplow, L. (2000), 'Horizontal Equity: New Measures, Unclear Principles', Paper No. w7649, National Bureau of Economic Research.

Keister, L. (2000), *Wealth in America: Trends in Wealth Inequality* (Cambridge: Cambridge University Press).

Kelly, S., and Percival, R. (2009), 'Longitudinal Benchmarking and Alignment of a Dynamic Microsimulation Model', IMA Conference Paper. International Microsimulation Association.

Kennell, D. L., and Sheils, J. F. (1990), 'PRISM: Dynamic Simulation of Pension and Retirement Income', in G. H. Lewis and R. C. Michel, eds., *Microsimulation Techniques for Tax and Transfer Analysis* (Washington, DC: Urban Institute Press).

Kerkhof, A. C., Moll, H. C., Drissen, E., and Wilting, H. C. (2008), 'Taxation of Multiple Greenhouse Gases and the Effects on Income Distribution: A Case Study of the Netherlands', *Ecological Economics*, 67/2, 318–26.

Kilgarriff, P., Charlton, M., Foley, R., and O'Donoghue, C. (2019), 'The Impact of Housing Consumption Value on the Spatial Distribution of Welfare', *Journal of Housing Economics*, 43, Mar 118–30.

Kilgarriff, P., McDermott, T. K., Vega, A., Morrissey, K., and O'Donoghue, C. (2019), 'The Impact of Flooding Disruption on the Spatial Distribution of Commuter's Income'. *Journal of Environmental Economics and Policy*, 8/1, 48–64.

Kleven, H. J., Kreiner, C. T., and Saez, E. (2009), 'The Optimal Income Taxation of Couples', *Econometrica*, 77/2, 537–60.

Klevmarken, N. A. (1997a), 'Behavioral Modeling in Micro Simulation Models: A Survey', Working Paper No. 1997: 31, Department of Economics, Uppsala University.

Klevmarken, N. A. (1997b), 'Modelling Behavioural Response in EUROMOD', Paper No. 9720, Microsimulation Unit, Faculty of Economics, University of Cambridge.

Klevmarken, N. A., and Olovsson, P. (1996), 'Direct and Behavioural Effects of Income Tax Changes—Simulations with the Swedish Model MICROHUS', in A. Harding, ed., *Microsimulation and Public Policy* (Amsterdam: Elsevier).

Koh, K., Grady, S. C., Darden, J. T., and Vojnovic, I. (2018), 'Adult Obesity Prevalence at the County Level in the United States, 2000–2010: Downscaling Public Health Survey Data Using a Spatial Microsimulation Approach', *Spatial and Spatio-Temporal Epidemiology*, 26, Aug 153–64.

Koh, K., Grady, S. C., and Vojnovic, I. (2015), 'Using Simulated Data to Investigate the Spatial Patterns of Obesity Prevalence at the Census Tract Level in Metropolitan Detroit', *Applied Geography*, 62, Aug 19–28.

Labandeira, X., and Labeaga, J. M. (1999), 'Combining Input–Output Analysis and Micro-Simulation to Assess the Effects of Carbon Taxation on Spanish Households', *Fiscal Studies*, 20/3, 305–20.

Labandeira, X., Labeaga, J. M., and Rodríguez, M. (2009), 'An Integrated Economic and Distributional Analysis of Energy Policies', *Energy Policy*, 37/12, 5776–86.

Lahiri, S., Babiker, M., and Eckaus, R. S. (2000), 'The Effects of Changing Consumption Patterns on the Costs of Emission Restrictions', Massachusetts Institute of Technology Joint Program on the Science and Policy of Global Change, Report No. 64, Massachusetts Institute of Technology, Cambridge, MA.

Lambrecht, S., Michel, P., and Vidal, J. P. (2005), 'Public Pensions and Growth', *European Economic Review*, 49/5, 1261–81.

Larrañaga, O., Encina, J., and Cabezas, G. (2012), 'A Microsimulation Model of Distribution for Chile', Fiscal Inclusive Development: Microsimulation Models for Latin America, Mexico City.

Layard, R., Nickell, S., and Jackman, R. (1991), *Unemployment: Macroeconomic Performance and the Labour Market* (Oxford: Oxford University Press).

Leahy, E., Lyons, S., and Tol, R. S. (2011), 'The Distributional Effects of Value Added Tax in Ireland', *The Economic and Social Review*, 42/2, 213.

Leeuwen, E. V., Ishikawa, Y., and Nijkamp, P. (2016), 'Microsimulation and Interregional Input–Output Modelling as Tools for Multi-Level Policy Analysis', *Environment and Planning C: Government and Policy*, 34/1, 135–50.

Leontief, W. W. (1951), *The Structure of American Economy, 1919–1939: An Empirical Application of Equilibrium Analysis* (New York: Oxford University Press).

Leonard, B., Kinsella, A., O'Donoghue, C., Farrell, M., and Mahon, M. (2017), 'Policy Drivers of Farm Succession and Inheritance', *Land Use Policy*, 61, Feb 147–59.

Levy, H., Immervoll H., Nogueira, J. R., O'Donoghue, C., and de Siqueira, R. B. (2010), 'Simulating the Impact of Inflation on the Progressivity of Personal Income Tax in Brazil', *Revista Brasileira de Economia*, 64/4, 405–22.

Levy, H., and Mercador-Prats, M. (2002), 'Simplifying the Personal Income Tax System: Lessons from the 1998 Spanish Reform', *Fiscal Studies*, 23/3, 419–43.

Li, J., and O'Donoghue, C. (2011), 'Household Retirement Choice Simulation with Heterogeneous Pension Plans', IZA Discussion Paper No.5866. Bonn: IZA

Li, J., and O'Donoghue, C. (2012), 'Simulating Histories within Dynamic Microsimulation Models', *International Journal of Microsimulation*, 5/1, 52–76.

Li, J., and O'Donoghue, C. (2013), 'A Survey of Dynamic Microsimulation Models: Uses, Model Structure and Methodology', *International Journal of Microsimulation*, 6/2, 3–55.

Li, J., and O'Donoghue, C. (2014), 'Evaluating Binary Alignment Methods in Microsimulation Models', *Journal of Artificial Societies and Social Simulation*, 17/1, 15.

Li, J., O'Donoghue, C., and Dekkers, G. (2014), 'Dynamic Microsimulation Modelling', in C. O'Donoghue, ed., *Handbook of Microsimulation Modelling* (Bingley: Emerald Group Publishing), 275–304.

Li, J., O'Donoghue, C., Loughrey, J., and Harding, A. (2014), 'Static Models', in C. O'Donoghue, ed., *Handbook of Microsimulation Modelling* (Bingley: Emerald Group Publishing), 47–75.

Liberati, P. (2001). The distributional effects of indirect tax changes in Italy. *International Tax and Public Finance*, *8*(1), 27–51.

Lindgren, U. (1999), 'Simulating the Long-Term Labour Market Effects of an Industrial Investment: A Microsimulation Approach', *Erdkunde*, 53, 150–62.

Lloyd, R., Harding, A., and Hellwig, O. (2000), 'Regional Divide a Study of Incomes in Regional Australia', *Australasian Journal of Regional Studies*, 6/3, 271.

Lluch, C., Powell, A. A., Williams, R. A., and Betancourt, R. R. (1977), *Patterns in Household Demand and Saving* (Oxford: Oxford University Press).

Lomax, N., and Smith, A. (2017), 'Microsimulation for Demography', *Australian Population Studies*, 1/1, 73–85.

Loughrey, J., and O'Donoghue, C. (2012), 'The Welfare Impact of Price Changes on Household Welfare and Inequality 1999–2011', *The Economic and Social Review*, 43/1, 31–66.

Lovelace R, Birkin M, Ballas D, and van Leeuwen E. (2015), 'Evaluating the Performance of Iterative Proportional Fitting for Spatial Microsimulation: New Tests for an Established Technique'. *Journal of Artificial Societies and Social Simulation*. 18/2.

Lovelace, R., and Dumont, M. (2016), *Spatial Microsimulation with R* (Boca Raton, FL: CRC Press).

Lüpsik, S., Paulus, A., and Võrk, A. (2006), 'I-CUE Feasibility Study', Estonia (2005 Tax-Benefit System), EUROMOD Feasibility Study.

Lutz, W. (1997), *FAMSIM Austria: Feasibility Study for a Dynamic Microsimulation Model for Projections and the Evaluation of Family Policies Based on the European Family and Fertility Survey* (Vienna: Austrian Institute for Family Studies).

Ma, J., Heppenstall, A., Harland, K., and Mitchell, G. (2014), 'Synthesising Carbon Emission for Mega-Cities: A Static Spatial Microsimulation of Transport CO2 from Urban Travel in Beijing', *Computers, Environment and Urban Systems*, 45, May 78–88.

Madden, D. (1995a), 'An Analysis of Indirect Tax Reform in Ireland in the 1980s', *Fiscal Studies*, 16/1, 18–37.

Madden D. (1995b), 'Labour Supply, Commodity Demand and Marginal Tax Reform'. *The Economic Journal* 105/429:485–97.

Madden, D. (1996), 'Marginal Tax Reform and the Specification of Consumer Demand Systems', *Oxford Economic Papers*, 48/4, 556–67.

Maitino, M. L., Ravagli, L., and Sciclone, N. (2017), 'Microreg: A Traditional Tax-Benefit Microsimulation Model Extended To Indirect Taxes And In Kind Transfers', *International Journal of Microsimulation*, 10/1, 5–38.

Markham, F., Young, M., and Doran, B. (2017), 'Improving Spatial Microsimulation Estimates of Health Outcomes by Including Geographic Indicators of Health Behaviour: The Example of Problem Gambling', *Health and Place*, 46, Jul 29–36.

Martin, J. P. (1996), 'Measures of Replacement Rates for the Purpose of International Comparisons: A Note', *OECD Economic Studies*, 26/1, 99–115.

Martini, A., and Trivellato, U. (1997), 'The Role of Survey Data in Microsimulation Models for Social Policy Analysis', *Labour*, 11/1, 83–112.

Mason, C. (2014), 'Models', in C. O'Donoghue, ed., *Handbook of Microsimulation Modelling* (Bingley: Emerald Group Publishing), 306–23.

Mastrogiacomo, M., Bosch, N. M., Gielen, M. D., and Jongen, E. L. (2017), 'Heterogeneity in Labour Supply Responses: Evidence from a Major Tax Reform', *Oxford Bulletin of Economics and Statistics*, 79/5, 769–96.

Mathur, A., and Morris, A. C. (2014), 'Distributional Effects of a Carbon Tax in Broader US Fiscal Reform', *Energy Policy*, 66, Mar 326–34.

Matsaganis, M., and Flevotomou, M. (2007), 'The Impact of Mortgage Interest Tax Relief in the Netherlands, Sweden, Finland, Italy and Greece', EUROMOD Working Papers Series No. EM2/07, EUROMOD at the Institute for Social and Economic Research, Essex.

Matsaganis, M., Levy, H., and Flevotomou, M. (2010), 'Non-Take-Up of Social Benefits in Greece and Spain', *Social Policy and Administration*, 44/7, 827–44.

Matsaganis, M., O'Donoghue, C., Levy, H., Coromaldi, M., Mercader-Prats, M., Rodrigues, C. F., et al. (2006), 'Reforming Family Transfers in Southern Europe: Is There a Role for Universal Child Benefits?', *Social Policy and Society*, 5/2, 189–97.

Matsaganis, M., Paulus, A., and Sutherland, H. (2008), 'The Take Up of Social Benefits', Research Note No. 2(2008), European Observatory on the Social Situation and Demography.

McFadden, D. (1973), 'Conditional Logit Analysis of Qualitative Choice Behaviour', in P. Zarembka, ed., *Frontiers in Econometrics* (New York: Academic Press), 105–42.

Melhuish, T., King, A., and Taylor, E. (2004), 'The Regional Impact of Commonwealth Rent Assistance', Report No. 71, Australian Housing and Urban Research Institute.

Mertens, K., and Montiel Olea, J. L. (2018), 'Marginal Tax Rates and Income: New Time Series Evidence', *The Quarterly Journal of Economics*, 133/4, 1803–84.

Merz, J. (1991), 'Microsimulation—A Survey of Principles, Developments and Applications', *International Journal of Forecasting*, 7/1, 77–104.

Merz, J. (1994), 'Microsimulation—A Survey of Methods and Applications for Analyzing Economic and Social Policy', FFB Discussion Paper No. 9. Forschungsinstitut Freie Berufe (FFB), Department of Economics and Social Sciences, University of Lüneberg.

Michaud, P. C., and Vermeulen, F. (2011), 'A Collective Labor Supply Model with Complementarities in Leisure: Identification and Estimation by Means of Panel Data'. *Labour Economics*, 18/2, 159–167.

Mideros, A., Gassmann, F., and Mohnen, P. (2016), 'Estimation of Rates of Return on Social Protection: Ex Ante Microsimulation of Social Transfers in Cambodia', *Journal of Development Effectiveness*, 8/1, 67–86.

Mideros, A., and O'Donoghue, C. (2015), 'The Effect of Unconditional Cash Transfers on Adult Labour Supply: A Unitary Discrete Choice Model for the Case of Ecuador', *Basic Income Studies*, 10/2, 225–55.

Miller, E. J. (2001), *The Greater Toronto Area Travel Demand Modelling System Version 2.0*, i: *Model Overview* (Toronto: Joint Program in Transportation, University of Toronto).

Minot, N., Baulch, B., and Epprecht, M. (2003), *Poverty and Inequality in Vietnam: Spatial Patterns and Geographic Determinants* (International Food Policy Research Institute (IFPRI)).

Moisio, P., Lehtelä, K. M., and Mukkila, S. (2016), 'Poverty Reduction Effects of Taxation and Benefit Policies in Finland, 1993–2013', *European Journal of Social Security*, 18/1, 30–45.

Morduch, J., and Sicular, T. (2002), 'Rethinking Inequality Decomposition, with Evidence from Rural China', *The Economic Journal*, 112/476, 93–106.

Morgenroth, E. (2010), 'Regional Dimension of Taxes and Public Expenditure in Ireland', *Regional Studies*, 44/6, 777–89.

Morrison, R. (2000a), 'DYNACAN: The Canada Pension Plan Policy Model: Demographic and Earnings Components', *Contributions to Economic Analysis*, 247, 341–60.

Morrison, R. (2000b), 'Assessing the Quality of DYNACAN's Synthetically-Generated Earnings Histories', Paper Presented to the Sixth Nordic Workshop on Microsimulation, Copenhagen, June 2000.

Morrison, R. (2006), 'Make it So: Event Alignment in Dynamic Microsimulation', DYNACAN Team, Ottawa.

Morrison, R. (2008), 'Validation of Longitudinal Microsimulation Models: DYNACAN Practices and Plans', Working Paper No. 8, DYNACAN Team, Ottawa.

Morrissey, K., Clarke, G., Ballas, D., Hynes, S., and O'Donoghue, C. (2008), 'Examining Access to GP Services in Rural Ireland Using Microsimulation Analysis', *Area*, 40/3, 354–64.

Morrissey, K., and O'Donoghue, C. (2011), 'The Spatial Distribution of Labour Force Participation and Market Earnings at the Sub-national Level in Ireland'. *Review of Economic Analysis*, 3/1, 80–101.

Morrissey, K., O'Donoghue, C., and Farrell, N. (2014), 'The Local Impact of the Marine Sector in Ireland: A Spatial Microsimulation Analysis', *Spatial Economic Analysis*, 9/1, 31–50.

Mot, E.S. (1992), Survey of Microsimulation Models—Inventory and Recommendations, SEO, Tichting voor Economisch Onderzoek der Universiteit van Amsterdam, Amsterdam.

Muñoz, H., and Esteban, M. (2016), 'A Spatial Microsimulation Model for the Estimation of Heat Demand in Hamburg', in *REAL CORP 2016–SMART ME UP! How to Become and How to Stay a Smart City, and Does This Improve Quality of Life?, Proceedings of 21st International Conference on Urban Planning, Regional Development and Information Society* (Hamburg: CORP–Competence Center of Urban and Regional Planning), 39–46.

Myck, M., and Najsztub, M. (2014), 'Data and Model Cross-Validation to Improve Accuracy of Microsimulation Results: Estimates for the Polish Household Budget Survey', Discussion Paper No. 1368, German Institute for Economic Research (DIW), Berlin, https://ssrn.com/abstract=2,432,938 or http://dx.doi.org/10.2139/ssrn.2432938.

National Research Council (1997), *Assessing Policies for Retirement Income: Needs for Data, Research, and Models* (Washington, DC: National Academies Press).

Nelissen, J. H. (1995), 'Lifetime Income Redistribution by the Old-Age State Pension in the Netherlands', *Journal of Public Economics*, 58/3, 429–51.

Nelissen, J. H. (1996), *The Modelling of Institutional Households by Means of Microsimulation* (Tilburg: Tilburg University Press), 166.

Neufeld, C. (2000), 'Alignment and Variance Reduction in DYNACAN', in A. Gupta and V. Kapur, eds., *Microsimulation in Government Policy and Forecasting* (Amsterdam: North-Holland).

Newbery, D. M. G. (1995), 'The Distributional Impact of Price Changes in Hungary and in the United Kingdom', *Economic Journal*, 105, Jul 847–63.

Newbery, D. M. G., and Stern, N. (1987), *The Theory of Taxation for Developing Countries* (Oxford: Oxford University Press).

Nichèle, V., and Robin, J.-M. (1995), 'Simulation of Indirect Tax Reforms Using Pooled Micro and Macro French Data, *Journal of Public Economics*, 56/2, 225–44.

Nickell, S., and Layard, R. (1999), 'Labor Market Institutions and Economic Performance', in O. C. Ashenfelter and D. Card, eds., *Handbook of Labor Economics*, iii/B (Amsterdam: North-Holland), 3029–84.

Nolan, B., and Maître, B. (2000), 'A Comparative Perspective on Trends in Income Inequality in Ireland,' *The Economic and Social Review*, 31/4, 329–35.

Nolan, B., Whelan, C. T., and Willams, J. (1998), *Where Are the Poor Households? The Spatial Distribution of Poverty and Deprivation in Ireland* (Dublin: Combat Poverty Agency).

Norman, P. (1999), 'Putting Iterative Proportional Fitting (IPF) on the Researcher's Desk', Working Paper No. 99/03 ed., School of Geography, University of Leeds, Leeds.

Oaxaca, R. (1973), 'Male-Female Wage Differentials in Urban Labor Markets', *International Economic Review*, 14, Oct 673–709.

O'Donoghue, C. (1997), 'Carbon Dioxide, Energy Taxes and Household Income', Working Paper No. 90, Economic and Social Research Institute, Dublin.

O'Donoghue, C. (1998), 'Simulating the Irish Tax-Transfer System in Eur6', Working Paper No. MU/RN/26, Microsimulation Unit, Faculty of Economics, University of Cambridge.

O'Donoghue, C. (2001a), 'Dynamic Microsimulation: A Methodological Survey', *Brazilian Electronic Journal of Economics*, 4/2, 77.

O'Donoghue, C. (2001b), 'Redistribution in the Irish Tax-Benefit System', unpublished Ph.D. dissertation, London School of Economics.

O'Donoghue, C. (2002), 'Redistribution Over the Lifetime in the Irish Tax-Benefit System: An Application of a Prototype Dynamic Microsimulation Model for Ireland', *Economic and Social Review*, 32/3, 191–216.

O'Donoghue, C., Albuquerque, J., Baldini, M., Bargain, O., Bosi, P., Levy, H.,... Tsakloglou, P. (2002), *The impact of means tested assistance in Southern Europe* (No. EM6/01). EUROMOD Working Paper.

O'Donoghue, C. (2003), 'Redistributive Forces of the Irish Tax-Benefit System'. *Dublin: Journal of the Statistical and Social Inquiry Society of Ireland*, XXXII/2002/2003, 33–69.

O'Donoghue, C. (2011), 'Do Tax–Benefit Systems Cause High Replacement Rates? A Decompositional Analysis Using EUROMOD,' *Labour: Review of Labour Economics and Industrial Relations*, 25/1, 126–151, doi: 10.1111/j.1467-9914.2010.00501.

O'Donoghue, C., Farell, N., Morrissey, K., Lennon, J., Ballas, D., Clarke, G., and Hynes, S. (2013), 'The SMILE Model: Construction and Calibration'. in *Spatial Microsimulation for Rural Policy Analysis* (Springer: Berlin, Heidelberg), 55–86.

O'Donoghue, C., ed. (2014), *Handbook of Microsimulation Modelling* (Bingley: Emerald Group Publishing).

O'Donoghue, C., Morrissey, K., and Lennon, J. (2014), 'Spatial Microsimulation Modelling: A Review of Applications and Methodological Choices'. *International Journal of Microsimulation*, 7/1, 26–75.

O'Donoghue, C. (2017a), *Farm-Level Microsimulation Modelling* (New York: Springer).

O'Donoghue, C. (2017b), 'Spatial Microsimulation Model for Environmental Policy', in *Farm-Level Microsimulation Modelling* (Cham: Palgrave Macmillan), 283–319.

O'Donoghue, C. (2017c), 'Spatial Microsimulation of Farm Income', in *Farm-Level Microsimulation Modelling* (Cham: Palgrave Macmillan), 147–75.

O'Donoghue, C., Baldini, M., and Mantovani, D. (2004), 'Modelling the Redistributive Impact of Indirect Taxes in Europe: An Application of EUROMOD', Working Paper Series No. EM7/01, EUROMOD at the Institute for Social and Economic Research, Essex.

O'Donoghue, C., Ballas, D., Clarke, G., Hynes, S., and Morrissey, K., eds. (2012), *Spatial Microsimulation for Rural Policy Analysis* (Springer Science+Business Media).

O'Donoghue, C., Chyzheuskaya, A., Grealis, E., Kilcline, K., Finnegan, W., Goggins, J.,... Ryan, M. (2019), 'Measuring GHG Emissions Across the Agri-Food Sector Value Chain: The Development of a Bioeconomy Input-Output Model'. *International Journal on Food System Dynamics*, 10(1), 55–85.

O'Donoghue, C., and Dekkers, G. (2018), 'Increasing the Impact of Dynamic Microsimulation Modelling'. *The International Journal of Microsimulation*, 11(1), 61–96.

O'Donoghue, C., Hynes, S., Morrissey, K., Ballas, D., and Clarke, G., eds. (2013), *Modelling the Local Economy: A Spatial Microsimulation Approach* (Dordrecht: Springer-Verlag).

O'Donoghue, C., Lennon, J., and Hynes, S. (2009), 'The Life-Cycle Income Analysis Model (LIAM): A Study of a Flexible Dynamic Microsimulation Modelling Computing Framework', *International Journal of Microsimulation*, 2/1, 16–31.

O'Donoghue, C., and Loughrey, J. (2014), 'Nowcasting in Microsimulation Models: A Methodological Survey', *Journal of Artificial Societies and Social Simulation*, 17/4, 12.

O'Donoghue, C., and Loughrey, J. (2016), 'Now-Casting in Microsimulation Models: A Methodological Survey', *Journal of Artificial Societies and Social Simulation*, 17/4, 12.

O'Donoghue, C., Loughrey, J., and Morrissey, K. (2011), 'Modelling the Impact of the Economic Crisis on Inequality in Ireland', IMA 2011 Conference Paper. International Microsimulation Association

O'Donoghue, C., Loughrey, J., & Morrissey, K. (2013), Using the EU-SILC to model the impact of the economic crisis on inequality. *IZA Journal of European Labor Studies*, *2*(1), 1–26.

O'Donoghue, C., Loughrey, J., and Sologon, D. M. (2018), 'Decomposing the Drivers of Changes in Inequality During the Great Recession in Ireland Using the Fields Approach', *The Economic and Social Review*, 49/2, 173–200.

O'Donoghue, C., and Morrissey, K. (2011), 'Conditional Independence, Calibration and the Generation of Synthetic Spatial Labour Market Microdata', Working Paper, Teagasc Rural Economy Development Programme, Ireland.

O'Donoghue, C., Morrissey, K., and Lennon, J. (2014), 'Survey of Spatial Microsimulation Modelling', *International Journal of Microsimulation*, 7/1. 26–75.

O'Donoghue, C., Redway, H., and Lennon, J. (2010), 'Simulating Migration in the Pensim2 Dynamic Microsimulation Model', *International Journal of Microsimulation*, 3/2, 65–79.

O'Donoghue, C., and Sutherland, H. (1999), Accounting for the family in European income tax systems. *Cambridge Journal of Economics*, 23(5), 565–598.

OECD (1994), *The OECD Jobs Study* (Paris: Organisation for Economic Co-operation and Development).

OECD (1994b), *The OECD Jobs Study* (Paris: Organisation for Economic Co-operation and Development).

OECD (1996a), *Taxation, Employment and Unemployment: The OECD Jobs Study* (Paris: Organisation for Economic Co-operation and Development).

OECD (1996b), *Policy Implications of Ageing Populations* (Paris: Organisation for Economic Co-operation and Development).

OECD (1997), *Making Work Pay: Taxation, Benefits, Employment and Unemployment* (Paris: Organisation for Economic Co-operation and Development).

OECD (1999), *Benefit Systems and Work Incentives* (Paris: Organisation for Economic Co-operation and Development).

OECD (1999), *Benefit Systems and Work Incentives* (Paris: Organisation for Economic Co-operation and Development).

OECD (2011), *Pensions at a Glance 2011: Retirement-Income Systems in OECD and G20 Countries* (Paris: Organisation for Economic Co-operation and Development).

Oketch, T., and Carrick, M. (2005), 'Calibration and Validation of a Micro-Simulation Model in Network Analysis', in *Proceedings of the 84th TRB Annual Meeting* (Washington, DC: Transportation Research Board).

O'Leary, E. (2003), 'Aggregate and Sectoral Convergence among Irish Regions: The Role of Structural Change, 1960–96', *International Regional Science Review*, 26/4, 483–501.

Oliver, X., and Spadaro, A. (2017), 'Active Welfare State Policies and Labour Supply in Spain', *Hacienda Pública Española*, 222/3, 9–41.

Orcutt, G. H. (1957), 'A New Type of Socio-economic System'. *The Review of Economics and Statistics*, 39/2, 116–123.

Orcutt, G. H. (1960), 'Simulation of Economic Systems'. *The American Economic Review*, 50/5, 894–907.

Orcutt, G. H., Caldwell, S. B., and Wertheimer, R. (1976), 'Policy Exploration Through Microanalytic Simulation', Urban Institute, Washington, DC.

Orcutt, G. H., Franklin, S. D., Mendelsohn, R., and Smith, J. D. (1977), 'Does Your Probability of Death Depend on Your Environment? A Microanalytic Study', *The American Economic Review*, 67/1, 260–64.

Orcutt, G. H., Greenberger, M., and Rivlin, A. M. (1958), *Decision-Unit Models and Simulation of the United States Economy* (Mimeo, Harvard University).

Orcutt, G. H., Merz, J., and Quinke, H., eds. (1986), *Microanalytic Simulation Models to Support Social and Financial Policy* (Amsterdam: North-Holland).

Orsini, K. (2005), 'The 2001 Belgian Tax Reform: Equity and Efficiency', Discussions Paper Series No. (DPS) 05.04, Center for Economic Studies. KU Leuven Department of Economics.

Osei, R., Pirttilä, J., and Rattenhuber, P. (2017), 'Quantifying the Impacts of Expanding Social Protection on Efficiency and Equity: Evidence from a Behavioural Microsimulation Model for Ghana', WIDER Working Paper No. 2017/193. Helsinki: UNU-WIDER.

Osunde, O. O. (2015), 'Poverty, Demographic Change and Inequality in Nigeria: A Microsimulation Analysis', Ph.D. dissertation. National University of Ireland, Galway.

Pacifico, D. (2013), 'On the Role of Unobserved Preference Heterogeneity in Discrete Choice Models of Labour Supply', *Empirical Economics*, 45/2, 929–63.

Pacolet, J., Bouten, R., and Versieck, K. (2018), *Social Protection for Dependency in Old Age: A Study of the Fifteen EU Member States and Norway* (Abingdon-on-Thames: Routledge).

Palme, M. (1996), 'Income Distribution Effects of the Swedish 1991 Tax Reform: An Analysis of a Microsimulation Using Generalized Kakwani Decomposition,' *Journal of Policy Modeling*, 18/4, 419–43.

Panori, A., Ballas, D., and Psycharis, Y. (2017), 'SimAthens: A Spatial Microsimulation Approach to the Estimation and Analysis of Small Area Income Distributions and Poverty Rates in the City of Athens, Greece', *Computers, Environment and Urban Systems*, 63, May 15–25.

Pearce, D. (1991), 'The Role of Carbon Taxes in Adjusting to Global Warming', *The Economic Journal*, 101/407, 938–48.

Pearce, W., and Raman, S. (2014), 'The New Randomised Controlled Trials (RCT) Movement in Public Policy: Challenges of Epistemic Governance', *Policy Sciences*, 47/4, 387–402.

Pearson, M., and Scarpetta, S. (2000), 'An Overview: What Do We Know about Policies to Make Work Pay?', *OECD Economic Studies*, 31/1, 12–24.

Peichl, A., and Schaefer, T. (2006), 'Documentation FiFoSiM: Integrated Tax Benefit Microsimulation and CGE Model', FiFo-CPE Discussion Paper No. 06–10. University of Cologne

Pendakur, K. (2002), 'Taking Prices Seriously in the Measurement of Inequality', *Journal of Public Economics*, 86/1, 47–69.

Philips, I., Clarke, G., and Watling, D. (2017), 'A Fine Grained Hybrid Spatial Microsimulation Technique for Generating Detailed Synthetic Individuals from Multiple Data Sources: An Application to Walking and Cycling'. *The International Journal of Microsimulation*, 10(1), 167–200.

Phillips, D., Warwick, R., Goldman, M., Goraus, K., Inchauste, G., Harris, T., et al. (2018), 'Redistribution Via VAT and Cash Transfers: An Assessment in Four Low and Middle Income Countries', Paper No. 78, Department of Economics, Tulane University.

Picos-Sánchez, F., and Thomas, A. (2015), 'A Revenue-Neutral Shift from SSC to VAT: Analysis of the Distributional Impact for 12 EU-OECD Countries', *FinanzArchiv*, 71/2, 278–98.

Pissarides, C. (1986), 'Unemployment and Vacancies in Britain', *Economic Policy*, 3/1, 499–559.

Poltimäe, H., and Võrk, A. (2009), 'Distributional Effects of Environmental Taxes in Estonia', *Estonian Discussions on Economic Policy*, No 17.

Pratschke, J., and Haase, T. (2007), 'Measurement of Social Disadvantage and its Spatial Articulation in the Republic of Ireland', *Regional Studies*, 41/6, 719–34.

Propper, C. (1995), 'For Richer, for Poorer, in Sickness and in Health: The Lifetime Distribution of NHS Health care'. in J. Falkingham and J. Hills, eds., *The Dynamics of Welfare* (London: Pentice Hall Wheatsheaf).

Pudney, S. (1989), *Modelling Individual Choice: The Econometrics of Corners, Kinks and Holes* (Oxford: Blackwell Publishers), http://iserwww.essex.ac.uk/home/spudney/?page_id=61.

Pudney, S., Hancock, R., and Sutherland, H. (2006), 'Simulating the Reform of Means-Tested Benefits with Endogenous Take-Up and Claim Costs', *Oxford Bulletin of Economics and Statistics*, 68/2, 135–66.

Pudney, S., and Sutherland, H. (1996), 'Statistical Reliability in Microsimulation Models with Econometrically-Estimated Behavioural Responses', in A Harding, ed., *Microsimulation and Public Policy* (Amsterdam: Elsevier), 473–504.

Rahman, A. (2017), 'Small Area Housing Stress Estimation in Australia: Calculating Confidence Intervals for a Spatial Microsimulation Model', *Communications in Statistics-Simulation and Computation*, 46/9, 7466–84.

Rahman, A., and Harding, A. (2016), *Small Area Estimation and Microsimulation Modeling* (Boca Raton, FL: CRC Press).

Rahman, A., Harding, A., Tanton, R., and Liu, S. (2010), 'Methodological Issues in Spatial Microsimulation Modelling for Small Area Estimation', *International Journal of Microsimulation*, 3/2, 3–22.

Rake, K., Falkingham, J., and Martin, E. (1999), 'Tightropes and Tripwires: New Labour's Proposals and Means-Testing in Old Age', CASE Paper No. 23, London: School of Economics.

Ranđelović, S., and Rakić, J. Ž. (2013), 'Improving Work Incentives in Serbia: Evaluation of a Tax Policy Reform Using SRMOD', *International Journal of Microsimulation*, 6/1, 157–76.

Rao, M., Tanton, R., and Vidyattama, Y. (2015), 'Modelling the Economic, Social and Ecological Links in the Murray-Darling Basin: A Conceptual Framework', *The Australasian Journal of Regional Studies*, 21/1, 80.

Ravallion, M., and Jalan, J. (1997), 'Spatial Poverty Traps?', World Bank Policy Research Working Paper No. 1862, World Bank, Washington, DC, http://ssrn.com/abstract=597203.

Redmond G., (1999), 'Tax-Benefit Policies and Parents Incentive to Work. The Case of Australia, 1980–1997', SPRC Discussion Paper No. 104, Research Report for Australian Commonwealth Department.

Redmond, G., and Kattuman, P. (2001), 'Employment Polarisation and Inequality in the UK and Hungary', *Cambridge Journal of Economics*, 25/4, 467–80.

Redmond, G., Sutherland, H., and Wilson, M. (1998), *The Arithmetic of Tax and Social Security Reform: A User's Guide to Microsimulation Methods and Analysis*, lxiv (Cambridge: Cambridge University Press).

Rees, P., Wu, B., and Birkin, M. (2017), 'Moses: Dynamic Spatial Microsimulation with Demographic Interactions', in *New Frontiers in Microsimulation Modelling* (Abingdon On Thames: Routledge), 53–77.

Rephann, T. J., Mäkilä, K., and Holm, E. (2005), 'Microsimulation for Local Impact Analysis: An Application to Plant Shutdown', *Journal of Regional Science*, 45/1, 183–222.

Reynolds, M., and Smolensky, E. (1977), 'Post-Fisc Distributions of Income in 1950, 1961, and 1970', *Public Finance Quarterly*, 5/4, 419–38.

Rosas-Flores, J. A., Bakhat, M., Rosas-Flores, D., and Zayas, J. L. F. (2017), 'Distributional Effects of Subsidy Removal and Implementation of Carbon Taxes in Mexican Households', *Energy Economics*, 61, Jan 21–8.

Rosenzweig, M. R., and Wolpin, K. I. (2000), 'Natural "Natural Experiments" in Economics', *Journal of Economic Literature*, 38/4, 827–74.

Rowe, G., and Wolfson, M. (2000), 'Public Pensions—Candian Analyses Based on the LifePaths Generational Accounting Framework', Paper Presented to the Sixth Nordic Workshop on Microsimulation, Copenhagen, June 2000.

Rowntree, B. S. (1902), *Poverty. A Study of Town Life* (London: Thomas Nelson and Sons).

Rubin, D. B. (1987), *Multiple Imputation for Nonresponse in Surveys* (New York: John Wiley & Sons).

Ryan, M., O'Donoghue, C., and Kinsella, A. (2017), 'The Potential Impact of Differential Taxation and Social Protection Measures on Farm Afforestation Decisions', Irish Forestry.

Saez, E. (2010), 'Do Taxpayers Bunch at Kink Points?', *American Economic Journal: Economic Policy*, 2/3, 180–212.

Saez, E., Slemrod, J., and Giertz, S. H. (2012), 'The Elasticity of Taxable Income with Respect to Marginal Tax Rates: A Critical Review', *Journal of Economic Literature*, 50/1, 3–50.

Salomäki, A., and Munzi, T. (1999), 'Net Replacement Rates of the Unemployed: Comparisons of Various Approaches', Economic Papers No. 133, European Commission Directorate-General for Economic and Financial Affairs (DG ECFIN).

Sastre, M., and Trannoy, A. (2002), 'Shapley Inequality Decomposition by Factor Components: Some Methodological Issues'. *Journal of Economics*, 77(1), 51–89.

Salvini, P., and Miller, E. J. (2005), 'ILUTE: An Operational Prototype of a Comprehensive Microsimulation Model of Urban Systems', *Networks and Spatial Economics*, 5/2, 217–34.

Savage, M., Callan, T., Nolan, B., and Colgan, B. (2015), *The great recession, austerity and inequality: evidence from Ireland* (No. 499). ESRI Working Paper.

Scarpetta, S. (1996), 'Assessing the Role of Labour Market Policies and Institutional Settings on Unemployment: A Cross-Country Study', *OECD Economic Studies*, 26/1, 43–98.

Schläpfer, F. (2017), 'Stated Preferences for Public Services: A Classification and Survey of Approaches', *Journal of Economic Surveys*, 31/1, 258–80.

Schofield, D., Carter, H., and Edwards, K. (2014), 'Health Models', in C. O'Donoghue, ed., *Handbook of Microsimulation Modelling* (Bingley: Emerald Group Publishing), 421–47.

Scholz, J. K. (1996), 'In-Work Benefits in the United States: The Earned Income Tax Credit', *The Economic Journal*, 106/434, 156–69.

Scott, A. (2001), 'A Computing Strategy for SAGE: 1. Model Options and Constraints', Technical Note No. 2, ESRC–Sage Research Group, London.

Serret, Y., and Johnstone, N., eds. (2006), *The Distributional Effects of Environmental Policy* (Cheltenham: Edward Elgar Publishing).

Seven Countries Group (1996), 'Unemployment Benefits and Social Assistance in Seven European Countries', Werkdocumenten, No. 10, Ministerie van Sociale Zaken en Werkgelegenheid, The Netherlands.

Scholz, J. K. (1996), 'In-Work Benefits in the United States: The Earned Income Tax Credit', *The Economic Journal*, 106/434, 156–69.

Scott, S. (1992), 'Theoretical Considerations and Estimates of the Effects on Households', in J. FitzGerald and D. McCoy, eds., *The Economic Effects of Carbon Taxes*, Policy Research Series Paper No. 14, Economic and Social Research Institute, Dublin.

Shapley, L. S. (1953), 'A Value for n-Person Games', in H. Kuhn and A. W. Tucker, eds., *Contributions to the Theory of Games*, ii (Princeton: Princeton University Press).

Shorrocks, A. F. (1980), 'The Class of Additively Decomposable Inequality Measures', *Econometrica, 48*/3, 613–25.

Shorrocks, A. F. (1982), 'Inequality Decomposition by Factor Components', *Econometrica*, 50/1, 193–211.

Shorrocks, A. F. (1984), 'Inequality Decomposition by Population Subgroups', *Econometrica*, 52/6. 1369–86.

Shorrocks, A. F. (1999), 'Decomposition Procedures for Distributional Analysis: A Unified Framework Based on Shapley Value', Mimeo. Department of Economics, University of Essex.

Shorrocks, A. F. (2013), 'Decomposition Procedures for Distributional Analysis: A Unified Framework Based on the Shapley Value', *Journal of Economic Inequality*, 11/1, 99–126.

Shorrocks, A., and Wan, G. (2005). 'Spatial Decomposition of Inequality'. *Journal of Economic Geography*, 5/1, 59–81.

Shrestha, S., Barnes, A., and Ahmadi, B. V., eds. (2016), *Farm-Level Modelling: Techniques, Applications and Policy* (Wallingford: CABI).

Smith, D. M., Clarke, G. P., and Harland, K. (2009), 'Improving the Synthetic Data Generation Process in Spatial Microsimulation Models', *Environment and Planning A*, 41/5, 1251–68.

Smith, S. (1992a), 'Distributional Aspects of Taxes on Energy and the Carbon Content of Fuels', *European Economy*, special ed. no. 1, 241–68.

Smith, S. (1992b), 'Taxation and the Environment: A Survey', *Fiscal Studies*, 13/4, 21–57.

Smith, S. (1995), 'The Role of the European Union in Environmental Taxation', *International Tax and Public Finance*, 2/2, 375–87.

Smith, D. M., Harland, K., and Clarke, G. P. (2007), SimHealth: Estimating small area populations using deterministic spatial microsimulation in Leeds and Bradford. University of Leeds School of Geography, Working Paper 07/06.

Snower, D. J., and de La Dehesa, G., eds. (1997), *Unemployment Policy: Government Options for the Labour Market* (Cambridge: Cambridge University Press).

Spadaro, A. (2001), 'Microsimulation and the Analysis of Redistributive Policies', DELTA Working Papers No. 2001-14, Paris.

Spielauer, M. (2007), 'Dynamic Microsimulation of Care Demand, Health Care Finance and the Economic Impact of Health Behaviours: Survey and Review', *International Journal of Microsimulation*, 1/1, 35–53.

Spielauer, M. (2011), 'What is Social Science Microsimulation?', *Social Science Computer Review*, 29/1, 9–20.

Stirling, T., and Lazutka, R. (2006), 'I-CUE Feasibility Study', Estonia (2005 Tax-Benefit System), EUROMOD Feasibility Study.

Stock, J. H., and Wise, D. A. (1990), 'The Pension Inducement to Retire: An Option Value Analysis', in Schulz J.H. ed., *Issues in the Economics of Aging* (Chicago: University of Chicago Press), 205–30.

Stone, R. (1954), 'Linear Expenditure Systems and Demand Analysis: An Application to the Pattern of British Demand', *The Economic Journal*, 64/255, 511–27.

Stroombergen, A., Rose, D., and Miller, J. (1995), *Wealth Accumulation and Distribution: Analysis with a Dynamic Microsimulation Model* (Wellington: Business and Economic Research).

Sutherland, H. (1995), 'Static Microsimulation Models in Europe: A Survey', Discussion Paper No. 9523, Microsimulation Unit, Faculty of Economics, University of Cambridge.

Sutherland, H. (2002), 'Indicators for Social Inclusion in the European Union: The Impact of Policy Changes and the Use of Microsimulation Models', *Politica Economica*, 18/1, 117–20.

Sutherland, H., and Figari, F. (2013), 'EUROMOD: The European Union Tax-Benefit Microsimulation Model', *International Journal of Microsimulation*, 6/1, 4–26.

Sutherland, H., Taylor, R., and Gomulka, J. (2002), 'Combining Household Income and Expenditure Data in Policy Simulations', *Review of Income and Wealth*, 48/4, 517–36.

Sutherland, H., and Figari, F. (2013), 'EUROMOD: The European Union Tax-Benefit Microsimulation Model'. *International Journal of Microsimulation*, 6/1, 4–26.

Symons, E., Proops, J., and Gay, P. (1994), 'Carbon Taxes, Consumer Demand and Carbon Dioxide Emissions: A Simulation Analysis for the UK', *Fiscal Studies*, 15/2, 19–43.

Symons, E., Speck, S., and Proops, J. (2002), 'The Distributional Effects of Carbon and Energy Taxes: The Cases of France, Spain, Italy, Germany and UK', *European Environment*, 12/4, 203–12.

Tanton, R. (2014), 'A Review of Spatial Microsimulation Methods', *International Journal of Microsimulation*, 7/1, 4–25.

Tanton, R. (2018), 'Spatial Microsimulation: Developments and Potential Future Directions', *International Journal of Microsimulation*, 11/1, 143–61.

Tanton, R., and Clarke, G. (2014), 'Spatial Models'. in O'Donoghue (ed.), *Handbook of Microsimulation Modelling* (Emerald Group Publishing Limited).

Tanton, R., and Edwards, K., eds. (2013), *Spatial Microsimulation: A Reference Guide for Users* (Netherlands: Springer).

Tanton, R., Vidyattama, Y., Nepal, B., and McNamara, J. (2011), 'Small Area Estimation Using a Reweighting Algorithm', *Journal of the Royal Statistical Society: Series A (Statistics in Society)*, 174/4, 931–51.

Tanton, R., Williamson, P., and Harding, A. (2007), 'Comparing Two Methods of Reweighting a Survey File to Small Area Data: Generalised Regression and Combinatorial Optimisation', First General Conference, International Microsimulation Association, Vienna.

Tanton, R., Williamson, P., and Harding, A. (2014), 'Comparing Two Methods of Reweighting a Survey File to Small Area Data', *International Journal of Microsimulation*, 7/1, 76–99.

Tesfatsion, L., and Judd, K. L., eds. (2006), *Handbook of Computational Economics: Agent-Based Computational Economics*, ii (Amsterdam: Elsevier).

Theil, H. (1972), *Statistical Decomposition Analysis* (Amsterdam: North-Holland).

Thoresen, T. O., Jia, Z., and Lambert, P. J. (2016), 'Is There More Redistribution Now? A Review of Methods for Evaluating Tax Redistributional Effects'. *Finanz-Archiv: Zeitschrift für das Gesamte Finanzwesen*, 72/3, 302.

Thoresen, T. O., and Vattø, T. E. (2015), 'Validation of the Discrete Choice Labor Supply Model by Methods of the New Tax Responsiveness Literature', *Labour Economics*, 37, Dec 38–53.

Timmins, K. A., and Edwards, K. L. (2016), 'Validation of Spatial Microsimulation Models: A Proposal to Adopt the Bland–Altman Method', *International Journal of Microsimulation*, 9/2, 106–22.

Tirachini, A., Sun, L., Erath, A., and Chakirov, A. (2016), 'Valuation of Sitting and Standing in Metro Trains Using Revealed Preferences', *Transport Policy*, 47, Apr 94–104.

Todd, P. E. (2007), 'Evaluating Social Programs with Endogenous Program Placement and Selection of the Treated', *Handbook of Development Economics*, 4, Jan 3847–94.

Toder, E., Nunns, J., and Rosenberg, J. (2013), 'Updated Tables for "Using a VAT to Reform the Income Tax"', Urban Institute and Brookings Institution Tax Policy Center, Washington, DC.

Tsakloglou, P. (1996), 'ELDERLY AND NON-ELDERLY IN THE EUROPEAN UNION: A COMPARISON OF LIVING STANDARDS', *Review of Income and Wealth*, 42/3, 271–91.

Tsakloglou, P., and Mitrakos, T. (1998), 'On the Distributional Impact of Excise Duties: Evidence from Greece'. *Public Finance = Finances publiques*, 53/1, 78–101.

Tu, G., Abildtrup, J., and Garcia, S. (2016), 'Preferences for Urban Green Spaces and Peri-Urban Forests: An Analysis of Stated Residential Choices', *Landscape and Urban Planning*, 148, Apr, 120–31.

Van Klaveren, C., Van Praag, B., and van den Brink, H. M. (2008), 'A Public Good Version of the Collective Household Model: An Empirical Approach with an Application to British Household Data'. *Review of Economics of the Household*, 6/2, 169–191.

Van de Ven, J., Hérault, N., and Azpitarte, F. (2017), 'Identifying Tax Implicit Equivalence Scales', *The Journal of Economic Inequality*, 15/3, 257–75.

Vandyck, T., and Van Regemorter, D. (2014), 'Distributional and Regional Economic Impact of Energy Taxes in Belgium', *Energy Policy*, 72, Sep, 190–203.

Van Ruijven, B. J., O'Neill, B. C., and Chateau, J. (2015), 'Methods for Including Income Distribution in Global CGE Models for Long-Term Climate Change Research', *Energy Economics*, 51, Sep, 530–43.

Van Soest, A. (1995), 'Structural Models of Family Labor Supply: A Discrete Choice Approach', *Journal of Human Resources*, 30/1, 63–88.

Van Tongeren, F. W. (1995), *Microsimulation Modelling of the Corporate Firm* (Dordrecht: Springer Professional).

Vedung, E. (2017), *Public Policy and Program Evaluation* (Abingdon: Routledge).

Vega, A., Kilgarriff, P., O'Donoghue, C., and Morrissey, K. (2017), 'The Spatial Impact of Commuting on Income: A Spatial Microsimulation Approach', *Applied Spatial Analysis and Policy*, 10/4, 475–95.

Verbič, M., Čok, M., and Turk, T. (2015), 'An Exact Analytical Grossing-Up Algorithm for Tax-Benefit Models', *Informatica*, 39/1, 23–34.

Verbist, G. (2004), 'Redistributive Effect and Progressivity of Taxes: An International Comparison Across the EU Using EUROMOD', EUROMOD Working Paper Series No. EM5/04, EUROMOD at the Institute for Social and Economic Research, Essex.

Verbist, G., and Figari, F. (2014), 'The Redistributive Effect and Progressivity of Taxes Revisited: An International Comparison Across the European Union', *FinanzArchiv*, 70/3, 405–29.

Voas, D., and Williamson, P. (2000), 'An Evaluation of the Combinatorial Optimisation Approach to the Creation of Synthetic Microdata', *International Journal of Population Geography*, 6/5, 349–66.

Wachter, K. W., Blackwell, D., and Hammel, E. A. (1997), 'Testing the Validity of Kinship Microsimulation', *Mathematical and Computer Modelling*, 26/6, 89–104.

Waddell, P. (2002), 'UrbanSim: Modeling Urban Development for Land Use', *Transportation and Environmental Planning. Journal of the American Planning Association*, 68/3, 297–314.

Waddell, P., Borning, A., Noth, M., Freier, N., Becke, M., and Ulfarsson, G. (2003), 'Microsimulation of Urban Development and Location Choices: Design and Implementation of UrbanSim', *Networks and Spatial Economics*, 3/1, 43–67.

Waduda, Z., Noland, R. B., and Graham, D. J. (2008), 'Equity Analysis of Personal Tradable Carbon Permits for the Road Transport Sector', *Environmental Science and Policy*, 11/6, 533–44.

Wagenhals, G. (2001), 'Incentive and Redistribution Effects of the Karlsruher Entwurf zur Reform des Einkommenssteuergesetzes', Diskussionspapiere aus dem Institut für Volkswirtschaftslehre der Universität Hohenheim 194/2001, Department of Economics, University of Hohenheim, Germany.

Wagenhals, G. (2011), 'Dual Income Tax Reform in Germany. A Microsimulation Approach', *International Journal of Microsimulation*, 4/2, 3–13.

Wan, X. (2018), 'Micro-Simulation Model as a Tool for Evaluating the Reform of China's Personal Income Tax', in *International Conference on Applied Human Factors and Ergonomics* (Cham: Springer), 254–61.

Watson, D. (2005), *Mapping poverty: National, regional and county patterns* (No. 37). Combat Poverty Agency.

Watson, D., Whelan, C. T., Willams, J., and Blackwell, S. (2005), 'Mapping Poverty: National Regional and County Patterns', in *Combat Poverty Agency Research Series No.* 34. Dublin: Combat Poverty Agency.

Wei, F. Y. W. (2012), 'The Relationship Between VAT and the Income Distribution of Rural and Urban Citizens: From 1995 to 2010', *Reform*, 11, 10.

Wertheimer, R., Zedlewski, S. R., Anderson, J., and Moore, K. (1986), 'DYNASIM in Comparison with Other Microsimulation Models', in G. H. Orcutt et al., eds., *Microanalytic Simulation Models to Support Social and Financial Policy* (Amsterdam: North-Holland).

Whitworth, A., Carter, E., Ballas, D., and Moon, G. (2017), 'Estimating Uncertainty in Spatial Microsimulation Approaches to Small Area Estimation: A New Approach to Solving an Old Problem', *Computers, Environment and Urban Systems*, 63, May 50–7.

Will, B. P., Berthelot, J. M., Nobrega, K. M., Flanagan, W., and Evans, W. K. (2001), 'Canada's Population Health Model (POHEM): A Tool for Performing Economic Evaluations of Cancer Control Interventions'. *European Journal of Cancer*, 37(14), 1797–1804.

Williamson, P. (2009), 'Creating Synthetic Sub-Regional Baseline Populations', Paper Presented to ESRC Microsimulation Series, 9 April 2009, London.

Winder, N. (2000), 'Modelling within a Thermodynamic Framework: A Footnote to Sanders (1999)', *Cybergeo: European Journal of Geography*, article 138, http://cybergeo.revues.org/2289, doi: 10.4000/cybergeo.2289, accessed 9 June 2012.

Wong, D. W. S. (1992), 'The Reliability of Using the Iterative Proportional Fitting Procedure', *The Professional Geographer*, 44/3, 340–48.

Wood, G. A. (2000), 'Effective Capital Gains Tax Burdens under Alternative Tax Rules: Microsimulation Results for Real Estate Investments', Economics Department, Murdoch University.

Woolley, F. R., and Marshall, J. (1994), 'Measuring Inequality Within the Household', *Review of Income and Wealth*, 40/4, 415–31.

World Bank. (2004), *The Microeconomics of Income Distribution Dynamics in East Asia and Latin America* (The World Bank).

Wright, G., Noble, M., Barnes, H., McLennan, D., and Mpike, M. (2016), 'SAMOD: A South African Tax-Benefit Microsimulation Model: Recent Developments', WIDER Working Paper No. 2016/115.

Wright, G., Noble, M., Dinbabo, M., Ntshongwana, P., Wilkinson, K., and Le Roux, P. (2011), 'Using the National Income Dynamics Study as the Base Micro-Dataset for a Tax and Transfer South African Microsimulation Model', Report Produced for the Office of the Presidency, South Africa.

Wu, B. M., Birkin, M. H., and Rees, P. H. (2008), 'A Spatial Microsimulation Model with Student Agents'. *Computers, Environment and Urban Systems*, 32(6), 440–453.

Wu, L., and Wang, Y. (1998), 'An Introduction to Simulated Annealing Algorithms for Computation of Economic Equilibrium', *Computational Economics*, 12, 151–69.

Yitzhaki, S. (1983), 'On an Extension of the Gini Inequality Index', *International Economic Review*, Oct 617–28.

Yusuf, A. A., and Resosudarmo, B. P. (2007), 'On the Distributional Effect of Carbon Tax in Developing Countries: The Case of Indonesia', Working Papers in Economics and Development Studies (WoPEDS) No. 200705, Department of Economics, Padjadjaran University, Bandung, Indonesia.

Yusuf, A. A., and Resosudarmo, B. P. (2015), 'On the Distributional Impact of a Carbon Tax in Developing Countries: The Case of Indonesia'. *Environmental Economics and Policy Studies*, 17/1, 131–156.

Zaidi, A., and Rake, K. (2001), 'Dynamic Microsimulation Models: A Review and Some Lessons for SAGE', Discussion Paper. No. 2, Simulating Social Policy in an Ageing Society (SAGE Research Group), London School of Economics.

Zaidi, A., and Scott, A. (2001), 'Base Dataset for the SAGE Model', Technical Note, Simulating Social Policy in an Ageing Society (SAGE Research Group), London School of Economics.

# Index